Tom Wright and The Search For Truth

A Theological Evaluation

Tom Holland

*'There comes a time when the chess pieces have to be put back on the board
so that the game may restart.'*

Robert Morgan cited by Tom Wright—*Paul in Fresh Perspective,* 19.

Copyright

Endorsements

Tom Holland provides a long overdue and thorough critique of the biblical scholarship of Tom Wright. Holland poses many excellent questions that point to fundamental, unrecognized, and potentially very damaging flaws in many of Wright's methods and arguments. In an uncomfortable number of instances, Holland argues, Wright is just plain old wrong! Holland particularly identifies how the Second Temple Literature, as well as Hellenism as a whole, provides an unnecessary and unjustified foundation for Wright's interpretations, especially of Paul. Holland does more than simply show how and where he believes Wright is in error; he presents numerous constructive and viable alternatives that merit further consideration. Regardless of whether one accepts these alternatives, if Holland is right in his fundamental criticisms, then Wright has a lot of explaining (and revising) to do!

- Stanley E. Porter, President and Dean, Professor of New Testament, Roy A. Hope Chair in Christian Worldview, McMaster Divinity College, Hamilton, Ontario, Canada

I have long felt that someone ought to write a comprehensive, probing critique of N. T. Wright's theological thought. I'm very grateful to Tom Holland for tackling this challenging, yet much-needed task. Holland rightly, I believe, raises serious concerns regarding Wright's methodology, which tends to elevate Second Temple literature above the Hebrew Scriptures. While Wright is correct in his efforts to peel back layers of Reformation tradition in reading Paul, Holland shows that Wright's own methodology does not always live up to the noble aims of the critical realism he espouses. No doubt there is much to learn from Wright's scholarly contribution. The way forward, however, I believe, is subjecting Wright's work to the kind of constructive critique Holland has provided. It is my hope that this volume marks the beginning of an even more thoroughgoing scrutiny of Wright's reconstructed synthesis-with the result that Paul's thought can be discerned more cogently from the New Testament documents against the most important ancient background, which surely must be the inspired canonical contributions of the Old Testament writers. Even the most ardent followers of Wright, not to mention Wright himself, will want to take note of this measured, yet pointed and sustained interaction.

The Search for Truth

- Andreas J. Kostenberger, Senior Research Professor of New Testament & Biblical Theology, Southeastern Baptist Theological Seminary and Founder of Biblical Foundations (www.biblicalfoundations.org)

As one who was among the first to alert the evangelical world to some of the dangers in Tom Wright's views, I was fascinated to read Tom Holland's careful analysis of Wright's methodology in interpreting New Testament material as well as on his understanding of justification. Dr Holland's study continues to develop the exegetical insights he has presented in previous works. While I have concerns about some of his conclusions, I greatly appreciate the way he has scrutinised Wright's sources and has shown how we should understand Pauline themes such as redemption against the background of the Passover and the prophecies of Isaiah and Hosea. New Testament scholars cannot afford to ignore this radically fresh and biblical perspective.

- Philip H. Eveson, Former Principal of the London Seminary and Director of the John Owen Centre for Theological Study

In this corner we have a veritable library made up of N. T. Wright's numerous books. And in this corner, now we have Tom Holland's Tom Wright and the Search for Truth, which offers a ringside view of a sometimes-bruising collision of perspectives. Holland presses some issues that echo queries already posed. Yet he offers a sustained critique of Wright's exegesis and its informing premises that breaks new ground. Particularly insightful is his demonstration of ways Second Temple sources control Wright's interpretations when New and Old Testament writings more likely furnish interpretive keys. Where Wright prefers a monolithic definition of "covenant," Holland shows the varying meanings Paul (and other biblical writers) conveys with the word. While Holland is appreciative of Wright at many points, and while there is much more to say in assessment of Wright pro and con, Holland's probing and robust, Old Testament-based alternatives to Wright's often shaky and tendentious reconstructions will stimulate scholarship. Holland's book will free some readers from unwarranted enchantment with Wright and enable them to arrive at more fruitful understandings of especially Pauline texts and their redemptive message.

- Robert W. Yarbrough, Professor of New Testament, Covenant, Theological Seminary, St. Louis, MO, USA

Various new perspectives on Paul have made a huge impact on New Testament studies in the last forty years. In his scholarly work N.T. Wright has had perhaps the most influence on a wider readership. In this accessible treatment of Wright's output, Dr Holland presents a careful, eirenic, and thorough examination of the influences and assumptions that have shaped Wright's approach to the theology of Paul. He treats his arguments to critical but fair scrutiny. It is important that widely popular claims are made accountable in an informed manner. In achieving this Dr Holland provides us with a resource that will prove invaluable for reaching a coherent evaluation.

-   Dr Robert Letham, Director of Research, Senior Lecturer in Systematic and Historical Theology, Union School of Theology

N.T. Wright has perhaps received more critical engagement than any other biblical scholar in this generation. These critiques often focus on the fruit of Wright's theology rather than its root. In contrast, Tom Holland's work levels a critique that goes all the way to the methodological roots. On the surface, the reader will find that Holland's theology is similar to Wright's in many ways—Paul is essentially a Jewish theologian, the New Exodus theme is a key component to Paul's theology, Paul emphasizes the corporate nature of salvation—but the roots of Holland's theology are drinking from a different stream. The fruit of Holland's Tom Wright and The Search for Truth provides refreshing and innovative insights paired with keen theological precision. Holland's critique of Wright is marked by humility and kindness, and his own positive contribution is a rich feast for the heart and mind. I hope The Search for Truth finds wide acceptance in Pauline studies.

-   Mark Baker, Books at a Glance

You are probably reading this book because of your interest in Tom Wright, but who is the author, Tom Holland? He is a British scholar who is the Senior Research Fellow of Union School of Theology, Oxford, UK. He has spent 40 years researching in the specialized field of Paschal New Exodus Theology, the field that is very close to what Tom Wright engages in. Holland is recognized as the world's leading scholar in this discipline. The following endorsements of his work come from a wide range of internationally respected scholars and commentators. 'there is a remarkable thesis being presented here that demands scholarly attention'. He has certainly produced a strong argument for a much greater influence of Passover typology than has generally been thought to be the case, and his arguments for the atoning sacrificial understanding of the original Passover sacrifice powerfully support the case argued by J. Jeremias and L. Morris'. Dr Holland has produced a stimulating volume which deserves the most careful scrutiny from

The Search for Truth

New Testament students. It is a remarkably fresh and creative study which makes one re-think familiar passages in new ways.

- The late Prof H I Marshall, Aberdeen University, *Evangelical Quarterly*

It provides a fresh and useful treatment of Pauline theology, and many of its arguments offer corrections to widespread misunderstandings of Paul'.

- Prof Anthony C. Thiselton, Nottingham University, Expository Times

It should be compulsory reading for any who feel in any way seduced by the arguments of either liberal or 'New Perspective' theologians on the origins and content of Paul's theology. It presents compelling evidence that Paul's theology was thoroughly rooted in the Old Testament.

- Robert Strivens, The Banner of Truth

This is certainly radical, and it boldly pushes forward an idea that has not really been discussed in Pauline scholarship.

- Tan Kim Huat, Trinity Theological Journal

A welcome and important contribution to the controversial area of Pauline theology'.

- Bill James, Reformation Today

Contours of Pauline Theology is a valuable tool for those in the Messianic movement who want to understand the New Testament, and those in the wider body of Messiah who are confused because they have been taught to read a thoroughly Jewish book through Greek lenses'.

- Richard Gibson, *Chai Magazine*

The strengths of the book are its robust challenge to many scholarly presuppositions and an impetus to new research on Paul's debt to the Old Testament...There is much that is very good and stimulating in this book'.

- Anthony Bash, European Journal of Theology

He has pointed to an interesting and important motif in the OT, in early Judaism and in Paul's theology, which needs to be studied more systematically and in depth. Many of his challenges of recent scholarship on Paul and suggestions of his own are worth pondering.

- Christoph Stenschke, Themelios

Those who would seek to discredit Pauline theology will appreciate Holland's scholarship and the sound arguments on Paul's behalf. Those who ascribe to Paul as an apostle of Jesus Christ will appreciate Holland's apologetic prowess and find Paul's Jewish hermeneutic illuminating'.

- The American Journal of Biblical Theology

I am thankful to Dr Holland for he has renewed my desire to study Paul's writings and to understand afresh the glorious gospel that animated the life and ministry of this apostle'.

- Peter Misselbrook, Evangelicals Now

If Tom Holland's conclusions are accepted, then it would mean a radical rethinking in the way we approach some of the well-known passages of Paul's letters.

- Philip Eveson, Evangelical Times

Generally speaking, conservative Reformed criticisms of the new perspective on Paul strike me as lacklustre and predictable. That cannot be said, however, of Tom Holland's new book, which is bound to shake loose some long-standing presuppositions in Pauline studies. Holland's book raises enough questions about traditional assumptions to clear the way for ground-breaking research, and his approach does allow for a rigorous re-examination of the degree to which Paul is indebted to texts like Isaiah and the Pentateuch.

- Mark Mattison, The Paul Page

The present reviewer, an Old Testament specialist, finds Holland's arguments as largely compelling and would suggest that Holland has re-integrated the faith of Old and New Testaments in a manner that serves effectively to emphasise the unity of Scripture.

- Stephen Dray, Evangel

The new perspective has both helpful insights and troubling implications—so we should do our best to reflect on it. To this end, Holland's book has been one of the best helps I have come across. It is readable, scholarly, imaginative and stimulating. All in one book!

- Chris Sinkinson, Congregational Concern

This is a book to be placed in the hands of serious academics, Jewish or Christian, who are interested in Pauline studies and the relationship between Christianity and Judaism.'

The Search for Truth

Contours of Pauline Theology is an important and brilliant book. I recommend it to all prospective students of theology to read and study before they go to university.

It is refreshing to read something radically new in such a popular area as Pauline studies. So often what promised new perspectives, new insights, turns out not to be essentially different. Tom Holland's original and creative approach to Paul does not fall into this category. Here Paul is not the innovator of Christian doctrine—he received his theological model from his Jewish upbringing in which he was taught that Yahweh would bring about the promised New Exodus. Paul came to realize that this had been inaugurated by the paschal death of Christ. Thus, Holland maintains that there existed a common hermeneutical model for both Judaism and the New Testament church, i.e. the New Exodus. Justification is not a declaration of being in the covenant but refers back to the creation of a covenant between Yahweh and His people. This view of justification fits in with Paul's doctrine of corporate baptism, the washing of the believing community accomplished by the Spirit through the death of Christ. Paul's theology is not individualistic, but corporate, so it is believers collectively as the church and not the believer's individual body which comprise the temple of the Holy Spirit. I anticipate that if it finds acceptance, the proposals of this book should provide a timely and fruitful alternative to some of the theological emphases that have guided the church for too long.

In his Contours of Pauline Theology Dr Holland argues forcefully that the main contours of Paul's thought can only be understood when we understand Paul as an exegete and theologian of the Old Testament, with the hoped-for New Exodus, now fulfilled in Christ, at the centre of his reading strategy. This approach finds corporate and covenantal themes to lie at the very heart of Paul's concerns. In constant critical engagement with the whole range of contemporary scholarship Holland maps out for himself and his readers new ways of understanding Paul and offers new insights into a range of absolutely vital issues from justification to Christology, and new insights into Pauline texts from Romans to Colossians. Challenging, unsettling and infuriating Dr Holland's tour de force cannot be ignored.

First Word

Biblical exegetes are not immune from the temptation to choose or create methods which lead to predetermine results.[1]

- Markus Barth, 'Christ and All Things,' *Paul and Paulinism: Essays in Honour of C.K. Barrett*

The author appreciates you taking the time and making the effort to read this book. He requests that if you found it helpful, or if you had any strong disagreements, that you post your impressions on Amazon.com, Amazon.co.uk, Barnes and Noble and Goodreads as well as any other sites that share reviews. You don't have to have any qualification to justify doing this, just that you have an opinion.

Thank you

Tom

---

[1] Markus Barth, 'Christ and All Things,' in Hooker, Morna, Stephen Wilson and C.K. Barrett, Paul and Paulinism: Essays in Honour of C.K. Barrett (London: SPCK, 1982), 162.

Acknowledgements

The writing of this book has drawn on the kindness, knowledge and skills of many people, and for this I am indebted.

Jonathan Stephen, the retired principal of Union School of Theology, initially encouraged me to write this book; while Iwan Rhys Jones, its Old Testament and Hebrew specialist, regularly checked

to see if OT scholarship would support my understanding of Paul's Hebraic mind. This was such a great help and avoided unsubstantiated claims being made

Donald Mitchell, the School's librarian, not only repeatedly hunted down material but also read the text and made helpful suggestions.

Tony Hate, a retired solicitor, applied his amazing attention to detail to the text, picking up on grammatical and typographical errors. Roy Harries, a retired accountant, also used his training and

highly-developed attention to detail to read the text and offer helpful suggestions. Also, Ann Weaver read the earlier draft and made very helpful suggestions.

Of course, I am deeply grateful to Prof Stanley Porter, Prof Andreas

J. Kostenberger, Prof Bob Letham, Prof Robert W. Yarbrough, Rev Philip Eveson and Mr Mark Baxter for reading the book, providing endorsements and giving much-appreciated advice.

To all the above, and to others who have kindly supported my endeavours, I extend my heart-felt thanks.

Tom Holland

Union School of Theology Reformation Day

500th Anniversary 2017

Preface

My introduction to Tom Wright goes back to 1977 when, as a young Baptist pastor, I was working in a small town twenty- five miles from Cambridge. I had been preaching through Romans and had become increasingly concerned about the way that numerous commentators of all theological traditions had resorted to overriding the clear meaning of the Greek text when it challenged their understanding. When their expected reading of a passage did not fit the Greek terms Paul used, they would say something like: 'While Paul uses this term, it doesn't properly convey what he wants to say. What he intends to say is ...'[2]

This common practice made me uncomfortable. It was like stopping someone during a conversation and saying, 'I think you have used the wrong word; what you meant to say is ...' To interrupt a person in such a way would be the height of rudeness, implying the person did not know what they were talking about. This widespread practice made me determined to read the text as it stood and not resort to textual corrections that could not be justified. Having studied the Greek text of Romans for my BD, I had engaged with a wide range of commentators, whose arguments left me dissatisfied and confused. As already noted, they modified and glossed over the clear meaning of the Greek text with little seeming concern.

But the more I considered Paul's Jewish heritage, the more I came to see that the problem with the then-prevailing understanding was the idea that Romans should be read as if it were the product of a Greek writer. I began to realize that Romans was far more akin to a Hebrew document than a Greek one. This perspective led me to focus on how it related to the Old Testament and I came to see that Paul used precisely the right vocabulary for his arguments. With this recognition came the discovery that the message of his letter to the Romans contained far greater insights and promises than I ever imagined!

---

[2] As for example, C. H. Dodd, (1934), *The Epistle of Paul to the Romans*. London: Hodder and Stoughton

I sent these initial conclusions to my undergraduate New Testament teacher, Dr Donald Guthrie. He advised me to get in touch with a young man who was also doing research on Romans and studying for a DPhil at Oxford, Tom Wright. I wasn't able to actually meet Tom, however, until 1979.[3] By then he had moved to Cambridge to complete his research while serving as the chaplain of Downing College and I was only a 30-minute drive away, which made it possible for us to get together for a conversation about our mutual interests. In that meeting, I shared how I had come to see that the New Exodus promises—made by the prophets to Israel when she was in exile—were taken over by the New Testament writers. These promises were the key to identifying the context of the themes that controlled Paul's thinking.

I recall pointing out that Paul's description of himself as a *doulos* ('slave') of Christ should be read in the light of how the LXX used *doulos* to translate the Hebrew word ebed, 'servant.' Paul was identifying himself not as a slave in Roman terms, the understanding that then prevailed, but as a servant of Christ, just as the prophets saw themselves as servants of Yahweh. Paul's use of the Servant Songs in 2 Corinthians 6:1–2 and the account of his 'conversion' (which linked his future ministry with the task given to the Servant of Isaiah, see Acts 26:15–18) were evidence of how he thus saw himself. On hearing this, Tom got up from his chair, went to a bookcase that was next to the window and, taking one of the volumes down, flicked through the pages for a few minutes, then looked up and said, 'No one has seen this. I'll be glad to supervise you to do an MPhil.'

I declined this very kind and unexpected offer, explaining that there were bigger issues I was anxious to pursue. I was focused on following through on my interest in Paul's anthropology, as I was convinced this was a key topic for understanding much of the apostle's salvation imagery. As I was leaving Tom's study in Downing College after several hours of scintillating discussion, I recall him saying, 'The problem I have with your suggestions is that there are no loose ends; theological study is not like that—there are always loose ends.'

Later, I obtained a copy of Tom's thesis after its award and was delighted to see how he had identified the Jewish Messianic theme that flows through Romans. He showed that the title, Christos, had a distinct Messianic content,

---

[3] The following details are not reliant on memory but on correspondence with Tom Wright and others from that time.

something that scholarship had debunked decades earlier because of their emphasis on Paul's Hellenistic mindset. They had argued that the word Christos became nothing more than a surname. Tom's identification of the Jewish nature of the letter was confirmation that I had at long last met someone who was looking in the same direction as I was. Eventually, I too completed the work I had sought to do and was awarded a Ph.D. from the University of Wales.[4]

As Tom began his writing career, I followed his publishing and the development of his ideas with interest. It became obvious that we shared the same perspective in believing that Paul was essentially a Jewish theologian who saw that the promises Israel's God made to his people in exile were an important key to understanding how the apostle developed his theology. As Tom expanded his thinking in an ever-increasing number of published writings, he began to identify the importance of the New Exodus theme that had been part of our discussion in his study in Cambridge. I also noticed there were some critical differences in our conclusions, but I could not immediately put my finger on why this was so.

Over time, I came to pinpoint the reason—I realized we were using different theological approaches or methods. The fact is that all of our theological understanding depends on how we interpret Scripture, and a big part of this relates to the way we approach this task. Tom Wright is very serious about the importance of correctly interpreting the Christian Scriptures. He argues that what Paul says in his debates with his opponents can only be constructed by understanding his detractors' arguments. This explains why Tom is eager to engage with the texts of Paul's opponents as well as the wider cultural context such as the Wisdom of Solomon and Books of the Maccabees; in his view, this will equip him to expound Paul's letters. This is one of the main reasons Tom Wright is intrigued with the intertestamental texts of Judaism's second-temple period—he believes they reflect the issues that the Jewish community debated at the time of the birth of the church, and therefore, had a shaping influence on the New Testament writers, especially

---

[4] Thomas S Holland, 'The Paschal New Exodus Motif in Paul's Letter to the Romans with Special Attention to its Christological Significance' (PhD thesis, University of Wales, Lampeter, 1996)

Paul. He argues that reading Paul's writings through this lens will open up new avenues of understanding.[5]

I don't deny these texts have value in shedding light on the cultural backdrop of the day, but I am concerned that this relatively new method of reading the New Testament through this lens has inadvertently opened the door for this literature to have an undue influence on Tom Wright's interpretation of the New Testament. In personal conversations, I have shared my concerns with him, but he has remained steadfast in believing in the benefits of this approach.[6] According to Tom, he only uses these texts to provide parallels that show how these primitive Jewish texts support his understanding of New Testament teaching. He claims they do not add to what he says characterized Paul's thought. Rather, in his view, intertestamental literature simply provides insight into how other Jews thought about the topics Paul was dealing with.

I believe however, that by using these extra-biblical sources, Tom Wright has added extraneous thoughts and concepts to Paul's theology resulting in a loss of clarity regarding the apostles teaching. I have no reason to doubt the sincerity of his intention to keep Paul within his Jewish heritage, but I do not believe he has achieved this goal and that his construction of some of Paul's arguments can only be sustained by appealing to intertestamental writings. Without these extra-biblical texts, several of the very important claims Wright makes for Paul's theology simply cannot be supported. In the end, I suggest that he has given us 'What Saint Paul Ought to Have Really Said' rather than 'What Saint Paul Really Said'. This claim is the burden of this book, and I believe I can provide the evidence from Wright's writings to substantiate it. Wright claims his reading of Paul is rooted in the Old Testament.

I will seek to show that while this is clearly one of Tom's sources, the most decisive influence on the outcome of his interpretation is intertestamental literature. He assumes that Paul bought into Hellenistic

---

[5] N.T. Wright, "Jesus and the Identity of God", http://ntwrightpage.com/2016/07/12/jesus-and-the-identity-of-god/. Originally published in *Ex Auditu* 1998, 14, 42–56.

[6] He was offered a copy of the first draft with an invitation to write the last chapter. He indicated that he would not have time but wanted to know what I would do with anything he disagreed with and I said I would endeavour to include it in the text of the book to let the reader hear his concerns. I will refer to his email from time to time to allow his concerns to be heard.

Judaism and therefore, looks to texts written from this perspective for insight into the apostle's mindset and theology. My case is that Paul was never drawn in that direction. I believe it can be proven that before his conversion to Christ, he was driven by the message of the Old Testament and that after his conversion those same biblical texts, and those alone, continued to drive him.

The reason for making the effort to open this discussion is because intertestamental literature figures not only in Tom Wright's theological constructions but in the writings of hundreds of other scholars as well. As I have stated and will show throughout the book, I believe using this material as an interpretive lens distorts the apostles teaching in significant ways. I have sometimes been asked why I have chosen Tom Wright as a subject when there are many other scholars who also engage with second-temple literature in their interpretation of New Testament texts. My first reason is that most other scholars are very open in acknowledging why they value their chosen method as compared to Tom Wright. These other scholars are mostly comfortable in saying that Paul deliberately developed the Christian message by infusing Hellenistic ideas into Hebraic teaching, and they have no difficulty in saying that Paul deliberately Hellenized the Christian gospel. Tom, however, says he only searches for parallels that support his interpretation of Paul and not for material to add to the apostle's constructions. While I support Tom's desire to show that Paul taught a Jewish message, I also believe the way he uses intertestamental literature has unwittingly produced an inaccurate version of Paul's teaching.

Another reason for choosing to examine Tom Wright's theology is that my early entry into this same field over forty years ago has given me an advantage above most others who are following this same line of thought. Because we started exploring the Jewish context of Paul's writings around the same time, I have not been trying to catch up with Tom Wright but have made my own pathway within our commonly agreed paradigm. Like Wright, I have a deep commitment to the Old Testament's New Exodus model as a key part of what has produced Paul's theology. However, the conclusions that I have reached disagree with his, which makes for an interesting comparison. The fact that our work shares a common emphasis on the New Exodus theme gives me an opportunity of showing the benefit of my methodology against his.

Tom Wright is also a natural subject because his stream of publications makes following his reasoning and the progression of his thought possible. This is not true of most other scholars many of whom joined the debates later in the discussion have not done the same level of groundwork necessary for building an original case. Having bought into the prevailing body of wisdom perspectives concerning their specialization, they have added their own understanding to it. This can be valuable, of course, but Wright is one of the few who has worked his position out from first principles, and that makes interacting with him more rewarding.

Another reason for choosing Tom Wright's work as the subject of this study is that I am repeatedly asked in what way my views agree or differ with his. It can be tedious to get into the level of detail that's needed to answer this simple question. The danger is that some enquirers may wish they never asked after hearing the more technical explanations. I hope that by writing this book I can tell future friends who may ask about this where they can find the answer, so they don't regret bringing it up!

And finally, I had hoped that others would have engaged with Tom's work at a level that, in my opinion, is necessary in order to maintain the high view of scripture that many in our tradition claim to hold. I have been disappointed, however, with earlier attempts to move the discussion forward. I am now retired, and if I do not add my concerns while I am able, they may never be heard and considered. I have sought to talk with Tom about the issues on which we disagree, but he is convinced his understanding is the correct one. This is perfectly acceptable, for that is the nature of theological debate, but his perspective is not the end of the discussion. It is also right for any who are interested in learning more about the wider issues and methods that shape his work to have the opportunity to explore viewpoints that may challenge his understanding. That is what I hope this book will provide.

There is a good deal of reluctance in publishing this work, for, if I am right, it will challenge the lifetime work of a good man, and that is never something that should be relished. Indeed, Tom Wright has proven himself not only to be a gifted theologian and Christian leader, but his kindness also has become legendary and I have been a recipient of his kindness. I am forever grateful for that day when he welcomed me into his study in Cambridge and treated the arguments of a young local pastor with a degree of respect that few others at that time gave, for they could not see the problems I was seeking to resolve. Over the years that same kind consideration has always characterized his dealings with others, even those with whom he has disagreed. I hope to emulate such a commendable spirit.

I hope that there is no sense of a personal attack or vendetta for that is not my intention. Rather, I hope this discussion will advance the cause of the same Christ whom we both seek to serve.

As we look at the theology of Tom Wright, I will highlight OT texts that he has not considered and show how his appeal to the writings of ITL have failed to bring greater clarity. I am not challenging Wright's use of the New Exodus model. Indeed, I use it more extensively than he has done.[7] Where I differ is in the question of our different methodologies. I believe that if his research had been properly controlled then his contribution would be of far greater value than it has been. It is my genuine hope that the potential of his work will be seen and valued despite those areas where I disagree and that the wider church might see the value of the research, he has spent his life doing, and yet read it with an awareness of the danger of using the sources that I wish he had not drawn on. I do not doubt that the saviour Wright seeks to serve will be loved more by his people better understanding who he is and what he has achieved through his life, teaching, death and resurrection. It is not that I am advocating the mistakes I consider Wright has made, but I am advocating the paradigm he has chosen, that of the New Exodus and its fulfilment in the ministry of Jesus.

Thus, I shall examine Tom Wright's theological presuppositions to understand how they have affected the way his arguments have developed. In addition to considering his methods and their impact, I shall examine his understanding of Christology, atonement, and justification to provide examples of what his methods have led to. I shall offer the reader different models created within New Exodus expectations and fulfilment and by so doing I shall reach somewhat different conclusions to those offered by Wright.

Before getting into the text of the book, it may help to see an example from Tom's latest book, The Day The Revolution Began, that shows why I am concerned about his methods. The book has received glowing reviews, with some evangelical leaders who had previously been suspicious of Tom's theology openly laying down their objections and raving enthusiastically over

---

[7] See Holland, Tom, *Contours of Pauline Theology: A Radical New Survey of the Influences on Paul's Biblical Writings* (Fearn, Ross-shire: Christian Focus Publications, 2004) and Holland, Tom, *Romans: The Divine Marriage: A Biblical Theological Commentary* (Eugene, Or.: Pickwick Publications, 2011).

it. While normally I would be delighted for an author of Tom's calibre to receive such high praise, it has intensified my deep concern that his exegetical method will become the model that others follow, especially those who lead the church and young men presently for Christian leadership. I foresee that an uncritical acceptance of his approach has the potential to seriously threaten the health and witness of the church. The passage I am quoting is from Tom's discussion of the details involving the last supper. He notices that each gospel writer used different words for the communion service, acknowledging this is difficult to explain. Offering his own solution, he says:

> Perhaps the best comment is that, given the subsequent events of that same night (not to mention the quantity of food and drink that had already been consumed), it isn't surprising to find various slightly different versions already current among Jesus's earliest followers these were strange and surprising words, sprung on them without warning at a moment of tension and excitement. What matters is that within the overreaching Passover theme of the meal, the whole occasion, and the events that would happen the next day, Jesus insisted that this new Passover would perform its freedom-bringing victory by means of the long-awaited final undoing of exile.[8]

If such casual exegesis is an example of treating the text with respect and holding a high regard for scripture as Tom has repeatedly claimed that he does, and if this is an example of serious scholarship, then I fear that I am not on the same page. Obviously, it is up to Tom to choose how he wants to interpret any biblical passage, but to my knowledge, no one has ever suggested that difficulties with the communion texts were the product of the apostles' diet and alcohol consumption! Even the most ardent liberal scholar has never challenged the apostles' accuracy, the reliability of their record or their teaching on such flimsy evidence. To propose that the account of the most sacred event in the entire Bible is at the mercy of the apostles' dietary preferences and the amount of alcohol they consumed exceeds any reasonable claim to be respectful of the text, which is why I find it difficult to accept that this is an example of sound exegesis. I just wonder where the Holy Spirit is in all of this? This is an example of what I mean by questionable methods. It is about careless and disrespectful exegesis, the sort that we will consider in the

---

[8] Wright, N. T, *The Day the Revolution Began: Reconsidering the Meaning of Jesus's Crucifixion,* HarperOne, London, 2016, pp 186-7. [sic] Emphasis added.

opening chapter of this book, and that are characteristics found throughout Tom Wright's work.

Writing this does not bring satisfaction, only sadness, but I genuinely believe that I have an obligation from the Lord to raise these issues. I recognize the many excellent qualities in Tom and the much good that he has done. But like Paul, I have to judge not on human ability or winsomeness, but on loyalty to the authority of Scripture, the Bible, the Word of God.

I offer this study in the hope that many will come to see the incredible consistency of the Scriptures and their message. Their unity is not a human invention; it is the revelation of the grace of God given in His Son, Jesus Christ our Lord.

Contents

The Search for Truth

The Search for Truth

Chapter 1:
Probing the Contours of Recent Research

The nineteenth century was the time of revolution not only for the natural sciences but also for theological understanding. From a position where most of Christendom afforded the Scriptures utmost respect and authority as the word of God, scholars in the German University of Tübingen took on board the newly constructed theories of Literary, Historical and Form Criticism. By using these methods of historical, literary construction, they argued that the Bible was not divinely inspired but was the result of borrowing from a wide range of teachings held by other religions in the ancient world.

Very soon these claims were embedded in the theological foundations of seminaries and university departments across Europe and North America, and it led to divine revelation being replaced by human ingenuity. This understanding had a profound effect on the authority of the Scriptures and in turn, on the life of the church as prospective pastors of the flock entered theological schools. The students learned that the Christian Scriptures have no more authority than the religious texts of other ancient religious communities. Many accepted this new way of understanding and went off into the pulpits of Christendom and taught these new insights as facts. They taught that the NT was nothing but a collection of foraged ideas that represented a whole range of sources which the NT authors had borrowed from and integrated into their writings. As a result of this change, scholarship increasingly focused on the religions and beliefs of the Greco-Roman world as the source of NT teaching. The mindset for NT studies for the next hundred years or so was set, and few had the confidence to challenge it. NT scholarship had become wedded to Hellenistic studies. The university system came to view anyone who disagreed with the new prevailing orthodoxy as oddities who were out of touch with intellectual reality.

Inevitably the authority of the Bible declined as the confidence of rationalism grew to the point that it became the dominant intellectual force in European society. Where once the praises of King Jesus were sung in the great cathedrals of Europe, he was increasingly being seen to be nothing more than a mystical figure whose only value was that he once taught an ignorant generation some useful lessons in morality. Obviously, and thankfully, there were exceptions who sought to challenge the new consensus.

A further influence on our understanding of the NT is the recent acceptance of the Jewish literature known as intertestamental literature (ITL). Much of this literature had been known for many centuries but because none of it was in Hebrew there was the fear that it not genuinely Jewish literature. It was seen to be probably much later and written mostly by Christian authors who wanted to show how Christ and his teaching had their roots in Judaism. This scepticism regarding dating and provenance all changed when the Dead Sea Scrolls (DSS) were found in 1947, with much more discovered in following excavations, and some of these previously known suspect texts were found in the Qumran community's collection. What was especially important was that they were written in Hebrew and dated before the emergence of Christianity! This is the evidence that was needed to accept that the previously doubted texts are genuine records of Jewish teaching in the first century. These texts, hailed as the greatest discovery of ancient texts ever made, became the focus of intense research with many scholars regarding them as the key to a correct understanding of the NT.

Interestingly one of the effects of the discovery of the DSS was that it provided ammunition for the growing number of scholars who found reading the NT from a Hellenistic mindset increasingly unsatisfying. Part of the argument for the NT being a collection of Hellenistic writings was the presence of terms that had been thought to be Greek and not Hebraic. The presence of these features, it was claimed, showed that the source of the thought patterns of the NT documents was from Hellenism. But the DSS showed these very terms, in the Hebrew equivalent, were present in Jewish literature that dated before the time of Christ. This discovery provided the evidence that was needed to challenge the Hellenistic reading and slowly a movement began to emerge that recognized the Hebraic origin and content of NT teaching.

Just as the still dominant aggressive scepticism was beginning to lose its appeal, Tom Wright entered his theological education and was soon to become a major voice that challenged earlier German assumptions.

The Contribution of Tom Wright

After graduating from Oxford, Wright stayed on and worked for his DPhil under the supervision of Dr G. B. Caird, who had a profound influence on his theological development. In preparation for the launch of Wright's book *Jesus and the Victory of God*, an unpublished draft of the book was given to Dr Peter Head, who was a member of the Tyndale Library in Cambridge where the book launch took place.[9] Dr Head had been given the 700-page script with a deadline of only a few days before the launch. At the crowded meeting, after introducing the author and before beginning his summary of the book, he gave the audience his advice. I recall him saying something like 'if you want to know what Wright is saying read Caird.' Such was the influence of the man who had just years earlier suffered an untimely death. It was Caird's work on the language of the Bible that directed Wright in his search for a better understanding of the Bible's message.[10] Caird's contribution, which deeply influenced Wright, is that much of the eschatological language found in the Bible is not literal but metaphoric.

There was another major influence that impacted Wright while he was doing his DPhil. It was at this time that the research of E. P. Sanders was published, three years before Wright submitted his thesis for his Oxford DPhil.[11] Sanders' book was to have a massive impact on the first-century Jewish studies; commonly called Second Temple Judaism (STJ).[12] Sanders claimed that he had shown that Israel's faith was not a legalistic system that promoted 'works righteousness' as understood by most Protestant scholars. Rather, he claimed, the historical, textual evidence of the first century showed that the Jewish community saw the law as being incredibly positive. This amended view challenged the understanding that many had of Paul speaking of the law as something that terrified and pursued the sinner. Sanders called for and produced a major rethink on the statements of Paul concerning the law. From this reappraisal, the 'New Perspective on Paul' was born.

This conclusion of Sanders supported Wright's growing conviction that the prevailing location of Paul's teaching was not to be found in Hellenism,

---

[9] N. T. Wright, *Jesus and the Victory of God. Christian Origins and the Question of God, Vol. 2* (London: SPCK, 1996).

[10] G. Caird, *The Language and Imagery of the Bible* (London: Duckworth, 1980).

[11] E. Sanders, Paul and Palestinian Judaism: A Comparison of Patterns of Religion. (London: SCM, 1977).

[12] Research on this period often focuses on the 4th century B.C.E. and following, and stretches into the 2nd century ce. It is sometimes mistakenly referred to as 'intertestamental.'

but in first century Judaism. Wright initially gave a strong endorsement to the findings of Sanders, but as his work was scrutinized and difficulties were raised concerning some of the evidence and his sweeping conclusions, his case began to weaken, and Wright modified his support.[13]

Despite Wright distancing himself from some of Sanders' claims, he continued to use the work to support his interest in researching the Jewishness of Paul's teaching. He continued to support the basic point that Sanders case rested on, that STJ was not legalistic and that it saw the law as God's greatest gift to his people. Sanders called this understanding of Judaism 'covenantal nomism' or 'covenant law,' nomos being the Greek word for law. This perspective informs Wright's understanding on Paul's teaching on the Law.[14]

It was Wright's research into the area of the law in Paul's thinking, and the conclusions he reached, that caused alarm to reformed Pauline scholars. He argued that the Reformers had misunderstood Paul's teaching. He claimed that Paul's doctrine of justification was not about how people are made right with God, i.e. a doctrine concerning salvation or soteriology, as had been taught by the Reformers and their descendants. Wright claimed that justification was, in fact, a relatively unimportant doctrine for both the Jewish community and also the church. He argued that it was an ecclesiological doctrine, being about who is in the church or covenant community. Unfortunately, this claim isolated Wright from the wider Evangelical community and his important message about the essential Jewishness of Paul's teaching took much longer to be received than might have otherwise

---

[13] Wright later wrote: 'Recent attempts to suggest a more variegated attitude to the Law than was allowed for by E.P. Sanders in Paul and Palestinian Judaism are undoubtedly right to stress variety, and undoubtedly wrong to use that as a way of smuggling back an anachronistic vision of a Pelagian (or semi-Pelagian) or medieval works-righteousness. I shall be in implicit debate, in the details of the exegesis and in the structure of thought, both with the so-called 'new perspective' and with its opponents; but I shall not have space for any hand-to-hand exchanges. My aim is a more strategic outflanking'. N. T. Wright, Paul in Fresh Perspective. (Minneapolis; London: Fortress Press; SPCK, 2005), 109.

[14] Interestingly Sanders finished up saying that Paul departed from his Jewish background to occupy an eclectic position in which he synthesised Hebraic and Roman Greco thought. See Sanders, Paul and Palestinian Judaism, 555.

been the case. Understandably, but regrettably his challenge of a central reformed doctrine caused many to see him as a threat to biblical truth.[15]

Wright continued his research into the Jewishness of Paul's teaching, and it opened up many interesting and valuable insights. Slowly the scholarly community began to open to his arguments, and his popular writings gave him an ever-growing following of thinking Christians who wanted to understand their Bibles better. Through his wide range of academic papers and books he has very effectively made his case and is now accepted in many institutions that once shut their doors to him. He regularly draws crowds of hundreds, if not thousands, to hear him when he gives public lectures. His deserved elevation to the bishopric of Durham gave him a platform to speak not only nationally but also internationally, and he has become one of the most recognized biblical scholars in the world today. His work as bishop was hugely valued, and many within the Anglican Communion were shocked and dismayed to hear that he had resigned from his bishopric to return to academia. He took this decision to complete his writing project, a five-volume work that rereads the Scriptures in the light of the paradigms he has identified as those which guided the early church in its understanding.

Much of what Wright has written has been excellent. He has helped Christians to see the importance of the OT for interpreting the NT. In his first major work, The New Testament and the People of God, he set out his case regarding the background of the OT and how the NT is related to it. He made it clear that this is only grasped by understanding the wider world of the New Testament writers which they sought to address. Wright claimed that a thorough knowledge of Greco-Roman texts and Jewish intertestamental literature was needed for it explained how the apostles were interpreting the Old Testament and its application to the world of the first century. One of his major contributions has been to challenge the scholarly grouping known as the Jesus Seminar, which met to decide which passages in the Gospels that recorded the words of Jesus were original and which had been 'created' by later generations of Christians as they sought to expand on Jesus teaching.

Wright, like Athanasius almost 1700 years before him, stood against this serious error. He demonstrated in his second major work, Jesus and the

---

[15] For an overview of the main contributors to the wider NPP debate and an analysis if their positions, see G. P. Anderson, *Paul's New Perspective: Charting a Soteriological Journey* (Downers Grove: Inter-Varsity Press, 2016), 92–152.

Victory of God, that the passages classified as later (Hellenistic) creations could only make sense in the time of Jesus's ministry as given in the Gospels. His point was that they could not be later works because they would have had not made sense, either to the supposed authors or their readers, for the issues they dealt with no longer applied. They only made sense in the time- frame indicated by the Gospel authors. Wright also wrote another hugely influential book, *The Resurrection of the Son of God*, which assured many of his orthodox credentials. He went on to write Paul and the Faithfulness of God, and The Day the Revolution Began, both of which have furthered his claims about how to correctly understand the teaching of Paul. These works have assured many that he is a trustworthy teacher of the church and for most, the early suspicions concerning his proposals concerning justification have evaporated. The consequence of this theological movement is that many no longer think that the Reformers are reliable authorities for guiding the 21st century church.

Wright's influence secured its place in contemporary scholarship not only through his writings but also through the positions he has held both in academia as well as the church.

Following undergraduate and then post graduate studies at Oxford, Wright taught at McGill University, Montreal (1981–1986). He returned to Oxford as chaplain, fellow and tutor at Worcester College and lecturer in New Testament in the University of Oxford (1986–93). He moved from Oxford to be Dean of Lichfield Cathedral (1994–99) and then returned briefly to Oxford as Visiting Fellow of Merton College, before taking up his appointment as Canon Theologian of Westminster Abbey 2000–2003. He became the Bishop of Durham 2003–2010. He retired from the See of Durham on 31 August 2010 and took an appointment as Research Professor of New Testament and Early Christianity at St Mary's College, St Andrews in Scotland.

Chapter 2:
Probing Saul and His Political Identity

On some occasions, when I have met a person who I had previously known only through email or phone, I found that they were nothing like I had imagined them to be! I'm pleased to say that usually such false anticipations have so far not had any far- reaching consequences.

When we come to study Paul and his teaching, we form a range of opinions about him. Some are very positive while others are fiercely negative—Paul tends to get the blame for perpetuating certain beliefs that have harmed many. Since Paul's writings remain central to the beliefs and practices of Christian churches across the globe, it is vital that we have a correct understanding of who Paul was and of what he meant by his letters. In other words, we must check that our impression of him is correct.

To be able to understand Paul at all, we must first ask ourselves some questions. How did he get his message? Was his evidence reliable or has he exaggerated his claims? Do we know what was behind his attempts to persuade gentiles to follow a Jewish Messiah? Do we know what he said about Jesus of Nazareth? Was it possible that Paul was deceived, confused, or worse still, a deceiver?

Since Paul is the apostle who handed on to the church the largest body of Christian teaching within the New Testament, it would not be too far off the mark to say that his teaching moulded the emerging church in the image of his understanding of Jesus and the way in which he had fulfilled God's purposes. For this reason, it is vital that we have confidence both in the reliability of Paul's message and also in our ability to properly understand it.

In this chapter, I want to ask if the Paul that Tom Wright has made popular is the same Paul who was such a mighty force in the development of the early church's worldwide mission. I shall investigate the accuracy of Wright's evidence to see if there may be any breaches between his understanding of Paul and what can be reasonably understood from the text of the New Testament. If there is any discrepancy, then we will need to ask how such a mismatch may have occurred, and what the consequences of it might be. Also, we must ask if there are underlying weaknesses in the way that Wright has constructed his arguments. I believe that there are several, and that these need to be identified and considered so that Wright's teaching on Paul might be carefully re-assessed. We might find that such a re-assessment challenges other aspect of his theological construction, and I will consider some of these aspects later.

Paul, Who He Was

Wright claims that before following Christ, Saul was a religious zealot of the extreme sort. He believes that the Old Testament hero traditions of Phineas, Elijah, and the Maccabean martyrs (traditions which were popular amongst the zealot community of first century Palestine) made a significant impression on him. His evidence for this claim comes from Paul's letter to the Galatians, as discussed in his paper, 'Paul, Arabia, and Elijah (Galatians 1:17).'[16]

Wright began his reconstruction of the apostle Paul by correctly noting that he never saw himself converting to any religion. He responded to Christ's claims as the Jewish Messiah and did not consider that he had in any way stepped outside of Judaism, which continued to be his natural home.

After meeting with the risen Jesus, Paul stayed on in Damascus and was nurtured by the people he had gone to harass. He soon found himself preaching to the Jewish community that they should also follow Jesus, who was the Messiah. Some reacted to him in the same way that he had previously behaved towards Jesus's followers: they sought his death. They even persuaded the governor, under King Aretas, to guard the city so that they could seize him;[17] but he escaped in a basket lowered from a window in the wall (Acts 9:23–25; 2 Cor 11:32–33). After fleeing, Saul went into Arabia before returning to Damascus. Three years later, he went up to Jerusalem to meet Peter and James, the Lord's brother (Gal 1:15–19).

So far, so good; all this follows the scriptural account. But where I think Wright begins to depart from a proper understanding of Paul is when he explores the significance of his statement about going to Arabia (Gal 1:17) with the reference to Sinai in Galatians 4:25. It says, 'Now Hagar is Mount Sinai in Arabia; she corresponds to the present Jerusalem, for she is in slavery

---

[16] N. T. Wright, 'Paul, Arabia, and Elijah (Galatians 1:17)' *N.T. JBL* 115 (1996) 683–692 (686).

[17] Note the power and influence of the Jewish community in the city of Damascus. Paul was now on the other side of the story; the persecutor had become the persecuted.

with her children.' Wright sees this to be a crucial clue as to where Saul in fact went. By linking the two passages (Gal 1:17 and Gal 4:25), Wright holds that Paul expected his readers to recognize that he had, in fact, gone to Sinai, and to draw from this fact inferences about Paul's connection with zealot convictions and practices.

Wright points out that this location with the story of Elijah's flight from Jezebel (1 Kings 19:2–8) and his encounter with God (1 Kings 19:8–18) at Horeb (Sinai) is crucially important. He claims that this was a deliberate link because in Romans 11:2–5 Paul cites this incident directly. Hence, Wright concludes that the apostle went into Arabia to re-enact the journey of Elijah and his meeting with God at Horeb. For Wright, this proves that Saul (like Elijah and Phinehas before him) was a zealot, and his journey to Horeb had the same significance for him as it had for Elijah.

A significant weakness in Wright's reading is that neither Elijah nor Phinehas are mentioned in the letter to the Galatians; indeed, Paul never directly links himself with either of them anywhere in any of his writings. It is true that in Romans 11:2–5, he cites from Elijah's complaint to Yahweh in 1 Kings 19:10 when Elijah thought that he was the only remaining prophet as a result of Jezebel's purge. But this citation has nothing whatever to do with Saul comparing his persecution of the believers with Elijah's confrontation with the prophets of Baal, as Wright claims, for that is not what he is saying in Romans. The comparison made in Romans 11:2–5 is between Jewish believers, who think that God has deserted them because of the growing and dominating gentile presence, and Elijah, who thought he was the only remaining prophet. Paul assures the Jewish believers that God will not allow them to be lost, citing how he protected his servants in the days of Elijah. The reference is not to do with Saul's re-enacting Elijah's journey but with fears of Jewish believers that the Jewish remnant might become extinct. He quells their fears by applying the reassurance Yahweh had given to Elijah, who had similar concerns. The citation is not about Elijah as a zealot but rather as a broken and depressed prophet; moreover, it does not typify Paul's experience, but that of the troubled Jewish believers in Rome.

Admittedly, there are places where Paul describes himself as 'zealous', but this, as I will show, is not the same as saying he was 'a zealot' in the sense that Wright has argued.

Thus, to recap Wright's argument: In Galatians 4:25, Paul tells his readers that he had gone into Arabia to meet with God. Wright sees this journey as a copy of the visit made by Elijah to Horeb hundreds of years earlier—and the Galatians are expected to have made this connection, even though Elijah is not once mentioned in the letter. Wright maintains that the Galatians would somehow understand this connection because Paul had referred to Elijah in his earlier letter to the Romans. But even if the Galatians knew the content of Paul's Roman epistle, how would they grasp the meaning which Wright ascribes to this chain of verses in Galatians? They would have needed to share Wright's view of how Romans 11:2–5 links Paul's journey with that of Elijah. This explanation fails because Romans 11:2–5 is not about Paul's experience, but rather the fear of the Jewish believing community in Rome. Paul's reason for quoting this incident concerning Elijah is to encourage the comparatively few believing Jews left in Rome that they were the faithful 'remnant', as were those of whom God had spoken to Elijah. Paul's reasoning is that they must not fear, for they were in God's care just like the remnant of Elijah's day.

One must question whether there would be any sense in Paul setting the Galatians the kind of exegetical puzzle which Wright suggests. If he had wanted them to know he had gone to Sinai, and that this was a significant point of his autobiography, why did he not just tell them plainly?

Wright sums up his case by saying:

> Saul saw himself, I suggest, acting out the model of Phinehas and Elijah. His zeal led him to physical violence against those whom he saw as the heirs and successors of the compromised Jews of Numbers 25 and the Baal worshipers of 1 Kings 18 (see Acts 22:3–5). He "was persecuting the church with great violence and was trying to destroy it" he again did what Elijah did. He went off to Mount Sinai.[18]

Evaluating Wright's Case

To achieve this narrative, Wright has brought Old Testament figures into his explanation, understanding them to be the models that motivated Paul as a zealot; even though there is no evidence that they held such a place in his thinking in any of his letters, nor in any of the recorded sermons that he delivered. It is pure conjecture that they were playing the parts that he has assigned to them as role models for the young Saul.

---

[18] Wright, 'Arabia', 68.

Rather than comparing his ministry to that of Elijah, Paul, in fact, compares it with that of Moses (2 Cor 3:1–4,18).[19] It would be more natural to say: 'Paul went to Sinai (if he ever did!), to re-enact the experience of Moses, and so become the servant of the new covenant.' Admittedly, Moses had slain an Egyptian before fleeing to Midian, but the tone of violence is not strong enough to justify the claim that he was a proto-zealot; and no one has ever suggested that Moses was somehow anticipating the zealot movement. On the contrary, Moses is remembered for being the meekest man on earth (Num 12:3).

So, what was Paul saying in the statement that he went 'away into Arabia' (Gal 1:17)? The answer is given in the previous verse: 'I did not immediately consult with anyone' (Gal 1:16). The fact is stated not to set up a mystery trail, but as evidence that he had gone into Arabia (exact location unknown, but an isolated location) to be away from others, especially those who sought his life. Because he was forced to leave the company of the Damascus 'Christian' leadership so soon after his conversion, he can say that his understanding of the gospel was not the result of his having been taught by men, but by revelation from God during his period of isolation. There is likely to be no other meaning intended by Galatians 1:17; and this fits in with what Paul was saying in Galatians 1:11–17a as a whole, that he did not receive the revelation of his gospel from man, but from God.

Wright's claim that Saul was a zealot significantly impacts the way in which he interprets Paul and his spiritual journey; it is the foundation of much of what Wright thinks explains the apostle's motives and message. If my concerns are valid, then these arguments will lose a good deal of their force.

Thus, Wright has sought to emphasize that Saul was a political zealot within Jewish society.[20] This foundation helps him to present Saul (and then Paul) as someone with clear political goals; an idea which merges well with what he assumes to be Paul's understanding of the eventual outworking of the gospel—challenging the Roman Empire by calling it to submit to Christ.[21]

---

[19] Admittedly he made this connection once he had become an apostle, not before.

[20] See, for example, N. T. Wright, *What Saint Paul Really Said: Was Paul of Tarsus the Real Founder of Christianity?* (Oxford: Lion, 1997), 26–27.

[21] See N. T. Wright, *Paul and the Faithfulness of God. Christian Origins and the Question of God Vol. 4* (London: SPCK, 2013), 1504. Barclay challenges

Conflicting Loyalties

A serious problem for Wright's view that Saul was an extreme zealot is that he must explain why such a committed zealot as Saul trained under the most liberal rabbi of his day. Saul had, at some point, left his home of Tarsus to live in Jerusalem where he trained to be a rabbi under his chosen teacher, Gamaliel (Acts 22:3). Gamaliel was one of the most distinguished teachers of the Jewish community. We know of him from the Acts of the Apostles, for it was he who advised the Sanhedrin to leave the Christian community alone, saying that the movement would soon come to nothing if it were not of God (Acts 5:34–39). Would a zealot deliberately put himself under such a teacher when their theologies would have been so very different?[22] Would Saul do that? Would he not rather assign himself to a teacher whose views reflected his own? Rabbinical students did not select their mentors solely to learn their teachings; they chose their mentor because they wanted to imitate their lives. More importantly, a rabbi accepted a student because he thought he would be a faithful disciple, one who would promote his reputation.

Wright acknowledges the difficulty of Saul being a student of Gamaliel and offers this solution. He says that it was not unknown for students to disagree with the teaching of their mentors. To prove this, he cites the case of Akiba, a rabbi who disagreed with his teacher Nehunya over his pacifistic commitment.[23]

The problem with this example is that Akiba left the teaching of his mentor only after leaving his school; indeed, decades after. By this time, he had become the leader of one of the largest rabbinical schools in Judaism.[24]

---

this understanding, saying that Paul did not have the sort of engagement with Rome that Wright claims. I will consider evidence that supports Barclay's case in chapter 4.

[22] As Wright acknowledges in *What Saint Paul Really Said,* 30.

[23] N. T. Wright, *The New Testament and the People of God* (London: SPCK, 1992), 198.

[24] In the following quote, Akiva is the same as the one referred to as Akiba above. 'The greatest tannaim of the middle of the 2nd century came from Akiva's school, notably Rabbi Meir, Judah ben Ilai, Simeon bar Yohai, Jose ben Halafta, Eleazar ben Shammai, and Rabbi Nehemiah. Besides these, Akiva had many disciples whose names have not been handed down, but the Aggadah variously gives their number as 12,000 (Gen R. lxi. 3), 24,000 (Yeb 62b), and 48,000 (Ned 50a)'. Source

Akiba felt compelled to abandon his former teacher's pacifist views because of the increasing persecution from Rome that his disciples were suffering. The Roman state had changed its tolerance to the Jewish religion because of the violence against Rome that some Jews were promoting. Rome's response had become less discriminating, so that the disciples of Akiba—who, like their teacher, were pacifists—were suffering because of Rome's indiscriminate military action. In this situation, Akiba's disciples defended themselves, and there came a point that Akiba found himself having to sanction his disciples' defensive response to their assailants. In other words, Akiba shared Nehunya's pacifist views when he became his student, but decades later, for the sake of his suffering disciples, he concluded that he was obliged to abandon his mentor's teaching.[25] This is not an example that matches Saul; for Wright is arguing that he became a disciple of Gamaliel whilst disagreeing with him.[26]

Hence Wright's solution to the problem has failed to address the difficulty satisfactorily. Universally, the idea of selecting a mentor or teacher in the ancient world was for the student to become a disciple of the teacher—certainly, he did not select him to be an opponent. The claim that Saul put himself under someone he strongly disagreed with is just not viable.

Finding Guidance

The relationship between a student and his teacher in first century Judaism is such an important barrier to Wright's reconstruction of Paul that I sought the view of an expert on the subject. Wright has himself acknowledged that the enormous amount of extra-biblical literature from New Testament times

---

http://en.wikipedia.org/wiki/Akiva_ben_Joseph.

[25] Akiva (aka Akiba) allegedly took part in the Bar Kokba revolt of 132–136. In 95–96 Akiva was in Rome (H. Grätz, Gesch. d. Juden, iv. 121), and some time before 110 he was in Nehardea (Yeb xvi. 7). During his travels, it is believed he visited important Jewish communities, The Baraita (Ber 61b) states that he suffered martyrdom on account of his transgression of Hadrian's edicts against the practice and the teaching of the Jewish religion. Jewish sources relate that he was subjected to Roman torture where his skin was flayed with iron combs. Source http://en.wikipedia.org/wiki/Akiva_ben_Joseph.

[26] L. Finkelstein, *Akiba: Scholar, Saint and Martyr* (New York: Atheneum, 1975), 235–277. 26 Wright, *People of God*, 100.

requires a lifetime of study.[27] I therefore consulted Dr David Instone-Brewer of Tyndale Library, Cambridge—a world-leading expert in the field of rabbinic studies—a scholar with a lifetime of study under his belt. The following is the question I sent to him and then his kind reply.

> Hello David,
>
> Can you tell me if there is any case where a student has chosen to study under a rabbi, he had a fundamental disagreement with on an issue of behaviour?
>
> I want to test the claim that Saul, as a zealot, would be happy to be taught by Gamaliel—someone who urged a much more tolerant position.
>
> Many thanks, Tom Holland

> Dear Tom,
>
> This sounds like an interesting question to pursue. The difficulty is, of course, that we know so little—much less than the enthusiastic books on background might suggest. One interesting insight into the extent and limitation of discipleship before 70 C.E. is seen in what happened soon after.
>
> You've probably seen Chilton and Neusner's chapter on Paul and Gamaliel in 'In Quest of the Historical Pharisees.' They point to the incident between Joshua and Gamaliel II in m.RH.2.7–9. Of course, this isn't the same Gamaliel, and it is after 70, so we have to see this as a contrast rather than illustration, but the presuppositions in the incident can teach us about what was normal at this time.
>
> On this occasion, Gamaliel II forced Joshua to comply with his ruling, and then greeted him as: 'My master in wisdom and my disciple in accepting my ruling'. In other words, Gamaliel II acknowledged the force of Joshua's argument and that he was (perhaps) wiser than himself. And yet he praises him for acting like a disciple and acquiescing to obeying the ruling that Gamaliel II had proclaimed.
>
> This means that Gamaliel II is willing to let his disciples have different opinions, and even to express them, so long as they behaved according to his specific rulings. Presumably (though this isn't stated) Gamaliel would also allow them to behave contrary to

---

[27] Wright, *People of God,* 100.

his wishes, so long as he had made no specific ruling about it.

Now, given that this is after 70 C.E when there was a huge push towards conformity and unity, this can tell us something about pre-70 standards. Presumably, it would have been even more acceptable for a disciple to hold different views than his master, and even to act differently to his master, so long as he didn't actually act contrary to an established ruling.

The established ruling of Gamaliel I was that you should not pull down altars of the pagans (Sifré Deut 61) and (if we accept the text of Acts) that you should not forbid public preaching in the name of Jesus. It would be arguable (though I hadn't considered it before you made your suggestion) that Paul was not breaking either of these specific rulings. He was persecuting Christians, but he didn't actually stop them preaching. This distinction sounds extremely legalistic, but then that's exactly the way they did think.

You could also argue that the small flurry of stories about disciplining disciples soon after 70 ce for disobeying the established united halakha implies that before this time every individual could follow their own rulings, independently of their master. This isn't a very safe argument because the normal way of seeing this mini-rebellion after 70 was that before 70 everyone could follow the halakha of their own master, but after 70 they had to follow the single halakha of the united majority.

I don't know if you can make anything of this—it will be interesting to see what you come up with.

All the best, David

Part of the answer may seem to support Wright's view—disciples could have been allowed to hold different opinions to their masters so long as they obeyed their rulings. On the other hand, as he admits, the answer is far from decisive. The fact remains that he knows of no specific case where a serious conflict of behaviour arose and where differences emerged during the time of training; never mind even during the application/selection process which was required to begin the training, as Wright claims were the case between Saul and Gamaliel.[28] Other texts we have access to show clearly that disciples were expected to conform to the practice of their mentors. The example found in the Mishnah illustrates this, saying:

---

[28] Wright never makes the claim that Saul became a zealot after he joined the school of Gamaliel, he seeks to justify why he would have chosen to be under such a man.

> When one is searching for the lost property both of his father and of his teacher, his teacher's loss takes precedence over that of his father since his father brought him only into the life of this world, whereas his teacher, who taught him wisdom [Torah], has brought him into the life of the World to Come. But if his father is no less a scholar than his teacher, then his father's loss takes precedence .... If his father and his teacher are in captivity, he must first ransom his teacher, and only afterward his father—unless his father is himself a scholar and then he must first ransom his father. (Bava Metsi'a 2:11)

If the thought that someone could ransom his teacher before his father seems shocking to us, it is because we don't understand the tremendous love and respect that disciples at that time—not to mention the community at large—had for their sages. Wright's claim that a student would disrespect his teacher and do the very opposite to his teaching appears to fly in the face of this convention. Without hard evidence to the contrary, and what Wright states is not hard evidence, it would be wise to pay due respect to the features of this relationship that would guide students to avoid clashing with their mentors.

Naturally, that Saul sought to kill personally the disciples of Jesus meant that he transgressed Gamaliel's instruction to the Sanhedrin. But this interpretation assumes that Saul killed believers. This interpretation is deduced from the fact that he said, 'I persecuted this Way to the death, binding and delivering to prison both men and women' (Acts 22:4 ESV). Clearly, Paul does not mean that he killed them and then bound them and cast them into prison! The ERV says 'I persecuted the people who followed the Way. Some of them were killed because of me. I arrested men and women and put them in jail.' I think that this represents more faithfully Paul's intended meaning, for there is no record that anyone was put to death by Saul or his supporters. Saul's intention was not to kill the disciples of Jesus, as a zealot would, but to bring them to trial where the appointed judges would make decisions on their behaviour. If this is correct, then Saul is not disobeying his teacher, for he does not violate his instructions but rather seeks to bring Jesus's disciples under the law, so that its representatives make legal decisions which (for the guilty) might result in death. This was not characteristic of zealot practices; zealots regularly took the law into their hands.

So, Wright's claim that Paul was a zealot despite being a disciple of Gamaliel has its problems. Considering that adequately explaining this relationship is crucial for Wright's case, the onus is on him to make a good argument, which I do not believe he has done. I am arguing that Saul was not behaving like a zealot who 'took the law into own hands'[29] but that he was acting as a servant of the Jewish establishment. He was behaving as a responsible Jew and, in this sense at least, his behaviour was not clashing with the teaching of his mentor, for whatever Gamaliel's personal preferences were, he would not have objected that his student was breaking the teacher/student code for following the requirements of the law. Gamaliel had not given the Sanhedrin authoritative instruction when he advised them to allow time to reveal if the Christian community's testimony was genuine or not. Saul was not facilitating the death of believers, although the court he delivered them over to have a history of finding followers of Christ guilty and sentencing them to death, as he knew from being present when the court's sentence on Stephen was carried out.

Palestinian Rabbinic Political Conflict?

Wright claims that Saul as a zealot would have held political views— his views forming his political perspective and vice versa. when he says that There is, of course, no difficulty with this generalized statement, but a problem arises when it is used to insinuate that Saul held one particular political view, i.e. that of a zealot. I believe that Wright has failed to establish that Saul was a zealot. Therefore, his premise that Saul had the political views he attributes to him are unfounded.

Wright's construction of Saul of Tarsus being a zealot is based on two facts, both of which are from Paul's writings. First, that he supported the persecution of the followers of Jesus and second, that he described himself as 'a zealot' or 'zealous' for the law and the traditions of the fathers. These two facts cannot possibly be contested—but are these facts being interpreted properly? We have already examined the evidence for Wright's claim that Saul was a practising zealot as well as a student of Gamaliel and found his evidence to be unconvincing. Now we need to ask whether Paul ever used the term 'zealous' in the specific hard-line way that Wright claims when he says that he was 'zealous' for the law.

Saul was a Pharisee, but he was also a student rabbi; meaning that he belonged to a rabbinic school. This might have helped us place Saul more

---

[29] Wright, 'Arabia', 685.

17

accurately as far as his views regarding violence are concerned, but the fact is that the rabbinic community was divided. The division was between those who followed Hillel, a liberal master who Gamaliel followed and who Paul studied under, and those who followed Shammai, who encouraged violent opposition towards Rome. The evidence from history suggests that the rabbis of Judea were normally the least interested in all the Jewish communities in political engagement. This fact was to be hugely significant not long after Paul's death.

The Jews suffered a humiliating defeat by the Romans in 70 C.E. when Jerusalem fell. The revolt that had brought this about was the result of zealot fervour. Despite the humiliation and desolation that this war produced for the Jews, a further uprising (the Bar Kokhba revolt in 120 C.E.) brought the wrath of Rome on the nation once again. This time, after quenching the rebellion, Roman officials identified a community of Jews which they considered to be trustworthy. They chose this group because its members had a history of non-violence, of not being involved in attempts to overthrow Roman rule. As a result, they were made the official representatives of the people. That community was the community of the rabbis![30]

Because of this, Rabbinic Judaism was elevated above all other Jewish groups.[31] This disinterest in the revolution was because the movement's only interest was the study of their sacred texts— and understandably Rome was happy with this focus. And so, a minority community became the official voice of second century Judaism. As a result of this arrangement, the

---

[30] The school of Akiba, based outside of Palestine, does not seem to have marred the reputation of Palestinian rabbinic Judaism.

[31] J. Fossum, 'The New Religionsgeschichtlíche Schule: The Quest for Jewish Christology' *SBL 1991 Seminar Papers*, ed. E. H. Lovering (Atlanta: Scholars Press, 1991), 638– 646. Page 643 says: 'the Pharisees made up only one of many parties or sects which existed within the spectrum of Israelite religion when the temple was still standing. It was actually unfortunate to refer to Israelite religion in that period as 'Judaism.' This usage inevitably creates the impression that the religion which was shaped by Pharisaic Rabbinism and is commonly called by the same name is the natural and legitimate outgrowth of the religion of Israel, whereas Christianity and other children of Rebbeca's are hybrids or bastards.' Fossum points out how unsustainable is the argument that Rabbinic Judaism represents Second Temple Judaism by pointing out that it would mean that the Jewish state was headed by someone from an opposing minority party—the High Priest.

rabbinical community came to play a dominant role in the life of the nation; a position that they continue to hold to this day. Whatever way the evidence is constructed, this historic choice made by Rome has to be considered when arguing about the characteristics of first century Palestinian Rabbinic Judaism.

The point is that having been thoroughly examined by the Roman authorities, there was nothing in Palestinian rabbinic history to exclude them from this important role. In fact, the rabbis were so concerned about how the Phinehas passage in Numbers 25:7–8 was being used as a model by the zealots to encourage violent opposition, that they removed it from their synagogue readings. Thus, rather than being characterized by violence, they were characterized by pacifism—a picture which does not match that painted by Wright when considering Saul, a key member of their admittedly earlier community.[32]

This designated status must feature in our reading of Paul's self-description as being zealous unless we are prepared to accept that a zealot would be elected to membership of such a distinguished ruling body as the Sanhedrin. Of course, Saul would have held political views, but they were most unlikely to have been the views of the zealots.

Conflict with Rome

Another fact that has to be considered as we try to identify the sort of man Saul was is that on his mission to Damascus, he was acting as the servant of the high priest. Taking letters from this puppet of Rome, Saul sets out for Damascus to round up the followers of Jesus; intending to bring them back to Jerusalem for trial (Acts 8:2–4; 9:21; 22:4–5). How can it be that a zealot would do the bidding of the high priest, who was a notorious stooge of the Roman Emperor?[33] Was this 'zealot' able to so control his loathing for Rome

---

[32] Wright does not consider the fact that Paul excelled above his peers in matters of the law (Gal 1:14) which suggests that he was valued and esteemed as a possible leader of Judaism. This would have been impossible if he was a known zealot.

[33] According to Josephus, Caiaphas was appointed in 18 C.E. by the Roman prefect who preceded Pontius Pilate, Valerius Gratus. In John's Gospel we find that Caiaphas considers, with 'the Chief Priests and Pharisees', what to do about Jesus, whose influence was spreading. They are concerned that if

that he was willing to make use of letters from the very person who served Rome's purposes? This Jewish leader was collaborating with an empire that used Jerusalem as a seat of local power from which to exercise its rule. This problem, of course, only exists if Saul was a zealot in the traditions of Phinehas, Elijah, and the Maccabees as Wright has claimed.

Zealot Claims and Roman Citizenship

A further difficulty for Wright's construction of Saul is the fact that Rome had a strict registration and taxation system. People who were Roman citizens had to register every five years and state their wealth for taxation purposes.[34] Failure to register and pay meant the loss of status and the privileges that went with it, and even, for some, death.[35] From this we can see that any suggestion that Paul had forgone his citizenship and then later taken it up again is wide of the mark. Rome had no tolerance for people who doubted the value of their privilege as the above details indicate; failing even to register could lead to death. To say that a zealot, jealous for his country, and fanatical about the independence of Israel, would turn up meekly every five years to ensure that

---

they 'let him go on like this, everyone will believe in him, and the Romans will come and destroy both our holy place and our nation.' Caiaphas makes a political calculation, suggesting that it would be better for 'one man' (Jesus) to die than for 'the whole nation' to be destroyed.'

[34] Claude Nicolet, *The World of the Citizen in Republican Rome* (Chicago: University of Chicago Press, 1988), 66. For more information see https://www.academia.edu/3793625/Paul_the_Roman_Citizen_Roman_Citizenship_in_the_Ancient_World_and_its_ Importance_for_Understanding_Acts_22_22-29 and http://www.roman-empire.net/society/ society.html

[35] Livy refers to a "law that threatened with death and imprisonment those [citizens] who failed to register." According to Dionysius, Romans were required to "register their names and give in a monetary valuation of their property. .... If any failed to give in their valuation, the penalty he [Servis Tullius] established was that their property should be forfeited and they themselves whipped and sold as slaves. This law continued in force among the Romans for a long time." Cicero says that: "By selling a man who has evaded the census, the state decrees that, whereas those who have been slaves in the normal way gain their freedom by being included in the census, one who has refused to be included in it although free has of his own accord repudiated his freedom."' Nicolet, The World of the Citizen, 61.

he continued to enjoy the benefits of being a Roman citizen is to ask us to accept something that is several steps beyond credibility!

This fact is a serious problem for Wright's construction because Paul claimed Roman citizenship as a result of birth. It is thought that his grandfather had been given the honour in return for something he had done that benefited the empire, its armies, or the Emperor directly. The requirement of repeated registrations would be an insurmountable problem for a zealot of the type advocated by Wright. Would such a zealot be willing to submit to these requirements for maintaining Roman citizenship? He certainly possessed this status later in his life but if he had refused to register, he would have lost it. While this is a real problem for the claims of Wright, it is not a problem for the understanding which the church has traditionally advocated.

The Meaning of Zealot

Returning specifically to Wright's case, we need to establish how Paul used the word 'zealot.' What did he mean by it? The correct meaning of this is important because Wright claims that it refers to Paul being a political zealot and, having asserted this, says that the traditional reading of Paul is, therefore, invalid. If this claim can be successfully challenged, then the construction of the mission of Saul as Wright interprets it collapses with it.[36]

In Acts 21 we have the account of Paul's arrest in the temple. As he was led from the temple to the garrison by a stairway, he was allowed by the commander of the guard to speak to the gathered crowd which was baying for

---

[36] Wright, What St Paul Really Said, 170 says, 'it is historically out of the question that Saul of Tarsus should have been a collaborator with Rome, a servant of the high priest. Wilson bases this conjecture on Acts 9:1–2, 14, 21; 26:10–12, which say that Saul obtained authority from the chief priest for his persecuting mission in Damascus. But this is completely to misunderstand the political situation and the different players in it. The Shammaite Pharisees, as we saw, were the hard liners, bitterly opposed to collaboration, and indeed fiercely supportive of revolutionary movement. This is what was meant by 'zeal', which the pre-Christian Saul of Tarsus possessed in abundance.' Without wanting to support Wilson's construction of Paul, it is not facing the evidence to assert that 'zeal' in Paul means he was a zealot and so change his theological position from a disciple of Gamaliel to the very opposite, that of a Shammaite. Then to argue that others followed two positions at the same time, with an example that had no relevance to support the claim because it came from a latter different century and situation. This is far from convincing.

his blood. Paul used the word 'zealous' to describe his commitment to Judaism before he became a follower of Jesus. He said:

> I am a Jew, born in Tarsus in Cilicia, but brought up in this city, educated at the feet of Gamaliel according to the strict manner of the law of our fathers, being zealous for God (ζηλωτὴς ὑπάρχων τοῦ θεοῦ) as all of you are this day. I persecuted this Way to the death, binding and delivering to prison both men and women, as the high priest and the whole council of elders can bear me witness. From them I received letters to the brothers, and I journeyed toward Damascus to take those also who were there and bring them in bonds to Jerusalem to be punished. (Acts 22:3–5).

Admittedly, Paul was speaking in Aramaic, and the account in Acts has been translated into Greek for readers who could not otherwise access it. Because of this, the commander is not likely to have understood him. In contrast, the Aramaic speakers in the crowd, who demanded Paul's death, would have immediately realized the significance of the claim. If it conveyed the meaning claimed by Wright, then Paul is admitting his involvement in violence and alleging their (v. 3b) involvement in anti-Roman behaviour![37]

This crucial confession, if Wright is correct in his understanding of what Paul meant by his use of the term zealot, would surely bolster the case of the mob against him because of his desertion of the anti- Roman cause and their demand for his execution! The fact is that they did not take Paul's defence to be an admission of political extremism speaks volumes. Instead, they took it the way it has always, until recently, been read: that Paul claimed that he loved and respected the Torah and sought to live by its precepts. Such an understanding of being 'zealous' or that he was 'a zealot' has nothing to do with being followers of Phinehas, as Wright has argued, but it has everything to do with bringing perceived law-breakers to trial within the Jewish system. This was what Saul did before his conversion—he saw himself as living under and according to the Torah and expected all Jews to do the same or suffer the consequences. It is surely significant that Ananias had earlier explained his fear concerning Saul's work when he said:

> "Lord, I have heard from many about this man, how much evil he has done to your saints at Jerusalem. And here he has authority from the chief priests to bind all who call on your name." But the Lord said to him, "Go, for he is a chosen instrument of mine to carry my name before the gentiles and kings and the children of

---

[37] Wright, Paul and the Faithfulness of God, 1306.

Israel." (Acts 9:13–15)

Thus, there is no suggestion that the believers believed that Saul was killing the disciples; they feared him because he handed them over to the legal authorities to consider if they were guilty of blasphemy. Such a mission in no way requires that he identified with the zealots.

Paul's Claim to be Zealous

In fact, Paul used the idea of zeal in exactly this same way as I am suggesting in some of his letters, including the letter to the Romans. Complimenting his fellow Jews, he writes:

> Brothers, my heart's desire and prayer to God for them is that they may be saved. For I bear them witness that they have a zeal for God (ζῆλον θεοῦ ἔχουσιν),[38] but not according to knowledge. For, being ignorant of the righteousness of God, and seeking to establish their own, they did not submit to God's righteousness. For Christ is the end of the law for righteousness to everyone who believes. (Rom 10:1 ESV)

> Do not be slothful in zeal, be fervent in spirit (τῷ πνεύματι ζέοντες), serve the Lord. Rejoice in hope, be patient in tribulation, be constant in prayer. Contribute to the needs of the saints and seek to show hospitality. (Rom 12:11–13)

To the Galatians, he writes:

> For you have heard of my former life in Judaism, how I persecuted the church of God violently and tried to destroy it. And I was advancing in Judaism beyond many of my own age among my people, so extremely zealous (περισσοτέρως ζηλωτὴς ὑπάρχων) was I for the traditions of my fathers. (Gal 1:13–14)

> They make much of you (ζηλοῦσιν ὑμᾶς οὐ καλῶς), but for no good purpose. They want to shut you out, that you may make much of them. It is always good to be made much of (καλὸν δὲ ζηλοῦσθαι) for a good purpose, and not only when I am present with you. (Gal 4:17–18)

The ESV masks the use of the term 'zeal', so I will provide the NIV translation of Galatians 4:17–18.

> Those people are zealous to win you over, but for no good. What they want is to alienate you from us, so that you may have a zeal

---

[38] I have italicized the appropriate word for the non-Greek reader to see that the same Greek word is used throughout.

for them. It is fine to be zealous, provided the purpose is good, and to be so always, not just when I am with you. (Gal 4:17–18 NIV) This translation of ζηλοῦσθαι as zeal in Galatians 4:17–18 is found in the ASV, KJV, and MEV translations.

In Philippians, Paul writes:

If anyone else thinks he has reason for confidence in the flesh, I have more: circumcised on the eighth day, of the people of Israel, of the tribe of Benjamin, a Hebrew of Hebrews; as to the law, a Pharisee; as to zeal, a persecutor of the church (κατὰ ζῆλον διώκων τὴν ἐκκλησίαν); as to righteousness under the law, blameless. But whatever gain I had, I counted as loss for the sake of Christ. (Phil 3:4–7)

In Acts, we read:

After greeting them, he related one by one the things that God had done among the gentiles through his ministry. And when they heard it, they glorified God. And they said to him, "You see, brother, how many thousands there are among the Jews of those who have believed. They are all zealous for the law (καὶ πάντες ζηλωταὶ τοῦ νόμου), and they have been told about you that you teach all the Jews who are among the gentiles to forsake Moses, telling them not to circumcise their children or walk according to our customs." (Acts 21:19–21)

I am a Jew, born in Tarsus in Cilicia, but brought up in this city, educated at the feet of Gamaliel according to the strict manner of the law of our fathers, being zealous for God (ζηλωτὴς ὑπάρχων τοῦ θεοῦ) as all of you are this day. I persecuted this Way to the death, binding and delivering to prison both men and women, as the high priest and the whole council of elders can bear me witness. From them I received letters to the brothers, and I journeyed toward Damascus to take those also who were there and bring them in bonds to Jerusalem to be punished. (Acts 22:3–5)

Could Paul appeal to the high priest and the whole council of elders for their testimony that he had served their purposes if he had been a zealot of the sort advocated by Wright? I find this to be an impossible hurdle for his claim that Saul persecuted the believers because he was a political zealot. Wright's understanding can only stand by ignoring all the evidence that speaks against it; but these same 'difficult texts' are a powerful support for the traditional view which has never claimed that the young rabbi was anything but a law abiding, God loving, Jewish rabbinical student.

Another fact that challenges Wright's reading of the evidence that Paul was a zealot is Paul's statement to the Galatians where he says:

> For you have heard of my former life in Judaism, how I persecuted the church of God violently and tried to destroy it. And I was advancing in Judaism beyond many of my own age among my people, so extremely zealous was I for the traditions of my fathers. But when he who had set me apart before I was born, and who called me by his grace. (Gal 1:13–14 ESV)

Paul links his esteemed status in Judaism with his persecution of the church. Such a status would not be conferred if he was a zealot, but only if he served under the law, according to the traditions of the fathers, not the zeal of the Maccabees. This clearly suggests that whatever he did, had the approval of the elders of the community; this favours the view that his persecution of the church consisted not in killing, but in bringing them to stand trial.

Conclusion

Finally, having identified Saul's role as a servant of the Jewish establishment, we can see how Wright is quite mistaken to see him as advancing the political agenda of the zealot extremists. In correcting this, we have removed the founding assumption that Paul, from his youth, had an antithesis toward the Roman State. Wright argues from this supposed zealot influence that the apostle had no difficulty in challenging Rome. There is no doubt that this might have been a consequence of his work, as he called people to worship Christ as Saviour and Lord, but there is no evidence that this was driven by a political agenda produced by his commitment to the zealot cause. Such a mission of deliberately confronting Rome quite simply contradicts what we have been able to establish about Paul and the theological convictions that created his understanding. We shall examine other evidence regarding Paul's self-identity in the next chapter, and we will find that it is rooted in the call of Israel's prophets to declare Yahweh's word to the nations. The Jews in exile were never encouraged to take their situation into their own hands; it was stressed to them again and again that their situation was Yahweh's judgment, and that they should humbly accept it. Unless we can provide clear evidence to the contrary, we should see Paul's exhortations in this light.

Some may ask, 'Why is this issue important, does it matter that Saul was a zealot or not?' We will see as we progress that it matters far more than we could anticipate. Wright argues that Paul was fully familiar with the content of these texts because as a zealot they inspired his thought and actions. This enables him to use these texts as key evidence to interpret Paul. He not only constructs Paul's understanding of the person of Jesus (Christology) through these, but also what the writers of the gospel understood the death of Jesus to have achieved (Soteriology), and how Jesus interpreted his own mission and person. Even Paul's doctrine of the resurrection, according to Wright, is rooted in the Maccabean tradition and without it some of Wright's key interpretations of Jesus and Paul cannot stand.

Chapter 3:
Probing Paul and His Theological Identity

The popular television series 'Who Do You Think You Are?' has caught the imagination of millions, making many reflect on the influences that have made them the people they are today. People have reconstructed their lineage with surprising, and sometimes painful, results. They have identified members of their family who had suffered dreadfully, sometimes unjustly, and there were members of the family tree who were nothing short of disreputable. But what would Saul of Tarsus answer to the question, 'Who do you think you are?'

The Theological Influence of Isaiah

I have tested Wright's case for Saul being a zealot, and I have not been persuaded by his argument. But is there anything else that we can bring that will test further the case that Wright has made? I think that there is, and it is an important thread to the identity of Paul and will help us to know who he thought he was. To get to this material and understand what Paul considered his identity to have been before he became a follower of Jesus, we need to examine his letters further and dig into the account of his conversion. The language that was used at that critical moment just does not fit with the claim that he was a zealot. We need somehow to enter the mindset of the future apostle to see if the mission he was commissioned to undertake was a natural transition from the work he had been doing as a supposed zealot. Could he really, immediately, step out of the life of a zealot into a role that was so dramatically different, i.e. serving Christ, with no suggestion that he was about to accept something that was an unbelievably different role to the one he had moments earlier been doing?[39]

---

[39] Wright objected to this observation, challenging me whether I did not think that conversion could be a radical transformation which would explain this change. My response is yes, it is a radical transformation, but not to the extent that it virtually obliterates the person who has been converted. Wright's own case for Paul denies this claim as he continually seeks to show progression rather than a 'destructive intervention' (my description). Of course, there were

The Search for Truth

Fortunately, we can locate the dominant influence on Paul's thinking, which is also the source from which he built his self- image. The book of Isaiah was the dominant influence on Saul as he trained to be a rabbi. It was not only required reading, it was the Old Testament book that supremely gave Israel her understanding of being called to be God's servant.[40] Such exposure should lead us to expect that it had a profound effect on him.

Hence—unlike in Wright's handling of the Second Temple literature— we do not guess at this influence, for, as we shall see, Paul deliberately and frequently quotes from Isaianic texts, and some of these quotations are used to refer to his missionary work. In other words, Paul recognized himself as fulfilling some of the prophecies that had been made many hundreds of years earlier, long before the theme of zealot martyrdom emerged.

The fact that one of these servant texts of Isaiah (Acts 26:15–18) was cited by Christ himself as he commissioned Paul (Saul) is hugely significant. There is no hint that he was surprised that this was to be his calling. This suggests that what he later described as his life's work had not changed in any fundamental way. He saw that he had been doing this as a servant of Yahweh before his encounter with Christ. His theological understanding regarding the general resurrection was essentially the same, but the realization that it had taken place in the resurrection of Jesus made him see that a whole range of prophecies was fulfilled. Significantly a key prediction in these prophecies was that the gentiles would share the blessings of the new covenant.

---

other former zealots in the apostolic community and they include Judas Iscariot and Simon the Zealot. But their pathway was nothing like that of Saul, for they had thought that Jesus was the political Messiah whom the crowds welcomed. When Judas, assuming that he had been a zealot as his name suggests, came to see that Jesus was not interested in taking power for himself as the Jewish Messiah the people wanted was expected to do, he turned to the authorities and sold his leader for thirty pieces of silver. In contrast, Saul turned from the promises of nationalism and popular Judaism and bowed to Jesus as the crucified and risen Lord. This resulted in the loss of the position he had held in Israel, a status which Judas craved for. Instead of being the darling of his people, Paul was consequently viewed as the scum of the earth (Phil 3:4–11).

[40] N. W. Porteous, 'Old Testament Theology', in M. Black, H. Rowley, and A. Peake, *Peake's Commentary on the Bible* (London; New York: Nelson, 1962), 151–159 [158].

The prophecy of Isaiah is almost certainly the major influence on Paul's thinking. He quotes from it more times than any other Old Testament book and the way its themes guide him gives many scholars confidence that his writings cannot be understood without a knowledge of Isaianic themes.[41]

The prophet clearly determined Paul's theology of salvation. For Isaiah, the key figure in his message of hope was someone known as the 'servant of the Lord.' The prophet's theological understanding on this issue was supreme amongst the Old Testament writers, especially his contribution to an understanding of Israel's call to servanthood. Porteous has noted that, 'Isaiah is the theologian par excellence of the Old Testament, but his importance for theology lies, not so much in any abstract formulations he may have reached about the oneness and creative power of God, as in the way in which he seems to have given living embodiment to his understanding of Israel's call to be God's servant in the world.'[42]

The reason for choosing to examine this theme at this point is two- fold. First, it illustrates how Hellenism has determined the way the New Testament has been, and still is, read. We will see that, once the idea of Greek control is removed, previously unrecognized Old Testament theological themes break out of the New Testament text. This discovery ought to give us confidence and appetite to explore other strands of Old Testament theology in the writings of Paul. Second, we will discover details that help us decide whether Saul would fit into the zealot community Wright supposes him to have adopted. These powerful chapters of Isaiah were Saul's training manual for his life-work as a Jewish rabbi. They tell us what fed his soul in those formative year; the years in which Wright believes him to have been active as a zealot. They will show if Wright's construction of the rabbinic student Saul of Tarsus is on or off target.

The Concept of the Servant in the Old Testament

An examination of the Old Testament Hebrew text of Isaiah shows that ebed, 'servant', was a title applied to a wide range of people. There were no

---

[41] See R. B. Hays, *The Conversion of the Imagination: Paul as Interpreter of Israel's Scripture* (Grand Rapids; Cambridge: Eerdmans, 2004), 25–49. Porteous, 'Old Testament Theology', 157

[42] Porteous, 'Old Testament Theology', 157.

alternative titles available for the Old Testament writers, so the variations in meaning had to be derived from the context in which the word was used.

Ebed was used for kings (Isa 37:24), prophets (Isa 20:3), the nation of Israel (Isa 41:8–9), the Messiah (Isa 42:1), and even ordinary Israelites (Isa 65:13–15). What can be said of ebed is that it spoke of someone who was subordinate to another, whether to God or man.

The Source of Confusion

Confusion arose when the Old Testament was translated into Greek. A study of the Hebrew text alongside the Greek translation shows that there was no consistency in the minds of the translators as to the choice of an appropriate Greek word for a particular type of ebed. The two principal Greek terms available were *doulos* and pais.

The evidence shows that pais was used not only for the ideal servant spoken of by Isaiah but also for Israel. It was used in such a way as to remind her of her unworthiness, for her 'unadopted' name 'Jacob' is used in parallel with the term (c.f. Isa 42:19; 44:1–2, 21; 45:4). Pais is also used of individual prophets (c.f. Isa 20:3; 44:26; 50:10). The problem appears to be even more complex because the term is applied to domestic servants and as a title for anyone who is in an inferior position to another (Isa 24:2; 36:11; 37:5).

The same meanings given for pais are given to the term *doulos*. So, we find *doulos* applied to the ideal servant (Isa 53:11), the nation (Isa 42:19; 48:2; 49:3, 7), and to domestic servants (Isa 14:2). In the Hebrew text, the term's context was clearly the key to its correct reading. The translators of the LXX evidently did not think it necessary to distinguish accurately between the various usages by designating one particular Greek word to correspond to each category of 'servant.'

The apparently arbitrary use of pais and *doulos* is not limited to the LXX. We also find the same range of usages for both terms in the New Testament. We find pais used for a domestic servant (Matt 8:6, 13), for Israel (Luke 1:54), and for David (Luke 1:69). We also find that *doulos* was used for an equally wide range of meanings. For a slave (Matt 8:9), for a domestic help (John 18:10), for a prophet (Rev 10:7), for Christians (Rom 6:17), and for Christ himself (Phil 2:7). It is clear that the arbitrary use of pais and *doulos* by the translators of the LXX influenced the practice of the New Testament writers. It would, therefore, be imprudent to attach any significance to the use of either term without deliberate reference to its context. It is thus the context alone that must determine how a particular use of a word should be understood.

Consequences of Confusion

This confusion has obscured the significance of the repeated use Paul makes of the term *doulos*. It has often been seen as a reference to a bond slave—someone without legal standing or personal claims and owned by another—since that is what the *doulos* was in Greco-Roman Society. This connection makes two fundamental assumptions. First, the Roman idea of *doulos* was the same as Paul's concept, and second, that Paul's concept was the same as the Old Testament concept.

The latter connection must be assumed to exist in Paul's thinking, in that his understanding of *doulos* is normally understood to be the same as that of the ebed/*doulos* in the Old Testament. However, it is a point in dispute as to whether Israel ever experienced slavery in the classical Greek or Roman sense amongst her own people.

An Example of Confusion

The French biblical scholar De Vaux summarizes the general picture:

> Certain writers and especially Jewish scholars have denied that
> real slavery ever existed in Israel; at least they maintain Israelites
> were never reduced to slavery. There is a semblance of
> justification for this view if we compare Israel with classical
> antiquity. In Israel and the neighbouring countries there never
> existed those enormous gangs of slaves which in Greece and
> Rome continually threatened the balance of the social order. Nor
> was the position of the slave ever so low in Israel and the Ancient
> East as in Republican Rome, where Varro could define a slave as
> 'a sort of talking tool' ('instrument genus vocale'). The flexibility
> of the vocabulary may also be deceptive. Strictly speaking ebed
> means slave, a man who is not his own master and is in the power
> of another. The king, however, had absolute power, and
> consequently the word ebed also means the King's subjects,
> especially his mercenaries, officers, and ministers; by joining his
> service they had broken off their social bonds. By a fresh
> extension of meaning, the word became a term of courtesy. We
> may compare it with the development of its equivalents 'servant'
> in English or *'serviteur'* in French, both derive from *servus*, a
> slave. Moreover, because a man's relations with God are often
> conceived on the model of his relations with his earthly sovereign,
> it became a title for pious men, and was applied to Abraham,

> Moses, Joshua or David, and finally to the mysterious servant of
> Yahweh. By 'slave' in the strict sense we mean a man who is
> deprived of his freedom, at least for a time, who is bought and
> sold, who is the property of a master, who makes use of him as he
> likes; in this sense there were slaves in Israel and some were
> Israelites.[43]

De Vaux then proceeds to make comparisons between the Semitic form
of slavery and the Greco-Roman form, to show how the former was much
more controlled and humane.

However, de Vaux has missed the essential difference between the
Hebrew slave, who was sold into the possession of another, and the slave of
Yahweh; it is not merely the status of the owner. The essential difference is
one of covenant. The king was the ebed of Yahweh because he had been
elected, called, and appointed to that office, and not because of anything less.

The ministers of the king, in turn, represented Yahweh and fulfilled the
purpose of the covenant, which was to establish righteousness. To fail to see
this is to miss the whole point of the ebed of Yahweh. In social terms, it
would be equivalent to seeing little difference between the role of a
housekeeper and the role of a housewife in Western society today. It would
also be foolish to think that the housekeeper could simply evolve into the
housewife. Language may evolve, but a covenant relationship does not; it
requires a decisive act of commitment and acceptance.

The Servant in the New Testament

We would expect that ambiguity in Old Testament theology would lead to
ambiguity in New Testament theology, and this is the very thing we find. For
example, C. K. Barrett notes an aspect of the problem when, in commenting
on Romans 1:1, he says:

> Paul describes himself in the first instance as a slave of Jesus
> Christ. This is a common term with him (c.f. especially Gal 1:10;
> Phil 1:1), imitated by other New Testament writers (James 1:1; 2
> Pet 1:1; Jude 1). It is particularly status and vocation. The
> description is more striking in a Greek work, such as this epistle,
> than in Semitic literature. A Greek did not think of himself as a
> slave (δοῦλος) of his ruler or king, nor did he think of himself as
> the slave of his divine king, or God, or speak of his service to the

[43] De Vaux, Israel, 80.

God as slavery. The Semitic king, however, was a slave (e.g. 2 Sam 9:19). Other distinguished members of the theocracy are described in the same terms (e.g. Ps 26:42; Amos 3:7). Thus Paul, as the slave of Jesus Christ, appears as a member of a people of God analogous to the People of God in the Old Testament.[44]

Barrett is suggesting that the Old Testament concept of the servant of Yahweh was based on the analogy of slavery, only elevated from a human situation. But this is not so, as we have seen. Barrett does, however, move in the right direction when he goes on to say that Paul 'appears as a member of a people of God analogous to the people of God in the Old Testament'. But, as we have seen, Barrett misunderstands the Old Testament theology of the servant ofGod.

Consequences of Confusion

If we follow the trend of de Vaux and Barrett and seek to work out a slave concept in the New Testament, there are some important questions which must be raised. Are we to conclude that Paul not only claims that he has no rights of his own (because he is in bondage to Christ) but also that he is serving Christ against his own will? If Paul is saying that he has no rights, how can he look forward to a reward or payment for his labour— 'a crown of righteousness' (2 Tim 4:8)? The slave concept totally precludes such a possibility.

Furthermore, when Paul's use of the term in Romans 6 is examined carefully, we come up against these same problems in specific statements. He writes, 'Do you not know that if you present yourselves to anyone as obedient slaves, you are slaves of the one whom you obey, either of sin, which leads to death, or of obedience, which leads to righteousness?' (Rom 6:16).

This type of slavery begins when the slave chooses which master he will serve and offers himself to him. This would never arise in the Roman practice of slavery. It may instead be argued that this is a reference to an Old Testament practice, when a slave could choose to stay with his master when the year of Jubilee arrives, having his ear bored to signify that he would be his lifelong possession (Deut 15:16–17).

Even this argument, however, fails to resolve the problem. First, it moves between Hellenistic or classical concepts and the Semitic concept, without any indication as to which practice is being followed in which part of the

---

[44] C.K. Barrett, Romans, 15–16.

illustration. Also, the basic meaning of *doulos* is that of one born into slavery. Under the controlled form of 'slavery', which the Old Testament permitted for those needing to sell themselves into service for a period of time to recover from debt, children were not born into permanent slavery. In such a case, the 'slave' was released, along with all that was his, in the year of Jubilee (Lev 25:39–43).

Finally, at the conclusion of the chapter, Paul states, 'For the wages of sin is death, but the free gift of God is eternal life in Christ Jesus our Lord' (Rom 6:23). It is most unlikely that Paul would speak of a wage being paid in a slave relationship. In contrast, in the Old Testament, Israel, God's servant, is continually promised blessing and exaltation as a reward for obedience to Yahweh (Deut 30:19–20; Ps 91:16; Isa 38:17).

New Testament Terms

Before we attempt to unravel the information available to us, it would be helpful to clarify the terms found in the New Testament that speak of Christian service, setting them alongside their corresponding Greek terms and assessing their relevance for our present enquiry.

The first term to note is the verbal form of *doulos*, *douleuo*. What becomes apparent from an examination of the use of this verb throughout the New Testament is that it is never used of unwilling service. It always describes service, regardless of motive, which may be either moral or immoral, as willingly rendered.

So, the elder son in the parable of the prodigal son says, 'All these years I've been slaving (*douleuo*) for you and never disobeyed your orders' (Luke 15:29 NIV). The translators of the NIV may feel justified in rendering *douleuo* as 'slaving', to emphasize the bitter feelings of the son at the father's generosity towards his unworthy brother. He is arguing that what was being spent on him was rightfully his property because his younger brother had already taken his portion. In addition, he had worked for his father, and had earned, by his devoted work, what was now being 'misused'. Paul testifies to the Ephesian elders, that he had been 'serving (*douleuo*) the Lord with all humility and with tears and with trials that happened to me through the plots of the Jews' (Acts 20:19).

He exhorts the Romans, 'Do not be slothful in zeal, be fervent in spirit, serve (*douleuo*) the Lord' (Rom 12:11. See also Luke 16:13; Rom 6:6, 22; 9:12; 12:11; 14:18; 16:18; Gal 4:8; 5:13; Eph 6:7; Phil 2:22; Col 3:24; 1 Thess 1:9; 1 Tim 6:2; Tit 3:3).

34

The use of the verbal form of *doulos*, therefore, suggests a situation quite different from a bond slave concept. There are other terms which Paul employs regarding serving, but these relate to appointed tasks within the Christian community, such as *latreuo* (a task done solely for God), *diakonia* (a spiritual ministry), and *diakonos* (the position held by someone who serves). *Diakoneo* is the verbal form used for the outworking of the position that the diakonos holds as in Matt 20:28, 'even as the Son of Man came not to be served but to serve, and to give his life as a ransom for many' (see also Matt 4:11; 8:15; 27:55; Mark 1:13, 31; 10:45; 15:41; Luke 4:39; Acts 19:22; 2 Cor 3:3; 2 Tim 1:18; Phlm 13; Heb 6:10; 1 Pet 1:12; 4:10, 11).

Now, while all these references to the deacon or minister (*diakonos*) pinpoint his position and the work he does, they fail to make specific reference to the relationship that exists between him and the Lord he serves. These terms tell us nothing about that aspect. In the LXX, *doulos* can have a range of meanings, from a slave made so by being taken as a prisoner of war, to one who serves Yahweh in the context of the covenant. We have also seen that, in the New Testament, *doulos* suggests willing service and that there are also statements made by Paul that seem to conflict with a slave situation.

Paul the Servant of the Lord

How then did Paul understand *doulos*? Did he see it in some 'adjusted' classical sense, as Barrett suggests, or was there some other perspective from which he viewed it? Paul's claim to be a Hebrew of the Hebrews not only points to competence in the Hebrew language but also a zeal for the Hebrew culture. What did he intend to convey to those who could not share directly in his training but had to be taught through the medium of a common language?

It would be natural to expect Luke, Paul's biographer, to use *doulos* in the Greek sense when referring to him. Instead, we find him placing Paul in the Hebrew theological mould of the Old Testament. Luke saw Paul's calling to be the shadow of his master, Jesus, who so clearly fulfilled Old Testament expectation of the ideal servant. In Acts, Paul is constantly robed in the mantle of Christ, being separated to do the messianic covenant work spoken of by Isaiah, as a light to the nations (Acts 9:15; 13:47). He is rejected, especially by his own countrymen, as was Christ (Acts 9:29; 13:50; 14:19; 17:13; 22:17–21).

As Bornkamm points out, there is a parallel in the offence their work brings. Christ was rejected because he sought to win sinners; Paul was rejected because he sought to win gentiles, who, to the Jews, were sinners. The preaching of Christ and of Paul produced the same effects in those who do not believe, namely blindness and hardening, and both outcomes are based on the predicted results of Isaiah's ministry in Isaiah 6:9–10 (Luke 8:10; c.f. Acts 28:26). Furthermore, Paul's journey to Jerusalem may be seen as providing a parallel with Christ's last journey to Jerusalem, since both men were rejected by the populace (Luke 9:51–53; 18:31–33). What is more, both Jesus and Paul were subjected to similar exhortations to consider the unreasonableness of their missions (Luke 13:31; Acts 21:10–14).

Finally, just like Christ, Paul is misrepresented by the leaders, hounded by the mob, and tried by the governor of Jerusalem (Luke 23:1; Acts 25:1–2). Here the parallels end, for Christ's death outside Jerusalem was foreordained; Paul's was not. What was predetermined for Paul was that he would eventually stand before kings and rulers (Acts 9:15), which he did when he finally arrived in Rome.

Wider Support

This picture of Paul as the servant in the Hebraic theological sense is no coincidence. It is supported by his own description of his ministry. He considered his call, described in Galatians 1:15, as being set apart from birth—a call which parallels that of the Old Testament prophets.

In 2 Corinthians, Paul was forced to defend his calling as an apostle. In chapters three to seven, he compares the old and new covenants and their ministries. In 3:6 Paul says, 'who (God) has made us competent to be ministers of a new covenant, not of the letter but of the Spirit. For the letter kills, but the Spirit gives life'. In 2 Corinthians 4:1, Paul says, 'Therefore, having this ministry by the mercy of God, we do not lose heart'.

Paul then proceeds to develop his comparison between the two covenants with reference to the motive of his ministry. He says, 'for the love of Christ controls us, because we have concluded this: that one has died for all, therefore all have died; and he died for all, that those who live might no longer live for themselves but for him who for their sake died and was raised' (2 Cor 5:14–15). This reference to the death of 'one for all' echoes Romans 5:12–19, a passage accepted by some scholars as referring to Isaiah 53. That this Corinthian passage also reflects that same prophetic passage is a fact borne out by the way in which Paul proceeds to speak of the new creation (2 Cor 5:17), which is brought about by Christ's representative death (2 Cor 5:21). This is the theme of Isaiah, for he too goes on to speak of all things being made new (Isa 65:17) in the context of the new covenant, which the servant's death establishes.

Thus, Paul sees his ministry as proclaiming the fulfilment of all that Isaiah had predicted. He is elevated above the evangelical prophet in that he proclaims the fulfilment and not just the expectation.

Perhaps the most significant passage of 2 Corinthians is chapter 6. Paul starts the section, which describes his sufferings, by quoting from the Servant Songs and concludes with a further quotation from them (Isa 49:8; 52:11).

> Working together with him, then, we appeal to you not to receive the grace of God in vain. For he says, "In a favourable time I listened to you, and in a day of salvation I have helped you. Behold, now is the favourable time; behold, now is the day of salvation". (2 Cor 6:1–2)

It is evident that Paul saw his own ministry as that of a servant of the new covenant, just as Moses, Isaiah, and the nation of Israel were the servants of the old covenant. As the prophets addressed Israel, appealing for fidelity, Paul appeals to the church at Corinth. The credentials of his ministry, as outlined before his appeal for separation, are that he is fulfilling all that the suffering servant suffered in his ministry to Israel.

Christian Suffering

The question is, does Paul view himself as a suffering servant because he is an apostle; or because he is a Christian? The reason for the question is this: if it is because he is an apostle, then it follows that his experience of suffering is part of the apostolic office and need not apply to Christians in general. If, however, it is because he is a Christian, then all Christians are called to this same realm of suffering. So, if *doulos* is applied to Christians, as in Romans 6, it is not to be equated with slavery but with the covenant figure of the servant of the Old Testament.

It is beyond doubt that Paul never saw his sufferings as unique. They were part of the sufferings to which the corporate servant, the church, was called:

> For you, brothers, became imitators of the churches of God in Christ Jesus that are in Judea. For you suffered the same things from your own countrymen as they did from the Jews, who killed both the Lord Jesus and the prophets, and drove us out, and displease God and oppose all mankind. (1 Thess 2:14–15)

Paul warned those he visited during his tour of the churches that they must, through much suffering, enter the kingdom of God (Acts 14:22). Clearly, he presupposed the inevitability, if not the necessity, of suffering.

This suffering was something to be endured, for it actually formed part of the will of God (2 Thess 1:4–5). This suffering is in no way vicarious, as was Christ's passion, but it is essentially the same as the sufferings that Christ experienced during his ministry of proclamation. Because of this, Paul frequently links his own suffering, and that of other believers, with Christ's. To be God's servants means being rejected by those who insist on walking in darkness.

> Now I rejoice in my sufferings for your sake, and in my flesh I am filling up what is lacking in Christ's afflictions for the sake of his body, that is, the church, of which I became a minister according to the stewardship from God that was given to me for you, to make the word of God fully known, the mystery hidden for ages and generations but now revealed to his saints. To them God chose to make known how great among the gentiles are the riches of the glory of this mystery, which is Christ in you, the hope of glory. (Col 1:24–27)

Such suffering is not endured in isolation, for the believer is part of Christ's body of which Christ is the head. 'And he said, "Who are you, Lord?" And he said, "I am Jesus, whom you are persecuting"' (Acts 9:5). Again, Paul says, 'that there may be no division in the body, but that the members may have the same care for one another. If one member suffers, all suffer together; if one member is honoured, all rejoice together' (1 Cor 12:25–26).

For Paul, suffering is not merely a sign of being part of the kingdom of God. It is a means of spiritual maturing and preparation for the glory and splendour of Christ's appearing. This parallels the theme of Isaiah, who saw Israel's suffering as necessary for the bringing in of the Messianic kingdom (Isa 40:1–10; 53–54).

> More than that, but we rejoice in our sufferings, knowing that suffering produces endurance, and endurance produces character, and character produces hope, and hope does not put us to shame, because God's love has been poured into our hearts through the Holy Spirit who has been given to us. (Rom 5:3–5)

> And if children, then heirs—heirs of God and fellow heirs with Christ, provided we suffer with him in order that we may also be glorified with him. For I consider that the sufferings of this

38

present time are not worth comparing with the glory that is to be revealed to us. (Rom 8:17–18)

The Fellowship of Suffering

There is deep significance in the passages that speak of the suffering of believers. The theme of suffering for the believer in Romans goes back to Romans 5:3–5. Not that this is the first reference to suffering. In Romans 4:25, Paul has affirmed that Christ 'was delivered over to death for our sins and was raised to life for our justification'.

Some see Romans 4:25 and Romans 5:15–17 to be reflecting Isaiah 53. If this is so, Paul is linking all believers (as he does in 5:12ff.) with the suffering of their representative. They will not only be his servants (6:14) but will also share his rejection and suffering. This is the theme of 5:3–5 and of chapter 8, where Paul emphasizes the relationship and its blessings. Believers are in Christ; they have no condemnation, but they do share in his sufferings as the 'suffering servant'. This is seen in two ways.

First, we may note how Paul linked his own suffering with those of other believers, 'For I consider that the sufferings of this present time are not worth comparing with the glory that is to be revealed to us' (8:18); 'likewise, the Spirit helps us in our weakness' (8:26); 'if God is for us, who can be against us?' (8:31); 'we are more than conquerors' (8:37). This attitude is quite different from that which Paul adopts towards the Corinthians and Galatians, who had moved from the truth of the gospel because of its intellectual or religious offence. In letters to them he set his sufferings against their allegedly superior position (2 Cor 10–11; Gal 2:17–3:5). He relates to the Thessalonians and the Philippians as he does to the Romans, because they are partakers of the sufferings of the gospel (Rom 8:22–38; 1 Thess 2:14ff.; Phil 1:2, 9ff.).

Second, Paul quotes from Psalm 44:8 (Rom 8:6). Examination of this Psalm shows that it summarizes the message of Isaiah 40–66; its message being to those suffering in exile. The same historical background is alluded to and the same language. Paul seems to be deliberately linking the experience of the church—which is awaiting the consummation of its salvation—with the faithful Jews who were awaiting their deliverance from exile to return to the place of promise.

It is no coincidence that Paul selects Psalm 44. This is shown by the fact that in Romans 10, where he goes on to describe the work of the church in proclaiming its message, he quotes from Isaiah 52:7. This is a passage that presents a similar picture to that painted by Psalm 44, but which tells of the work of the faithful remnant who had waited for God's redemptive act. They are God's servants, chosen to proclaim the message of deliverance and renewal.

> How then will they call on him in whom they have not believed? And how are they to believe in him of whom they have never heard? And how are they to hear without someone preaching? And how are they to preach unless they are sent? As it is written, "How beautiful are the feet of those who preach the good news!" (Rom 10:14–15)

Bornkamm sets the original passage in Isaiah in its context when he says:

> In its original context the quotation describes the situation of the few who at the time of the exile stayed on in Jerusalem after it was laid waste and eagerly awaited the return of the exiles from Babylon. Watchmen were posted on the heights surrounding the city and looked forward to seeing the forerunners of the return. At long last the first messenger appeared afar off on the mountains. There upon watchtower the watcher broke into shouts of rejoicing. These passed from mouth to mouth. The forsaken city resounded with jubilation. Their tidings of joy were the dawn of Jerusalem's salvation. This, as Paul sees it, is the condition of the whole world; the message about Christ which sets men free is to sound to the ends of the earth (Rom 10:18) with its citation of Psalm 19:4.

Thus, Paul is not merely quoting the prophecy of Isaiah but drawing his theology from it. This is illustrated by the constant use he makes of the prophet to support his argument and how he uses these quotations as the scaffolding of his letter. Just as Jerusalem was under judgment for sin in Isaiah's time, so now Paul sees the whole world under condemnation; and as Yahweh reserved a remnant for himself in those days, so he has done now. Similarly, as it was the task of the faithful remnant of Israel (distinct from the rest of the populace and denoted by the title 'servant') to announce the restoration of Israel, so it is the church's task to prepare all people for the coming of God's kingdom.

If Paul is so anxious to use the writings of Isaiah in a credible manner—being so faithful to his message that he merely adjusts Isaiah's chronological perspective as to the timing of fulfilment—then we ought to expect him also to have remained faithful to Isaiah's concept of servant-hood. And that is precisely what we find. The threefold use of the 'servant' in the Old Testament, found with particular clarity in Isaiah, is in Paul's mind when he uses *doulos*. Paul sees Christ, the apostles, and the church to be cast in the same mould as Isaiah saw the Messiah, the prophets, and Israel. The term that distinguished Paul and his ministry from other servant believers is that he was an apostle, one who was sent to bear witness to Christ amongst the nations. His status was like all other believers, but his calling to mission amongst the gentiles was not the same.

The Servant and Jesus

It has long been thought that Isaiah 53 was a key text for the theology of the early church and was understood to be the controlling text for the way in which Jesus's death was interpreted as a vicarious atonement. Yet this widely accepted notion might easily be called into question when one considers that Isaiah 53 is used so sparsely in the New Testament. That a text of such importance is quoted so little leads some to suppose that substitutionary atonement theology could not have been a foundational belief in the early church's theology.

I want to suggest that there was a deliberate avoidance of this text by the New Testament writers; and that this refrainment was not because they failed to view Jesus's death as a vicarious atonement. The lack of citations of Isaiah 53 does not prove that they had not noticed its rich suggestiveness; nor does it indicate that they were not interested in the subject. I believe the reason they avoided using this key text for interpreting Christ's death was because of the way the doctrine of the servant had been understood until then.

As we have seen, the servant role was not limited to Jesus; it was shared by the whole people of God, and it was this fact that made it difficult for the early church to use the text. The apostles knew that if they used Isaiah 53 to interpret the significance of the death of Jesus, the servant, then it might consequently be used to interpret the significance of the sufferings of the church, the corporate servant of the Lord. The trouble with this is that if the servant's (Christ's) sufferings were declared to be vicarious, then the church's sufferings might also be thought of as vicarious, for she also was a servant.

This was far too great a price for the early church to pay for explicitly using the text, when that same text implicitly speaks to believers, as it has to countless millions throughout the church's history, without the need for numerous overt references to it.

I am not suggesting that either Jesus or the apostles had no theology of vicarious atonement, only that they purposely avoided using this most suggestive of texts for their model. In fact, they did not need to use it for, as we shall soon see, they had a much more powerful and totally uncomplicated model to use—the Passover. We shall see in chapters seven and eight that this neglected model is the paradigm that was used by Jesus and the apostles to interpret his death.

Conclusion

Our study has shown that Paul's self-identity was bound up with his conviction that he was a servant of Christ, and that his mission was to take the good news to the gentile world. While all this would have become clearer once he became a follower of Jesus, the concept was far from innovative. His rabbinic studies meant that he was constantly engaging with the writings of Isaiah, and so he would have seen his call as a fulfilment of Israel's calling to be a light to the gentiles.

He would also have understood from these same Scriptures that the gentiles would one day become equal heirs of the covenant promises. This interpretation is supported by the fact that as soon as he responded to the call of the risen Christ, he was commissioned to take the good news to the nations. Paul did not utter a word of protest when given this assignment, which might indicate that the gentile mission is what he expected all along once the Messiah had come and his kingdom was established; for it was all foretold in the Law and the Prophets. For Paul, the prophetic Scriptures made clear that the gentiles would be welcomed without circumcision and that they were not required to bear the same visible identity mark as Israel.

In the light of this, we need to ask if Saul saw himself as a zealot in the way that Wright has claimed. Is it possible that a man burning with such anger and hatred could change in a matter of hours and without any theological instruction to help him see how wrong he had been in his previous understanding? Was it further possible that such a man could respond, without any evidence of the slightest theological problem, to the call to be a light to the gentiles which the risen Christ commissioned him to be?

In concluding our study of Paul's use of *doulos*, we have identified a fundamental error in the understanding of many scholars regarding its use and meaning in the New Testament. Wright's ambivalence on Paul's status suggests that he has moved from the traditional slave reading for some key passages.[45] Despite this welcome change, he still, unfortunately, retains what was the traditional reading for *doulos* in some places, and this results in confusion, especially in that it suggests that Paul was indifferent to the terms he used to describe his ministry.

The traditional Hellenistic setting for *doulos* is not adequate if we wish to explain the theological implications that surround its use. Paul follows the New Exodus model, consistently seeing humanity in Adam to be the slave of sin just like Israel in Egypt was the slave of Pharaoh, but those who are in Christ as God's servant are just like Israel was when she was released from slavery in Egypt and brought into covenant with God. A Semitic setting proves itself to be authentic for interpreting many of the concepts that Paul has allegedly lacked in clarity. Paul, like any Christian, is not a slave of Christ, but a servant; with all the dignity and privileges that such a high calling carry. This demonstrates the erroneousness of the assumption that Paul was Hellenistic in his thought-patterns and the inaccuracy of the claim that Greek or Greco-Roman influence formed the basis of his theological constructions. It is this clarity that Wright lacks as he oscillates from describing Paul as a servant and then as a slave having no possessions and no rights. He is failing to observe his own warnings by arguing for two distinct meanings to be within the one term, even though he has argued that these meanings must never be confused. Here again in the Greek *doulos* (slave/servant) is a word that has a range of contradictory meanings and so the correct translation can only be decided by closely considering the theological and cultural context. Surprisingly, it was this very theme that I raised with Wright on that morning in his study back in 1978, and it is clear that while he was enthusiastic to supervise me to do further research into the theme, he never got around to clearing it up himself.

Thus, Paul's theology was deeply rooted in the Old Testament idea of the servant, and there is no place in the Scripture where the servant, called to be a light to the nations, was called to function as a zealot. Once we see the servant theology of Isaiah, Jeremiah, and Ezekiel we see that Israel, as Yahweh's servant, was also called to submit to the prevailing order. This was the case, even when pagans administered the nation; for this was the out-working of Yahweh's sovereign will and was part of his punishment and correction of his wayward people. To introduce a zealot theology into this stream of

---

[45] See N. T. Wright, Justification: God's Plan and Paul's Vision (Downers Grove: IVP, 2009), 142–3.

understanding would be to violate the powerful OT tradition that was already firmly established.

Thus, our study of the use of *doulos* in Paul's letters shows that he saw himself, from the very beginning, to be a servant of Christ. This was not an idea he had stumbled across in some post-conversion enlightenment; it was part of 'who he thought he was'. He was essentially a biblical theologian who knew his place in the purposes of God, even as a student rabbi. That Paul's identity was rooted in Hebraic prophetic tradition challenges Wright's claims of his promotion of an anti-Empire position. Paul never encouraged such an attitude. Indeed, he could not, because the prophets warned the exiled Jews not to seek to undermine the status of the Babylonians or Persians. They knew that the exiles were experiencing the outworking of divine discipline, which was not to be resisted but rather patiently accepted until Yahweh responded to their cry and gave them the deliverance that he had promised. Wright's assumptions that Paul was a zealot just does not fit the written and oral evidence which Paul provides concerning his self-understanding.

Finally, having identified Paul's role, we can see how Wright is quite mistaken to see him as advancing a political agenda to challenge the state.[46] There is no doubt that this might have been a consequence of his work, but it was never specifically his intention. Such a mission quite simply contradicts what we have been able to establish about Paul and the theological convictions that created his understanding. The Jews in exile were never encouraged to take their situation into their own hands; it was stressed to them repeatedly that their situation was Yahweh's judgment, and that they should accept it humbly. Unless we can provide clear evidence to the contrary, we should see Paul's exhortations in this light.

---

[46] Wright, Justification, 153, 'Part of the reason of Romans is to challenge, at several levels, the ideological foundations of Caesar's empire.' This is far too specific; Paul's thesis is to challenge every form of authority which challenges Yahweh's rightful rule over his creation.

Chapter 4:
Probing Paul and His Intellectual Identity

Wright, along with the clear majority of current academic opinion, considers that the identity of Paul's thought world has been settled. As indicated earlier there was a time when most scholars thought that his thinking was essentially Greek and used that culture as the key to interpret Paul's teaching. The major benefit of the New Perspective on Paul movement was that it showed Paul to be thoroughly Jewish. However, Wright warns of the danger of thinking that the Jewish world was cut off from the intellectual movements of the first century Rome and the Hellenistic culture which drove its administration and education system.

Wright has said:

> The Pagan world looked back to Homer, Iliad. Writings of Plato and Aristotle. Dense philosophical works which teach us how to think about the world. In the hundreds of years between Plato, Aristotle, and Paul ... various groups: Stoics, Epicureans, academics, sub groups. Paul grew up in Tarsus—SE Turkey, which is a university town. Paul pretty certainly knew that stuff first-hand. We don't know if he actually studied it but when you compare some of Paul's writing with works like somebody like Epictetus who is on the border between a Stoic and Cynic, they are talking a similar language. They argue the same way. First time I read Epictetus, I thought this fellow lived next door to Paul, or at least they certainly met in the pub frequently. That is how people thought, so Paul is using the tools of thought from the Hellenistic world; not, I would say, to turn Christianity into a form of Stoicism, but to engage with those thought forms. Paul says that whatever is true, lovely, and of good report, think on these things. He isn't saying all the truth in the world is what we've got in our pockets, and there's nothing good out there. It needs to be baptized and needs to be brought to serve Christ, but it can do that. So, Paul, the Jew looks at the Hellenistic world and says, 'right' we can do business here, and there's stuff we've got to share, and we may learn some new tricks in the process.[47]

---

[47] N.T. Wright, *Tom Wright The Shape Of Paul's Theology: Paul and the*

Elsewhere Wright is more specific as to the parallel between Paul and Epictetus. Paul uses diatribe as his preferred method of debate (as found in Romans 2)[48] and this was a feature of the teaching method of Epictetus. So, Wright deduces that the style found in this chapter reflects Paul's indebtedness to the wider culture of the university town he was raised in.[49]

The difficulty with this suggestion is that Hellenism is not the only source for diatribe. It is in fact found in the Jewish Scriptures.[50] This fact demonstrates the danger of assigning influences too hastily when there could be other sources to consider that might make better sense of the material being considered. It is my concern that Wright is prone to this, and his confident assertions as to sources and the consequences of their acceptance opens the door to some serious ramifications.

So, we need to consider this claim and look at the topic of Paul's assimilation of/into the Hellenistic world.

Paul and Hellenism

Wright understands that there were three worlds that Paul lived in and conversed with. The first was the world of the Jewish Scriptures, what is the Christian Old Testament. These give Israel the record of her ancient history and within that collection of books is the record of Yahweh's dealings with the nation. This began with her election and the establishing of covenants that assured Israel of her special status among the nations. Into the Mosaic covenant was embedded the laws that Israel was obliged to keep as people of the covenant. The historic section of the OT told of Israel's disobedience and the inevitable correction that was meted out as Yahweh sought to call her back to covenant faithfulness.

Wright correctly sees these writings as controlling Paul's theology. But alongside these, he brings Greco-Roman history with its culture, which he says Paul used as a tool to engage with the gentile world. He adds to these

---

faithfulness of God 2011, StJohns Timeline, Aug 12, 2011, http://www.youtube.com/watch?v=jN_LSIF9ySk.

[48] Wright, *Faithfulness of God,* 224.

[49] Wright, *The Shape of Paul's Theology.*

[50] Gerhard von Rad, *Old Testament Theology Vol. 2* (Edinburgh: Oliver and Boyd, 1965)

two sources the insights that the study of the literature of Second Temple Judaism has uncovered. While Wright believes the issues found in this literature have a bearing on Paul's teaching, in that he was aware of the issues they debated, he does not claim that Paul had read them and even less likely that he studied them—yet these are the key to correctly understanding Paul, says Wright, for they show us how his fellow Jews were using key terms found in his letters.[51]

The reason why Wright is so confident that Paul engaged with Hellenism is because of the research of the German scholar Martin Hengel.[52] Hengel's work related to the impact of Hellenism on Judaism and he has shown—through his meticulous analysis of legal documents, inscriptions, cemetery memorials, and other sources— that first century Palestine was far from being the location of an unspoiled Jewish heritage. Instead, Hellenism had been assimilated into every part of the nation's life. This led most scholars

---

[51] See also, Wright, *Faithfulness of God*, 1366 where he says, 'I would not myself build too much on this one way or another. Paul's use of the "diatribe" does not mean, on the one hand, that he was smuggling in Stoic logic by the back door or, on the other hand, that he was simply being inconsistent, leaning on a stick he had himself declared to be broken. His claim to understand—indeed to possess!—'the mind of the Messiah' was not a claim that he and his congregations now knew everything there was to know, and had no need to think things through. Rather, his claim was that his, and their human minds were being transformed by the spirit so that they were able at least to understand the full, deep truths about the world. But for that one needed to think clearly, which is where the "diatribe" could help.' I find Wright's explanation of 'having the mind of Christ' as relating to understanding the deep truths about the world and the need to be guided by insights from Stoic logic surprising. Are those who have never been trained in Stoicism forever barred from the mind of Christ? Surely Paul refers to understanding how Christ was guided by the Scriptures and the Spirit to understand how redemptive history was to be completed by his death and resurrection. In fact, the passage where Paul uses this expression, 1 Cor 2:16, speaks about those who have not received Christ not being able to understand the things of the Spirit and 1 Cor 2:6–10 makes it clear that unbelievers cannot share in the mind of Christ. To suggest that the mind of Christ is learned from consulting the sciences is quite simply not what Paul is about!

[52] M. Hengel translated by J. Bowden, *Judaism and Hellenism: Studies in their Encounter in Palestine during the Early Hellenistic Period. 1st English edition*. (London: SCM, 1974). See also M. Chancey, *Greco-Roman Culture and the Galilee of Jesus SNTS* (Cambridge: Cambridge University Press, 2005), 134

(including Wright) to conclude that Hellenism was a part of Saul's educational upbringing and mindset. It was, therefore, something from which he could not have escaped, even in Jerusalem. This position is so widely accepted that one is considered odd if one questions it.

Interestingly, and rarely noted, is that Hengel's work contributed to the need to reconsider the claims for the evolution of Christian teaching. The descendants of the Tübingen School claimed that there was in the New Testament a core of Palestinian material which most scholars accepted as being reasonably accurate. This material was free from Hellenisms, and this was its distinguishing feature—and most textual specialists agreed that only 18% of the material found in the Gospels belongs to this category. Then came another layer of explanation which had to be added to help Diaspora Jews who had believed on Jesus. Because these Jews had a different cultural context from those in Palestine, they needed help to understand the customs and theology of Palestinian Christianity. Finally, there was the further development that virtually re-wrote the story and significance of Jesus for the sake of the gentile believers. It was thought that, since these knew nothing of Palestinian Christianity, they needed a 'different kind' of Saviour—one that could match the Greek and Roman gods who challenged Jesus for pre-eminence. To meet this need, it was thought that the early communities expanded the story of Jesus to create their own narrative, elevating the status and significance of their founder beyond anything which the early believers in Palestine might have recognized. These three stages of the development of the early Christian message would have identified—it was claimed—the extent to which the influence of Hellenism could be found in the text. Of course, the scholarly consensus was that this material was brought together and edited to produce the Gospels we now have.

Hengel's work provided a serious challenge to this view, for if the Hellenization of Palestine had occurred before the New Testament texts were written, then the case for an evolutionary explanation of the New Testament is considerably weakened. Nevertheless, the assumption now prevails that Hengel's work has provided conclusive evidence that Saul was Hellenized to an undefinable level at all stages of his intellectual development. While Hengel's thesis has been adopted by most New Testament scholars the claim needs to be examined. What Hengel has certainly done, is to place the earlier theory of the development of Christian teaching, identified through Tübingen's religion historical method, in the waste paper bin. Instead of the message of Jesus being Hellenised by the church's teachers, Hengel had shown that Judaism itself was Hellenised long before Jesus walked the roads of Palestine. Thus, any Hellenization could have happened in the church's earliest years. However, the question is, did it?

Cultural Assimilation and its Limits

Even though Hengel's work has given invaluable insight into the general situation of Hellenization in Palestine in the first century, it must be remembered that such a study could never be the basis for interpreting the mindset of an individual who lived within that system. For that, an altogether different methodology would be needed. The fact that Saul lived in the university city of Tarsus does not necessarily mean that he was bound to engage with the philosophical ideas that were in circulation there; nor does the fact that he lived in a Jewish city known to be extensively Hellenised confirm his assimilation into Hellenism. This fact has been overlooked by most NT scholars who assume that the question of Paul's engagement with Hellenism is established. I have sat as the observing supervisor in several PhD vivas in recent years where one of the examiners has begun, with the second examiner agreeing, saying something like: 'Well, we do not need to discuss Paul's engagement with Hellenism, Hengel has settled that for us.'

But there are many examples where communities live with the benefits of the dominating culture, while at the same time hating what it has brought. Someone reading the Jerusalem Post would find very different views about modern Israel from those held by the Orthodox community. While America's mainstream media pours out the message of capitalist America, there are many thousands who still live in the past and continue to fight the civil war, refusing to accept the versions of history that are agreed to be accurate by most historians. What I am saying is that there is a danger in assuming that the majority worldview is the one that is shared by all people living within a certain demographic, while in fact, there are many views— some of which strongly oppose the majority view.

Paul's testimony concerning his early life reveals that he was concerned to please his God in every minute detail of the law (Phil 3:4–6). Yet clashing with this picture are several statements that Paul has made that suggests that he valued Hellenism as a vehicle of intellectual development and as a tool for communication, but I want to suggest that these texts have not been adequately scrutinised.

Is it possible that in his views about Saul's early life, Wright has inadvertently re-created the young rabbi in his own image? An admirably well-balanced young man who studied the widest possible curriculum to prepare himself for a career that would value such training? While such a route is entirely valid for the modern scholar, I believe matters were very different for trainee rabbis of the first century, especially if they belonged, as Wright claims Saul did, to the Shammite group, who were staunchly nationalistic. In trying to credit Saul with this sort of intellectual equipment, scholars are, I would suggest, doing what King Saul did when he attempted to dress the young David with his royal armour for his impending battle with Goliath. If Wright has done this, he is not the first person to fall at this hurdle, most of us do this sort of thing, i.e. create in our mind's eye an image of someone that we fail to properly appreciate. I intend to show that the arguments that have been used to prove Paul's Hellenistic credentials are not as convincing as have been assumed, and I want to argue further that reading Paul's writings from an exclusively Hebraic perspective make much better sense of his arguments.

Other Examples of Failed Cultural Assimilation

On Thursday, July 7th, 2005 four Islamist terrorists each detonated a bomb in central London—three on Underground trains and the other on a double-decker bus. As well as the four bombers, fifty-two civilians were killed and over seven hundred were injured.

Another bombing took place almost two years later. On Saturday, June 30th, 2007, the target was Glasgow airport, when a dark-green Jeep Cherokee loaded with propane canisters was driven towards the glass doors of the terminal and set ablaze. Security bollards stopped the car from entering the terminal, although the doors were damaged. The car's driver was severely burnt in the ensuing fire, and five members of the public were injured.

It was not long after each attack before the bombers' identities were revealed to a bewildered British public. Neither gang contained any who might obviously be taken for extremists. Most of them had not been identified as threats by the security forces; they included a primary school worker, a surgeon, and an anaesthetist and some were married with children.

To everyone who knew the bombers, they appeared to be well- integrated into wider society—but this was clearly not the case. There was something very different about them—they claimed to be soldiers fighting a war against those who supported the British government which they saw as responsible for the deaths of Muslims in Iraq and Afghanistan—in short, they had a different value system and worldview from that of the general population.

Since those attacks the activities of militant Islam have hardly been out of the news. Almost daily there are new reports of bombings and shootings, and the same story is frequently reported. The terrorist lived as a normal, well-balanced member of society, and no one saw anything that would have suggested that he or she had been radicalized. In one case, the bomber was a young man who lived in his parents' home. They were horrified to find that he had been arrested for planning to detonate a bomb, they had no idea of his extreme views, even though they shared the same house. These people appeared to fit into the communities in which they lived and worked. In the case of the UK terrorists their children went to British schools and universities, they had British bank accounts and owned British property. They carried behind their names strings of qualifications from Western Universities. However, the reality was that their belief system was different. They had public images that were light years away from where their minds and hearts really were.

The Windows of the Mind

Here is a question pertinent to our theological discussion: how might the Glasgow or London bombers have been identified as extremists by the security services? I would suggest that this could only have been through the careful reading of their private letters and online correspondence. It is only here, in communications written to people who shared the same values as themselves, that evidence would be found to show that they were not assimilated into British life, no matter what assumptions to the contrary their peers, neighbours, or even their parents had made about them.

In first century Palestine, there must have been many who were deeply unhappy because of the direction the nation had taken. The Roman control of their homeland and the subsequent erosion of their cultural and religious identity as a fiercely independent nation under the rule of God would have offended the greater part of the population. The fact that the zealots could muster support for their cause in the years leading up to 70 ce is evidence of this underlying resentment. Again, should we wish to identify those who were amongst this disgruntled group, then only an examination of their private correspondence could bring us into their thought-world and allow us to understand the mindset that it had created.

So, it is not the prevailing cultural influence that tells us about the mindset of Paul the apostle, but his personal writings; of which, thankfully, a sufficient sample for such an exploration has survived. Even though Palestine itself was permeated with Hellenism, this does not prove anything about Paul's personal beliefs. Paul's correspondence and preaching alone divulge to us the way he saw the world and how he understood and related to his God.

After reading the first draft of this book, Wright accused me of 'operating with a very blunt instrument of a Hellenic/Hebrew dichotomy.' Wright's logic concerning this is stated in his book *Paul and the Faithfulness of God*, where he concludes that 'hopefully, we can leave such dichotomy behind forever', he goes on to say:

> . . . the sterile antitheses which have dogged the footsteps of Pauline scholarship ever since F. C. Baur squashed Paul, and the rest of early Christianity, into the two boxes demanded by his Hegelian ideology. Not only are the labels 'Judaism' and 'Hellenism' dangerously anachronistic, as we saw earlier. Not only do we now know that Paul's 'Jewish' world was firmly and irrevocably part of wider 'Hellenistic' culture, which itself was anything but monolithic. Much scholarship is now well aware that ignoring these problems produces gross and distorting historical oversimplification. The deeper problem is that those two labels, with their apparent but pseudo-historical validation, have been used to designate two competing ideologies, setting up a Procrustean bed on which different thinkers can be placed and to whose shape they can be fitted by a process of philosophical, cultural and not least historical torture. The protests against all of this have increased in recent years, though even those who have voiced them have not, I think, seen all the ramifications of following through a genuinely historical investigation.[53]

Wright goes on to acknowledge that this synthesis in Paul's thinking must not allow us to ignore the historically grounded evidence for the real antithesis which manifested itself at the time. He says that 'We cannot, for instance, simply ignore the Maccabean literature, or 4 Ezra. We cannot pretend that the Roman-Jewish war of 66–70, or the great revolt of 132–5, were simply outbreaks of ordinary anti-imperial revolution, though of course, they were that as well.'

These observations are perfectly reasonable by the evidence that exists, but what they must not be used to claim is that everyone in Judaism was characterized by the same general cultural/religious mindset. While clearly, we must not claim that Baur was right in his dichotomy between Judaism and

---

[53] Wright, *Faithfulness of God*, 1357

Hellenism, modern scholarship is equally at fault in demanding that all were synchronized and shared in this integrated worldview. It is this position that Wright seeks to promote when he says:

> It will not do to recognize and reject the nineteenth-century distortions and then to pretend that the first century was simply a flat landscape on which various odd people did various odd and interlocking things. To go in that direction would, in fact, impose another ideology—that of late modern or postmodern relativism in place of the Hegelian one. As usual, it is the Jewish evidence that will suffer most on that new Procrustean bed.[54]

The implication of this statement is that we must not argue that Paul stood outside of this theological/philosophical synthesis because if we do, we are assigning him to the company of these various odd people who did various odd and interlocking things! Such a claim is equally as damaging as any that were made by Hengel and his associates. I believe that this will become clear as we probe further into the theological constructions of Paul.

Probing Paul's Use of Greek Language and Model

Without considering the evidence given above, it is easy to see why many scholars have thought Paul was a Hellenist. For example, he writes in Greek. For many this fact overrides statements that Paul made about his identity, such as being of the tribe of Benjamin and a Hebrew of the Hebrews (Phil

---

[54] Wright, Faithfulness of God, 1358–60. The difficulty in identifying with Wright's position is that he is adamant that Paul remained rooted in the OT for his theological understanding while at the same time engaging with Hellenism. He is convinced that this process had no effect on Paul, as he (Wright) interprets him (Paul). My position is that Paul did stay rooted in the OT and that he did not engage with the philosophers as Wright claims. I claim this because I do not find the evidence that Wright produces to be convincing as I will demonstrate in the coming pages. Wright assumes that since Judaism had already been Hellenised, so Paul was by default Hellenised. I am saying that the evidence does not support the claim that Paul read the OT through the lens of Hellenistic Judaism, but that he interprets the OT both by an internal hermeneutic methodology and through the fulfilment of the promises it contains in the Christ event. This method totally bypasses any need for Hellenistic support or influence and, I would claim that this reading not only gives a clearer understanding of what Paul was teaching but that it has a dimension of authority way beyond what Wright is claiming for his own reading.

3:4–6). Also, Paul seems to adapt Greek models to convey the truths he seeks to share with his readers.

Some years ago, I gave a paper at a theological conference in London. I was making the point of the importance of recognizing the Jewishness of Paul's theology. At the end of the paper, one of the staffs from the department of theology in the host university stood up and with a condescending tone mocked me saying I had shot myself in the foot. 'You're obviously wrong,' he said, 'Paul spoke and wrote in Greek. Obviously, he was Hellenized.'

I was expecting to hear other voices join the protest and challenge me on what I had said and prepared my mind to answer. Instead, to my surprise, the entire audience turned to the one who from the back of the gathering had made the statement and, rather than adding their voices to his, they said, 'but you cannot say that because a person uses a language it means that they share its cultural mindset'. The young scholar, who had just been appointed to a prestigious role in a different leading UK university, was stunned by this outcry and sat down, possibly seeing that he had, in fact, shot himself in the foot!

Paul's self-designation in Phil 3:4–6 is normally seen as an assertion that Paul was a Hebrew speaker, something that was relatively rare in the first century ce. It would be similar, for example, to a Welshman asserting he was not only of Welsh stock but also a Welsh speaker. Such a claim probably indicates that such a person wishes to conserve their national identity and culture. Similarly, Paul's claim to be a Hebrew of the Hebrews linked Paul and his contemporaries who used their ancient language, to a particularly conservative strand of Judaism, which was fiercely proud of its national heritage.

Paul is not describing his past experience, but his present status. The statement would have little value if it was known that Paul had abandoned his heritage, and there would be no point in using the claim as an appeal to the Philippians to resist circumcision. The appeal he made could be paraphrased: 'as one who has this status, I appeal to you to recognize that it does not make you right with God'. There is no suggestion that Paul ever gave up this heritage but viewed it through the Christ event; and he interpreted that event through the lens of the Scriptures that had foretold it. As we shall soon see, his teaching never went outside the Jewish Scriptures but continually cited them to support his theology.

Of course, because he could only communicate with a minority of Jews through the medium of Hebrew, Paul was constrained to use Greek as his language of evangelism and teaching. Of course, I am not saying Paul could not make use of features of Greek society, such as the writing style that was common in his day, and even the form of greeting that was normal. But there is a huge difference between making use of cultural norms of the prevailing culture and using the literature and its presupposition in philosophy etc. to build his theological models. They are very different activities indeed. There is the earlier example of the Islamists making wide use of Western society for their own advantage, using its banking system, its transport system, and its learning centres, but never accepting or valuing its culture. Accepting the necessity of using the language of Hellenism was not evidence of how Paul explored its learning to build his theology. I can give a modern example of this.

I am an Englishman, but I have lived in an English-speaking part of Wales for some years. However, if I were to visit a predominantly Welsh-speaking area, I would find people with immense pride in their cultural heritage and their ancient language. They only use English when necessary for the sake of non-Welsh speaking visitors, they certainly prefer to use their own language and certainly do not see English culture as superior to their own. Far from it, for them the Welsh culture is rich and diverse, and Welsh speakers have no need to turn to English history or culture to provide moral or historical lessons for their children. I suggest that this same dynamic was at play in the life of Saul/Paul; the fact that he spoke Greek tells us nothing of his engagement with Hellenism. His first language and his first choice if he were intelligible in using it, would always have been Hebrew.

The evidence normally cited to support Paul's Hellenistic education is his quotation of their poets in the opening of his message on Mars Hill in Acts 17:28, 'even some of your own poets have said, "For we are indeed his offspring".' Wright makes much of the Athenian speech (Acts 17:22–31) claiming that it was probably a summary of a much longer message that reveals Paul's polemic against idolatry and shows his ability to converse meaningfully with Hellenists.[55] This claim of

Wright, concerning Paul's ability to engage the Greek philosophers, requires that Paul, whatever his level of understanding when growing up in Tarsus, was by this time in his life thoroughly familiar with Hellenism and

---

[55] Wright, *Perspectives,* 105

this is significant. Wright has moved from Paul as someone who had a street awareness of Hellenism because of his upbringing in Tarsus to be a man so conversant with the Greek philosophers that he was able to stand before intellectual Greeks and expose the failures of their teachers' arguments. It would have been utter folly to have attempted this engagement if he had not developed his understanding from a street level to a thorough intellectual competence.

In response to this confident use of a very brief quote from a Greek poet, I consider that it is hardly proof that Paul had developed a higher than average degree of familiarity with Greek literature/ culture. If one conducted a census in London, New York, or even Paris, and asked members of the public to recite a line from Shakespeare, the majority would probably be able to cite something, even if it was only from Romeo and Juliet! However, to claim that they were, therefore, conversant with English literature would be quite ridiculous. Their responses merely indicate that some Shakespearean sayings have penetrated popular culture and nothing more. They certainly are not prepared to enter a serious discussion on, for example, personality development in the writings of Shakespeare, or some other analysis of the bard's thought. Likewise, Paul's quote of a few words from a Hellenistic source is not proof that he was familiar with the literature and philosophy of Hellenism and to enter serious engagement through this cultural/intellectual medium. To argue otherwise stretches the evidence way beyond reasonable limits.

Despite what is normally perceived, the fact is that Paul used incredibly little of such material. Even on the only occasion that he did use Greek literature (Acts 17), he immediately led his hearers from it to a hermeneutic based on the Old Testament teaching of sin and judgment; and went on to explain God's solution in the cross (Acts 17:29–32). This cannot possibly be described as engagement through Hellenism, as Wright argues (believing that what Acts records is but an introduction to Paul's detailed critical analysis of the pagan gods).[56] As we shall soon consider, even his presentation to Agrippa (Acts 26:1–32) is completely void of Hellenistic material. If Wright is correct in his construction of Paul, then such a lack of material is very surprising, since Agrippa was a gentile ruler who would have been highly-trained in Hellenistic culture. Instead, Paul again gives a very Jewish presentation that reflected those given on the Day of Pentecost by the

---

[56] Wright, *Perspectives,* 105

apostles. This hardly demonstrates Paul's engagement with the Hellenistic world—an assumption that has been held by many scholars since the Enlightenment.

Paul and His Engagement with Hellenism

While he argues for the essential Hebraic roots of Paul's theology, Wright is persuaded that Paul did not limit himself to OT texts as he engaged the Greco-Roman world of his readers. Wright sees this policy of intellectual engagement when in 2 Corinthians he said:

> For though we walk in the flesh, we are not waging war according to the flesh. For the weapons of our warfare are not of the flesh but have divine power to destroy strongholds. We destroy arguments and every lofty opinion raised against the knowledge of God, and take every thought captive to obey Christ, being ready to punish every disobedience, when your obedience is complete. (2 Cor 10:3–6)

Wright thinks that Paul is here justifying his method of evangelistic engagement by which he demonstrates the superiority of the gospel over competing ideologies. Wright also takes this as a justification for his own ministry and method; for he claims to keep faithful to the apostle's Hebraic heritage, arguing that he engaged with Hellenism as a tool of evangelism and teaching without allowing Hellenism to influence the message he delivered. Thus, he is very clear that the illustration or example that Paul used has never become part of Paul's theology, it is nothing more than a bridge to help the understanding of the Greeks. This is what I am challenging, for I do not accept that Paul's method, as understood by Wright, would have preserved the purity of his Hebraic heritage in which Paul glories (Phil 3:4–6). If this is correct, then what we now have is a Hellenistic contribution that is hidden in the produced theology. It is this methodological error, which is a Trojan horse that I am most concerned about, for it has profound theological implications. I hope that by this analysis the reader will reflect on his/her own methodological presuppositions and develop a more thought out strategy of interpretation.

Thus, I must question Wright's claim that 2 Corinthians 10:3–6 demonstrates how Paul engaged with Hellenism. Paul's statement that he 'sought to take every thought in subjection to Christ' is not about intellectual activity at all. The wider context of the passage shows that Paul was not fighting an intellectual war with Hellenism but that he was in a battle in which he sought to demolish the Corinthians' self-belief regarding their superiority.

This becomes clear from the flow of his argument. He says: 'I, Paul, myself entreat you, by the meekness and gentleness of Christ' (10:1); 'when they measure themselves by one another and compare themselves with one another, they are without understanding' (10:12); 'it is not the one who commends himself who is approved, but the one whom the Lord commends' (10:18). The thoughts referred to are thus not intellectual but spiritual. Paul is not engaging in a philosophical nor even (directly) a theological debate; rather he is presenting an attitude which his opponents do not share—the attitude of submission and servanthood, where Christ is submitted to as Lord.

This understanding is supported by the context in which Paul compares his ministry of servanthood with the self-promotion of his opponents. If this reading is correct, then there needs to be better evidence to show that Paul, when he debated with the Hellenistic world, adapted, and used its philosophical and literary heritage to claim the minds of pagan hearers for Christ, building arguments that become part of the case supposedly being presented. The arguments that come out of such a hermeneutic are no longer essentially Hebraic; rather, we allow Hellenism to hold the reins of our exegesis. I intend to show that this is happening in Wright's construction of Paul's theology. Thus, while it is found to a lesser degree in Wright than in the works of most others, it is still found, and Wright has not recognized it. He is confidently saying that the teaching which he claims Paul gave to the churches was not influenced by Hellenism. I am saying that as Wright has constructed it, it most definitely is; and to a significant degree.

Paul's Supposed Ongoing Exhortation to Engage with the Best of Hellenism

Wright has made a similar point concerning how he sees Paul's exhortation in Philippians 4 where he says:

> Finally, brothers, whatever is true, whatever is honourable, whatever is just, whatever is pure, whatever is lovely, whatever is commendable, if there is any excellence, if there is anything worthy of praise, think about these things. (Phil 4:8)

Wright says this is evidence that Paul valued truth, beauty, and learning wherever he found it, and he used it in the service of Christ.[57] However, there

---

[57] Wright says, 'Paul is a Jew who looks out on the Hellenistic world and says, "we can do business here, there is stuff that we have got to share and we may learn some new tricks in the process."' Wright, *The Shape of Paul's Theology*.

is a problem with this reading as there is with his reading of 2 Corinthians 10:3–6. We have found that that in the Corinthian passage Paul was not speaking of intellectual debate as claimed by Wright, but about modelling a servant lifestyle and attitude. So, it is in Philippians. Once again, the passage is not an encouragement to accept truth wherever it is found, but it is part of an appeal to live like Christ, preferring one another above themselves. The context makes this very clear:

> I entreat Euodia and I entreat Syntyche to agree in the Lord. Yes, I ask you also, true companion, help these women, who have laboured side by side with me in the gospel together with Clement and the rest of my fellow workers, whose names are in the book of life.
>
> Rejoice in the Lord always; again I will say, rejoice. Let your reasonableness be known to everyone. The Lord is at hand; do not be anxious about anything, but in everything by prayer and supplication with thanks giving let your requests be made known to God. And the peace of God, which surpasses all understanding, will guard your hearts and your minds in Christ Jesus.
>
> Finally, brothers, whatever is true, whatever is honourable, whatever is just, whatever is pure, whatever is lovely, whatever is commendable, if there is any excellence, if there is anything worthy of praise, think about these things. *What you have learned and received and heard and seen in me—practice these things, and the God of peace will be with you.* (Phil 4:2–7 emphasis added)

The final italicized words of the paragraph make the context of Paul's appeal in the following verse (Phil 4:8) clear. It was not to make use of truth wherever it was found, but it was about following the example of those who put Christ first above their personal interests and feelings. He had been saying this throughout the letter, in chapter 2 he wrote:

> So if there is any encouragement in Christ, any comfort from love, any participation in the Spirit, any affection and sympathy, complete my joy by being of the same mind, having the same love, being in full accord and of one mind. Do nothing from selfish ambition or conceit, but in humility count others more significant than yourselves. Let each of you look not only to his own interests, but also to the interests of others. Have this mind among yourselves, which is yours in Christ Jesus, who, though he was in the form of God, did not count equality with God a thing to be grasped, but emptied himself, by taking the form of a servant, being born in the likeness of men. And being found in human

form, he humbled himself by becoming obedient to the point of death, even death on a cross. Therefore God has highly exalted him and bestowed on him the name that is above every name, so that at the name of Jesus every knee should bow, in heaven and on earth and under the earth, and every tongue confess that Jesus Christ is Lord, to the glory of God the Father.

Therefore, my beloved, as you have always obeyed, so now, not only as in my presence but much more in my absence, work out your own salvation with fear and trembling, for it is God who works in you, both to will and to work for his good pleasure.

Do all things without grumbling or disputing, that you may be blameless and innocent, children of God without blemish in the midst of a crooked and twisted generation, among whom you shine as lights in the world, holding fast to the word of life, so that in the day of Christ

I may be proud that I did not run in vain or labour in vain. Even if I am to be poured out as a drink offering upon the sacrificial offering of your faith, I am glad and rejoice with you all. Likewise you also should be glad and rejoice with me. (Phil 2:1–18)

Moreover, again in chapter 3 he has exhorted them saying:

Brothers, join in imitating me, and *keep your eyes on those who walk according to the example you have in us.* For many, of whom I have often told you and now tell you even with tears, walk as enemies of the cross of Christ. Their end is destruction, their god is their belly, and they glory in their shame, with minds set on earthly things. But our citizenship is in heaven, and from it we await a Saviour, the Lord Jesus Christ, who will transform our lowly body to be like his glorious body, by the power that enables him even to subject all things to himself. (Phil 3:17–19 emphasis added)

I have deliberately chosen to put the text before you rather than simply citing number references which will not make the impact of how the appeal to 'think on these things' is not an appeal to an intellectual exercise but something far deeper and profound. The italicized passage shows that Paul's concern was that the Philippian believers lived lives worthy of the Lord, who had saved them, this was the focus of his exhortation to be selective in their thinking.

Thus, it was not a call to cross-cultural, intellectual appreciation and engagement, but rather a call to focus on the qualities found in Christ and to let this mould their mindset so that they became like him in life and death.

These are simply not texts that show that Paul urged his disciples to engage in apologetic evangelism but to live as the one they are called to commend.

The Hybridization of Paul's Theology

Wright's claim that Paul's theology is essentially Hebraic is a claim that I totally support, I had come to this understanding years before I met with Wright and shared it with him back in 1978. But sadly, despite Wright claiming that he has constructed a Hebraic picture of Paul's theology, I have to challenge his understanding that he has achieved what he has claimed, for I am sure that his construction of Paul's theology is eclectic. Over the years, I shared my concern with him, but he has disagreed with my conclusions. Wright continues to claim that while Paul used the language and imagery from these sources, it never changed his OT theology which controlled all that he did.[58] I do not see Paul using the sources that he says that he used i.e. from the Hellenistic and Jewish second temple world, and I, therefore, consider they are an unnecessary and damaging intrusion into what otherwise would be an excellent insight of New Testament teaching for Wright to give to the church. My concern is that the (unintended) intrusion of this material has some very important consequences for the outcomes that Wright seeks to promote.

I do want to make it clear that Wright is not the only theologian that accepts and works on these assumptions. The clear majority, including those who would consider themselves to be the modern equivalents of being a Hebrew of the Hebrews in their theological standing, also do. So, while Wright is the subject of this book, I ask all those who have opposed him to reflect on their own way of doing theology, for it may lack the foundations that have been assumed and be found to be built on unsupported

---

[58] Paul is at home, in fact, in the same street-level world of Hellenistic discourse, while being aware of the need, as he puts it, to "take every thought captive to obey the Messiah." He makes fruitful use of the language and imagery of the pagan moralists while constantly infusing it with fresh content. Nor is this simply a matter of accommodating to another culture, of playing at both ends of the field at once. Precisely because his Jewish tradition taught him that all human beings were made in his imagery, he, like some of his contemporaries such as the author of the Wisdom of Solomon was able to mark out a firm platform within Jewish thought from which to address the inhabitants and indeed the rulers, of the rest of the world.' Wright', *Perspectives*, 4.

presuppositions. Rather than being built on the rock I fear much modern theology, of the evangelical kind, is built on sand. I repeat the gist of what I said in my PhD thesis. 'We would be horrified to discover how Hellenistic thought has controlled so much of Christian thought and in doing this, it has left us with a message that is a distortion of the Gospel.' Thankfully, it has not obliterated that message, but it has certainly blurred and confused it. Claiming that we hold to the authority of Scripture does not help us if we are irresponsible in the way we interpret it.

I want to make it clear that I share completely with Wright the importance of the New Exodus motif that he holds. Having said that, I think that he has failed to see just how pervasive the paradigm is. He often misses the theme in important sections of the New Testament which I intend to show in coming chapters. I do not describe my own understanding simply as New Exodus understanding or theology but as 'Paschal New Exodus theology' because I understand that the Passover and the promised exodus from Babylon are at the very heart of Paul's theological understanding. This narrative is at the heart of redemptive history and is provided entirely from the Old Testament sources that the early church gloried in. Once this has been identified, it produces a compelling and self-authenticating reading not only of Paul's letters but of the entire New Testament. Nothing has to be added or brought in from outside to clarify or expand the truth the apostles were teaching to the fledgling church. Thus, I cannot agree with Wright that he succeeded in describing a theology of the apostle that is thoroughly Hebraic and free from extra-biblical intrusions; instead what we have is a distortion of Paul's message. I do of course recognise that Paul writes in Greek and even uses Greek letter styles such as the salutation, but this is not bringing any Greek ideas into the theology that Paul constructs. I acknowledge that having been brought up in the university town of Tarsus he is likely to be aware of at least the rudiments of Hellenistic thought. But however much of this material he knew, what is abundantly clear to me is that when constructing his theological arguments, he always draws from the Old Testament Scriptures and it is a Hebraic mindset that controls his thought processes. Introducing anything post Old Testament distorts Paul's message, for it is entirely rooted in the law and the prophets.

Tracing Intrusions and their Consequences

To demonstrate an example of intrusion I need to show that under Wright's construction he has Paul assimilating Hellenism and then constructing a new theology. I believe an important example of this is provided when Wright explores Paul's teaching on the Torah. In Romans 2 and 7 Wright sees Paul to be answering the questions of Jews and the gentiles concerning the law. He says:

> . . . one obvious passage in which Paul appears to be echoing several pagan moralists is Romans 7, where Paul joins a long line from Aristotle onwards in complaining [through the medium of the first person singular, the 'I', which like many exegetes I understand as a rhetorical ploy rather than actual autobiography] that 'I don't do the good thing I want to do, but I end up doing the evil thing I don't want to do.' This is the classic problem of akrasia, 'weakness of will'. It has been proposed that Paul, here and perhaps elsewhere, is claiming as a major point that being 'in Christ' enables one to attain the self-mastery at which the philosophical schools, especially Stoicism, were aiming. There is a sense in which I agree with this, but only in the following way[59]

Wright then goes on to describes his nuanced position saying that the passage is not about the issues that the philosophers struggled with but the issues the covenant people struggle with and outlines the pattern of the history of redemption which he sees Paul is reflecting on.[60] This is all very good and helpful, but I think he trips over it when he sums up his understanding on Romans 7:7:

> The crucial point for the present chapter is that Paul has carefully and deliberately set out his retrospective theological analysis of the plight of the devout Jew under Torah in terms of the well-known dilemma of the pagan moralist.[61]

Wright goes on to say:

> All this demands, I think, that we read certain Pauline texts in at

---

[59] Wright, *Faithfulness of God,* 1376–77.

[60] 'His head-on confrontation with paganism did not mean that he was not able to affirm the reuse of elements of it within his own thought. As he says, he "takes every thought captive to obey the Messiah." (2 Corinthians 10:5), and when it comes even to pagan political rulers he is clear that God wants the world to be ruled in an orderly way (Romans 13:1–7; Colossians 1:15–20), since the alternative is chaos come again. Confrontation does not mean dualism.' Wright, *Perspectives,* 105.

[61] Wright, *Faithfulness of God,* 1378. Emphasis Wright's.

least a bifocal fashion.[62]

Such a statement leaves one asking, 'whose view of sin is Wright responding to'? Can the two views be mixed without one or both of them being compromised and how could a moral pagan possibly understand the wider canvas of the covenants that Paul has drawn his analysis on? I have no problem with Wright's Jewish reading of the text and have argued for a very similar understanding elsewhere,[63] but not for a 'bifocal reading' simply because the proposed solution creates more problems than it solves. A further problem that the proposed reading presents is who decides what is and what is not bifocal reading? This is an important question because any claim is likely to be challenged by others. Indeed, this is the very thing I am doing in this discussion!

Another problem for this bifocal reading that Wright considers essential to understand Paul is the question 'What is the purpose of Paul linking his argument with the philosophers?' The letters of Paul were written to the churches he was linked with. They were not private correspondence and teachings in which he was exploring philosophical niceties, they were letters that were read to the entire congregation. It is clear that those in the Roman church had welcomed the gospel with its understanding that righteousness did not come by the law but by grace which produced faith and obedience. This fact must control the argument that Paul is making concerning the law. He is not writing evangelistic tracts or an apology for the law to win gentiles over by claiming that it was the fulfilment of all that the gentiles had sought. Certainly, this was an argument that Justyn Martyr was eventually to make as he engaged with his gentile readers, but it has no place in this passage. Rather, in Romans 2 and 7 Paul is seeking to explain how believers, both Jewish and gentile, relate to the law. By introducing the teaching of the philosophers into Paul's discussion Wright loses Paul's clear purpose of helping the mixed community to understand how they are all 'under the law' in the same way and how both sections of the new covenant community depend on the same grace of God for acceptance.[64] This is an unfortunate observation to have to

---

[62] Wright, *Faithfulness of God*, 377. Emphasis mine.100

[63] Holland, *The Divine Marriage*, 203–250.

[64] Wright argues that because Paul believes in 'the rehumanizing power of the gospel of Jesus and the gospel is meant to renew people in this genuine image-bearing humanness 'we should expect then, to find that standards emphasized in the finest contemporary philosophers would be echoed by

make on the work of one who has done so much good work on the law in Paul.[65] If there is any echo of the philosophers, it would be coincidental rather than forming part of the argument.

The claim of Wright, that Hellenism never became part of Paul's argument and that it was only used as a means of comparison does not seem to be working out here. Indeed, because he sees the presence of Hellenistic arguments in these chapters Wright has to appeal for a 'bifocal reading'.[66]

The Case of the Firstborn King

A similar interaction between Paul's Jewish message and Hellenism is seen in his explanation of Paul's meaning of the term 'firstborn' when applied to Christ in Colossians 1:15. Wright says:

> Near the heart of Paul's view of Jesus is the sense, easy to spot but hard to analyse, that like many Jews of his day he saw God's wisdom as a quasi—independent power, as in Proverbs 1–9, Ben Sira 24 and the Wisdom of Solomon, going out to create a beautiful world, to enable humans to be genuinely and gloriously human, and to live, in particular in Israel, in the Temple, in and through the Torah (Ben Sira is particularly clear on this).[67]

He goes on to say:

> ...with this theology in his head and heart, [Paul] took a flying leap into a view of Jesus, his identity, his mission from the Father, and his role in the new creation. This enabled him to draw freely on 'wisdom' ideas, relocating them in and around Jesus, and to invite those who belonged to Jesus to discover in him the personal presence of the Divine Wisdom, God's second self, doing at least what Temple, Torah and 'Wisdom' might have been supposed to do but what they had not succeeded in doing.

I will consider this passage from Colossians in chapter seven but what I want to note here is that Wright understands Paul to be doing something

---

Paul.' Wright, *Faithfulness of God,* 1376. But this ignores the fact that what Paul as a Christian Jew considers renewal to be, and what the Greek philosophers considered it to be, are very different. Here Wright has chosen the Greek meaning.

[65] See N. T. Wright, *The Climax of the Covenant: Christ and the Law in Pauline Theology* (Edinburgh: T&T Clark, 1991).

[66] Wright, *Faithfulness of God,* 1377.

[67] Wright, *Justification,* 132–3.

similar to what goes on in Ben Sira 24 and the Wisdom of Solomon, both of which are Hellenistic Jewish texts. Wright sees this as an example of Paul using the best of what he finds in Hellenism to convey his message. Clearly, Wright is not Hellenizing Paul in this observation, but he is saying that Paul has used a text that others have Hellenized. In other words, Paul created a further synthesis between Hebraic and Hellenic culture! This 'flying leap' is into a view of Jesus that has added to Paul's Hebraic background. This statement is contrary to Wright's claim that Paul's teaching remained Hebraic. For most the definition of Hebraic is what is found in the OT, not what is found in the Hellenized theology of Second Temple Judaism. This example shows if we accept Wright's reading of the evidence, not only that Paul accepted Hellenistic influences, and he was, therefore, Hellenized which Wright denies! Therefore, Paul's theology was clearly shaped by Hellenism and this, if the method is accepted, most definitely contributed not only to Paul's theology but also to Wright's theology of Paul.

This incarnation of wisdom, quite different from the incarnation of the Logos in John which has been shown to be directly based on Genesis 1 and is thoroughly Jewish, is used to explain the imagery of Christ ascending and descending in Romans 10. I have dealt with this elsewhere and have shown that the passage is fully understood as an expansion of the New Exodus theme.[68]

Probing the Parousia and the Imperial Coming

Another clear example of the presence of Hellenism is found when Wright explains the meaning and significance of Paul's reference to the return of Christ as being his *Parousia*.[69] Wright notes that the term was a technical term used in the Roman Empire to speak of the coming of the emperor or some other senior figure whom the populace must prepare to welcome. [70]Wright

---

[68] Wright also recognises the presence of this important New Exodus theme in the introduction to the hymn (vvs.13–14) but does not see how it should carry on into the hymn and control its meaning.

[69] Wright, *Justification,* 142 notes that the Greek term in nowhere found in the LXX.

[70] 'The word parousia itself, and the language of meeting which Paul uses in 1 Thessalonians 4.17, is not, like so many of his key terms, familiar from the Septuagint. It evokes the scene, familiar from much Hellenistic and Roman writing, of a king or emperor paying a state visit to a city or province. As he approaches, the citizens come out to meet him at some distance from the city,

builds on this widespread understanding of the term to argue that Paul is adopting Hellenistic imagery to describe the coming of Christ. He then appeals to the work of Oaks to show that there is similar imperial imagery found in Philippians.[71]

But the presence of the Greek word *Parousia* does not present the evidence that Wright claims for it. That the word never occurs once in the LXX, does not mean that it must be Hellenistic in its significance and meaning. Once it is recognized that there are other Greek words that have no LXX history but that do very clearly carry clear Hebraic 'adopted' meanings, Wright's argument fails. For example, the word υἱοθεσία...a (*huiothesia*, 'adoption') is found nowhere in the OT, and Paul uses it to describe the relationship believers have with God. Wright is clear that the term does not carry the Hellenistic understanding of adoption that many scholars hold.[72] This is because he recognizes the continual relationship between adoption and being sons of Abraham/God. Such an interpretation allows the OT content to dominate the Greek word to the extent that there is nothing of the Greek term's original meaning left. OT theology and not the Greek dictionary prevails.[73]

---

not in order then to hold a meeting out in the countryside, but to escort him into the city. 'Meeting the Lord in the air' is not a way of saying 'in order then to stay safely away from the wicked world'. It is the prelude to the implied triumphant return to earth where the Messiah will reign, and his people with him, as Lord, saviour and judge. And in that context parousia means what it means to imperial rhetoric. The royal presence of the true Lord as emperor. This points on to the theme of the next chapter, since precisely in Thessalonians as in Philippians and Romans, we find clear signs that Paul's gospel of Jesus the Messiah claims to be the reality of which Caesar's empire, with all of its trappings, is simply a parody.' Wright, Perspectives, 55–6.

[71] Peter Oaks has shown how much imperial imagery is in the Christ hymn of Philippians 2, this points to contrast between the salvation Jesus offers won through his weakness and that which Caesar offers, which was won through his might: Wright, *Perspectives,* 72–3.

[72] T. J. Burke, Adopted into God's Family: Exploring a Pauline Metaphor (Downers Grove: InterVarsity, 2006).

[73] Elsewhere, Wright, Perspectives, 26, has argued, 'Exegesis needs the concordance, but it cannot be ruled by it. It is no argument against calling Paul a covenant theologian to point out the scarcity of diathekē in his writings. We have to learn to recognise still more important things, such as implicit narrative and allusions to large biblical themes' (Emphasis added). In

As Wright holds to this understanding of adoption, he ought to have no difficulty accepting that the term Parousia could be based on an OT model. Paul has attached Parousia to the theme and in so doing he has caused the term, if it was not already, to be severed entirely from its original Greek meaning and bestowed on it the biblical meaning that the OT return of Yahweh theme supplies. If we look at the race illustration in 1 Cor 9:27, we will find that Paul does the same thing again.[74]

There are some problems with Wright's interpretation of Parousia that he has missed. It is understandable why he thinks that imperial language is embedded in 1 Thessalonians, but there are problems that need to be resolved before endorsing it. Oaks notes the difficulty of applying the imagery to people going out to meet the emperor with the observation that it would need the people to lead Christ back to earth.[75] For this reason, Oaks is not as committed to the imagery as Wright is. A significant 'glue' that has held the Hellenistic model together in 1 Thessalonians is the assumption that the judgment that is brought at the second coming, in the Parousia, is modelled on the application of Roman law to the rebels. In other words, it was believed that Paul's use of law in 1 Thessalonians was based on Roman law. However, Matt Arnie has researched this understanding, and he has established that the references to law in the Thessalonian correspondence is not Hellenistic but

---

other words, a particular word must not dominate the interpretation of a text, its context and the themes within it are more significant.

[74] There are other examples of this practice in the Pauline letters. So, as we have already noted, Paul does it with *doulos*, adoption (*huiothesia*) and Parousia.

[75] Peter Oakes, 'Re-mapping the Universe: Paul and the Emperor in 1 Thessalonians and Philippians,' *JSNT* 27.3 (2005): 301–322. Oakes says: 'For most Christians, the imperial cult was probably a less pressing issue than other cults in which they had previously participated. At Philippi, even though the imperial cult temple occupied a prominent place in the forum, the cult has only a minor place in the overall collection of inscriptions that testify to the religious life of the people of the city.', 313. Oakes goes on to say, 'A further difficulty for reading great significance into the two "political" terms is the fact that they sometimes occur in non-political senses. A third difficulty is that v. 17 does not fully fit the pattern of civic greeting, because, in v. 17, the Christians appear to stay in the air, which would be the equivalent of staying outside the city after greeting an official. What happens long-term is unclear, but if Paul intended a parallel with civic greeting, we might have expected the Christians to lead Christ down to earth.', 316.

from the themes of judgment in the OT when the curse of the law will be brought on those who disobey.[76] Thus, the imagery is not from Hellenistic sources but OT ones. Furthermore, when we examine the letter to the Philippians, we note that Oaks has again shown some reservations about linking parts of the letter to Hellenistic practices.[77] But Oaks and Wright (surprisingly, considering his positive attitude to the exodus theme in Paul's letters) have overlooked what is said immediately after the hymn in Phil 2:4–11.

> Let each of you look not only to his own interests but also to the interests of others. Have this mind among yourselves, which is yours in Christ Jesus, who, though he was in the form of God, did not count equality with God a thing to be grasped, but emptied himself, by taking the form of a servant, being born in the likeness of men. And being found in human form, he humbled himself by becoming obedient to the point of death, even death on a cross. Therefore God has highly exalted him and bestowed on him the name that is above every name, so that at the name of Jesus every knee should bow, in heaven and on earth and under the earth, and every tongue confess that Jesus Christ is Lord, to the glory of God the Father. (Philippians 2:4–11)

Paul then goes on to use the example he has given of Christ saying:

> Therefore, my beloved, as you have always obeyed, so now, not only as in my presence but much more in my absence, work out your own salvation with fear and trembling, for it is God who works in you, both to will and to work for his good pleasure.

> Do all things without grumbling or disputing, that you may be blameless and innocent, children of God without blemish in the midst of a crooked and twisted generation, among whom you shine as lights in the world, holding fast to the word of life, so that in the day of Christ I may be proud that I did not run in vain or labour in vain. Even if I am to be poured out as a drink offering upon the sacrificial offering. (Philippians 2:12–18)

In other words, rather than the hymn being a comparison between Christ and Caesar, as claimed by Wright, it is written as an example for the believers to follow, and the language is clearly New Exodus. The passage speaks of

---

[76] Matthew D. Aernie, *Forensic Language and the Day of the Lord Motif in Second Thessalonians 1 and the Effects on the Meaning of the Text. West Theological Monograph.* (Oregon: Wipf & Stock, Reprint 2011).

[77] Oaks, 'Re-Mapping', 315.

The Search for Truth

shining as lights in the dark world, the very imagery that Isaiah uses to describe the ministry of the faithful remnant on their pilgrimage. We will soon see that the imagery of running the race is again a New Exodus theme. In light of this, we can see how Paul, referring to his possible death and his willingness to submit to it in the context of the New Exodus, echoes the role of the servant whose suffering brought about the Second Exodus from Babylon. Clearly, we know that Paul never saw his own possible death as a sacrifice with anything like the significance of Christ's death, but the sacrificial imagery is used throughout the New Testament to highlight the ultimate act of witnessing about Christ.

While it is widely understood that 'our citizenship is in heaven' is seen to be comparing Romans citizenship with citizenship of heaven (so Wright), I would question why there is nothing in the letter that explicitly supports this reading, beyond importing the recognized status of the city into the passage. However, this is not the only possible reading and lacks specific support from within the letter. This statement could be comparing the citizenship of heaven with what the believers are promised if they embrace Judaism. What supports this is Paul's reasoning in Galatians:

> Now Hagar is Mount Sinai in Arabia; she corresponds to the present Jerusalem, for she is in slavery with her children. But the Jerusalem above is free, and she is our mother. For it is written, "Rejoice, O barren one who does not bear; break forth and cry aloud, you who are not in labour! For the children of the desolate one will be more than those of the one who has a husband." Now you, brothers, like Isaac, are children of promise. But just as at that time he who was born according to the flesh persecuted him who was born according to the Spirit, so also it is now. But what does the Scripture say? "Cast out the slave woman and her son, for the son of the slave woman shall not inherit with the son of the free woman." So, brothers, we are not children of the slave but of the free woman. (Gal 4:25–31)

Paul was facing this issue throughout the churches he had founded. Judaizers, or zealous gentile converts to Judaism, who had possibly previously confessed Christ, were seeking to win converted gentiles to Judaism on the promise of a greater citizenship. Wright acknowledges that Paul has described his own journey from Judaism as part of the covenant people and should have no difficulty in applying the same metaphor to the Christian community as a whole. As part of that journey, he gave up his identity and status as a Jew, and with all that he had once held dear (Phil 3:2–11). The context of his statement concerning his credentials is to stress how he values his new identity in Christ, and he uses it as a warning that his readers must not become ensnared by those of the circumcision. He testifies that the inheritance he has in Christ is beyond anything that Judaism gave him, and that he now considers what he once had as refuse compared to what he has gained in Christ. It is such a reading, I would suggest, that makes better sense and is consistent with the purpose of the letter and the actual opponents who he mentions. They are not Roman officials but zealots, servants of the circumcision party.[78]

So, returning to Paul's use of Parousia that we considered earlier, the term is not linked to the arrival of the emperor but of the pilgrim community which is led by their Saviour Lord, Jesus, who is the Christ, who delivered them from the kingdom of darkness and had brought them to his own kingdom. The final entrance into the kingdom of God has yet to happen; their intermediate state is being members of the body of Christ, and they enter the kingdom of God with all others on the resurrection day.[79] Then all who are in the grave will be caught up with him and be led in triumphant majesty as the whole of creation welcomes its crucified, risen and triumphant Lord. It's the presence of the Creator of all things that the term Parousia relates to and this is loaded with OT meaning and imagery.

The Case of the Unidentified Babysitter

In Galatians 3:24–25 Paul says:

> So then, the law was our guardian until Christ came, in order that we might be justified by faith. But now that faith has come, we are no longer under a guardian,

The use of the Greek term *paidagōgos* was seen to refer to the law as a jailer keeping the unbeliever in check until Christ came. But the idea of the *paidagōgos* being a jailer was eventually seen by some as being too harsh. Even before the birth of the New Perspective on Paul there were those who were uncomfortable with such a harsh depiction of the role of the law. The suggestion was made that Paul's use of the word related to the role of the *paidagōgos* in a Greek household. Such people were slaves who the

---

[78] See Eph 2:11–22 where he describes how the gentiles are now members of the new covenant community and Gal 4:21–31 for membership of different covenant communities.

[79] Acts 14:21–22; 1 Cor 15:24–28; Eph 5:5.

householders used, not primarily for domestic duties, but to guide the development of their children. These slaves were thought to teach the child and so the translation 'the law was our schoolmaster to bring us to Christ' was the agreed meaning.

This view prevailed until Conzelmann objected because he realized that the *paidagōgos* was a figure who was despised for his cruelty. Hellenistic artists represented him as a harsh figure who was often uneducated and uncouth. He was presented as having a rod which he used as an instrument of punishment if the child did not keep up with his lessons. He was widely despised and was mocked in the theatres as an objectionable figure. Conzelmann argued that such a picture could not be intended by Paul, as no pious Jew would represent the law in a manner that mocked it. If Paul had intended such imagery, he would have so deeply offended his fellow Jews that he would have damaged the credibility of his message. It was, for this reason, Conzelmann suggested that instead of being a teacher, the *paidagōgos* spoke of one who managed the child in taking him to school and ensuring that his homework was done. This readjustment was welcomed as a solution to a problem that many had recognized to be within the earlier interpretations of the text.

But Wright has challenged this understanding, and without giving his reason he has said that he prefers to see the *paidagōgos* as a nurse looking after the child.[80] By bringing in this image he has certainly softened the picture that Paul is understood to be intending. Thus, the condemning aspect of the law's role was replaced by the much softer and attractive role of the nurse with her loving concern for the child that was in her charge. Jewish readers of the letter certainly would not object to this very positive role for the law which they had always been taught expressed God's love for them.

But all the above solutions with their welcome progression to a more positive role for the law failed to take into account one obvious problem. The theology of Galatians is essentially the history of salvation explaining how God had always planned for the gentiles to be part of the new covenant

---

[80] 'The Torah was our nanny, our baby sitter, the slave hired to look after us while we were young and at risk, so that we might make it through to the coming of Messiah, when God's people would be defined, justified, declared to be God's people, indeed, on the basis of faith. Paul is not saying, as traditional readings have had it, that the law was a hard taskmaster, driving us to despair of ever accomplishing its demands, so that we would be forced to flee to Christ and find an easier way, namely faith'. Wright, Justification, 10.

community. The argument is built up by painstaking exegesis of OT texts. To find this introduction of a Greek figure to play the role of the law in Jewish history is such a sharp contrast to the OT exegesis that has laid the foundation for the argument suggests that Paul has had a very unwelcome brainwave. Why would he explain the role of the law in a way that was bound to be unattractive to both Jews and gentiles? This it would seem is the issue that Wright has struggled with before suggesting his reading of the *paidagōgos* is intended to refer to a babysitter.

While undoubtedly a better solution than earlier attempts, the weakness of Wright's proposal is the lack of support from ancient texts, either biblical or secular. There is no evidence that a *paidagōgos* ever acted as a babysitter. The term that denotes one who cared for the baby and a more appropriate term for such a person is τροφός (*trophos*), the child's nurse. Wright's proposal leaves one asking why Paul has chosen *paidagōgos* and not *trophos*? In 1 Thessalonians 2:7 Paul says, 'But we were gentle among you, like a nursing mother taking care of her own children.' Here Paul uses *trophos,* so he is aware of the word and it would be the most natural word for describing the role of the law if that is what he intended. I want to suggest that Wright is in danger of missing the importance of this passage for Paul's theology, claiming that his babysitter theme; 'turns out to be a major motif.'[81] As we are about to see, the term relates to something far more glorious than what Wright has suggested.

The Paidagōgos and Redemptive History

The theological stream in which a term is used must determine how we interpret individual terms within an argument, not the range of possibilities that Hellenism was familiar with. In the following discussion, I will argue that Paul understands that the law functioned in an OT sense and one that the Greek *paidagōgos* did not reflect. The theological stream that Galatians is part of is that of redemptive history. Paul's argument is that the law was a gift from God to his people and given so that it could bring his people to her loving God. The law has brought the elect community to Christ, but Christ has been snatched away and he has now put his Spirit in charge. It is he, the Spirit, who now guides the covenant community. It is with him that they must keep in step, and it is his authority that they are to submit to as they continue

---

[81] Wright, *Justification,* 115.

their pilgrimage to the bridegroom. Christ has been snatched away, but the church waits for her perfection at the Parousia.

Perhaps this two stage pilgrimage needs expanding. We know that Jesus said his disciples could not fast because the bridegroom was among them. He then said the day would come when they would fast because the bridegroom had been snatched away. If we think of the divine marriage in Western categories, we are very unlikely to follow what is going on. In the East, marriage started with the groom coming from his father's home to that of the bride where a week of celebration was held before he finally left for his father's home with his bride where the marriage was consummated. Once the marriage celebration had begun, in the home of the bride, nothing, not even the news of the death of the bride's father, was allowed to stop the celebration. It was for this reason that Jesus said it was not appropriate that his disciples should mourn, for the bridegroom was with his bride and the marriage had begun.

But Jesus anticipated that the marriage would not be consummated in the immediate future. He would be snatched away. The bride would be left without the groom. Then it would be appropriate for her to mourn and fast. It is this reality that explains the two parts of salvation history. The first part relates to the role of the law bringing the elect to Christ, the second relates to the elect community continuing her pilgrimage, having been delivered from the Egypt of the kingdom of darkness, looking for her bridegroom who she has been assured will come again. Then the marriage will be consummated. Thus, law and Spirit are two distinct phases of salvation history.

To further aid our understanding of the law in Paul we need to remind ourselves that Galatians is an abbreviation of the letter to the Romans. Arguments that are made in one letter should, therefore, be transferable to the other. The expanded form of the argument that is normally found in Romans ought to provide insight into the abbreviated form of the argument found in Galatians. This may be the clue we need to decide what being 'under sin' means and how it relates to the imagery of being under the *paidagōgos*. Here in Galatians Paul speaks about being shut up under sin (Gal 3:23). Reading a range of modern translations will show how the translators remain unclear as to what this means.

For most translators and commentators, the idea of being 'under sin' suggests the idea of imprisonment. But that understanding is not necessarily in the text, it is being assumed, and it in fact directly violates the meaning given to *paidagōgos* in the following verse. If the presently preferred understanding of *paidagōgos* is correct and corresponds to what Paul intended, then he creates a very real tension by describing the law as a jailer and then as a teacher. But such ideas, of the prison service reforming prisoners through education, did not exist in the first century. Nothing so enlightened as prison reform emerged in that period of history.

The Law of Marriage

But we might get some help from Paul's argument from Romans 6 and 7. In the first of these chapters Paul has argued that the unbeliever serves Sin. As we have seen, commentators agree that in chapter 6 the word sin in the singular is not about the violation of the Mosaic law. Rather, it is a pseudonym for Satan. So, Paul is not saying those in Christ cannot commit sins, but that those in Christ cannot be in the service of Sin. They cannot willingly do the will of Satan. Paul extends this argument in chapter 7 where he explains how a woman is bound to the law of her husband as long as he lives. But if her husband dies, Paul says, she is free from the law of her husband. He then tells the Romans that they have in fact died, by the body of Christ, that is, by his physical death, and so they are free to marry another, even Christ.

Clearly, if they have been freed from the law of the first husband, and they are now married to Christ, then they come under his law, i.e. the law of Christ. This suggests that the law of sin is not essentially about sin somehow lording it over people making them do whatever it wants. It is a far bigger picture than this. It is corporate; it is about those who were once the bride of the former husband who have now been freed through Christ's death. But who is the former husband? He is Sin. Paul has been saying this all the time. Formerly they belonged to Satan, and this union was one of the covenants. Like the Jews, Adam made a covenant with Satan. This is what Hosea accused the Jews of doing in their pursuit of other gods; they were repeating the sin of Adam.[82]

---

[82]The passage is a problem for many scholars because there is no mention of covenant in Gen 1–3. For this reason, some identify Adam with a non-descript village called Adam, so 'At Adam they broke the covenant; Oh how they were unfaithful to me!' (NET). However, this is not the problem that the translators have thought. Hosea had already turned the Exodus into a marriage occasion so why could he not develop the significance of Adam's sin so that it was portrayed as a violation of the divine marriage? The former development

In Romans 7:1–4 Paul is not speaking about the individual's experience; it is about the community that is in Christ, those who have been liberated by his death, now actually becoming his bride. Nowhere in any part of Scripture is the marriage analogy ever used to describe an individual's relationship with God. It is always a corporate analogy. This imagery is clearly behind what is said in Ephesians 5:25–27. Paul says, 'Husbands, love your wives, just as Christ loved the church and gave himself up for her to make her holy, cleansing her by the washing with water through the word, and to present her to himself as a radiant church, without stain or wrinkle or any other blemish, but holy and blameless.'

To repeat what I have said above when it says in Galatians 3:22 that the law has shut us up under sin, we need to recognize that the flow of the argument is the same as that found in Romans 6 & 7. The law, God's law, whether it be in its Mosaic form or simply the principle of truth and righteousness expressed in other laws, not only forbids adulterous relationships, it also recognizes all covenant relationships. The law respects the law of the husband, upholding his authority in the covenant relationship, which can only end through death.

If we keep in mind that the former husband in Romans 7 is sin, and sin is another term for Satan, then Paul sees unredeemed mankind in a relationship with Satan of the same nature as he was created to have with God. In the former relationship, the husband was sin (Satan), so the law of the husband is the law of Sin. Just like in a marriage it would be possible to speak of the authority or law that Joe Smith has over his wife Ann Smith, so Paul speaks about how sin has authority over those who are his. This is more than legal authority, it is covenanted authority, and it is this authority that the legal system has to recognize, and that is what Romans 7:1–6 is all about. It is the law of sin and death, both terms being pseudonyms for Satan in biblical literature. It would be the same as speaking of the law of Joe Smith, her husband. The compound designation being used to make clear who this husband was—the law of sin and death, of Satan. So, what does it mean that the law has put us under sin as found in Galatians 3:23? In the light of the above, it means that the law itself, God's law, agrees with the claim of sin

---

logically required the development of the later suggestion. See Colin Hamer, *Marital Imagery in the Bible, An Exploration of Genesis 2:24 and its Significance for the Understanding of New Testament Divorce and Remarriage Teaching, Apostolos Old Testament Studies* (London, 2015),144–45.

(Sin) to be the rightful owner of those who are in Adam. They are Satan's (i.e. Deaths) by the covenant established through Adam's disobedience.

An Alternative Understanding of the Paidagōgos

I am arguing that the statement about the law being a *paidagōgos* has been interpreted without proper reference to the redemptive- historical context. The prevailing view of the *paidagōgos* ignores the condition the son is held in, described just a few verses later. In Galatians 4:2 he says that the heir is subject to guardians and trustees until the time set by his father. This subjection was only until Christ came and then they received the adoption of sons (vv. 4–7) which is evidenced in that they have received the Spirit of adoption. It is clear that the argument is that the *paidagōgos* role of the law has finished since Christ has come. This would suggest that the role of the law was not about bringing individual sinners to Christ through making them aware of their guilt and need for forgiveness but was somehow preparatory for Christ's historic appearing.

The supplementary description of *paidagōgos* given in 4:2 designates him as a guardian and trustee. This is an important window into Paul's understanding that ought not to be overlooked. Calling the law a nurse fails to take cognizance of this statement. The description strongly militates against all the understandings of the *paidagōgos* that have been discussed earlier. In the imagery of guardians and trustees, there is a far more positive understanding of what the role of the *paidagōgos* was for Paul. In this imagery, there is a relational aspect that the Hellenistic *paidagōgos* would rarely have fulfilled.

When we examine the OT, we find that the steward acted as a guardian who also took part in the choice and care of a spouse for his master or his son. Abraham sent his servant Eleazer to find a wife for Isaac; he then brought her to him. In Esther, the king appointed servants who were to seek a bride for him, although admittedly he This role of the servant being responsible for choosing, protecting, and bringing the bride to her husband is possibly echoed in John the Baptist's saying that:

> A person cannot receive even one thing unless it is given him
> from heaven. You yourselves bear me witness, that I said, 'I am
> not the Christ, but I have been sent before him.' The one who has
> the bride is the bridegroom. The friend of the bridegroom, who
> stands and hears him, rejoices greatly at the bridegroom's voice.
> Therefore this joy of mine is now complete. He must increase, but
> I must decrease." (John 3:27–30 ESV)

It is interesting to note that John was regarded as the last representative of the law. And as such, he describes himself as the friend of the groom, i.e. the best man.

This interpretation certainly fits the New Exodus theme that I am suggesting is the theological framework of the letter. At the heart of the exodus event is the divine marriage, when Israel is presented before her groom, Yahweh. In the New Exodus, the law acts in a way like the 'best man' or guardian. The *paidagōgos* is responsible for the bride. In this sense, the law brings us to Christ, not by driving us, but by teaching us and telling us of the grace that welcomes us.

While the law has brought a greater knowledge of sin (Rom 5:20), it is that greater knowledge that in turn magnifies the grace of the bridegroom in that he gave himself up for his defiled and unworthy people (Eph 5:25). This is not denying that the law may have to speak harshly and sternly to the elect community, I will say more of this in a moment, in our guilt and lostness, but in no way does it attempt ultimately to do anything other than to glorify the grace of God. Paul's concern here is not about two ways of salvation, one by keeping the moral precept of the law and the other by God's free grace.

This marital theme is so embedded in the exodus imagery that to leave it out is to miss the very purpose of the exodus; for it was Yahweh wooing his people into the wilderness where he spoke tenderly to her and took her as his bride (Hos 2:14–16). To miss the presence of the divine marriage in Gal 3:24 is missing the very heart of Paul's explanation of the role of the law. There ought to be no surprise to find it present and just to make sure you do not have the suspicion that a rabbit has been pulled out of the hat by sleight of hand, reflection on Galatians 4 ought to neutralize this suspicion.

The allegory of Sarah and Hagar is powerfully used by Paul to make this theological point. He wants to know whose children the Galatian believers are. Are they Sarah's children, the children of promise, or are they Hagar's children, produced by man's intervention, adding to the promise in an attempt to help the promise be fulfilled? The children of the promise are born out of the covenant relationship that God had made with Abraham and was fulfilled in Sarah. The child born through Hagar was not born in that covenant sworn by Yahweh, but one created by man. Sadly, it could hardly be called a covenant, for all that happened was this poor Ishmaelite was used and then discarded.

But the point is that the covenant with Abraham had to culminate in marriage through which Abraham was given offspring. Marriage is essential to the story. This is driven home by the application of Isaiah 54:1 in Galatians 4:27. Isaiah speaking on behalf of Yahweh says to Israel:

> For it is written, "Rejoice, O barren one who does not bear; break forth and cry aloud, you who are not in labor! For the children of the desolate one will be more than those of the one who has a husband." (Gal 4:27 ESV).

The prophet speaks of Israel as the bride of Yahweh, and Paul uses the same text to illustrate the church's relationship to Christ. It is the same bridal imagery that I am suggesting is embedded in 3:24. If the letter is based on the New Exodus paradigm, then it is not the perspective that I am arguing for that needs defending, but justification for missing it out that needs to be provided!

In fact, *paidagōgos* is used in only one other place in the NT, and it is again found in Paul. In 1 Corinthians 4:15 Paul says: "For though you have countless guides (*paidagōgos*—guardians NIV) in Christ, you do not have many fathers. For I became your father in Christ Jesus through the gospel" (1 Cor 4:15 ESV). Paul is saying that he takes seriously his role of caring for them to the point that he fulfils the function of a father. In fact, Paul, in his second letter says something of what this function means. He says: "For I feel a divine jealousy for you, since I betrothed you to one husband, to present you as a pure virgin to Christ". (2 Cor 11:2 ESV). Certainly, one of the tasks of the *paidagōgos* was to guard the moral integrity of his charge. Paul in 1 Corinthians 4:15 seems to be saying that the care he has for them is not just what a *paidagōgos* is expected to have, but what a father has. This salvation history picture, of the law bringing the covenant community to her Saviour to be his bride, is further borne out by those who have noticed that the passage is not speaking about the individuals being brought to Christ, but the community. What is in the background to all of this is that Christ has acted as the church's redeemer, securing her release and taking her to himself in a Levirate marriage just as he promised he would do for widowed Israel (Isa 54:1–8).

I want finally to draw your attention to the rich OT background for the concept of the *paidagōgos*. It forms part of the OT redemptive- historical paradigm. The word is part of the semantic domain of the paida root which (paida)gōgos shares. It is used throughout the OT for the law in its teaching role.

Know then in your heart that, as a man disciplines his son, the

> Lord your God disciplines you. (Deut 8:5)

> And consider today (since I am not speaking to your children who have not known or seen it), consider the discipline of the Lord your God, his greatness, his mighty hand and his outstretched arm. (Deut 11:2 NET)

> Out of heaven he let you hear his voice, which he might discipline you. And on earth he let you see his great fire, and you heard his words out of the midst of the fire. (Deut 4:36 NET)

> Hear, O heavens, and give ear, O earth; for the Lord has spoken: "Children have I reared and brought up, but they have rebelled against me. (Isa 1:2 NET)

> When I please, I will discipline them, and nations shall be gathered against them when they are bound up for their double iniquity. (Hos 10:10)

> Sow righteousness for yourselves, reap unfailing love. Break up the unplowed ground for yourselves, for it is time to seek the Lord until he comes and showers deliverance on you. (Hos 10:12)

The term translates the Hebrew *musat* which conveys the idea of instruction, correction, and chastisement, even punishment if the earlier warnings are not headed. These meanings lie in the LXX use of the paida words and they carry the same range of meanings.

Thus, these meanings range from instruction through to correction. If the lesson is not accepted, then the threat is finally extended to punishment. The meaning must be derived from the context. So, the law is a musat, a paida or *paidagōgos* which teaches, corrects, and even punishes if necessary. It is this range of roles we find attributed to the law by Paul in Galatians 3. It teaches, encourages, shuts up and if necessary, exercises judgment by imposing the appropriate sentence.

As I conclude, we could note something in Isaiah 53:5 'But he was pierced for our transgressions; he was crushed for our iniquities; upon him was the chastisement that brought us peace, and with his wounds we are healed (Isa 53:5).' He bore our chastisement, or correction, musat or paida. The servant's sufferings are essential for Israel to be redeemed and restored to her proper relationship with Yahweh. Part of this relationship is her being re-established back in Zion where she will worship Yahweh in truth, the very reason that the Egyptian exodus took place. There she will be the bride of her Redeemer.

So here, the servant suffers, bearing Israel's correction, dictated by the law that she had rejected, and she is then brought not just to Yahweh, but to her husband Yahweh (Isa 54:1–8).

So, what is the *paidagōgos* in Paul's understanding? It is the Torah itself. It does not need to be compared to the slave who in a very faint way fulfilled some of the functions of the law; he can never convey the magnificent richness of the OT model. This *paidagōgos* not only brings the elect community to her lover but before they meet, he has required and sentenced to death the beloved as the means by which the holiness of God can be satisfied, and the justification of Yahweh and his people can be achieved in the same amazing redemptive, atoning death.

The *paidagōgos* of which Paul spoke required the death of the true teacher of righteousness, the one who said, 'I am the Way, the Truth and the Life. No one comes to the Father but by me'. No slave ever got close to teaching such a foundational truth of redemption history nor did any nurse prepare her charge for the life that it required.

This was the antitype of the great exodus type, the fulfilment of the Passover type, the time of Israel's marriage to Yahweh and the feast when Israel was united with Moses and he became their representative. In this antitype that Paul has followed, the entire remnant community, which included all believing Jews and gentiles, slaves and free, male and female, were united with Christ as he died. This was not only the moment of unity through death but also through marriage for she was being cleansed to become Christ's bride (Eph 5:27; note how the book of Revelation starts with redemption and finishes with the divine marriage Revelation 1:4–8 and Revelation 18).[83]

This is of course the very model that guides the book of Isaiah (Isa 61:10; 62:5) where the redeemed community becomes the bride. This is the same pattern of the argument that goes on in Galatians 3:23–29, broken relationship, promise, corporate baptism, union with Christ, one flesh status (i.e. not is not the product of a physical sexual relation but being one flesh speaks of a covenant being made that is not conditional on gender) between Christ and his people. With this narrative in place, we can see that the law functions as a best man, a guide, a mentor, the protector who brings the bride

---

[83] Wright comes very close to identifying that the death of Christ was not only the occasion of the baptism of his people, 'into his death', but also the moment of the divine marriage. Wright, Faithfulness of God, 950.

to her groom. In such an understanding, in which the law is preparing the remnant community for the momentous event of meeting and becoming one with her groom, the law is doing the sort of thing it was always intended to do, to guide the community so that she lived according to her Creator's will and honoured him through her loving, obedient life which the law was given to guide her in. Wright was thrown off this understanding because although he promoted a positive view of the law, he never left what he objected so strongly to when he says that the law was given to keep Israel in check.[84] This was never the law's intention; it was given as a wedding gift to Israel and because that was always its purpose it was helpless in dealing with sin when it appeared in the Jewish community for it had never been intended to fulfil such a role. Following Israel's yet again adulterous behaviour at Sinai the law had to function in a role that was not its primary intended function, of controlling Israel's wayward behaviour and eventually after repeated warnings bring her under the curse that the covenant terms prescribed.

---

[84] Wright's major oversight was not to recognise how the adoption theme was transformed by Hosea to present the Exodus event being much more than Israel becoming Yahweh's son, she was his bride.

Chapter 5:
Probing Further Uses of Hellenistic Language and Imagery

There are other passages that are often seen to contain Hellenistic imagery that Wright does not directly deal with as regarding discussing the origin of their content. But while Wright has not directly commented on the origin of the following passages, it is reasonable to suggest that by comparing other passages that deal with the same or related themes that he deals with we can identify clues to what Wright's view is likely to be if we assume consistency in his exegesis.

Slave Market Imagery

In 1 Corinthians 6, Paul uses language that most scholars take as evidence that he used Hellenistic culture and imagery to convey his message. He wrote:

> "All things are lawful for me," but not all things are helpful. "All things are lawful for me," but I will not be dominated by anything. "Food is meant for the stomach and the stomach for food"—and God will destroy both one and the other. The body is not meant for sexual immorality, but for the Lord, and the Lord for the body. And God raised the Lord and will also raise us up by his power. Do you not know that your bodies are members of Christ? Shall I then take the members of Christ and make them members of a prostitute? Never! Or do you not know that he who is joined to a prostitute becomes one body with her? For, as it is written, "The two will become one flesh." But he who is joined to the Lord becomes one spirit with him. Flee from sexual immorality. Every other sin a person commits is outside the body, but the sexually immoral person sins against his own body. Or do you not know that your body is a temple of the Holy Spirit within you, whom you have from God? You are not your own, for you were bought with a price. So glorify God in your body. (1 Cor 6:12–20)

Wright does not follow the traditional understanding which sees the term 'redemption' (bought with a price) to have come from the Corinthian slave market where slaves became the property of a different master as a result of paying an agreed price. Wright ignores commenting on the widely held

Hellenistic background of the term but correctly identifies that the temple theme found in the passage is derived from the OT. However, what Wright does say is that Paul describes the individual's body as a temple of the Holy Spirit, which is impossible to support from the Greek.[85] The loss of this corporate reading has consequences for how the text and its wider theology is interpreted.

I have dealt with this passage in detail elsewhere,[86] so I will only indicate the salient points. Because of the presence of the words 'temple' (v. 19) and

---

[85] ἢ οὐκ οἴδατε ὅτι τὸ σῶμα ὑμῶν ναὸς τοῦ ἐν ὑμῖν ἁγίου πνεύματός ἐστιν οὗ ἔχετε ἀπὸ θεοῦ, καὶ οὐκ ἐστὲ ἑαυτῶν (1 Cor 6:19 BGT). N. T. Wright, 'Mind, Spirit, Soul and Body: All for One and One for All, Reflections on Paul's Anthropology in his Complex Contexts', *Society of Christian Philosophers: Regional Meeting, Fordham University,* March 18, 2011 says: 'Paul's statement in verse 19 is normally translated in the singular "do you not know that your body is a temple of the Holy Spirit." This is normally interpreted as a reference to the believer's body being the dwelling place of the Holy Spirit, but this overlooks the fact that sōma (body), is singular, whereas humōn (your), is plural. It is their corporate body, themselves as a Church, not their individual bodies that Paul is referring to as the temple of the Holy Spirit. Indeed, the traditional individualistic interpretation is contrary to all other usages of the New Testament writers in regard to the concept of the living temple. Elsewhere this concept is always applied to the Church, never to the individual. The only occasion that it is used of the individual is when it refers to Christ's own body (John 2:18–21)'. In his lecture on anthropology Wright said, 'The body of the Christian is already a Temple of the Holy Spirit, and as God had promised in Jeremiah, Ezekiel and elsewhere that the Temple would be rebuilt after its destruction, so Paul envisages the rebuilding of the body-Temple after its bodily death (Romans 8:5–11; the language of 'indwelling' is Temple-language). This body, as we have seen, will no longer be merely *psychikos,* soulish; it will be *pneumatikos,* spirit-ish, animated by and indwelt by God's spirit. The fact of fluidity in Paul between the human spirit and the divine spirit ought to alert us, I think, not to a confusing linguistic accident but to the possibility that Paul may envisage the human spirit in terms of the human as open to God— but, within his essentially biblical mindset, as the whole human open to God, not the human with one "part" only available to divine influence or transformation.' In this statement, Wright shows his confusion concerning Pauline anthropology for he compresses the glorious truths of the corporate reality and experiences of the church into a description of truth concerning the individual believer. In doing this Christian truth has been badly skewed and is recreated beyond any recognition of biblical reality.

[86] Holland, *Contours,* 111–139

'bought' (v. 20), most scholars conclude that the passage reflects Corinthian cultic and slave market imagery.[87]

But if Paul is using the slave market imagery, he has made an obvious mistake. His reference to being 'bought with a price' is normally seen as a reference to the practice of 'sacral manumission', whereby a slave could bring money to the temple and deposit it there so that the god of the temple might purchase him from his existing master—this was a transaction no owner could legally refuse. Having been thus been fictitiously purchased by the god, the erstwhile slave walks away from the temple a freeman. He was now in theory the property of the god, but in reality, the transaction did not tie him to the deity and had no further significance for the way in which he lived his life.

The idea that Paul intends to use the custom of sacral manumission to illustrate his message seems rather incongruous when one realizes that his appeal to moral rectitude is seriously damaged by this illustration. This is because in the first instance, it implies that the sinner can purchase his own salvation, since at the heart of the practice was the concept of the slave himself providing the means for obtaining his own freedom. Secondly, an illustration where ownership by the temple god is regarded as merely technical cuts right across Paul's argument that the Corinthians should live as those who genuinely belong to the true and living God. Indeed, the illustration of sacral manumission is quite possibly the worst that Paul could have chosen to elucidate how the gospel brings salvation and changes lives—which is what he is anxious to teach the church.

To Wright's credit, he has avoided using sacral manumission language as the key to this passage and links the theme of the temple with the Old Testament predictions of Yahweh dwelling amongst his people. However, he misses applying the Paschal New Exodus context provided by 1 Corinthians 5:7 (even though he applies it to his interpretation of paschal context of the Lord's Supper in 1 Corinthians 11) and fails to follow the clear meaning of the Greek text by saying, with most others, that the reference is to the believer's body being the temple of the Holy Spirit.[88]

---

[87] So R. Ciampa and B. S. Rosner, *The First Letter to the Corinthians* (Nottingham: Eerdmans, 2010), 265; A. Thiselton, *The First Epistle to the Corinthians* (Grand Rapids: Eerdmans, 2010), 275; H. Conzelmann and G. MacRae, *1 Corinthians* (Philadelphia: Fortress, 1975), 113.

[88] Wright, *Faithfulness of God,* 712.

There is a much better explanation of what Paul is doing here. If we examine the background of the above passage more closely, we will discover that the verses immediately preceding 6:19–20 (vv. 13–17) conveys strong imagery of marriage. Moreover, if we look back to 1 Corinthians 5:7, we find Paul specifically saying that, 'Christ, our Passover lamb has been sacrificed'. Passover was the time when the Jews understood that their marriage to Yahweh as their God had taken place. This idea of corporate marriage language linked with the reference to the Passover points to the Old Testament source of the theology behind the language of 1 Corinthians 6:19–20. In the Old Testament, this divine marriage motif sees Yahweh paying the price of his own costly involvement to save Israel; she not only became his bride but also the place in which he dwelt (his temple, see Ps 114:1–2). In this model, there is no confusion over the status or contribution of the Corinthian believers; for in the Old Testament the work of salvation is entirely the work of God.

This marital imagery is important because in Paul's view of human marriage, it is the husband—not the bride—who owns her body; the husband's body being similarly claimed by his wife (1 Cor 7:3–5). It is, therefore, most natural for Paul to talk about the body of Christ in relation to the bride figure, who has been redeemed to be the bride of her redeemer. The redeemer-husband owns the body of his wife, and so Paul confidently describes the church as the body of Christ.

It is within the context of such rich imagery that the associated themes mentioned above most naturally arise. The bride (the church) has been given the Spirit as a down-payment for her eventual marriage to Christ (Eph 1:14; 5:25–27). It is the consummation of this marriage that is the church's eschatological hope, for after this event she will never again be parted from her Lord. The Aristotelian imagery, which some have suggested is the origin of Paul's body metaphor, is totally bereft of these ancillary themes. While Wright has avoided this Hellenistic connection through his identification of the Old Testament background of the promised eschatological temple, he has failed to see the divine marriage context which 1 Corinthians 5:25–27 cries out for.[89]

---

[89] See Wright, *Faithfulness of God,* 927, 979.

Jewish Hellenistic Wisdom Literature

He is the image of the invisible God, the firstborn of all creation.
For by him all things were created, in heaven and on earth, visible
and invisible, whether thrones or dominions or rulers or
authorities—all things were created through him and for him. (Col
1:15–16)

I will deal with this in some detail in chapter seven. For now, it suffices to say
that the Greek understanding of Wisdom, which is believed to be behind the
term 'firstborn' in v. 15, is diametrically opposed to that which a Jew might
recognize as Wisdom. [90] Incarnation, which is thought by many to be
reflected in the hymn's thought, cuts right across the dualistic nature of Greek
thought, where anything 'physical' is intrinsically evil and anything 'spiritual'
is true and pure.

A major problem for this interpretation is that the connection of firstborn
(prototokos) with Wisdom cannot be established because the only link is
through the fact that Philo spoke of the *protogonos* (elder son) being a
reference to Wisdom. The argument is that the two words are sufficiently
similar for the meaning of the one word to be transferred to the other. The
legitimacy of such a transfer of ideas between the use the terms, prototokos
and *protogonos* on such flimsy evidence is a complete violation of linguistic
rules.[91] Just imagine the consequences of saying that rain is similar to reign,
and they, therefore, have a similar meaning!

The Old Testament repeatedly states that God was satisfied with his
creation, declaring it to be good. This judgment concerning the worth of

---

[90] G. Fee, *Pauline Christology: An Exegetical-Theological Study* (Peabody,
MA: Hendrickson, 2007). Fee, 'Wisdom and Christology in Paul' in *WWIS*,
251–79 commenting on claims that Paul links up with the theme of Wisdom
incarnation says: 'there is nothing even remotely like it in the Jewish wisdom
traditions'.

[91] Wright, *Justification,* 61 indicates why the church has lost the threads of a
proper biblical theology when he says, 'The church can and must, under the
guidance of the Holy Spirit, develop words, concepts, discourse of all sorts,
out beyond the narrow confines of exegesis. It will imagine itself to have
biblical warrant for its own ideas, when all it actually has is 'unbiblical'
echoes of its own voice.' While clearly the church must speak in the language
of the present generation to communicate its message, it must be a message
that is faithful to that which was preached by the apostles, anything less will
give birth to syncretism.

creation does not change because of the sinfulness of humanity; it does not become intrinsically sinful, even though affected by the consequences of Adam's sin. It is for this reason that, throughout the Old Testament, we find the continual expectation and hope of creation's redemption; hence, the resurrection. This was something that a Greek mind could never accept. Such ideas are contrary to the ideas conveyed by a Greek understanding of Wisdom, even if the questionable transfer of meaning explained above was allowed.

Military Procession Imagery

> Already you have all you want! Already you have become rich! Without us you have become kings! And would that you did reign, so that we might share the rule with you! For I think that God has exhibited us apostles as last of all, like men sentenced to death, because we have become a spectacle to the world, to angels, and to men. We are fools for Christ's sake, but you are wise in Christ. We are weak, but you are strong. You are held in honour, but we in disrepute. To the present hour we hunger and thirst, we are poorly dressed and buffeted and homeless, and we labour, working with our own hands. When reviled, we bless; when persecuted, we endure; when slandered, we entreat. We have become, and are still, like the scum of the world, the refuse of all things. (1 Cor 4:8–13)

Many see that in this passage Paul is comparing his experience to the life of the Greek philosophers in their struggles in search of truth. Their work brought them into suffering and misunderstanding.[92]

The reference to being sentenced to death (v. 9) is seen to refer to criminals, taken prisoner in military campaigns, being led behind the victorious emperor as he enters his capital city in pomp and splendour to affirm his greatness. Such criminals were used to entertain the populace as they were sent into the arena to compete with wild animals.[93] In this illustration, the 'super apostles' have been exalted to sit in the stands of the

---

[92] H. Conzelmann, *1 Corinthians,* 88.

[93] Thiselton notes the term used for exhibited is used in the context of displaying theatrical entertainment or gladiatorial shows. A. Thiselton, *The First Epistle to the Corinthians* (Grand Rapids: Paternoster, 2000), 359. So also R. B. Hays, *First Corinthians* (Louisville: John Knox Press, 1997), 181.

Coliseum, from where they watch the authentic apostles being devoured by wild beasts.

While some have seen the use of boasting in this section to refer to the super apostles, others have more recently seen it to be referring to members of the Corinthian church who looked on Paul with disdain. It is argued that they saw themselves as having a greater understanding of the gospel than Paul because, unlike Paul, their 'super apostles' had been trained in 'wisdom'. This knowledge imparted by their teachers, they reasoned, propelled them to the front of the band of believers as they took possession of the spiritual gifts that they had been taught was their inheritance.

The difficulty with this Hellenized reading is that it produces imagery which conflicts with and challenges the surrounding themes that are present in the passage. The thought of the 'spiritual ones' being removed from the band of prisoners and given seats of honour in the stadium is stretching the imagination too far.

Bringing the experience of the philosophers into the same model is not convincing either, for what is the connection between the criminal, brought as part of the booty of war, and the philosophers, who struggle to promote noble thinking and living? There is too much conflict between the parts of this construction for it to be convincing, and so it fails one of the most basic tests of authenticity.

However, when we identify the ongoing theological theme that Paul has developed in the immediately preceding chapters, we can identify his pattern of thought, and the illustration fits better. Chapter 2 of First Corinthians is soaked in the language of Isaiah's promise concerning the Second Exodus (1 Cor 2:6–10), in which the Spirit guides and instructs the community; chapter 3 deals with the divisions that existed in the Corinthian community (1 Cor 3:1– 9). In this chapter, Paul asserts that the apostles are God's fellow workers (1 Cor 3:9), and that the Christian community is God's building (temple). Paul warns of the danger of destroying God's temple (1 Cor 3:17) and makes it clear that this could happen if the Corinthians imposed the world's standards of wisdom on the Christian community rather than the wisdom of the cross (1 Cor 3:18–23).

This, then, is the context of the passage we are considering in 1 Corinthians 4:8–13. The language is not military language at all,[94] but rather the language of pilgrimage. Members of the Corinthian church had been persuaded that they had a greater wisdom than the apostles, allowing them to reach the goal of their pilgrimage ahead of the true apostles, who were, by their own admission, still striving to attain maturity. Having accelerated themselves to the finishing line because of their superior spirituality, the Corinthians became disdainful of the very apostles who had brought them the gospel in the first place.

Paul describes the apostolic band as those who are struggling and humiliated, but still on their pilgrim journey. Meanwhile Paul employs strong irony to expose how the Corinthian church no longer identifies with the shame of a crucified Messiah, because its members are reigning even now. They were no longer on a pilgrimage, in need of the apostles' help, for they had achieved their eschatological goal of wisdom. The illustration is not, therefore, taken from Roman military victory processions;[95] it is exodus imagery, albeit employed ironically, where some of the pilgrims have raced ahead to secure their inheritance. They have arrived in Zion, whilst the weaker, less enlightened, struggling apostles have yet to receive their inheritance. Of course, the reality is that Paul's words emphasize the deficiency of those who thought they had arrived.

Being under the sentence of death does not necessarily convey military imagery either. In a pilgrimage, those who are at the back of the procession are those who are in danger of being attacked by bandits and wild animals. Paul is saying that the apostles deliberately put themselves at risk to protect the weak of the community as they journey toward their eschatological hope. The Corinthians fail to see the reason for this 'slow' progress, glory in their achievements, and focus on their own self-promotion.

A second widely recognized military metaphor is found in the second letter to the Corinthians, and it reads:

> But thanks be to God, who in Christ always leads us in triumphal procession, and through us spreads the fragrance of the knowledge of him everywhere. For we are the aroma of Christ to God among those who are being saved and among those who are perishing, to

---

[94] N. T. Wright, *Paul for Everyone: 1 Corinthians. (New Testament for Everyone). Second Edition* (London: SPCK, 2003), 4.
[95] Ibid.

one a fragrance from death to death, to the other a fragrance from
life to life. Who is sufficient for these things? For we are not, like
so many, peddlers of God's word, but as men of sincerity, as
commissioned by God, in the sight of God we speak in Christ. (2
Cor 2:14–17)

Most see the background of 2 Corinthians 2:14–17 to be the same as 1
Corinthians 4:8–13 which we have just considered, and so perceive it to be a
reference to the procession of a Roman Emperor returning from his conquests
with the booty of war.[96] Such theatre allowed the emperor to impress on his
subjects his greatness and dominance.

However, not all are convinced by this setting. Thrall examines a wider
range of possibilities than most and, whilst she is not decisive in drawing her
conclusions, she leaves a trail of interesting possibilities. She thinks that Paul
might see himself as a lieutenant, supporting his victorious general, and
bringing up the rear of the procession.[97] She asks how Paul's presentation of
himself as a socially-shameful figure in v. 14 could be recognised by the
readers without any assistance from the immediate context, which he fails to
give.[98] She notes that the display of the power of the gospel is its ability to
deliver from death, not to hand a person over to it.[99] While she also
acknowledges that the reference to fragrances could point to the perfumes
used to give pleasure to the participants in the victory celebrations, she also
shows how it might conceivably be a reference to the Old Testament
sacrifices, where the offerings were intended to be a sweet-smelling savour to
God.

Furthermore, beyond what Thrall has noted, when we reflect that the
verses under consideration are set in a passage concerned with personal
relationships, we discover a setting that hardly supports slave imagery. In 2
Cor 2:1–11, Paul deals with the issue of forgiveness amongst the members of

---

[96] M. J. Harris, *The Second Epistle to the Corinthians: A Commentary on the
Greek Text* (Grand Rapids: Paternoster, 2005), 42; S. J. Hafemann, *Suffering
and Ministry in the Spirit: Paul's Defence of his Ministry in II Corinthians
2:14–3:3* (Carlisle: Paternoster, 1990), 34. Wright, *Faithfulness of God,* 1117
follows this understanding of the passage being about Christian suffering,
rather than victory, which is what the New Exodus motif turns it into.

[97] M. Thrall, *A Critical and Exegetical Commentary on the Second Epistle to
the Corinthians Vol.2* (Edinburgh: T&T Clark, 2000), 192.

[98] Ibid., 194.

[99] Ibid., 195.

the community, and concludes that, on his part, he forgives any who may have sought him harm. He is anxious that Satan does not outwit the church or gain an advantage over them by his schemes (2 Cor 2:11).

As Wright acknowledges, the passage which immediately follows 2 Corinthians 2:14–17 does not support the military theme either. 2 Corinthians 3:1–18 is very much based on exodus imagery, as Paul compares his own calling and ministry with that of Moses. He explains that the new covenant, of which he is a servant, is open—that is, one in which nothing is hidden. It does not have a fading glory that must be disguised, as in the case of the Sinai covenant (2 Cor 2:15); it is characterised instead by the glorious presence and ministry of the Spirit. Despite this correct theological context, Wright sees the imagery of suffering in this passage to be taken from the military procession imagery.[100]

Paul continues the defence of his ministry in chapter 4 and explains that the god of this world seeks to thwart his God-given ministry as he proclaims Yahweh's salvation (2 Cor 4:3). He speaks of his sufferings in the apostolic ministry (2 Cor 2:12), whilst emphasizing that he must and shall continue his ministry nonetheless, because of its importance (2 Cor 4:16–18).

Chapter 5 is recognized as being full of new covenant imagery. The declaration that 'if anyone is in Christ he is a new creation' (2 Cor 5:17) brings us right to the heart of the new creation promise that is part of the new covenant.

Wright acknowledges the New Exodus content of the early chapters of both 1 and 2 Corinthians, but when it comes to the two passages we have considered as being exodus processional imagery he identifies Roman military imagery as the origin. Thus, he has made it clear that the language of triumph and rejoicing has within it Roman celebratory themes.[101] He has seen Paul to view his life in terms of martyrdom and understands the sacrificial

---

[100] Wright, *Paul for Everyone: 2 Corinthians. (New Testament for Everyone). Second Edition* (London: SPCK, 2003), 2–4.

[101] Wright, *Fresh Perspective,* 55. In coming to this conclusion Wright has violated his own rubric, for he has said 'Exegesis needs the concordance, but it cannot be ruled by it. It is no argument against calling Paul a Covenant theologian to point out the scarcity of *diathekē* in his writings. We have to learn to recognize still more important things, such as implicit narratives and allusions to large biblical themes.' Wright, *Justification,* 26.

imagery to be drawn not only from Old Testament imagery but also from pagan sacrificial practices.[102]

So, with all of these themes forming the surrounding literary and theological context of the supposed military illustration of 2 Corinthians 2:14–17, one might very well reflect upon whether its proper context has been missed; I would suggest that it has.

The passage is not about being led by Christ in the way that a Roman emperor or general led his procession into the Coliseum, but about being led by Christ in the way that Moses led the children of Israel out of Egypt. This was not an event of suffering and humiliation but of redemption and triumph. This construction explains the ongoing comparison of the two covenants in the following chapter and illuminates the key statements in the passage being considered. So, for example, the fragrance description echoes the tribes of Israel travelling through the wilderness and regularly setting up camp with the tabernacle in the centre. It was here that the sacrifices were offered, and their smell would have wafted for many miles through the desert,[103] announcing to all that Israel and her God were present. The response of the surrounding nations to the children of Israel and to their God's presence among them could be (and was) one of two alternatives. In unbelief, they would oppose God and hinder Israel's progress, in which case the aroma (the sign of God's presence among them) would signal their approaching death—God was among them to punish the evil-doer. On the other hand, if they came in faith, as some did, seeking to make their peace with Yahweh and obey his commands, the smell of sacrifice, the signal of God's presence among his people would be an aroma of life, for God's presence among them preserved the faithful. This fits the on-going exodus typology perfectly.

---

[102] Wright, *Faithfulness of God,* 987. See also Wright, *Perspectives,* 72 where he says that Paul spoke of the 'resurrection which marked out the martyrs in particular. This, it seems, is what he was telling the Philippians to imitate.' Wright appeals extensively to the Maccabean martyr theology which originates in Hellenism. See J. J. Williams, *Traditions,* 33 for support of Wright's position.

[103] A recent BBC programme gave disturbing interviews with the soldiers who liberated Bergen-Belsen concentration camp at the end of World War Two. One soldier told how the stench of burning flesh could be smelt 30 miles away from the camp. The burning of the sacrifices in the desert probably went even further as the breeze would blow it across the open spaces of the desert.

I have suggested that the two passages we have just considered are, rather than being comprised of military metaphors, better understood as reflecting the widely-acknowledged New Exodus pilgrimage theme found throughout the New Testament. It is this same theme that we find in Hebrews, and in this passage, there is certainly no suggestion of a Roman military metaphor being present.

> For you have not come to what may be touched, a blazing fire and darkness and gloom and a tempest and the sound of a trumpet and a voice whose words made the hearers beg that no further messages be spoken to them. For they could not endure the order that was given, "If even a beast touches the mountain, it shall be stoned." Indeed, so terrifying was the sight that Moses said, "I tremble with fear." But you have come to Mount Zion and to the city of the living God, the heavenly Jerusalem, and to innumerable angels in festal gathering, and to the assembly of the firstborn who are enrolled in heaven, and to God, the judge of all, and to the spirits of the righteous made perfect, and to Jesus, the mediator of a new covenant, and to the sprinkled blood that speaks a better word than the blood of Abel. See that you do not refuse him who is speaking. For if they did not escape when they refused him who warned them on earth, much less will we escape if we reject him who warns from heaven. At that time his voice shook the earth, but now he has promised, "Yet once more I will shake not only the earth but also the heavens." This phrase, "Yet once more," indicates the removal of things that are shaken—that is, things that have been made—in order that the things that cannot be shaken may remain. Therefore let us be grateful for receiving a kingdom that cannot be shaken, and thus let us offer to God acceptable worship, with reverence and awe, for our God is a consuming fire. (Heb 12:18–29)

Whilst it is true that the themes in this passage—pilgrimage (v. 18), the spectacular welcome (v. 19), the festal gathering (v. 22), and the citizenship of the heavenly Zion (v. 23)—all reflect the themes found in the Corinthian 'military' passages, at the same time these themes form part of a letter that is recognized by all as being heavily bathed in Old Testament imagery. In view of this, I would like to suggest that the Old Testament is the source of the language found in the Corinthian passages, and not Greco-Roman literature as is so often assumed.

Christian Armour Imagery

Wright references Ephesians 6:10–20 when he deals with Christian warfare and identifies the origin of the imagery as reflecting Isaiah 4–5; 49:2; 52:7.[104] He comments: 'Interestingly, if this is so, he is taking passages that appear to speak of the Messiah, clothed with righteousness and faithfulness, striking the earth with his word'. Many scholars have explained the language of the Christian armour in Ephesians 6 as representing Paul's reflection on the armour of one of the soldiers guarding him.[105] Whilst this idea is both possible and understandable (since the assumed source was so immediately available to Paul) another possibility is that the imagery Paul is employing might be inspired by the book of Isaiah. As we have noted in the above examples, most of what Paul has been saying has a New Exodus context, and here again in Ephesians we discover possible indications that the apostle is using Old Testament imagery.[106]

In Ephesians 5:14 Paul cites Isaiah 60:1 ('Arise, shine, for your light has come, and the glory of the Lord has risen upon you'), and this is clear Second Exodus language where Yahweh exhorts Israel to wake up from sleep. Paul applies this exhortation to the Ephesian church and follows it with guidance concerning the way in which their behaviour must be modified when they wake up. Their marriage relationships will be changed (Eph 5:22–33), their relationships with their children will be different (Eph 6:1–4), and their relationship with slaves, who are part of their households, will be transformed (Eph 6:5–9).

Having explained the transformative effects of 'waking up' to spiritual realities and responsibilities, Paul proceeds to warn the Ephesians that such a renewal will bring them into direct conflict with the evil spiritual powers, who

---

[104] See N. T. Wright, *Paul for Everyone: The Prison Letters: Ephesians, Philippians, Colossians, and Philemon. (New Testament for Everyone)* Second Edition (London: SPCK; 2002), 75.

[105] E. Simpson and F. F. Bruce, *Commentary on the Epistles to the Ephesians and the Colossians* (London: Marshall, Morgan & Scott, 1957). *The New International Commentary on the Old Testament* does not mention Isaiah as the source nor does Lincoln in A. T. Lincoln, *Ephesians* (Dallas: Word, 1990), 442.

[106] For Isaiah's influence on Ephesians, see Richard M. Cozart, *This Present Triumph: An Investigation into the Significance of the Promise of a New Exodus of Israel in the Letter to the Ephesians* (Eugene: Wipf & Stock, 2013).

would be exceedingly opposed to the believers' zeal for Christ. In view of this he exhorts them to, 'put on the full armour of God, that you may be able to stand against the schemes of the devil' (Eph 6:11), using the Isaianic imagery described above.[107]

Wright has also embraced this Isaianic origin of the imagery for the armour of God. What is surprising is that he has not kept to this imagery of the victorious Messianic community arriving in the heavenly city but in 1 Corinthians 14:16 has allowed Classical military history to control Paul's meaning. All three passages are based on New Exodus imagery and there is no reason to remove the Old Testament background that has rightly been seen to control the meaning of pilgrim language in Ephesians 6:10–17.

Greek Anthropological Tripartite Language

> Now may the God of peace himself sanctify you completely, and may your whole spirit and soul and body be kept blameless at the coming of our Lord Jesus Christ. He who calls you is faithful; he will surely do it. (1 Thess 5:23–24)

Many have understood this passage to reveal Paul's essentially Hellenistic anthropology, the tripartite view of man as body, soul, and spirit. Schweizer[108] argued that the liturgical setting of the statement means that this should not be taken as a precise description of the constitutive parts of human nature; and

---

[107] Wright discusses the passage but rather than ref Cozart, *This Present Triumph.* See also J. Muddiman, *Ephesians* (London: Continuum, 2001), 287 (who also sees the same theme in Wisdom of Solomon 5:17, 20a). So also K. Snodgrass, *Ephesians* (Grand Rapids.: Zondervan, 1996), pp. 338–9, who helpfully says 'we usually interpret this as if they were addressed to individuals, but without denying their relevance for individuals, we should understand them as Paul's instructions for the church to collectively put on God's armour and stand as one person, erring to the Isaianic passage as the key he focuses on the setting of the cell from which Paul writes his letter and the threatening circumstances that engulf Paul. In this the positive message of the New Exodus is missed.

[108] E. Schweizer, 'πνεῦμα', *TDNT* 4:435.

the same position has been taken by Best,[109] Wanamaker,[110] Malherbe,[111] and Green.[112] The point on which all these authorities agree is that, while Paul uses familiar Hellenistic terminology in 1 Thessalonians 5:23, he does not thereby endorse the Greek understanding of human nature; his words merely serve to emphasize that his prayer is for the Thessalonians' complete protection.

These same scholars argue that other texts—such as the theological argument in 1 Corinthians 7:34—demonstrate that Paul embraced a Hebraic anthropology.[113]

Wright's solution to the 1 Thessalonians 5:24 conundrum is to note that Paul uses a dozen terms to refer to what humans are and what they do and suggests that these terms have been subsumed under these three headings to give the text greater depth and meaning.[114] While Wright has offered a way out of the problem, he has still left a modified Hellenistic view of man and he

---

[109] E. Best, *A Commentary on the First and Second Epistles to the Thessalonians* (London: Black, 1972), 243.

[110] C. Wanamaker, *The Epistles to the Thessalonians* (Grand Rapids: Paternoster, 1990), 206.

[111] A. Malherbe, *The Letters to the Thessalonians in The Anchor Bible* (New York: Doubleday, 2000), 339.

[112] G. Green, *The Letters to the Thessalonians* (Grand Rapids: Eerdmans, 2002), 268.

[113] Hebraic anthropology considers the body of man/woman to be intrinsically good although made weak by the Fall whereas Hellenism, because of its dualism (i.e. matter is evil, and spirit is good), has an anthropology that sees the human body as being intrinsically evil. In the former, humans cannot be truly human apart from relating to others and therefore a person is identified through the community they belong to. Greek anthropology sees man in a much more individualistic way.

[114] Wright, Mind and Spirit, 1. See also Wright's explanation of Paul's use of flesh and body when he says: 'Paul does not mean by "flesh" simply physical substance. For that he normally uses soma, usually translated "body". For him, the word "flesh" is a way of denoting material within the corrupt world and drawing attention to the fact that it is precisely corruptible, that it will decay and die. From that point Paul's usage expands one more level, to include the moral behaviour which, consequent upon idolatry, is already a sign of, and an invitation to, that progressive corruption hence the "works of the flesh".' Wright, *Perspectives,* 35.

has not explored the Old Testament in any depth beyond the widely-accepted fact that Hebrew thought does not view man as being a tripartite being.

However, what is generally overlooked is that the construction of Paul's prayer clearly suggests that he is not praying primarily for the individual believer in Thessalonica, but rather for the community as a whole. Paul writes, 'May God himself, the God of peace, sanctify you through and through. May your whole spirit, soul and body be kept blameless at the coming of our Lord Jesus Christ' (1 Thess 5:23 NIV).

The Greek reads:

Αὐτὸς δὲ ὁ θεὸς τῆς εἰρήνης ἁγιάσαι ὑμᾶς ὁλοτελεῖς, καὶ ὁλόκληρον ὑμῶν τὸ πνεῦμα καὶ ἡ ψυχὴ καὶ τὸ σῶμα ἀμέμπτως ἐν τῇ παρουσίᾳ τοῦ κυρίου ἡμῶν Ἰησοῦ Χριστοῦ τηρηθείη (1 Thess 5:23 BGT)

Paul prays that God would sanctify ὑμᾶς ('you'—pl.), by keeping ὑμῶν ('your'—pl.) πνεῦμα ('spirit'—sing.), ψυχὴ ('soul'—sing.), and σῶμα ('body'—sing.) blameless. In other words, Paul's prayer is not for the sanctification of the individual believers' spirit, soul, and body; it is for the sanctification of the spirit, soul, and physical wellbeing of the community, the church.[115]

Once again, this is in keeping with Old Testament thought. For example, in Isaiah 57:15 Yahweh says, 'For thus says the One who is high and lifted up, who inhabits eternity, whose name is Holy: "I dwell in the high and holy place, and also with him who is of a contrite and lowly spirit, to revive the spirit of the lowly, and to revive the heart of the contrite"' (Isa 57:15 ESV). Here, the element רוח (ruach, 'spirit') is by the LXX translated as ὀλιγοψύχας, indicating that Yahweh cares for the spirit of the community; that community being the servant whom Yahweh encourages. While the individual is clearly included, it was the nation which had acted unrighteously (vv. 9–10) and so was called to humble itself.

---

[115] Wright, *Faithfulness of God,* 492 fn 99 commends the work of R. Jewett, *Paul's Anthropological Terms: A Study of their Use in Conflict Settings* (Leiden: Brill, 1971) as a 'back marker' on Paul's anthropology and proceeds to unpack Paul's anthropology from Jewett's arguments. The weakness of this is that Jewett's position is completely eclectic, moving repeatedly from Hebraic to Hellenistic sources and back again without any reflection on the serious differences between the two positions. For a specifically Hebraic anthropology see Holland, *The Divine Marriage,* 203–226

Furthermore, in Isaiah 58:11 the prophet says, 'The Lord will guide you always; he will satisfy your needs נַפְשֶׁ֑ךָ (*nephesh*, 'soul') ['desire' in RSV, ESV and NAS; 'needs' in NJB and NIV; 'soul', KJV] in a sun- scorched land and will strengthen your frame'. Again, it is the nation that is addressed (v. 2), but the call expects individual Jews to respond. In the LXX, נַפְשֶׁ֑ךָ is translated ψυχή. (For similar uses when the spirit and the soul of the church are referred to see 1 Cor 6:20 and 1 Pet 2:11.)

These same Hebrew and Greek terms רוּחַ (*ruach*) and πνεῦμα (spirit) are used in Deuteronomy 6:5, 'you shall love … with all your soul'. We have already seen elsewhere that σῶμα ('body') is normally used with a corporate meaning.[116]

Clearly, the very same terms which Paul uses in 1 Thessalonians 5:23 are used within the Old Testament to apply to the community as a whole. Thus, Paul is not praying for the believers as tripartite beings but for the community, that they will be preserved and blessed. As individuals, they would know the blessing of sanctification (sanctify you—pl.) as the community experiences God's blessings.

The point of this observation is that Paul, by his use of the singular along with the plural, is shown to be referring to the constituent parts of the believing community and not the tripartite nature of man. Such a focus is typical of Hebraic understanding and is rarely found in Greek thought.[117]

---

[116] For the same use in the LXX, see J. Ziesler, 'Soma in the Septuagint', *Novum Testamentum 2* (1983):133–45.

[117] Wright seeks to avoid the Hellenism that imposes a dualistic definition on man, but because he does not read the text corporately he has to say: 'I therefore read Paul's various summary statements, not least the famous tripartite one in 1 Thessalonians 5.23, not as a trichotomous analysis, but as a multi-faceted description of the whole. His language there is, in any case, holistic: may the God of peace sanctify you wholly, *holoteleis*, and may your spirit, soul and body be preserved (*teretheie*) whole and entire (*holokleron*) unto the royal appearing of our Lord Jesus the Messiah. If Paul had wanted to say that he saw these three aspects of humanity as separable, or, particularly, as to be ranked in importance over one another, he's gone about it in a very strange way. It seems to me, then, taken all together, that when Paul thinks of human beings, he sees every angle of vision as contributing to the whole, and the whole from every angle of vision. All lead to the one, the one is seen in the all. And, most importantly, each and every aspect of the human being is

The Term 'Body of Sin'

> We know that our old self was crucified with him in order that the body of sin might be brought to nothing, so that we would no longer be enslaved to sin. (Rom 6:6)

Wright sees the term 'our old man' which he understands to be 'old human' to refer to the life his readers had in Adam which came to an end through baptism.[118] Wright does not address the meaning of the 'body of sin' seemingly assuming that it has the same meaning as 'old man—old human'. The use Paul makes of the expression 'body of sin' here suggests to many readers that Paul imagined the human body to be sinful.[119] This in turn suggests that he held to a Greco- Roman anthropology in which man's physical condition is seen to be intrinsically evil. Over the centuries, such an interpretation has caused massive pastoral problems within the Christian church, not least because it controls the way Paul's teaching concerning salvation and sanctification is viewed.

Since I have dealt with this question elsewhere,[120] I will deal with it only briefly here. Suffice it to say that this confused state of affairs has arisen entirely as the result of failing to appreciate the thoroughly Hebraic concepts which control Paul's thinking and teaching. For this reason alone, there is a

---

addressed by God, is claimed by God, is loved by God, and can respond to God. It is not the case that God, as it were, sneaks in to the human being through one aspect in order to influence or direct the rest. Every step in that direction is a step towards the downgrading of the body of which I have already spoken. And that downgrading has demonstrably gone hand in hand, in various Christian movements, with either a careless disregard for the created order or a careless disregard for bodily morality. Or both.' N. T. Wright, 'Mind, Spirit, Soul and Body: All for One and One for All, Reflections on Paul's Anthropology in his Complex Contexts'. *Society of Christian Philosophers: Regional Meeting*, Fordham University, March 2011.

[118] Wright, *Faithfulness of God,* 893.

[119] Wright's claim that Paul uses soma when speaking about physical substance is contrary to the studies that have been done on this term. R. Bultmann and K. Grobel, *Theology of the New Testament. 2nd rev. edition* (Waco: Baylor University Press, 2007), pointed out that when Paul uses the term, unless he makes it clear otherwise, it is always a corporate term. For a more recent and fuller study see Holland, Contours, 85–110.

[120] See Holland, ibid

desperate need to sort through some of the claims that are commonly made regarding Paul's mindset.

So then, to be brief, I view Paul's use of the term 'the body of sin' as a corporate description and to be the opposite to the term 'the body of Christ'. It describes the human condition in Adam, and all of Adam's offspring are born into this community. Paul's use of the term conveys the essential meaning of inherited sin; it is a state of alienation as a result of belonging to a community that has rejected the claims of God's love. Since there is no other place in the entire Bible where the term is used, it is therefore vitally important to understand how the meaning of the term is controlled by the flow of the argument provided by the context. The background of Romans 6 is, as Wright recognizes, of course, Romans 5, and in that passage, Paul has described two communities, one in Adam and the other in Christ. The latter is designated by Paul as 'the body of Christ', whilst the former is designated as the body which is in Adam— 'the body of sin'. This has the advantage over Wright's reading that Adam is never referred to as sin[121] or death[122] which is the term used in 7:1–4 which Wright appeals to for support.[123] But these terms are used as deliberate designations of Satan who Adam had put himself and all of his offspring under. Wright has missed this covenantal dimension thinking that covenantal imagery was limited to Israel's relationship with God, when it was not!

By identifying the body of sin as a community the window opens to understanding that this is a community that is owned by, in a covenantal relationship with sin (Sin, i.e. Satan), something that Wright has not recognized and thus offers explanations of following texts that lack this vital insight. I have dealt with this elsewhere and leave the interested reader to

---

[121] So, the references to sin throughout chapter 6 which are widely recognised as a pseudonym for Satan. See E. P. Sanders, Paul: *A Brief Insight* (New York: Oxford University Press, 1991; representing, New York: Sterling, 2009), 57, 59 and Dunn, *Theology of Paul,* 70; Wright himself has acknowledged this in Wright, 'The Letter to the Romans,' in R. W. Wall, J. Paul Sampley and N. T. Wright, *New Interpreter's Bible: Romans.* Edited by L. E. Keck. (Nashville: Abingdon, 2002), 539.

[122] See Rev 6:8 and Isa 28:16 where Israel is rebuked for her intended covenant with death, seen by commentators to refer to Isis the god of death in the Isaianic passage.

[123] Wright, *Faithfulness of God,* 893.

consult the argument that has been made.[124] Essentially the imagery draws on Israel's unfaithfulness to Yahweh and of her entering covenant relationships with other gods. Through this imagery, we can identify who the two husbands are in 7:1–4.

Such an understanding as that outlined above does not require Paul to have imbibed the principles of Hellenism. Instead, it is a fully Hebraic concept of a community linked in covenant with its representative head, and through that head to the God who has appointed him. In this model, 'inherited sin' is not based on a biological understanding of inheritance, but on the concept of covenantal relationships.

The Greek Games

> Do you not know that in a race all the runners run, but only one receives the prize? So run that you may obtain it. Every athlete exercises self-control in all things. They do it to receive a perishable wreath, but we an imperishable. So I do not run aimlessly; I do not box as one beating the air. But I discipline my body and keep it under control, lest after preaching to others I myself should be disqualified. (1 Cor 9:24–27)

Wright references 1 Corinthians 9:24–27 merely as evidence of the effort required by a disciple of Christ, making no mention of the source of the imagery which Paul has used. However, elsewhere he makes it very clear that Paul used athletic metaphors.[125] As he has made no attempt to correct the widely accepted Hellenistic origin, we shall assume that such is his understanding here.

---

[124] See Holland, *Contours,* 85–139.

[125] Wright, *Faithfulness of God,* 1113 on Phil 3:12–14, he says that 'Knowing where one is within the essentially Jewish story-line is now further defined by the Messiah's death and resurrection commits one also to a sober assessment that one has not yet arrived at the destination, is not yet perfect.' He goes on to explain that 'Chasing towards the line: one of Paul's various athletic metaphors, indicates that the "not yet" of eschatology does not mean hanging around with nothing to do.' Paul is warning that 'certain present lifestyles' are 'simply incompatible with being part of that future' and that those who indulge in these fleshly lifestyles 'will not inherit God's kingdom'. Wright, *Faithfulness of God,* 1113–4.

Some have suggested that the reference to Paul's disciplining and buffeting his body in this way is because of its sinful tendencies. This view of the sinfulness of the body is a very Hellenistic concept.

However, this explanation completely ignores the context in which Paul describes the Christian as an athlete, as followed by Wright,[126] or, possibly, a pilgrim. Whatever the imagery chosen, people are exerting effort and making their bodies weary and tired in the process.[127] If being tired—as Christ was in John 4:6—is sinful, then it could be argued to support a Hellenistic understanding of the sinfulness of the body; but most would find that a very strange claim to make. Rather than assuming that Paul's anthropology is Hellenistic and so understanding the verse in terms of the body having to be kept under control because of its sinfulness, let us see what a Hebrew mind might consider he is saying.

On first sight, the description of Paul's efforts as well as his vocabulary suggests a reference to the Greek games, and this is understandable. However, when passages that seem to have strong links with Hellenism are examined more closely, particularly in the context of the ongoing theological motifs that surround them, we have seen that they have a possible origin and significance that takes them back into the Old Testament for their conceptual roots. I want to suggest that the same may be true for this passage also.

The ongoing arguments of 1 Corinthians 5–9 have clearly developed Old Testament themes. In 5:7, we have the reference that Christ, our Passover lamb has been sacrificed, and in chapter 6, contrary to the views of most interpreters, we have discovered the presence of divine marriage imagery. Within this theme there is the warning to those members of the community who are acting like Israel in the wilderness (1 Cor 10:1–10). They had been redeemed at a price (1 Cor 6:20), and together they were the temple of God (1 Cor 6:19). Paul threatens them that, if they were to continue to behave like disobedient Israel, he would hand them over to Satan (1 Cor 5:3), delivering them to the harlot community, the body of sin (1 Cor 6:16).

---

[126] Wright, *Faithfulness of God,* 1113.

[127] R. B. Hays, *First Corinthians* (Louisville: John Knox Press, 1997), 156 reminds us that Paul's argument does not suggest that the body is the enemy of the spiritual life; buffeting refers rather to the gruelling training for the contest.

Chapters 8 and 9 are about Yahweh's exclusive claims over those whom he has redeemed; whilst in 1 Corinthians 9:1–23, Paul writes about his own behaviour and the rights he surrenders to be an effective servant of the gospel.

We then encounter the verses about 'running the race', which are immediately followed by an exposition of exodus typology (1 Cor 10:1–10). The passage speaks of Israel asserting her own rights and freedom in a way that resulted in judgment and the loss of her calling to be a light to the nations. In view of this, should it not be thought strange that Paul should introduce into this strongly redemptive historical narrative an entirely unconnected illustration from the Greek games? Perhaps light can be gained by observing the way in which Isaiah uses similar language and imagery to describe those who pursued the Second Exodus.

> Why do you say, O Jacob, and speak, O Israel, "My way is hidden from the Lord, and my right is disregarded by my God"? Have you not known? Have you not heard? The Lord is the everlasting God, the Creator of the ends of the earth. He does not faint or grow weary; his understanding is unsearchable. He gives power to the faint, and to him who has no might he increases strength. Even youths shall faint and be weary, and young men shall fall exhausted; but they who wait for the Lord shall renew their strength; they shall mount up with wings like eagles; they shall run and not be weary; they shall walk and not faint. (Isa 40:27–31)

Elsewhere, Paul uses similar sporting imagery in a way which suggests a strong Old Testament background. In Romans, he says, 'So then it depends not on human will or exertion, but on God, who has mercy' (Rom 9:16–17); where exertion reflects Psalm 119:32 (LXX 118:32), 'I will run in the way of your commandments when you enlarge my heart!' [128]

We must ask the question whether Paul— 'a Hebrew of the Hebrews'— would be more likely to see himself as being engaged in the Greek games rather than in the promised eschatological pilgrimage? Moreover, would he be more likely to keep to the wider theological context that he has built up in his letter, which naturally fits into the fulfilment of the promises given by the prophets of a new heaven and new earth, than to take an unprepared for turn into the theme of an individual in competition with all other contestants striving for the only prize? Such excessive individualism is one of the main reasons Paul wrote to the Corinthians in the first place, as many saw

---

[128] J. Piper, *The Justification of God: An Exegetical and Theological Study of Romans 9:1–23. 2nd Edition* (Grand Rapids: Baker, 1993), 152.

themselves better than others—something which Paul felt he had to correct. In the light of this, it would appear strange for him to promote just such a mentality here. Is he not rather referring to that pilgrim community which was anticipated by the experience of the Old Testament church?

Before we can be sure of this, however, we must ask whether the Corinthians would understand this Old Testament setting as being Paul's intention? The clue to this must surely be found in the large number of typological references within the letter that requires that the readers have an understanding of the Old Testament in order for them to follow the argument. As the Second Exodus illustration is followed throughout the letter, Paul clearly expected his readers to follow his argument, perhaps because he was confident that the church's Jewish teachers would expound this to the gentile believers.

A similar pilgrimage/race illustration is found in the letter to the Hebrews, which is saturated with Old Testament typology. This shows that a Jewish community would have no difficulty understanding the imagery and its source. The writer says:

> Consider him who endured from sinners such hostility against himself, so that you may not grow weary or fainthearted. In your struggle against sin you have not yet resisted to the point of shedding your blood. And have you forgotten the exhortation that addresses you as sons? "My son, do not regard lightly the discipline of the Lord, nor be weary when reproved by him. For the Lord disciplines the one he loves, and chastises every son whom he receives." It is for discipline that you have to endure. God is treating you as sons. For what son is there whom his father does not discipline? If you are left without discipline, in which all have participated, then you are illegitimate children and not sons. Besides this, we have had earthly fathers who disciplined us and we respected them. Shall we not much more be subject to the Father of spirits and live? For they disciplined us for a short time as it seemed best to them, but he disciplines us for our good, that we may share his holiness. For the moment all discipline seems painful rather than pleasant, but later it yields the peaceful fruit of righteousness to those who have been trained by it. Therefore lift your drooping hands and strengthen your weak knees, and make straight paths for your feet, so that what is lame may not be put out of joint but rather be healed. Strive for peace with everyone, and for the holiness without which no one will see the Lord. See to it that no one fails to obtain the grace of God; that no "root of bitterness" springs up and causes trouble, and by it many become

defiled; that no one is sexually immoral or unholy like Esau, who
sold his birthright for a single meal. For you know that afterward,
when he desired to inherit the blessing, he was rejected, for he
found no chance to repent, though he sought it with tears. (Heb
12:3–17)

There are many parallels between this passage and 1 Corinthians 9:24–
27, where it is thought that Paul is speaking of the Christian as an athlete. The
immediate context, which is found in the opening of chapter 10, relates to the
chastisement of the Jews in the desert; Paul is urging the Corinthian church
not to fall under the same discipline. The passage in Hebrews, which uses
language of the race in the context of the pilgrim community, also speaks of a
prize—the peaceful fruit of righteousness—which requires discipline in order
to be obtained (Heb 12:11). There is also the exhortation to strive (Heb
12:14), and the warning that some could fail the grace of God and thereby not
receive the inheritance (Heb 12:15).

The Jewish community who received the letter to the Hebrews would be
able to follow the meaning of the passage with its strong exodus imagery.[129] It
follows that the Jewish teachers in the Corinthian community would be able
to explain the meaning to those who would otherwise have missed the
background.

But despite the very strong wider theological support for the idea that the
passage fits into the New Exodus paradigm, there appears to be one word that
suggests Paul is quite intentionally encompassing both concepts. It is his use
of the word 'stadium', which occurs in 1 Corinthians 9:24, as follows:

Οὐκ οἴδατε ὅτι οἱ ἐν σταδίῳ τρέχοντες πάντες μὲν τρέχουσιν, εἰς
δὲ λαμβάνει τὸ βραβεῖον; οὕτως τρέχετε ἵνα καταλάβητε. (1 Cor
9:24)

It is the use of σταδίῳ (*stadiō*, 'stadium'), the word used for the Greek
athletics stadium; indeed, from it our English word 'stadium' is derived. At
first sight this term does not appear to fit into the New Exodus model; but in
fact, there is some evidence to suggest that Paul intends us to read it in this
way.

When we considered Paul's imagery in 1 Corinthians 4:8–13 and 2
Corinthians 2:14–17 we saw that, despite widespread acceptance of a military
setting for these metaphors, there were features that suggested a Second

---

[129] B. C. Shin, *New Exodus in Hebrews* (London: Apostolos, 2016).

Exodus background was more appropriate. Hence it is possible that the stadium, rather than being the location of the celebration of a military victory, is a metaphor for the heavenly city of Zion where the triumphant pilgrim community is welcomed. The 'contestants' are thus neither slaves nor athletes, but pilgrims.

If this is the correct setting for two these passages, then the use of the term 'stadium' is not such a problem as was initially thought. It links the 'stadium'—the meaning of which must be understood from its context—with the parading pilgrims, as was seen earlier in 1 Corinthians 4:8–13 and 2 Corinthians 2:14–17.

So, the conclusion of the 'pilgrim race' takes place in a rather different stadium to the one used by the Greek athletes; it is the place where the crown of life is presented to the people of God. Whilst a technical term for the athletics stadium is being used by Paul, he does not focus on the imagery of athletics nor on the earthly stadium, but on the toil and demands of being eschatological pilgrims and their triumphant entrance into the eschatological Zion, where they receive their prize.

Scrubbing Language

This kind of transfer of a technical term to a more general use is common. A recent discussion on BBC radio featured linguistic experts exploring how numerous words have changed their meaning. The experts spoke about how the original meanings 'have been scrubbed' over time, departing from their original meaning by a considerable margin to serve different needs. While we have no evidence of how the term 'stadium' developed in the ancient world, words are very flexible and adapted by writers from the strict sense that they originally had. The theological weight for linking the term 'running' with the pilgrim New Exodus tradition suggests that it is this context that controls how Paul uses the word 'stadium'. If this is so, then in 1 Corinthians 9:24 the term could reasonably be understood to signify the place where the pilgrimage, like the marathon, ends and where the prizes are presented. Of course, all this discussion should not surprise us for James Barr had raised this very issue decades earlier when he warned of the danger of relying on the etymology as the key to understanding the meaning of a word.[130] Only the context, he argued, can give a word's intended meaning. In this passage, the

---

[130] J. Barr, *The Semantics of Biblical Language* (Oxford: Oxford University Press, 1961).

overwhelming contextual evidence supports Paul to have been referring to the triumphant arrival of the New Exodus community.

In this New Exodus tradition, this place is the New Jerusalem, which the community will enter with great joy upon the completion of its pilgrimage. There the pilgrims receive their crowns. Indeed, as Paul goes on to describe the behaviour of the original pilgrim community, it could be said that they had forfeited their crowns by turning from Yahweh their Redeemer (1 Cor 10:1–10). As this is the illustration that follows on immediately from his use of 'stadium' it is an important part of the evidence for Paul's use of this term.

This understanding is confirmed by what Paul says in Philippians 2:

> Do all things without grumbling or disputing, that you may be blameless and innocent, children of God without blemish in the midst of a crooked and twisted generation, among whom you shine as lights in the world, holding fast to the word of life, so that in the day of Christ I may be proud that I did not run in vain or labour in vain. Even if I am to be poured out as a drink offering upon the sacrificial offering of your faith, I am glad and rejoice with you all. Likewise you also should be glad and rejoice with me. (Phil 2:14–18)

The description of the community as children of God who shine as lights in the world clearly echoes the description of the pilgrim community given by the prophets. It is in terms of this community's responsibility to represent Yahweh to the nations that Paul speaks of his anxiety about whether he has run or laboured in vain.

Earlier in the chapter Paul had written:

> Therefore God has highly exalted him and bestowed on him the name that is above every name, so that at the name of Jesus every knee should bow, in heaven and on earth and under the earth, and every tongue confess that Jesus Christ is Lord, to the glory of God the Father. (Phil 2:9–11)

This passage has strong links with Isaiah 45:23 where every knee will bow to Yahweh; a passage that is rooted in Second Exodus thought. This suggests that the two passages may share a common pilgrim theme. It is in the context of this clearly established motif that the running imagery can be found and explained. It has nothing to do with Greek athletics but portrays eager pilgrims whose progress on the journey is described as running.

Administrator Imagery

A recent work to support the use Paul is thought to make of Hellenistic imagery focuses on the word *oikonomoi* in 1 Cor 4:1–2[131] and 1 Cor 9:17.[132] In classical Greek the term was used of an administrator who functioned in ancient regal, municipal, and private administrative roles. Because Paul has used this term of himself, it has been claimed that he intended to suggest to the Corinthians that he was called to a similar role in the church and that the authority that came with such an important secular position informed the church of the role and authority that Paul was given as an apostle of Christ. It is claimed that by examining how the role was bestowed, asserted, and contested, the model provided insight into Paul's role and authority.

Certainly, the suggestion is novel, and the thesis introduced the reader to realms of Corinthian life that had been hidden in obscurity, but the question is whether too much has been loaded onto this term. It has the 'smell' of some of the other examples we have looked at where the context appears to be ignored in the excitement of catching an original thought or insight. As we have noted, the warning of James Barr in his ground-breaking application of linguistics to biblical studies has largely been forgotten for it is not the history or etymology of a word that decides its meaning but its context. In this argument, there has been no recognition of the context which begins back in chapter two with a reference to the prophecy of Isaiah which speaks of the new creation:

> Yet among the mature we do impart wisdom, although it is not a wisdom of this age or of the rulers of this age, who are doomed to pass away. But we impart a secret and hidden wisdom of God, which God decreed before the ages for our glory. None of the rulers of this age understood this, for if they had, they would not have crucified the Lord of glory. But, as it is written, "What no eye has seen, nor ear heard, nor the heart of man imagined, what God has prepared for those who love him"—these things God has revealed to us through the Spirit. For the Spirit searches everything, even the depths of God. (1 Cor 2:6–10)

---

[131] 'This is how one should regard us, as servants of Christ and stewards of the mysteries of God. Moreover, it is required of stewards that they be found faithful.'

[132] 'For if I do this of my own will, I have a reward, but if not of my own will, I am still entrusted with a stewardship.'

In chapter 3 Paul moves his exhortation describing his work in building the church to be like that of a master builder (1 Cor 3:10) and goes on to remind them of their importance to God for:

> Do you not know that you are God's temple and that God's Spirit dwells in you? If anyone destroys God's temple, God will destroy him. For God's temple is holy, and you are that temple.
>
> Let no one deceive himself. If anyone among you thinks that he is wise in this age, let him become a fool that he may become wise. For the wisdom of this world is folly with God. For it is written, "He catches the wise in their craftiness," and again, "The Lord knows the thoughts of the wise, that they are futile." So let no one boast in men. For all things are yours, whether Paul or Apollos or Cephas or the world or life or death or the present or the future— all are yours, and you are Christ's, and Christ is God's. (1 Cor 3:16–23)

So, coming into chapter four and meeting the term oikonomoi we need to make sure that the meaning we ascribe to it is part of the argument that Paul has been developing. Indeed, Paul goes on to describe his ministry of caring for the church by saying that the apostles were less than others because they had been put at the back of the procession while the Corinthians saw themselves to have arrived at their heavenly heritage (1 Cor 4:8–13). Such a position in the pilgrim community hardly matches a privileged and highly esteemed administrator.

The fact that Paul aligns himself and his ministry with that of the suffering servant and that he sees himself to be among the unworthy hardly suggests the confidence and status of an administrator in the Corinthian local government.

When we read Paul's presentation of the same themes to the Roman church the argument flows very similar. He will judge no one but leave this to God to do on the last day (Rom 14:10–12).

Paul then says that Christ became a servant to the circumcised to show God's truthfulness (Rom 15:8) and then says that he has also been appointed to be a servant (Rom 15:16) and explains what being a servant means. It is about fulfilling a priestly ministry.

> But on some points I have written to you very boldly by way of reminder, because of the grace given me by God to be a minister of Christ Jesus to the gentiles in the priestly service of the gospel of God, so that the offering of the gentiles may be acceptable,

sanctified by the Holy Spirit. In Christ Jesus, then, I have reason
to be proud of my work for God. For I will not venture to speak of
anything except what Christ has accomplished through me to
bring the gentiles to obedience—by word and deed, by the power
of signs and wonders, by the power of the Spirit of God—so that
from Jerusalem and all the way around to Illyricum I have
fulfilled the ministry of the gospel of Christ; and thus I make it my
ambition to preach the gospel, not where Christ has already been
named, lest I build on someone else's foundation. (Rom 15:15–
20)

It is surely significant that the New Exodus theme is clearly part of the
narrative of 1 Cor 1–5 and in that passage the church is described as God's
temple. Such places do not have administrators of the Hellenistic kind.
Instead, they have servants of the priestly kind, and this is confirmed by Rom
15:15–20. It is highly unlikely that Paul would create metaphors to describe
his own ministry from local practices as he moved around the Roman world,
and still more unlikely that he would use one metaphor when writing to the
church in Rome and another when writing to the Roman city of Corinth.[133] In
view of the explicit use of the priestly servant metaphor theme in Romans and
the powerful use and control of New Exodus themes in both 1 Corinthians[134]
and Romans[135] as well as Paul's clear dependence on the OT servant theme,[136]
a theme that was used not only to describe the ministry of Jesus but that of
himself and the ministry of all other believers,[137] I conclude that the evidence
to support Paul's use of the Greco-Roman administrator metaphor used in
Corinth has been shown to be misplaced.

Evidence of Paul's Hebraic Mind-set from His Own Testimony

In attempting to reconstruct Paul's mindset, there is a source of evidence
which carries far more weight than any of the constructions which can be
placed on his general statements, and that is from his personal testimonies

---

[133] See John Goodrich, 'Paul as an Administrator of God in 1 Corinthians.'
Society for New Testament Studies Monograph Series, volume 152
(Cambridge: Cambridge University Press, 2012).

[134] Holland, *Contours,* 157–182.

[135] Holland, *The Divine Marriage,* 73–104.

[136] Holland, *Contours,* 69–82.

[137] Rom 12:1–2.

which he gives in his letters on some occasions. From these, we can ascertain that Paul saw himself as a servant of the new covenant, just as Moses was the servant of the former covenant, and in this role, Paul seeks to advance the kingdom of his Saviour.

Paul's Written Testimony

> For I would have you know, brothers, that the gospel that was preached by me is not man's gospel. For I did not receive it from any man, nor was I taught it, but I received it through a revelation of Jesus Christ. For you have heard of my former life in Judaism, how I persecuted the church of God violently and tried to destroy it. And I was advancing in Judaism beyond many of my own age among my people, so extremely zealous was I for the traditions of my fathers. But when he who had set me apart before I was born, and who called me by his grace, was pleased to reveal his Son to me, in order that I might preach him among the gentiles, I did not immediately consult with anyone; nor did I go up to Jerusalem to those who were apostles before me, but I went away into Arabia, and returned again to Damascus. (Gal 1:11–17)

This is an important statement from Paul. He says that what characterized his life in Judaism, before he became a follower of Jesus, was that he excelled in the traditions of his fathers. His conversion to become a follower of Christ did not mean that the teaching of the fathers was terminated, but that his energies were now focused on proclaiming the one who the fathers had looked forward to. There is no suggestion here that Paul was focused on evangelizing gentiles, at this stage of his experience his ministry was focused on the diaspora, the Jews who lived among the gentiles. Thus, there was no need to contextualize the message of the gospel to fit with a gentile mindset.

This aspect of his personal history was so widely known that Paul was confident that even his Galatian readers had heard of his youthful Pharisaic zeal, expressed in his persecution of the church. At first reading, this could be taken as an admission by Paul that he had once been a zealot. However, the wider evidence shows that such is not the case—for example, in Romans 10:2 when he describes the nation as sharing in this fervour, he was surely not suggesting that Israel was a nation of zealots!

Furthermore, it is widely accepted that in stating that he was set apart before he was born, Paul is identifying his call with those of the Old Testament prophets; he uses similar language to describe his call to preach the message of Christ as the prophets did regarding their call to preach the message of Yahweh.

We find more of Paul's self-understanding disclosed in his Philippians letter:

> Though I myself have reason for confidence in the flesh also. If anyone else thinks he has reason for confidence in the flesh, I have more: circumcised on the eighth day, of the people of Israel, of the tribe of Benjamin, a Hebrew of Hebrews; as to the law, a Pharisee; as to zeal, a persecutor of the church; as to righteousness under the law, blameless. But whatever gain I had, I counted as loss for the sake of Christ. Indeed, I count everything as loss because of the surpassing worth of knowing Christ Jesus my Lord. For his sake I have suffered the loss of all things and count them as rubbish, in order that I may gain Christ and be found in him, not having a righteousness of my own that comes from the law, but that which comes through faith in Christ, the righteousness from God that depends on faith—that I may know him and the power of his resurrection, and may share his sufferings, becoming like him in his death, that by any means possible I may attain the resurrection from the dead. (Phil 3:4–11)

These are not the words of a man who has acquired a competence in Hellenism to be able to evangelize the Greek world in the way that Wright implies. Rather, Paul was so zealous concerning his Jewish heritage that his life revolved around it, and he was determined to protect it. The discovery of how God's promises had been fulfilled in Christ caused Paul to re-evaluate his understanding of Israel's heritage so that he came to see that all which he had held dear was worthless if he failed to enter into its fullness in Christ. The law had prepared the way for the coming of Christ, and his coming brought far greater riches than the law was ever able to give. It is not clear how these could be the words of one who gathered truth from wherever it was found, as claimed by Wright. They are the confession of a man who says that his earlier years had focused on doing the will of God according to a certain type of Pharisaic understanding of the law— 'the traditions of the fathers.'

Finally, we can now understand the way in which Paul ends his letter to the Roman church. Having not visited Rome before, he wants to explain his ministry in the hope that they will support in his evangelistic venture in Spain. This mission would depend on their willingness to help; not only through their encouragement but quite possibly by them sending gifted men and women with Paul to Spain.

Paul lays out the credentials of his mission in Old Testament terms, with not a hint of a development of his message to meet the mindset of the people he wants to reach or of those he wants to support him. He wrote saying:

113

> I myself am satisfied about you, my brothers, that you yourselves are full of goodness, filled with all knowledge and able to instruct one another. But on some points I have written to you very boldly by way of reminder, because of the grace given me by God to be a minister of Christ Jesus to the gentiles in the priestly service of the gospel of God, so that the offering of the gentiles may be acceptable, sanctified by the Holy Spirit. In Christ Jesus, then, I have reason to be proud of my work for God. For I will not venture to speak of anything except what Christ has accomplished through me to bring the gentiles to obedience—by word and deed, by the power of signs and wonders, by the power of the Spirit of God—so that from Jerusalem and all the way around to Illyricum I have fulfilled the ministry of the gospel of Christ; and thus I make it my ambition to preach the gospel, not where Christ has already been named, lest I build on someone else's foundation, but as it is written, "Those who have never been told of him will see, and those who have never heard will understand." (Rom 15:14–21)

This summary of his message and his resources for his intended mission could have been given on the Day of Pentecost! Not once is there a suggestion that he is equipped because he has developed a cross-cultural strategy that is attractive to the gentile world. His work is not that of a Christian philosopher, but of one who fulfils a priestly ministry in teaching the nations how they can return to their Creator God, who calls them out of darkness into the light of Christ. This conflicts with Wright's claim that Paul presented himself as a slave in his opening salutation.[138] Indeed, I find it startling that in a letter to a predominantly gentile church (forty to fifty thousand Jews having been expelled from the city by Emperor Claudius in 49 ce) we find a remarkable deficiency of arguments that might be thought of as reflecting a Hellenistic mind. Instead, we find a teacher who is saturated with the message of the Old Testament, and who seeks to make that message clear to the church he hopes to visit.

Paul's Oral Testimony

Paul gave his testimony before Roman officials on two occasions before he was—because of his appeal to Caesar—sent to Rome for trial. These are two crucial records, for nowhere else do we hear Paul making a presentation to people whose education and training in Hellenism would be essential as part of their vocation. Acts 24 records:

---

[138] Wright, 'Romans', *NIB,* 415.

And when the governor had nodded to him to speak, Paul replied:
Knowing that for many years you have been a judge over this
nation, I cheerfully make my defence. You can verify that it is not
more than twelve days since I went up to worship in Jerusalem,
and they did not find me disputing with anyone or stirring up a
crowd, either in the temple or in the synagogues or in the city.
Neither can they prove to you what they now bring up against me.
But this I confess to you, that according to the Way, which they
call a sect, I worship the God of our fathers, believing everything
laid down by the law and written in the Prophets, having a hope in
God, which these men themselves accept, that there will be a
resurrection of both the just and the unjust. So I always take pains
to have a clear conscience toward both God and man. Now after
several years I came to bring alms to my nation and to present
offerings. While I was doing this, they found me purified in the
temple, without any crowd or tumult. But some Jews from Asia—
they ought to be here before you and to make an accusation,
should they have anything against me. Or else let these men
themselves say what wrongdoing they found when I stood before
the council, other than this one thing that I cried out while
standing among them: 'It is with respect to the resurrection of the
dead that I am on trial before you this day. (Acts 24:10–21)

Wright has argued that Paul was uniquely prepared to engage with the
Hellenistic world because of his familiarity with it.[139] If this were so, one
might expect Paul to use this knowledge when standing before a Roman
governor who had the advantage of the highest education of his day and the
power of life and death in his hand. Surely here, if anywhere, we should see
Paul engaging with Hellenistic ideas. However, instead, when his life was in
the balance, Paul remained silent about anything Hellenistic as he reasons
with this Roman official. What he presents instead is perhaps as Jewish a
presentation of the gospel as one is ever going to find. If he fails to give a
Hellenized version of his gospel to a Roman governor, who on earth is he
going to present it to?

Shortly after his testimony to Felix, Paul presents his defence again, this
time to Agrippa. Once again, his life is at stake, and there can be no room for
confusion regarding his message. He must make his message as clear as
possible, and so he recounts his experience of meeting the risen Jesus on the
Damascus road. He said:

In this connection I journeyed to Damascus with the authority and

---

[139] Wright, *Faithfulness of God,* 78.

commission of the chief priests. At midday, O king, I saw on the way a light from heaven, brighter than the sun, that shone around me and those who journeyed with me. And when we had all fallen to the ground, I heard a voice saying to me in the Hebrew language, 'Saul, Saul, why are you persecuting me? It is hard for you to kick against the goads.' And I said, 'Who are you, Lord?' And the Lord said, 'I am Jesus whom you are persecuting. But rise and stand upon your feet, for I have appeared to you for this purpose, to appoint you as a servant and witness to the things in which you have seen me and to those in which I will appear to you, delivering you from your people and from the gentiles—to whom I am sending you to open their eyes, so that they may turn from darkness to light and from the power of Satan to God, that they may receive forgiveness of sins and a place among those who are sanctified by faith in me.' Therefore, O King Agrippa, I was not disobedient to the heavenly vision, but declared first to those in Damascus, then in Jerusalem and throughout all the region of Judea, and also to the gentiles, that they should repent and turn to God, performing deeds in keeping with their repentance. For this reason the Jews seized me in the temple and tried to kill me. To this day I have had the help that comes from God, and so I stand here testifying both to small and great, saying nothing but what the prophets and Moses said would come to pass: that the Christ must suffer and that, by being the first to rise from the dead, he would proclaim light both to our people and to the gentiles. (Acts 26:12–23)

This testimony provides a very different picture of Paul to that painted by those who say that Paul saw himself as an international negotiator, building bridges with the gentile world and constructing a teaching system that avoided offending pagans by demonstrating that Jesus was at least as great as their own gods.[140] I am not suggesting that Wright has this understanding; he continually stresses Paul's Old Testament roots. Nevertheless, what I observe is that his idea of Paul engaging with Hellenism as a tool for teaching and

---

[140] O. Chadwick, 'All Things to All men' (1 Cor 1X, 22) *NTS 1* (54–55) 261–275, 273 says: 'The eschatological and apocalyptic character of the primitive Palestinian Gospel was a grave liability in preaching the Gospel of Christ to an audience of Hellenistic intellectuals. He boldly reinterpreted the Gospel so as to put into the background the concept of the end of the world, and interpreted the supremacy of Jesus Christ in terms of Cosmic Wisdom, the agent of God in creation.'

engaging with the nations tends towards a similar conclusion.[141] The hard evidence that we have from Paul's writings and those of his traveling partner, Luke, demonstrate clearly that he declared fearlessly that Yahweh, Israel's God, who is the God of the whole earth, called all people to repentance and faith in his Son. This message was not presented in any other way than what the average committed Hebrew believer could copy and likewise present, for there is nothing of Hellenism, other than Acts 17, that has been adopted as a vehicle for the message.

In this testimony before Agrippa, there is absolutely no attempt to engage this cultured Roman governor in the Hellenistic terms with which he was most at home. Instead, Paul addressed him in Old Testament terms, explaining how his call was to fulfil the ministry of the Old Testament prophets. So here again, where we would expect Hellenistic engagement, we find none! Instead, we find Paul standing before Agrippa as Yahweh's servant, fearlessly declaring the word of the Lord to a gentile ruler.

What we have discovered instead is that while it is reasonable to claim that Judaism as a whole had become Hellenized, the lack of evidence of such Hellenization in Paul's writings and sermons suggest that he was one of those who had chosen not to follow the theological consequences of this cultural change.

Conclusion

We have looked for evidence that would demonstrate that Paul had utilized what he had learned from a 'Hellenist' education to confront pagan culture with the message of the gospel, and we have found nothing that supports such an argument. This outcome will be difficult for many scholars to come to terms with. Those who have advocated this view of Paul as one who was educated in Hellenism and of him using it to construct his theology have led their followers along a road which Paul never trod, and to admit this will be extremely difficult. I have sympathy for those who must face the dilemma they are in. But if prejudice is put aside and hard facts are examined and weighed, there is simply no evidence for the construction Wright gives of Paul engaging in Hellenistic ideas in order to express new covenant themes.

---

[141] The reason Wright does not totally abandon Paul to this sort of reconstruction is that he keeps him in many areas rooted in the Old Testament, even though he often lets intertestamental texts control his own, and Paul's, interpretation.

Hence, to continue to hold on to this idea will not only prevent us from gaining a better understanding of the apostle's teaching; it will just continue to leave him speaking words 'not easy to understand'!

At the start of his academic writing, Wright reflected on the difficulty of persuading fellow scholars that their reading of Jesus outside of his distinctively Jewish setting was the cause of many of the problems they encountered in their gospel studies. He wrote: 'One sometimes wonders whether certain scholars would recognize a reduction ad absurdum if it came and bit them on the nose. To change the metaphor, when an argument has hit the buffers in this fashion, we should be honest and admit that it was travelling on the wrong track'.[142]

This sentiment expresses perfectly the frustration I feel when I hear that the evidence of Paul's Hellenization is beyond challenge. I want to address in the same sentiment: 'Just how many bites on the nose are required to put this same sort of fallacy into its proper place as an example of bad exegesis that scholarship has swallowed for far too long?'

Instead, we must interpret Paul in the context of the sources we know that he knew and which he repeatedly cites; namely, the Old Testament Scriptures. This is not about reverting to an outdated method, but about using all our improved understanding of Old Testament biblical theology and interacting with it in a responsible manner. In doing this we are only keeping to what the evidence points to, we are treating Paul as a single-minded expounder of the Jewish Scriptures, we are allowing him to be what he claims to be, 'A Hebrew of the Hebrews.'

To demonstrate where this can lead to, I offer the reader several chapters (see chapters 7–8) on selected themes from Paul's gospel to show how much has been missed through the dominant hybrid methodology and how much can be gained by a more responsible Old Testament based exploration of Paul's understanding. But before we can do that, we must first examine Wright's use of and claims for extra-biblical literature to see what use it can play in biblical studies see chapter 6.

---

[142] Wright, *Victory of God,* 488.

Chapter 6:
Probing Paul's Use of Second Temple Literature

The court was silent as judge Thokozile Masipa prepared to deliver her verdict. She had listened to weeks of evidence, which had gone through the most stringent testing, and had reflected on the claims and counter-claims made by the prosecuting and defending lawyers.

Millions watched through the TV broadcast as she began to give her judgment; but before she gave it, she took the court and the waiting world through an explanation of how she had evaluated the evidence. In just a matter of a few sentences she swept away weeks of testimonies and cross-examinations on the grounds that the people called to witness were not actually present at the crime scene; nor did their evidence agree.

The key to her decision was that the only evidence that could be relied on was the hard evidence of a series of telephone calls that had been made, the times of which could be proven. The judge concluded that only the stories or testimonies that fitted into these fixed facts should be considered.

This left just a few testimonies as relevant to the case and on these she based her judgment. She found Oscar Pistorius not guilty of the murder of Reeva Steenkamp but guilty of culpable homicide and reckless endangerment with a firearm at a restaurant.

Her verdict was immediately questioned, and the high court judges eventually intervened as there was a national and international sense of a miscarriage of justice. The verdict was overturned, and Pistorius was pronounced guilty of murder, not manslaughter. What was never questioned by the supreme court was the correctness of how the value of the evidence was determined, only the decision concerning the verdict was challenged.

I want to draw attention to the way in which judge Masipa applied one crucial principle in the examination of the evidence that was before her. In a difficult, much publicized and emotionally charged case, her judgment hinged on the quality of the evidence, not the volume of witness statements that had been brought to the court.

As we consider any argument, the judge's example is a pattern for us to follow. The first and most important question that can be asked is 'what is the quality of the evidence?'

In writing this book, I do not deny that Tom Wright has done some truly excellent work, introducing millions of people to a greater knowledge of Christ and challenging many cherished ideas that needed to be reconsidered. The thrust of my argument is, however, that some of his solutions are badly constructed and that they need to be subjected to the same detailed examination which he performs on other peoples' writings.

Agreeing Procedures

We must decide how to examine Wright's teaching. As is the case in a court of law, legal rules regarding evidence need to be followed. Often, these rules infuriate litigants because they seem unnecessary hurdles to negotiate, reducing the volume of evidence presented to the court. But these rules of evidence are vitally important. They have been devised to make sure that the evidence heard may be legally accepted; that which is less than reliable has to be removed. If the evidence is from witnesses, it must be direct—no witness can bring hearsay as evidence. Where the evidence is based on written texts, they must be subjected to every possible scrutiny to confirm their genuineness.

These rules also apply to an argument that is brought by all theologians when building their case. If this procedure is not followed, unreliable evidence could sabotage the argument that has been constructed, causing what appeared to be solid to completely fall apart. I want to make the case that the quality of some of Wright's supporting evidence has not been adequately examined. When it is, it is found to be suspect. Because of this weakness, some of his key arguments are left without foundation. I have applied some of these rules of evidence in the previous chapters and they were so obvious that they did not need to be defined. What amazes me is that no one (to my knowledge) has challenged Wright on the quality of the evidence he has built his case on.

We are now moving into an area of evidence whose appropriateness and authenticity require particular attention—Paul's sources. It has become almost the new orthodoxy in academia that Paul's theological ideas may be seen to have developed through his engagement with the intertestamental texts. It is claimed that knowledge of these texts is an essential part of our achieving an authentic understanding of the teaching of the New Testament. Without embracing this idea, one is left outside of the discussion, since to lodge a counter-claim would be seen as evidence of gross ignorance. Whilst I feel at risk of imprisonment in this lonely cell of questioning, I must speak out against what I consider is this ill-judged and ill-founded practice.

Before discussing these widely-employed sources of evidence, we need to consider the laws of evidence which we shall apply to them, and we must also agree on how to deal with apparently conflicting evidence.

Rules of Evidence

In exploring the beliefs of the early church, we are dealing with the convictions of individuals and communities who lived two thousand years ago. Clearly, we have no oral evidence, but we do have some of their writings (the primary evidence) as well as some documents produced by others who either supported or rejected their teachings (secondary evidence). In any type of research, it is the primary evidence that is always given the greatest weight when assessing the value of an historical construction.

So, what are the rules which should control the submission of material as evidence when examining the beliefs of the early church? I would suggest that the first rule of evidence is that the raw material should be accurately dated. To introduce texts as evidence that were not in existence at the time of Jesus or Paul is unacceptable, for these certainly cannot be presented as evidence of what Jesus or Paul thought or knew.

This rule is so obvious that it should not need to be stated; but there have been times when dates of evidence have been assumed, rather than tested, and only later have these assumptions been shown to be wrong. We will find that Wright violates this rule on at least one occasion.

This was the case in the arguments made by the brilliant German scholar Rudolf Bultmann, who was professor of the famous department of theology at the University of Marburg in the early part of the twentieth century. Bultmann's teachings were read everywhere and they had massive influence across Europe and beyond. They changed attitudes to the way the New Testament was regarded, and his arguments were taught as facts in universities and seminaries worldwide. As student pastors were taught and then graduated, they took his extreme views into the pulpits of Christendom and from it congregations were fed a diet of soul-destroying scepticism. And what was the consequence of his framework of understanding? It was a church that lost and denied her spiritual heritage.

But Bultmann's conclusions were seriously flawed. His argument was that the presence of common terms in the New Testament and the Gnostic writings was proof that the writers of the NT had borrowed ideas from Gnosticism. He therefore claimed that the absence of these documents from the interpretations of his peers and predecessors had left their understanding seriously weakened.

The problem with Bultmann's argument was that—as it was eventually shown—the Gnostic documents on which he depended did not exist in the first century; they were the product of the movement's second century teachers. So, it turned out that, rather than the early Christians borrowing from the Gnostics, the Gnostics had probably borrowed from Christian writings. When scholars eventually established this, the value of Bultmann's work crashed and he has little influence today.

So, the correct dating of secondary supporting texts is vital; they cannot be assumed. Any failure to establish the correct dating will produce a serious weakness in the argument.

But it is not only dating that has to be considered. The availability of the secondary writings to the New Testament authors must also be considered. Only if it can be reasonably supposed that the New Testament writers had actually read these secondary texts can they be useful in identifying the links and meanings which an understanding of them might give to a New Testament scholar.

An example of how unrealistic this sort of evidence can become is the case of one scholar who was explaining what the word 'head' (*kephale*) meant in the letter to the Colossians. Apparently a very rare text had been found on the northern border of ancient Iran, and this particular scholar argued that the writer of the Colossian letter intended to use the term in an unusual way, just as the writer of the obscure Iranian text had done. Before such an argument could be accepted, it would have to be proven that this extra-biblical text really was available for the author of Colossians to read. He would then have to show that the Colossian community was familiar with the unusual meaning of this word or the explanation would be worthless. Since there was no evidence to substantiate either acquaintance, the suggestion of this scholar was rightly rejected by the vast majority of those, including the distinguished

British scholar, F. F. Bruce, who regarded it as just too speculative to be trusted.

So, dating and provenance (the history, authorship and location of the text) are two important pieces of evidence that must be considered in any argument built around the existence of secondary literature. If these details cannot be established, then the argument produced will be seriously suspect.

Of course, it is much safer when a scholar argues that the writer of a New Testament document has deliberately quoted from an Old Testament text. This is much easier to establish because these ancient texts were read publicly in synagogues throughout the Roman Empire every Sabbath day. As the Christian congregations had their beginnings in these Jewish communities— and many continued their ties with them, even though they had come to definitive views about who Jesus was—they were all sharing the same literary heritage and would be much more likely to recognize intended, and even unintended, echoes from these Scriptures. The importance of these Old Testament texts for the early Christian community does not need to be debated because the general consensus is that these were believed to be the sacred Scriptures through which God had spoken to his people

In terms of identifying the likelihood of an Old Testament text being referred to or alluded to by Paul, New Testament Professor Richard Hays has done an invaluable service in his book, Echoes of Scripture in Paul.[143] This linking up of texts, an Old Testament one with one quoted in Paul's arguments, is known as intertextuality, and understanding how it works has brought a much deeper appreciation for what the apostle was intending to say. Hays sought to establish when it could be accepted that an Old Testament text or even an allusion to one was present the New Testament.

The seven criteria Hays laid down for deciding the probability of deliberate intertextuality are as follows:

Availability

Hays considers that a key element for a case of intertextuality is whether the proposed source of the echo in the text of Paul's letter was available to the apostle and his original recipients. He points out that Paul was clearly acquainted with the Old Testament, even before the collection of texts was

---

[143] R. Hays, *Echoes of Scripture in the Letters of Paul* (New Haven: Yale University Press, 1989).

formally acknowledged as a canon by the leaders of Judaism. He argues that Paul expected his readers to be familiar with these texts as well.

Hays also raises the subject of Paul's knowledge of the teaching of Jesus. He suggests that although the gospels were written too late to have been the source of Paul's message, the possibility that Paul was drawing on an oral tradition of Jesus's teaching should not be discounted (although this is far more difficult to establish). However, this might need to be re-examined as a recent thesis has been published that suggests that at least one of the gospels could have been circulating among the churches when Paul was writing his letters.[144]

Frequency

Hays points out that when there is a number of citations of any given Old Testament text in the New Testament, they become an important indicator of its intertextual use. However, it is not sufficient simply to discover that there are significant terms common to both the source text and the passage which echoes it; it is just as vital to examine whether the theological context of the source is clearly present in the vicinity of text in the NT in which it is being cited. So, for example, if the key words in Paul's argument are 'light' and 'darkness', it may be reasonable to see an intertextual use of the creation narrative, especially if the theme of the passage in which Paul uses these terms is that of new creation.

Recurrence

If Paul is exploring an Old Testament passage such as the giving of the law (see 2 Corinthians 3), then terms occurring in Paul's argument that are part of the original exodus narrative should give the Old Testament passage additional credence as an intended case of intertextuality.

Thematic Coherence

Does the theme of the context of the alleged Old Testament echo support the background theme of the passage in which the supposed allusion appears? Does the thematic background of the borrowed text parallel and support the argument that is being made by Paul?

---

[144] S. Lauer, 'Traces of a Gospel Writing in 1 Corinthians: Rediscovery and Development of Origen's Understanding of 1 Corinthians 4:6b' (PhD thesis, University of Wales Trinity Saint David, 2011).

Historical

Another piece of evidence is historical plausibility. Would, or could, Paul have understood the subject he is supposed to be writing about? Remembering that Paul was a first century Jew, it would not be sensible to suggest that he was teaching something that only emerged centuries later in the understanding of the church.

Interpretation

Have any other readers throughout the church's history identified this reading as being one produced by intertextuality. Hays points out that as time went on 'a radically divergent social and religious context engendered a major hermeneutical revision by locating Paul's letters within a different intertextual space: the space defined pre- eminently by the four canonical Gospels and the Acts of the Apostles. A historically sensitive exegesis can recover echoes previously dampened or drowned out.'[145]

These guidelines are eminently sensible and most scholars, with some small revisions relating to identifying the correct reading from textual variations, have gone along with them. But if these rules are important for establishing claims of the New Testament's usage of Old Testament texts, then it is far more important that they are applied to the claim that echoes of other literature are to be found in the New Testament. This includes intertestamental literature (ITL), which is mostly a collection of Jewish writings from shortly after the end of the Old Testament period to 200 C.E.

Further, it would be helpful to know how much the emergence of later Christian writings cemented Greek ideas into the developing understanding of the early church, which was increasingly dominated by gentile converts. The shift into Hellenistic thinking needs to be defined and incorporated into the adopted hermeneutic. For most scholars, it is assumed that this development was well under way before the texts were written, but in my opinion this assumption needs to be demonstrated rather than assumed. This is a view that is shared by Alister McGrath, noting that 'The translation of a word into a different language inevitably involves a distortion of the semantic field.'[146]

---

[145] Hays, *Echoes,* 31.

[146] Alister McGrath, *Iustitia Dei: A History of the Christian Doctrine of Justification, 2nd edition.* (Cambridge: Cambridge University Press, 1998), 5 9.

Wright's Rules of Evidence?

But what does this have to do with Wright's arguments? It is that Wright purports to see the influence of intertestamental literature in Paul's letters. Yet such a claim should be approached with extreme caution; for if the use of Old Testament texts by New Testament writers has to be so carefully scrutinized, how much greater must the scrutiny be when it is claimed that the influence of a non-biblical text is present in the New Testament?

Unlike establishing the presence of Old Testament citations or allusions in the New Testament with the help of Hays' rules, there are no recognized and published guidelines for accepting the influence of non-biblical texts. The absence of such agreed guidelines ought to demand caution when many are readily accepting their presence and influence on either Paul or his audience.

Wright—like many others who follow the same method—has never applied any of the rules listed by Hays to the intertestamental texts he has identified as sources for Paul's teaching. In regard to this I sent an email to Prof James Davila, a world-leading authority of Jewish intertestamental texts. In my email, I asked if he knew of any study of intertestamental literature similar to the one by Hays for identifying Old Testament sources in the New Testament. I wanted to know if he knew of any work which had been done to identify ITL in the New Testament. He replied, 'I am not aware that my New Testament colleagues think that there is a problem'. The tone of this response showed that he was not in the least concerned that such an analysis ought to be provided for intertestamental literature; his colleagues had never raised the issue as a problem that needed to be addressed. Thus, while there are strict guidelines provided by Hays for identifying the presence of an Old Testament citation or allusion in the New Testament, there is no need for such guidance to identify a text from the ITL in the New Testament! The point is this: that the issue needs to be addressed urgently, or scholars will continue to work on their gut instinct, something that should not control scholarly methodology.

The presence of one word, or even a string of words, found in both the intertestamental literature and a writing of Paul or any other apostle is insufficient to allow Wright to utilize these texts as supporting evidence for his views concerning the teachings of the primitive apostolic church.[147] When

---

[147] See for example Wright, *The Meaning of Jesus,* 94 where such literature changes the meaning of New Testament teaching.

he makes such claims for dependency, they can often be shown to be superficial, if they are even there at all.[148] Often there is serious conflict between his chosen intertestamental literature text and the New Testament text, yet the intertestamental literature meaning normally prevails in his exegesis. We will look at some examples of this later, suffice it to say at this point that Wright is far from alone in using this practice, for it has come to dominate New Testament research and is rarely, if ever, challenged.

Yet this now widespread practice of using extra-biblical texts to explain what the New Testament teaches is a very new phenomenon.[149] It hardly existed before the discovery of the Dead Sea Scrolls in 1949. Before then, many of the texts we are now familiar with existed only as translations of texts originally written in an unknown language. Because the origin of these texts was unknown, scholars rightly avoided integrating them into their writings as examples of early Christian thought.

However, when the Dead Sea Scrolls were found, some of the intertestamental literature texts were found within this unique ancient collection. This established their original Hebraic origin and character, and the gloves were taken off! They soon became the measure of historic intellectual credibility, to the point that you cannot get a PhD without serious engagement with them. In fact, these documents have become so important that they are now present in virtually all recent academic papers, monographs, and biblical commentaries to a degree that is not normally appreciated.

For example, the index of citations at the back of Wright's Jesus and the Victory of God shows Wright's practice very clearly. There you will find ten pages of Old Testament citations, ten pages of New Testament citations, and nine pages of citations from extra- biblical sources. Now some of these citations are historical details, acquired by reading such works as those of the Jewish historian Josephus. Obviously, such citations are legitimate; but many others are not providing historical details and are being used by Wright as theological Rosetta stones. They have become indispensable tools for authoritatively interpreting the New Testament. If the proposed meaning of a New Testament text clashes with the assumed meaning of the intertestamental text, the trend is very definitely to correct the established New Testament

---

[148] See discussion on Col 1:15, p. 243.

[149] Other than rabbinic texts, which have been appealed to long before the discovery of the Dead Sea Scrolls.

interpretation to conform to the meaning claimed to be in the intertestamental literature.[150] Does this method of interpretation recover lost meanings that would stay forever gone without such engagement? Should the previous two thousand years of Christian scholarship be relabelled as 'the Extra-Long Dark Ages' because these texts were either not known or were being ignored?

This is not to deny there has been a progressive clearer understanding through the past two thousand years, but never before has the increase in understanding been dependent on anything other than a better understanding of the New Testament texts themselves. This reliance on intertestamental literature is totally different from anything that the church or academia has ever before claimed or adopted.

I want to make it clear that my concern about the use of these texts is not because they are not Scripture; in other words, this is not a confessional issue. It is at a scholarly level that I raise this matter, because these texts never belonged to the early Christian community at all. In saying this, I acknowledge that the case has been made for a much wider range of people calling themselves followers of Jesus than those who received the New Testament letters. Some of these may well have been writers or receivers of these recently embraced texts. If our interest lies in the rise of this wider 'Christian' community, then all is well and good as long as the research is done according to best practice. But to suggest that these communities and their documents are the key to understanding the teaching of the apostles would be seriously off target. Many of these groups were openly opposed to the early church and its message of Jesus; can they really be reliable witnesses to the apostles' teaching? Even if we postulate the possibility that the apostles knew and used these works as part of their polemic—in order to refute them—this possibility has yet to be verified. Another important requirement is to recognize that we cannot take texts that share a common term and construct a meaning which then determines what Paul meant when he used the same word.

To indicate how badly designed this methodology is, we could consider a modern example. If a person came to the minister of an Evangelical church

---

[150] See for example N. T. Wright, *The Resurrection of the Son of God, Christian Origins and the Question of God, Vol. 3* (London: SPCK, 2003), 147–150 where he uses Maccabean material to establish new meaning in the Old Testament and also as the foundation for the New Testament doctrine of the resurrection.

and asked about water baptism, would it be suggested to him that he should read the book of Mormon or the Jehovah Witness' magazine 'Watch Tower' for helpful insights into evangelical thinking? Indeed, would a Presbyterian minister even send the enquirer to a Baptist church, a Methodist church, or a Salvation Army citadel? If there would be reluctance to expose a seeker to another legitimate Christian body, how much more unlikely would he be sent to those whom they considered to be their theological opponents!

Let us take this back to the New Testament era. When the apostles, who claimed to speak for Christ, taught the fledging congregations, would they integrate the teachings of other religious groups into their writings? To be more precise, would they use the writings of groups which they had denounced as heretics and enemies of the gospel of Christ in order to teach the church? You don't have to agree with the apostles' insistence that the believers should have nothing to do with these groups, you only have to recognize that this was the position which they held and ask whether they would have spent their time reading their literature in a deliberate attempt to integrate it with their study of the Old Testament Scriptures. Of course, such a suggestion assumes that they knew of the writings' existence in the first place— and the evidence for this is far from established.

So, here is one of my concerns about Wright's teachings. They are littered with viewpoints gleaned from extra-biblical texts, which he claims bring crucial details to light so that we might have a proper understanding of the New Testament.

This trend in scholarship has been noted by those who specialize in the content, dating, and significance of intertestamental writings. They are increasingly concerned over the poor scrutiny that has been given prior to their use for interpreting the New Testament.[151]

There is one specific detail that I think provides decisive support for the concern I am expressing. Until very recently it was thought that Paul regularly used his rabbinic training when making his arguments. But closer scrutiny has challenged this claim, and Wright himself has raised his voice against it.

One example that seemed to have survived this scrutiny is Galatians 4:7–8, where Paul appears to give a typically rabbinical allegory as part of his argument. But even this occasion is now being questioned. There is growing

---

[151] S. Sandmel, 'Parallelomania', *JBL* 81 (1962)1–13.

recognition that this section of the Galatian letter is nothing more than an intertextual reflection on Isaiah 54:1, which Paul had earlier quoted.[152] This was nothing less than the application of the observations Hays had made years earlier in Echoes of Scripture in Paul.

Now, if this is a correct understanding, then what we are witnessing is that Paul actually follows the exegetical method of Jesus. He no longer relates his thinking to the traditions of the elders, which he was taught, but goes straight back to the Old Testament text and asks the question, 'What does the Scripture say?' He handles the text in the same compelling way as Jesus and his followers did and experienced the totally liberating method of exegeting the Old Testament texts on their own soil.

Evidence for Apostolic Mixing of Intertestamental and Biblical Texts

A very simple rule I suggest for deciding if a correct merging of texts has taken place is that we ask if the proposed reading makes sense. By this I do not mean to the one who proposes it, but can the case be made that the original recipients would have immediately grasped the point being made? Far too much of the fruits of intertestamental intertextuality have required the original recipient community to contain some people equivalent in their training to the modern equivalent of PhD graduates to help them make the connections that are claimed to exist. The truth was that most in the churches had no formal education of any kind, so how were they expected to handle all this material, which they probably had never heard of, and so follow the incredibly complex claims for intertestamental intertextuality being made? Wright is guilty of this speaking down to his readers when he says such things as 'all of this is incredibly dense but what Paul is really saying is ....' It is the equivalent of 'trust me, I'm a doctor'. If the argument is above the intellectual ability of the people Paul wrote to, it is likely to be the wrong argument.

The Intertestamental Texts

One of the major sources that Wright relies on for his novel reinterpretations of Paul is the literature of Second Temple Judaism. When he wrote his

---

[152] See Karen H. Jobes, 'Jerusalem, Our Mother: Metalepsis and Intertextuality in Galatians 4:21–31' *WTJ* 55 (1993):299–320. See also Matthew S. Harmon, 'She Must and Shall Go Free: Paul's Isaianic Gospel in Galatians.' *BZNW* 168 (New York: de Gruyter, 2010).

doctoral thesis at Oxford University, he had very little engagement with this literature. However, soon after graduation he was given a teaching post and then moved on to teach at McGill University in Canada. At both institutions, he was asked to teach courses on intertestamental Judaism. It was through reading the literature of this period that he became convinced that he had found a major key for interpreting the New Testament documents. From then on, he began to construct his theological arguments in a way he had not previously attempted, relying heavily on the texts with which he had recently become acquainted. The extent of this influence, as noted already, can be seen by examining the index of citations at the back of his book Jesus and the Victory of God. There are ten pages of OT citations, ten pages of NT citations, and nine pages of intertestamental citations, an incredible contrast to the percentage ratio he cited in his DPhil thesis.

Of course, Wright was far from the first to discover the wealth of material that exists in this collection of texts. Many of them had been known since the second century, but prior to the discovery of the Dead Sea scrolls the texts were not in Hebrew, they were only known in preserved languages such as Egyptian, Syriac, and other ancient forms. There was no certainty that they had existed in the apostolic age or whether, as was claimed, they were Hebrew documents written by Jews who adopted the nom de plume of a key historical Jewish figure. In this collection were found writings such as the Wisdom of Solomon, The Book of Enoch, and The Gospel of Thomas. Many documents were titled to suggest that they were written by a revered Old Testament leader, while some claimed Christian authorship. Because of the uncertainty of their origin, scholars were reluctant to depend on them as evidence when interpreting the New Testament.

However, all of this changed with the discovery of the Dead Sea scrolls; a discovery which has been described as the greatest discovery of ancient texts ever made. Soon claims were being made that these scrolls showed that Christianity was not the faith its leaders claimed it to be. These texts, it was argued, showed that the early Christians had invented the accounts of Jesus. They had borrowed from the writings of other Jewish groups of the time, and the evidence was there for all to see in these newly-discovered documents!

Eventually, reason began to prevail. It was realized that, while these texts were testimony to a far greater diversity in first century Judaism than had previously been appreciated, they were not the source of the writings of the New Testament writers. They represented the writings of other Jewish groupings whose identities are mostly unknown.

These writings give a fascinating insight into the Jewish world of the intertestamental period, but the evidence that could be reliably drawn from them to help understand the message of the New Testament is open for challenge. To this newly discovered collection of texts the long known wider collection of Jewish Second Temple texts was added to make up the corpus of intertestamental texts that scholars rely on. So, what are these intertestamental texts and what are they called?

The Jewish Targums

During this period, the rabbis collected their oral traditions together and these were eventually put down in written form in the 3rd century C.E. The oral traditions were assigned to different stages of Jewish history and they were given appropriate labels to designate their believed origin. These sayings, which were believed to have originated during the time Israel was in captivity in Babylon, are called the Babylonian Targum; those believed to have originated in Jerusalem after the return from exile are called the Palestinian Targum.

As these traditions were not written down until the end of the third century ce, there are some scholars who are very wary of using them as evidence of the meaning of Old Testament sayings. Others have no hesitation in using them, saying that these oral traditions were deeply respected and faithfully transmitted from generation to generation. Most of them, they claim, were in existence at the time of both Jesus and Paul, and they would have made reference to them and might even have borrowed from them.

The eminent scholar W. D. Davies believed these texts provided a key for interpreting Paul. Davies wrote a book, Paul and Rabbinic Judaism, in which he attempted to show how Paul had used these traditions.[153] Yet, despite the fact that Paul was a trained rabbi who would probably have known considerable sections of these traditions, the book failed to convince the scholarly world of his dependence on this rabbinic material. This is a judgment that Tom Wright, along with others, endorsed. This is an interesting observation, for Wright discounts the rabbinic writings, the sources of which we can be very confident he would have engaged with as a student rabbi, as being a major influence on Saul, yet he is convinced that the writings of 'heretical' Jewish groups are important.

---

[153] W. D. Davies, *Paul and Rabbinic Judaism: Some Rabbinic Elements in Pauline Theology. 3rd edition.* (Philadelphia: Fortress Press, 1980).

The Pseudepigrapha

The Pseudepigrapha is a collection of Jewish texts that were written mostly between 200 B.C.E and 200 C.E. They were written by a range of authors who, for whatever reason, attributed their work to one of the great Jewish figures of Israel's history. The writings were written as though they were the work of the figure whose name they bear, and it could be that the work was passed off as being authentically the work of the ancient leader. It is because the manuscripts are not ascribed to the actual author but to another figure that they are called Pseudepigraphal writing. What is now known as the Pseudepigrapha is not a fixed collection; when books are discovered from this period they are added to the list.

It is understandable if you say that you have never heard of these books, or that you are not very interested in them. However, what you do need to know, if you are a Christian, is that these non-Christian texts have now become massively influential for how commentators and experts understand the teaching of the New Testament. Moreover, the books written by these supposed 'experts' are the material that pastors and ministers read when they are preparing their sermons. Hence, without appreciating it, the views of these 'heretical' Jews are being introduced into the mind of the modern church in a verbal form of the Trojan horse!

Scholars read these texts avidly when they are trying to identify possible sources of Paul's expressions and images. My concern is not that scholars use them, but that they often use them very badly. The concern I am expressing may be appreciated if we imagine a contemporary, albeit rather foolish, situation.

A visitor to Scotland seeks to gain some understanding of the Scottish Presbyterian doctrine of the Holy Spirit. He begins his research with a survey of Scotland's view on the subject. Searches of past editions of newspapers are made followed by searches of the literature of other religious groupings within the country. Spiritualists, Mormons, Jehovah's Witnesses, Unitarians, Baptists, Methodists, Catholics, and so on are all consulted about their understanding of the Holy Spirit. With this contextual study completed, the writings of the Presbyterian divines are then considered.

If this method was followed, and the fruit of the wider study used to inform the primary texts, there would be no possible chance of understanding the distinctive doctrines of Presbyterianism. It should have been the theological differences that were the important points to study, not the similarity of vocabulary.

Much contemporary New Testament study conducts its research in a similar way. The fact that terminology in the texts is similar, or even identical, to that found in the New Testament is no guarantee that the meanings being expressed are the same. My concern is that ideas are being imported from these intertestamental texts into claims which are supposed to represent the ideas of the original NT author. I contend that rather than helping scholarship in its task, it does the very opposite, it confuses the picture of what the early church believed.

The trouble with the above illustration of someone seeking to understand the Scottish Presbyterian doctrine of the Spirit is that it fails to fully reflect the current situation in New Testament studies. To find a more direct equivalence we must imagine that our fictional researcher, after gathering all of his material, has a disastrous day. All of the search facilities he has employed fail, and they are never available for anyone ever to use again. He cannot recover his sources on his computer, and so his collection of written material is the only collection in the world.

To add to this, as he is working in his study with his window open, a gale develops outside and all of his written source material (which had been piled up according to origin and theological background) is blown across the room and out into the corridor so that it is now impossible to know what page belonged to which group. With this information gone, he can no longer ascertain what the terminology on the individual sheets of paper conveyed to the original reader. The ability to locate the sources of the information, and therefore the views that they represented, has been lost. There are now only piles of texts on the floor, which cannot be accurately labelled in terms of origin and whose original meaning can only be guessed at. But, undaunted, our researcher begins considering his material on the Presbyterian doctrine of the Holy Spirit!

This foolish story illustrates what I believe to be the situation in New Testament studies as far as the use of the Pseudepigraphal writings is concerned. Since we do not know the theological homes of these writings, we can only guess at their original meaning. Indeed, to make any sense of these

Chapter 6: Probing Paul's Use of Second Temple Literature

sources will demand incredible discipline and patience;[154] they cannot readily be pulled across as evidence into the field of Old Testament studies to show that they support a proposed exegesis. To use this method is to disregard the rules of historical research for admissible evidence.

A Test Case

If anyone supposes that the above conclusion is too harsh and that the Pseudepigrapha must have more value than the limited use I have conceded earlier, I might suggest that the situation is even more serious than I have indicated so far.

Even within the one community we can define, and whose literature we have access to (the Qumran community), the variations which exist between their extant texts prevent any firm conclusions being drawn concerning its belief system. The following extract shows why this is the case:

> It is not possible to do a simple, homogenous Qumran messianic belief without doing violence to the nature of the evidence. Nor, however, is it acceptable to make this variety of concepts the basis for working out a pattern of systematic development in chronological order for messianic beliefs at Qumran. We simply do not have sufficient information to allow precise dating of the Qumran works (essential for the construction of this kind of chronological schema), nor do we know enough about the interrelationship of the various Qumran writings.[155]

This is the argument that Barclay is highlighting in his ground-breaking book Paul and the Gift. He says: 'Grace is everywhere in Second Temple Judaism but not everywhere is the same.'[156]

If there is such uncertainty about interpreting the documents of a clearly defined community, what chance is there of understanding an array of texts that come from the widely diverse groupings (whose origins we don't even know) that existed within first century Judaism? The complexity of the

---

[154] Wright, *People of God,* 100 says that, 'Jewish sources alone are a lifetime's study.'

[155] A. Chester, 'Jewish Messianic Expectations and Mediatoral Figures and Pauline Christology' in *Paulus und das antike Judeatum,* Editors, M. Hengel and U. Heckel (Tübingen, 1991):17–89 [25].

[156] J.M.G. Barclay, *Paul and the Gift* (Grand Rapids: Eerdmans, 2015).

problem demands extreme caution when making any claims; yet such caution is very rarely exercised, even by those who say they recognize its need.

The warning I have just given would not come as something new to Wright, for it is not as though he has not already considered it and its dangers. Indeed, he has written concerning the intertestamental literature: 'We have learned that we must not glibly pass over differences of setting and time, imagining continuity of thought between documents of different provenance.'[157]

Yet even though he has giving this very clear warning, I believe that Wright repeatedly uses these texts in the very same irresponsible way that he warns us against.

Theological Diversity

Despite the above arguments, the Pseudepigraphal texts are often used as the key for understanding the meaning of the New Testament. This presupposes that they share the same theological outlook and that their meanings are transposable. But this is to ignore a fatal flaw. There were, and still are, many theologies within Judaism.[158]

The Pseudepigraphal documents represent different Jewish perspectives, many of which were distinct from, and in contradiction to, the others. This is made clear by Charlesworth, who, when commenting on the Pseudepigrapha, says:

> In these writings, as in the Dead Sea Scrolls, we are introduced to the ideas, symbols, perceptions, fears, and dreams of pre-70 ce Jews. Since none of them can with assurance be assigned to Pharisees, Sadducees, Zealots, or Essenes, it is wise not to describe early Judaism in terms of four such sects; rather we must now think of many groups and numerous subgroups.[159]

Not until the distinctive beliefs of each group are understood and their relationship to the New Testament established can they be safely used in New Testament exegesis. To put these texts heedlessly into footnotes or the text of commentaries in order to give supporting evidence is to do the very opposite

---

[157] Wright, *People of God,* 119.

[158] W. D. Davies, *Paul and Rabbinic Judaism,* 20.

[159] J. Charlesworth, *The Old Testament Pseudepigrapha and the New Testament* (Harrisburg: Trinity, 1980), 538–9.

of what is needed. Instead of moving New Testament studies on to a more scholarly footing, this practice ignores the complexity of these sources and unwittingly reads a particular theology into the text; the result is a pollution of the primary text, i.e. the NT text itself, which is the only starting point from which New Testament theology can be safely done.

Unheeded Warnings

Perhaps it is the eminent Jewish rabbinical scholar Neusner who has been most vocal in declaring the complexity of Judaism. Neusner's concern is that Judaism has been reduced, in the thinking of many scholars, to a homogeneous system. His particular aim is to establish that Judaism did not have common expectations concerning its coming messiah, but many, and sometimes conflicting, expectations. Indeed, Israel did not look for a Messiah but for messiahs.

Neusner says:

> What is wrong with the established view is simple. People join together books that do not speak the same language of thought, that refer to distinctive conceptions and doctrines of their own. If books so close in topic and sentiment as the four Gospels no longer yield harmonization, books so utterly remote from one another as the Mishnah and Philo and Fourth Ezra and Enoch should not contribute doctrines to the common pot: Judaism. But if we do not harmonize, then what we have to do is quite the opposite: analyse. In fact, all we propose is to describe things item by item, and to postpone the work of searching for connections and even continuities until all the components have had their say, one by one. For, as we see throughout this book, each of the components—the distinct books—makes its own distinctive statement.[160]

---

[160] 158 J. Neusner, W. Green and S. Frenchs, Eds., *Judaisms and Their Messiahs at the Turn of the Christian Era* (Cambridge: University Press, 1990), xiii. See also the warning given by R. J. Bauckham, *The Fate of the Dead: Studies on the Jewish and Christian Apocalypses* (Leiden: Brill, 1998), 114 who says: 'Heavily influenced by apocalyptic as primitive Christianity undoubtedly was, it was also highly selective in the aspects of apocalyptic which it took over. This is a fact about the Old Testament which can only be appreciated by diligent study of Pseudepigraphal works which do not look at all relevant to the New Testament.'

Charlesworth has given a similar warning concerning the diversity of Judaism:

> The contradicting ideas should not be explained away or forced into an artificial system. Such ideas in the Pseudepigrapha witness to the fact that early Judaism was not a speculative philosophical movement or theological system, even though the Jews demonstrated impressive speculative fecundity. The Pseudepigrapha mirror a living religion in which the attempt was made to come to terms with the dynamic phenomena of history and experience.[161]

Since we 'cannot identify with certainty any author of the pseudepigraphon as being a Pharisee or an Essene or a member of another sect',[162] we don't even know which theological school to assign each document to. This means we may never, with certainty, know the significance that should be given to the documents' theological terms, for the meaning of these may have differed from group to group.

Inadequate Samples

There is yet another limitation which needs to be recognized when it comes to using the intertestamental literature; for although the documents that we have represent a range of theological traditions, they each represent very limited samples of the tradition from which they come. How much of Paul's theology would we appreciate if we had only 1 Thessalonians in our possession?[163] It is only the multiplicity of documents addressed to different congregations and dealing with a wide range of issues that gives us reasonable grounds to believe that we can attempt to reproduce a genuine Pauline theology.

Obviously documents such as the letters of John, Peter, or James give us a more limited glimpse into the thinking of their authors. Although this may prove a major hurdle for scholarship, it is not a problem for orthodox

---

[161] J. Charlesworth, *The Old Testament Pseudepigrapha and the New Testament: Prolegomena for the Study of Christian Origins* (Cambridge: University Press, 1985), 54.

[162] Charlesworth, *Old Testament Pseudepigrapha*, 2: xxix.

[163] See G. Fee, *God's Empowering Presence: The Holy Spirit in the Letters of Paul* (Peabody: Hendrickson, 1994), 594. Fee argues against assuming that we have Paul's pneumatology sewn up: 'A text like this one alerts us that Paul's understanding is too large for us to encompass by merely collecting particular texts and looking at them.'

Christianity, which believes in the unity and inspiration of the Scriptures as written by men under the direction of the Spirit of Truth. From a confessional point of view, we do not, or should not, look to individual writings to provide a full Christian theology.

However, since they are part of the Christian Scriptures and thus can be assumed to share a similar mindset and system of beliefs, they can be interpreted from that wider perspective to which they also contribute. Obviously, such a claim would be invalid if they represented factions within the early church, but such suggestions are no longer acceptable in the light of the results of modern research.

Authenticity of Sources

De Jonge has raised other problems that add to the multiplicity of dangers inherent in relying on the intertestamental literature. Like Moore, back in 1920, De Jonge points out that the transmission of these texts was in the hands of Christians, and that they preserved them because they served their purposes. Hence, we have no idea how much material was discarded because it didn't serve the new movement's expectations.

In addition, there is the problem that many of these documents, despite the Hebrew confirmation provided by Qumran, are translations of the original texts, and we cannot be certain how accurate the translations are.

Also, it is difficult even to guess just how much tampering of these documents took place. Since we know from textual evidence that later generations of some Christian communities had been prepared to tamper with the New Testament documents themselves to promote their views, there is little doubt that at least the same amount of tampering would have taken place with the documents of the Pseudepigrapha. It is no wonder that De Jonge warns of the need of specialists to guide New Testament theologians in the use of these texts.[164]

---

[164] M. De Jonge, 'The Pseudepigrapha of the Old Testament and Early Christianity' in P. Borgen and S. Giversen, Eds., *The New Testament and Hellenistic Judaism* (Oxford: University Press, 1995), 59–71 [61–63]. L. Henninger, 'Zum Erstgeborenrecht bei don Semiten' im E. Gaf (Ed.) Fesschrift Werner Caskel zum Siebzigsten Geburstag (Leiden: Brill, 1966), 112–183 [176]. Henninger claims that there is little evidence of a religious significance in the extra-biblical sources.

The Relevance of the Documents

Even if it were possible to demonstrate theological equivalence between New Testament texts and the Pseudepigrapha, what would it prove? For example, how widely known were the Pseudepigraphal writings? How far had their message penetrated wider Judaism? Were they known beyond Palestine and how do we know that even the population of Palestine knew them? How can we know that an apparent reference, or even an echo, from the Jewish Pseudepigrapha, or later recorded rabbinic tradition for that matter, could have been recognized by the readers of the New Testament? How do we decide each individual New Testament writer's knowledge of the Pseudepigrapha?

Indeed, Dunn[165] claims that Luke, as a gentile, shows no evidence of being aware of intertestamental Judaism. Yet it is these writings that Turner[166] and Menzies[167] rely on in their attempts to understand Lucan theology of the Spirit, and, incidentally, they come to totally different conclusions! This provides an example of the danger of reading into the intertestamental texts one's own preferences and then using these very texts for understanding Luke's mindset. Indeed, even if Luke had been aware of these sources, we cannot know what relevance they would have had for him. He wrote his Gospel for gentile readers who, being scattered across the Roman world, could not possibly have known of their existence or contents. No one can seriously suggest that the Gospel writers expected these so-called allusions to intertestamental literature to be picked up by their readers. Such claims strain the evidence way beyond the point of credibility.

But even if there are echoes of these documents, could it not be that these extra-biblical writings are themselves echoing some other source that both the Pseudepigrapha and the New Testament writer were familiar with? In other words, they could both be echoing a commonly unknown source. It is easy to imagine that, in the process of usage, they both deviated from the common source they shared.[168] Are the Pseudepigraphal writings in the same

---

[165] J. Dunn, 'Baptism in the Spirit: A Response to Pentecostal Scholarship on Luke-Acts', *JPT*, 3 (193):3–27 [21].

[166] M. Turner, *The Holy Spirit and Spiritual Gifts: Then and Now* (Carlisle: Paternoster, 1996).

[167] R. Menzies, *Empowered for Witness: the Spirit in Luke-Acts* (Sheffield: Sheffield Academic Press, 1994), 6.

[168] See J. Fossum, 'The New Religionsgeschichtlíche Schule: The Quest for

theological stream as the writer of the OT text that they refer too, or have they drifted even further from the unrecognized source?

The way the Dead Sea Scrolls and the New Testament use the same Old Testament material in different ways raises the possibility that such a three-way relationship, the original OT text's meaning, the ITL understanding and the understanding of the NT writer who uses the OT text, exists between them. These are all questions or possibilities that are dangerously ignored by most scholars as they draw upon the texts in support of their interpretations.

Wright acknowledges the variety of beliefs in Judaism. He (correctly in my judgment) claims that, despite this variety, we can trace the outlines of a worldview and a belief system, which were shared by a large number of Jews at that time. What I think he fails to do is recognize that he is importing details into his own interpretation from these sources, rather than simply illustrating through them that similar, but far from identical, views were held by other Jews at the time.[169] Also, as we shall soon see, there are occasions when by his interpretation of the texts he has given meanings to these sources that are then made the evidence for interpreting the New Testament.

In fact, as I have indicated above, it is not possible to have any certainty as to the detailed meaning of these texts without knowing their original stable and without having a substantial collection of texts from the same source that deal with the same themes. In using the intertestamental literature in the way he does, Wright, along with a growing number of other scholars,[170] builds his exegesis on foundations that are unreliable. Wright's Wisdom Christology,

---

Jewish Christology', in E. H. Lovering, ed., *SBL 1991 Seminar Papers* (Atlanta: Scholars Press, 1991), 638–646 [643]. See also D. Carson, D. J. Moo and L. Morris, *An Introduction to the New Testament* (Grand Rapids: Zondervan, 1992), 122 for a similar discussion of sources in the early Church Fathers. The same difficulties apply to the Pseudepigrapha being identified as a source of common ideas in the New Testament.

[169] Wright, *People of God*, 338; see also R. B. Hays, 'Adam, Israel, Christ', in *Pauline Theology, Vol. III, Romans,* edited by D. M. Hay and E. E. Johnson (Minneapolis: Fortress, 1995), 79. interpretation of the texts he has given meanings to these sources that are then made the evidence for interpreting the New Testament.

[170] E.g. B. Witherington., *The Paul Quest: The Renewed Search for the Jew of Tarsus* (Downers Grove: IVP, 1998) and M. Turner, *Power from on High: The Spirit in Israel's Restoration and Witness in Luke-Acts* (Sheffield: University Press, 1996).

for example, relies heavily on these texts, despite his acknowledgement of the immense complexity of the material in question.[171]

Textual Certainties

But these observations are not meant to suggest that we languish in ignorance concerning the theology of the early church. Paul's use of the Old Testament prophets shows, without a shadow of doubt, the dependence of the early church on these writings. Indeed, we know that the whole of Judaism fed off these Scriptures. Every member of the covenant community drank in from its streams of warning, comfort, encouragement, and hope, gathering at least weekly to hear them read, be taught from their pages, and sing their Psalms in worship. It is these writings that saturate the New Testament literature.

Not only were the New Testament letters written to communities outside of Palestine, which had immediate access to the text of the OT, but it is these writings that Paul explicitly states are those which are fulfilled in the person and work of Jesus, the Son of David.[172] It is from these Scriptures that the apostles taught—not from any of the Palestinian perspectives, but from the perspective that Jesus himself had used.[173]

I want to make it clear that the problem I have is not with NT scholarship using the research being done in the area of intertestamental literature nor in Hellenism for that matter, but in the way that the research is used. Many of the arguments lack the rigorous scrutiny that is demanded if they are to be used as keys for understanding the New Testament.

Thus, I am not saying that ITL texts cannot help us to understand the Scriptures, for it is clear that they provide the historic context and details of wider cultural issues etc., but I am saying that they can help us to understand the theology that the apostles taught in only a very limited way. This is for the simple reason that these texts did not belong to the emerging Christian

---

[171] Wright, *People of God,* 119 says: 'We have learned that we must not glibly pass over differences of setting and time, imagining continuity of thought between documents of different provenance.'

[172] Rom 1:3ff.; 1 Cor 15:3.

[173] C. Dodd, *According to the Scriptures: The Substructure of New Testament Theology* (London: Nisbet, 1952), passim, acknowledges that the New Testament way of reading the Old Testament shows every evidence of being the interpretation of Jesus himself.

community but to other communities who were expressing their own theological convictions. These communities were often avowed opponents of the new movement and they denounced its teaching. To identify how they understood a term and then to transfer that meaning over as the/a key to support a preferred understanding of what the apostles taught makes no sense to me at all. My position is not that I am saying they cannot be used because they are not Scripture, I am saying that they have not emerged from the community that was taught by the apostles and that their narrative and inevitably their theology was different from that held by the Christian community. Because they were written in the same language and discuss the same subjects at about the same time, it is easy to think that the discussions are in parallel and the words that they use have the same meaning as those used by the apostles; but they rarely are.

The Example of Other Disciplines

An example of the danger of uncritically using this material can be given by comparing the research methods by a group of social anthropologists. Let us say that a group of researchers decide to study an unreached tribe in a remote area. The community has always lived in complete isolation, even from the nearest tribes. This people group had arrived by sea hundreds of years earlier and because of their aggressive rejection of anyone from outside their own community they had no social or intellectual contact with any other tribe in the locality.

These scholars amazingly find a way to contact the tribe and over a long period of time they win their confidence and are allowed first to visit them and then eventually to stay with them. First, they begin to observe the tribe's behaviour and customs, and then to try to interpret the meaning of their ceremonies. One of their number suggested the meaning of one of their rituals by drawing on what he has witnessed in a neighbouring tribe. The team leader immediately stopped the conversation, for he had seen the danger of this. He explained that a meaning provided by another tribe could not be the solution, for the ritual being observed had not originated with that other tribe. Only this tribe's explanation of what the ritual meant would be valid. If the other tribe's solution was taken as valid, no further attempt to get at the truth would be made, and so the danger existed that the actual meaning of the ritual would forever be lost to subsequent scholarship.

This is why I challenge the use of ITL as a key to NT studies. Through this literature, we do not hear the voice of the Christian community, we hear the voice of other communities and some are even their opponents. In thinking that an answer has been given we stop searching and this can be disastrous in scholarly terms.

So, my argument is not that these texts cannot be used because they are not inspired or because they are not Holy Scripture. My argument is applicable to any other discipline where texts from different communities are being used to find a greater understanding of the beliefs or understanding of a different community. In the case we are considering it is simply that texts that NT scholars are introducing are not the texts of the early Christian community. The early church lived under the authority of the apostles who in turn lived under the authority of Christ. He had taught them how they should read their own sacred texts, i.e. the OT, the writings of the Law and the Prophets. If we stop searching for better meanings within their heritage, we will be in danger of never being able to progress. This is because we will have discounted the prime importance of their own texts and of making the writings of other communities the hermeneutical key. We are in danger of constructing arguments that are not advancing our understanding of early Christian beliefs but of producing a regression from the correct understanding of the early communities' understanding. Thus, my case is not built on theological prejudice or naivety, it is built out a desire for scholarly integrity.

I can hear the cry 'but these primary texts have been studied for two thousand years and we have not advanced, how can we stay in this impasse for any longer'?

My reply is that I am not persuaded that we have studied the OT and it relation to the NT as thoroughly as we should. If you carry on reading this book you will find that I offer an understanding of the atonement that has not been offered before. It is based on what I see is a key text in the book of Ezekiel. I was asked recently why this text had been overlooked and its importance missed, and I could not answer. I decided to look into this and searched through the works of the Patristic fathers, then the reformers, and on into the puritans and I found something that surprised me. The book of Ezekiel had virtually been ignored by all of these good people. Vital texts that were crucial keys had not been considered. Clearly modern OT scholars have studied them, but they were not looking for how they supplied understanding to the New Testament writers.[174] Their interest had naturally been about how the people of Ezekiel's day would have understood the prophet. So, instead of focusing on OT texts, the texts that the early Christians were taught from and which they heard read to them every Sabbath, many scholars have turned to the ITL and constructed their understanding and answers with the aid of these writings.

Summing Up My Case

So, my case is that before the texts of any other community are used to understand the apostolic position, the full collection of the early church's sacred Scriptures should be searched and assessed for their influence on the apostolic teachers. I intend to show that when this is done, much more compelling arguments can be constructed from these sadly neglected sacred and authoritative texts of the early church than have been achieved by introducing the understanding of other Jewish communities.

Throughout this chapter, I have sought to help the reader understand how to think for themselves by understanding the issue of rules of evidence and how arguments are constructed, not only in the theological realm, but in all literary and historical research. My claim has been that Wright has inadvertently written views of Jesus and Paul that are flawed, that is, they would not be recognised by the apostolic church. This is since they did not appeal to the sources he cites and on which (despite his protestations to the contrary), he builds his case. In his use of ITL, Wright has made a statement that completely denies his claim that the ITL only illustrates his case and has not affected his view of either Jesus or Paul. Wright has written:

> So I believe the explosion of study of Second Temple Judaism in
> our day enables us to go behind the received ways in which we
> have understood the words, sentences, paragraphs, and chapters of

---

[174] The librarian of one theological school told me that students had noticed the separation of the disciplines in the thinking of their professors. They sought to correct this by putting up notices at the end of the library book stacks. The one at the end of the New Testament stack said 'To all New Testament staff, this way to the OT section' with an arrow to direct. They had also put a similar notice at the end of the Old Testament stack saying, 'To all Old Testament staff, this way to the New Testament section'. I am glad to say this is increasingly less characteristic of theological studies and that Wright is certainly one who knows the locations very well.

the NT. We are enabled to discover meaning in our beloved
Gospels, and hence meanings in our beloved Jesus, which we had
never suspected and which may again prove quite
revolutionary.[175]

What Wright says here is not about just identifying the correct context so
that we do not get things wrong. He is saying that by knowing non-Christian
texts, indeed in most cases the texts of communities that were avowed
enemies of the fledgling church enables us to 'discover meaning in our
beloved Gospels, etc.' He is contending that Second Temple literature
fundamentally changes our interpretations, and I cannot see how it can mean
anything less than that it changes the message the apostles delivered to the
church.

Thus, my case is that Wright, along with many other sincere believing
scholars engaged in biblical research, weaves ideas from extra-biblical
literature into the biblical (OT and NT) story line. This understanding is
falsely attributed to Jesus and Paul so transforming the actual worldviews of
them both, even though, supposedly, they have not actually read the texts. So,
in that sense, whether he means to or not, Wright is using ITL as an
interpretive tool. He goes beyond showing supposed helpful parallels to claim
that some of this ITL shaped Jesus' and Paul's mindsets. This alternative
mindset created through the influence of ITL on some very important issues,
clearly, from what Wright has stated, function as an interpretive key.

Conclusion

I have attempted to evaluate the value of intertestamental literature for New
Testament research, seeing that, while it appears to be a collection of
expectations shared by a number of distinct groups, the details were
interpreted by each group in its own distinct way. Their common terminology
is not evidence of a common theology, and therefore, intertestamental
literature is of only limited value for New Testament research.

What the intertestamental literature does provide is evidence as to how
widely different themes were used and discussed, but it does not give us the
details we need to map the theology of these documents accurately. We have
seen in chapters four and five that the key to the New Testament is the Old

---

[175] N.T. Wright, "Jesus and the Identity of God", *NT Wright Page,* Originally
published in Ex Auditu 1998, 14, http://ntwrightpage.com/2016/07/12/jesus-
and-the-identity-of-god/.

Testament. It is, therefore, the message of the Old Testament Scriptures that should be used as the theological key to New Testament and particularly Pauline thought.

But the introduction and acceptance of intertestamental texts into New Testament studies has not only led to confusion over what the apostles were teaching, it has given a platform for those who oppose the message of Scripture. Bart Ehrman, for example, has been able to marshal arguments that those believing scholars who have accepted the validity of these texts find very hard to refute. And they will continue to find their defence of the authority of Scripture overpowered because they have ceased to stand on the same ground that the apostles stood, in being totally committed to the Scriptures that the apostles were committed to. In accepting other texts as keys to the interpretation of the New Testament they have lowered the writings of the apostles to the same level as any other religious writer of the time, they have no divine authority for they merely express the opinion of humans.

The amalgamation of the texts of other communities with the Scriptures of the early Christian community has not enhanced the message of the latter nor has it clarified it for its adherents today; for, sadly, they have abandoned its unique authority and the power it brings to the lives of true believers. It is these same intertestamental texts that have opened the doors wide for radical feminists and other opponents of the authority of the Bible to again produce a 'Christian' message from the first century that is totally different from that which the apostles proclaimed, and which transformed individuals, communities and eventually nations.

Chapter 7:
Probing Paul's Understanding of the Person of Christ (Christology)

I understand Tom Wright to be a committed Trinitarian; indeed, there can be no doubt about this. He has consistently called his readers to submit to Christ's Lordship and claims for him the title of Lord of all Creation. There is nothing that I would want to challenge about his teaching in this area. Nevertheless, I feel that his dependence on the intertestamental texts as indicators of apostolic understanding has caused him to miss important parts of the Old Testament picture of Christ which I believe—contrary to the opinion of many—the early church would have grasped.

Wright sees Paul to have inherited his understanding of who Christ is from a range of sources. The first must be from his encounter with the risen Christ on the road to Damascus. The second came from his profound knowledge of the OT and the third from the traditions he inherited from the teaching of the apostles. Wright understands Paul took this 'primitive' understanding of the person of Christ and added to it by bringing his wider insights that he had developed through his knowledge of Hellenistic Judaism which produced an understanding of Christ that served the mission of evangelizing the gentiles more effectively. As Wright sees that Paul has built on this foundation it would be wise to examine the nature of these Hellenistic influences.

Like many others, and it is clearly part of the presentation made in all four Gospels, Wright identifies the importance of the Son of Man figure in Daniel 7:22 as the key Old Testament figure with whom Jesus identified.[176] The evidence that Jesus referred to himself as the Son of Man is supported by the title's inclusion in each of the four Gospels. It was once thought that the term was used as a cover for his divine identity, but in recent years, this 'incognito' explanation has been dropped as a result of closer research. I will return to this theme shortly as I think that Wright has not entirely grasped its

---

[176] See Wright, *Victory,* 501–2.

implication. Many understand the term as a reference to Jesus's humanity, but even this explanation does not match all the facts.

Wright has also identified the messianic significance of the title 'Christ'. Before his DPhil thesis in which he explored the significance and meaning of the term, it was seen by most to be nothing more than a surname for Jesus.[177]Wright, in his thesis, convincingly showed that the term was understood as a messianic title; so, the words 'Jesus Christ' conveyed the meaning 'Jesus who is the Christ.' This linked into the theme of the promised Davidic king, and so his observations expanded the significance of the references to Jesus being of the house of David. This understanding of Christ being a king has become widely accepted today, although when Wright wrote his thesis it was not so. This is another key area for which biblical scholarship is indebted to Wright.

Wright also recognized Paul's use of the Old Testament Shema, 'Hear, O Israel: The Lord our God, the Lord is one' (Deut 6:4) in 1 Corinthians 8:6, 'yet for us there is one God, the Father, from whom are all things and for whom we exist, and one Lord, Jesus Christ, through whom are all things and through whom we exist'[178] This was a huge contribution to the evidence that the early church had a Trinitarian-shaped understanding of the person of Jesus, for in this confession, he is identified with Israel's God in a full ontological sense.

An Incomplete Narrative

Having outlined Wright's superb contribution in this subject, why do I think Wright's understanding of the biblical evidence remains incomplete?

In Jesus and the Victory of God, Wright makes it clear that his goal is to locate Jesus's self-understanding in both the history of his growing self-awareness and in the context and limitations of first century Judaism. Guided by typical Enlightenment understanding (of which he is normally critical), he begins his construction of Jesus's understanding of himself by noting that he saw himself as a prophetic figure, with a mission to declare God's word to Israel; a message about the imminent coming of God's kingdom. I have no

---

[177] Wright, *The Messiah and the People of God: A Study in Pauline Theology with Particular Reference to the Argument of the Epistle to the Romans* (D.Phil., University of Oxford, 1980).

[178] Wright, *Victory of God,* 147–197.

problem with Wright picking up on this theme, it is certainly part of the evidence that must be considered, but by making this his starting point for Jesus self-awareness he has missed vitally important material that would have led to significant awareness in Jesus's self-understanding.

At some indefinable point, but linked with his impending journey to Jerusalem, Wright says that Jesus began to sense his call to be the Son of God. This term, used in all three of the Synoptic Gospels, has nothing to do with Jesus being the second person of the Trinity; it refers instead to the Old Testament king, who was titled God's son. This is shown in the coronation Psalm, where it says, 'I will tell of the decree: The Lord said to me, "You are my Son; today I have begotten you"' (Ps 2:7). With this awareness, he had a growing sense of the need or inevitability of his death to bring about the creation of a new community, which would be under a new covenant.

In attempting to explain how Jesus came to know he was the Son of God, Wright says that:

> Jesus did not, in other words, "know that he was God" in the same way that one knows one is male or female, hungry or thirsty, or that one ate an orange an hour ago. His "knowledge" was of a more risky, but perhaps more significant, sort: like knowing that one is loved. One cannot "prove" it except by living by it.[179]

In other words, Jesus was driven by something akin to a hunch. The problem with this is that many others have had similar senses of this awareness and were shown to be wrong. Obviously, the resurrection vindicated this conviction, but we are presented with a picture of Jesus, who before he was raised was very much in the dark as to who he was.[180]

---

[179] Wright, *Victory of God,* 653.

[180] I am not sure why Wright has built Jesus's call to be the King of the Jews on such a subjective model. His ancestry would surely have caused any Jewish boy to ask himself if he was the anticipated Messiah, and certainly what he would have learned about the prophecies given at his birth would have propelled him to such a conclusion. But Wright seems to overlap his definition of Jesus's self-awareness as the Messiah with that of the ontological meaning of the term. Wright describes Jesus' self-knowledge of his Messiahship as being rooted in his baptism and ties the experience into a sense of calling to be a prophet and king to Israel to bring God's word to her (*Victory of God,* 536). This understanding of Messiahship has absolutely no ontological significance, Jesus is nothing more than a man called to a

Thus, with the absence of a definite Trinitarian understanding in the Synoptic Gospels, Wright has chosen to follow the evolutionary model that others have followed to trace Jesus's spiritual development into full self-awareness.[181] The German scholars argued, as Wright has, that Jesus did not know himself to be God, but only knew of his identity as a prophet.[182] This is surprising because Wright distances himself from the methods that these scholars have developed. He goes on to diverge from the liberal view in holding that after his death and resurrection both he and the church came to see that he was more than a prophet or even a (the) messiah—claiming, contrary to liberal scholarship, that he came to know that he was God himself. According to Wright, both Jesus and the disciples arrived at this understanding at approximately the same time! Jesus immediately by his resurrection and the disciples from his presence, the Spirit, and their teaching and the insights of the Old Testament.

The traditional liberal argument is that it took decades for the church to elevate Jesus to the status of being God because of the need to present him as such to win gentiles. The Messiah they preached had to match the gods that the gentiles worshiped. Thus, the liberal argument is that Jesus did not understand his status in the way that the church later came to understand it—he was only a human being, albeit a human being with a divine call to be a

---

particular task. There is nothing in this evolutionary understanding that most liberal scholars would disagree with, even though they might argue that his sense of call was psychological rather than being a call from God. Wright is very clear that there was no awareness in Jesus's understanding concerning his eternal being or nature, Jesus's understanding is limited to a more developed understanding of Messiahship than any other had come to ('if Jesus was Messiah, he was a Messiah with a great difference. But Messiah was what he claimed to be' Wright, *Victory of God,* 539).

[181] Jesus did not, in other words, "know that he was God" in the same way that one knows one is male or female, hungry or thirsty, or that one ate an orange an hour ago. His "knowledge" was of a more risky, but perhaps more significant, sort: like knowing that one is loved. One cannot "prove" it except by living by it.' Wright, *Victory of God,* 653.

[182] This method of argument is followed by other modern scholars such as J. Dunn, *Christology in the Making: A New Testament Inquiry into the Origins of the Doctrine of the Incarnation. 2nd edition.* (London: SCM, 1989); M. Casey, *From Jewish Prophet to Gentile God: The Origins and Development of New Testament Christology* (Cambridge; Louisville, 1991); KT: J. Clarke & Co; Westminster/J. Knox Press; and Reginald Fuller, *The Foundations of New Testament Christology* (London: Lutterworth, 1965).

prophet. But somehow Wright stands with their evolutionary approach and this means that the disciples came to know more about the true person of Jesus only days after he had discovered it for himself through his resurrection!

Jesus and His Call to Preach

One important observation to note is that even in following this evolutionary model, Wright claims that Jesus's understanding of his mission and identity is rooted in his sense of a call to preach. This is surprising because he has ignored the important evidence that the birth narratives and Jesus's visit to the temple at the age of twelve provide. Elsewhere Wright has asserted his acceptance of the historicity of the birth narratives but claims that they could be removed, and it would not change his or the church's faith concerning the message of Jesus. I believe this is a fundamental error and will seek to show how important these texts are for establishing a correct understanding of the apostolic Christology.

Wright's construction has the church discovering these truths of who Jesus is very soon after the resurrection, but the model still sentences Jesus to ignorance over his true identity prior to his resurrection. This is most unfortunate because to his credit, not only does Wright reject the hypothesis that the later gentile communities composed the gospels, but his argument in Jesus and the Victory of God shows that he believes in the historic reliability of the Synoptic Gospels. He demonstrates throughout this work that statements attributed to Jesus could only make sense in the time-slot of Jesus's life—it would make no sense for them to have been invented by a later generation of Christians.

However, Wright's claim that Jesus's self-understanding was limited to the idea that he was a Jewish prophet/king who was dying for the sake of Israel, is for me, inadequate.[183] Wright says that in dying for Israel he was

---

[183] 'Jesus would die for Israel bearing her fate like the Martyrs', so Wright, *Victory of God*, 569, 582–4, 608. 'Jesus believed he would suffer the fate that was hanging over Jerusalem; indeed, that he would suffer so that she might avoid it.' Wright, *Victory of God,* 571 says that 'The saying does not carry any sort of atonement-theology such as characterized the church's understanding of Jesus' death from very early on. Indeed, it holds out no hope of rescue, only the warning that what is happening to Jesus is a foretaste of what will happen to many more young Jews in the not too distant future. It belongs, not with even the earliest post-Easter reflection on Jesus' crucifixion, but exactly where Luke places it. Its value in our current quest is therefore

liberating her to do God's work of taking the good news to the nations and in this sense he died for the world, but in Wright's opinion Jesus had no understanding of a developed doctrine of atonement, and saw his death as being for Israel alone.[184] Wright is clearly building here on an evolutionary understanding of Jesus growing self-awareness, and only in the restricted categories of the prophet and the king. Unfortunately, in seeking to limit his evidence to what is historically feasible to avoid clashing with historians claiming that he was building his argument on confessions rather than textual evidence, he has adopted some of the elements of the liberalism that he has rejected. Under this model, it was the early church that identified, at a remarkable speed, that Jesus is the incarnation of God. Wright says that this was something that Jesus never knew as a man on earth. I find serious tension here.

Wright's methodological decision of attributing to Jesus nothing more than a prophetic consciousness, has in my opinion, left a serious weakness in his work and its value is seriously reduced because it has left a door open for a view of Jesus that is not satisfactory. Knowing that historians would challenge confessional arguments concerning Jesus's self-understanding, he sought a way around the problem. His solution was to assert that Jesus would have known nothing more than what a deeply religious person, particularly one who thought he was called to be a prophet, might be reasonably supposed to have known in his circumstances.[185] Hence, Jesus could not have known of his 'divinity', but Wright was willing to accept that Jesus could have had

---

simple and powerful. It suggests, in its dark riddling way, that Jesus understood his death as being organically linked with the fate of the nation. He was dying as their rejected king, who had offered the way of peace which the city had rejected; as the representative king, taking Israel's suffering upon himself, though not here even with any hint that Israel would thereby escape.' Wright, *Victory of God,* 570 says that 'Jesus believed he would suffer the fate that was hanging over Jerusalem; indeed, that he would suffer so that she might avoid it.' And finally, Wright, says that 'Matthew is not suggesting that Jesus' death will accomplish an abstract atonement, but that it will be the means of rescuing YHWH's people from their exilic plight.' Wright, *Victory of God,* 561.

[184] Jesus, therefore, was not offering an abstract atonement theology: he was identifying himself with the sufferings of Israel.' Wright, *Victory of God,* 592.

[185] Wright states, 'I do not think Jesus knew he was God': N. T. Wright, *The Challenge of Jesus: Rediscovering Who Jesus Was and Is* (London: IVP, 1999), 121.

knowledge of future events which any prophetic figure might have had. Many, for instance, in both OT and NT predicted the eventual fall of Jerusalem, since due to Israel's increasing demand for independence, such an outcome could have been seen as inevitable.

In making these restrictions on the self-understanding and foreknowledge of Jesus, Wright has conceded far too much to the historical lobby and this concession was not necessary. For example, the Old Testament clearly predicted the inclusion of the gentiles into the new covenant community.[186] It is, therefore, reasonable to claim—even under the model Wright has chosen—that if Jesus was interpreting his death in the light of these Scriptures, then he could see that his death would have a 'universal' atoning significance. If the Jews needed to be reconciled to God, the gentles certainly did. Could Jesus really have thought that his death was needed to deal with Israel's sins but that it was not necessary for the sins of the nations? Wright's model means that Jesus saw that the gentiles would be saved in a different way from how the Jews were to be saved, for his death was for them alone. For Israel, the provision was a sacrifice of atonement, for the gentiles, an invitation to covenant membership without a sacrificial requirement.

Of course, the idea that Jesus was aware of his divinity is an issue that historians simply cannot pass judgment on for it is outside their field of competence. Their role is to investigate the quality of evidence for a claimed historical event and to draw conclusions with an open mind that must not be controlled by their prejudices. Once they have identified the validity of an event, are they are at liberty to interpret its meaning and significance, but they have no greater authority in this area than anyone else who gives an opinion. It would have been better for Wright to have acknowledged this and put the issue of Jesus's self-knowledge to one side. This would have been a more honest approach, but because he has chosen to construct a picture of Jesus that he thinks historians could accept he has spoiled the otherwise excellent work *Jesus and the Victory of God*.

At this point we must reflect on Wright's claim that Jesus saw his death to be about bringing to completion the New Exodus, for this requires some qualification. Wright claims that the Jews believed they were still in exile and from this he suggests that Jesus intended to end this exile through his example and death. However, there is no evidence that Jesus ever understood that either his death or his ministry was to bring about a political or geographical

---

[186] Psa 22:27; 45:17; 72:11; 86:9; Isaiah 1:10; 2:2; 42:1; 49:6; 52:15; 60:3.

solution to Israel's predicament. Jesus repeatedly rejected Jewish nationalism and the elevation of Israel, even though John the Baptist may have expected something like it (Matt 11:2–18). Jesus never shared this mindset; his mission was not about national political fulfilment but about bringing a remnant out from under the rule of Satan. While Wright does recognize that Jesus had come to do battle with Satan, who was behind Israel's condition, salvation is still about bringing Israel out of her exile.[187] For Jesus, the purpose of his death was far more significant than Wright claims.

Jesus bequeathed to the apostles a new way of understanding prophetic fulfilment which was not about vindicating Israel, but about judging Israel and bringing from her embers a new community in which gentiles shared as full members of the family of Abraham and that looked for an eternal city where they would know the presence of God. The exclusive attention to the salvation of Israel that Wright claims Jesus pursued is contrary to his teaching of the inclusion of the gentiles in the kingdom he had come to establish. This understanding is reflected in Matthew 19:28: 'Jesus said to them, "Truly, I say to you, in the new world, when the Son of Man will sit on his glorious throne, you who have followed me will also sit on twelve thrones, judging the twelve tribes of Israel'". Here, Jesus clearly anticipates the regeneration of all things (the KJV translates *paliggenesa* as rebirth or regeneration in Matt 19:28; see also Tit 3:5). This is a thread of the Pauline doctrine of the new creation (2 Cor 5:17), which is, again, heavily rooted in Isaianic new (second) exodus expectations. This rebirth is far more glorious than many Christians today believe it to be; it is the rebirth of the entire created order, as predicted by the prophet (Isa 11:6–9; 40:3; 41:18–20; 43:19–21).[188] It is clear that Isaiah saw the gentiles as equal partners in this new covenant community without converting to Judaism (Isa 2:1–5; 19:23–24). Jesus clearly held that the gentiles would also be part of this renewed people of God (Matt 24:14–31; 25:32; Luke 11:31; 14:15–24).

---

[187] As recognised by Wright, *Victory of God*, 462, but still focusing on the preservation of Jerusalem. See also Wright, *The Meaning of Jesus,* 48.

[188] Wright sees the essence of the new creation to be about people's hearts made new and learning to love others that bring about profound change in those they have contact with, See M. J. Borg and N. T. Wright, *The Meaning of Jesus,* (New York: Harper One, 1999), 105.

Jesus and the Maccabean Martyrs

Wright says that the source for Jesus's understanding of what his death was for and what it would achieve comes from the Jewish intertestamental book of Maccabees. The four books of Maccabees are crucial sources for Wright's analysis of Jesus's mindset. Two of these books are especially important, namely 2 and 4 Maccabees, which were about a group of men who lived about 200 years before Jesus and who led a rebellion against their Greek oppressors.[189] They believed that their sacrificial deaths could turn away God's wrath from Israel and so bring her salvation. Wright believes these stories influenced both Jesus's view of his person, (i.e. his own identity) and mission, as well as Paul's construction of the work of Christ. As this chapter is about Jesus's understanding and whether he viewed himself in the context of the Maccabean story, it is not appropriate to discuss Paul's perspective at this point, but I will do so in the next chapter. In fact, there is too much Maccabean material for this chapter without it becoming overly long, so I will briefly explore the heritage of the Maccabees now and save their history and theological significance for the next chapter where I will consider Paul's teaching on the atonement and how Wright claims that the apostle relied on the Maccabees story.

Wright claims that the Jewish Maccabean martyr story was widely known throughout Israel because of the annual celebration of the feast of Hanukkah.[190] This feast celebrated the rededication of the temple (Kislev 25,

---

[189] Fuller details are provided in the next chapter.

[190] 'He seems to have constructed his vocation in terms familiar in the stories of the martyrs. He would go ahead of the nation to take upon himself the judgment of which he had warned, the wrath of Rome against rebel subjects. That was what his royal vocation demanded. That, I believe, lies at the heart of the New Testament's insistence that Jesus died the death that awaited others, in order that they might not die it.' Wright, The Meaning of Jesus, 98. Wright does not claim that either Jesus or Paul had read these documents but he does insist that they would be aware of their contents. He says, 'We must remember too, that the Maccabeans were celebrated in the big annual feast of Hanukkah, causing their story to be widely known'. We will examine this claim later for it is disputed i) that the crucial 4 Maccabees had been written early enough to be part of this festival celebration in the time of Jesus and ii) That the celebration had two versions and the zealot version was not widely known as Wright claims. If Saul had not been a zealot as I have earlier argued, then the version of Hanukkah that he would have celebrated was the

165 B.C.E.) after it had been defiled by Antiochus Epiphanes. A key part of
the story was how Jonathan Maccabeus, one of the Jewish martyrs, prayed
that his death would atone for Israel's sins as he was being put to death. It was
this powerful example of self- sacrifice for the good of the nation, Wright
says, is what inspired Jesus to die for his people. Wright reasons that this
narrative profoundly shaped the thinking of Jesus as to how Israel's exile
would be ended. It explains why Jesus sought death, for he had the hope that
like the Maccabeans, his death would save the nation from God's wrath,
which was about to be poured out through a Roman invasion and as a reward,
as was expected by the Maccabeans, he would be raised from the dead by
God.[191] Jesus believed, claims Wright, that his death would prevent God's
judgment falling on the nation.1[192]

One of the problems with this construction is that it is all of a geo-
political nature that is basically nationalistic, and it gives no hope for those
knowing that they need to be made right with God. According to this
construction Jesus did not achieve his goal, for Jerusalem fell, and with it
huge numbers died.[193] This slaughter included many who were true believers
in Israel's God and the promises he had given to his people. As Wright claims
that the only understanding that Jesus had for the reason for his death was that
by it, he would save Jerusalem from judgment, then his mission was a total
failure. It follows that the apostles attempted to present a reconstruction of the
purpose of his death that sounds like a massive PR exercise to salvage
something from the embers of the tragedy.

---

one that ignored the military achievements. Neither Paul nor Jesus were
therefore exposed to the traditions that Wright has claimed moulded their
theological thinking.

[191] Wright, *The Resurrection of the Son of God,* 175.

[192] Wright claims that the Jewish community was familiar with the martyr
tradition because Hanukkah is based on it; therefore, even if Paul or Jesus
may have never read the books of the Maccabees, they, along with other
Second Temple Jews would be familiar with the story and be aware of the
'connection of revolt against the pagans, action in the Temple, and the
establishment of a royal house would be firmly impressed on the popular
mind.' This is contrary to the evidence, see Anderson, *4 Maccabees*, 535.

[193] 'Jesus believed he would suffer the fate that was hanging over Jerusalem;
indeed, that he would suffer so that she might avoid it', Wright, *Victory of
God,* 571.

Probing Jesus and the Maccabean Tradition

We need to note that in spite of Wright's repeated protestations that he does not integrate intertestamental understanding into his theology, he is clearly doing so here. He goes back to the Maccabean texts and makes them the foundation stone of Jesus's own understanding of his identity and calling, and then in turn, he makes them the key to understand Paul's doctrine of the atonement and as we shall see, of the resurrection as well. Although Wright insists that intertestamental literature does not influence his understanding of the teaching of either the gospels or Paul, his claim cannot be sustained. He has made this clear when he wrote:

> According to the Maccabean tradition, 'the suffering and perhaps death of certain Jews could function within YHWH'S plan to redeem his people from pagan oppression: to win for them, in other words, rescue from wrath, forgiveness of sins, and covenant renewal. This by itself, I suggest, would be enough to give us some substantial clues as to the world of thought within which a prophet and would-be Messiah, in the first third of the first century, might find his own vocation being decisively shaped.[194]

Appealing to the Maccabean martyrs might at first appear reasonable. But when one examines what Jewish scholars say about the feast that celebrated the achievements of the Maccabees and what it shows concerning their understanding of the traditions and their importance for Jewish piety, the likelihood of the possible influence reduces to almost zero. We will look at the reasons for this claim in a moment, but before we do, I want to make one thing very clear.

Wright does not obliterate the influence of the OT sacrificial system, he regularly refers to it, and especially Isaiah 53, all of which, he thinks, influenced the understanding of the Maccabees. But what is clear, as shown by the above quote, is that this Old Testament heritage fades significantly into the background and Maccabees has become Wright's dominant model.

Challenges to Wright's Foundation

For us to accept that the Maccabean tradition to have had such a powerful effect on the thinking of Jesus and his disciples, it has to be shown that they would have engaged with it at some level. Wright claims that this did happen because the Maccabean martyrdom story was widely known as a result of the

---

[194] Wright, *Victory of God,* 583–4, emphasis added.

important part it played in the feast of Hanukkah which celebrated the achievements of the Maccabeans and which was remembered annually throughout Judaism.

But contrary to Wright's confidence concerning the value of the Maccabean tradition, the rabbinic sources point out that Hanukkah was one of the least important of Jewish religious celebrations and that the books of the Maccabees have never been read during this holiday.[195] Since they were written after the prophets, they were never considered to be part of the Jewish canon and therefore they never had the same authority as Scripture in Second Temple times.[196] Because they were not Torah, the moderate rabbis would not even allow them to be read in their synagogues.

Unestablished Links

Wright's claim dealt with in chapter 3 is that Saul was a zealot before becoming a disciple of Jesus. So, Wright argues that the young Saul would have been fully aware of the Maccabean traditions because they were used as models to inspire commitment to the zealot cause. It is this claim, that Paul was a zealot before becoming a disciple of Jesus that forms the evidence that Wright now builds on as he uses the tradition to develop his understanding of the significance of Jesus's death.

But we have examined this claim, and we have found serious difficulties in accepting the case that Wright has made. Without rehearsing the detail again, we found that Wright had to ignore issues that are a serious challenge to his claims. If we are to allow this link between Paul and the zealot movement to stand, we must have a better argument built on a firmer foundation. Until this evidence is provided, we must be cautious about the

---

[195] 'There is no evidence that 2 Maccabees was read publicly during the feast of Hanukkah. It is also questionable whether the book was disseminated among private readers. There is no clear sign that Philo knew 2 Maccabees (*Quod omins probus liber sit* 13.88 does not constitute evidence), and Flavius Josephus, who used 1 Maccabees as a source, ignored 2 Maccabees.' Arnaldo Momigliano and Silvi Berti, *Essays on Ancient and Modern Judaism* (Chicago: University of Chicago Press, 1995), 45.

[196] Maccabees is not found with earlier LXX texts. When they are found, they accompany LXX texts that belong to the Christian community. They were therefore not repeatedly in the hands of the Jewish leaders and so reminding them of the traditions as Wright assumes they were.

claim that Paul knew the narrative of and built on the Maccabean details that Wright has claimed.

If we accept that Saul was a disciple of Gamaliel and that because of this he would have rejected the zealot movement, then he would have been protected from this deviant tradition and its propaganda. Jewish scholars point out how the mainstream rabbis downplayed the emphasis on the military aspect in the celebration of the feast of Hanukkah by shifting the focus away from the military achievements of the Maccabees which nurtured fanaticism, saying that the victory was about truth triumphing over error. These same rabbis also created the story of the one-day supply of oil lasting eight days as a way of introducing a miraculous element into an otherwise secular holiday. In this story, when the temple was dedicated following the Maccabean conquest, there was a need for oil to burn for eight days as part of the dedication. The victorious warriors could only find enough oil to last one day. The story is told that this became the focus of a miraculous intervention by God who caused the one-day supply to last the full eight days. So, in the Talmud, the role of the Maccabees was minimized with no reference to their military victory was made and the attention was turned to the miracle that God performed for the dedication service![197]

So, contrary to Wright's claims concerning the influence of the Maccabees, there is no evidence to support his contention that Jesus or his audience would have known the last line of Mattathias' speech 'to pay back the gentiles in full, and obey the commands of the law,' as recorded in 1 Maccabees for it was never part of the celebration of Hanukkah. Nor is his claim that the knowledge of the Maccabees was so widespread that 'Jesus's

---

[197] See Why is the Book of Maccabees not read on Chanukah?, *Jewish Values Online*, http://www.jewishvaluesonline.org/565 and the many links provided to Jewish scholarly opinion on this subject. Thus, there is no guarantee concerning what degree the Jews understood the details of the storyline as described in the books of the Maccabees or whether Jesus would have necessarily known the concept of martyrs dying to save Israel in the way that Wright suggests. There is no evidence that Paul, as an orthodox Pharisee, would have ever read the book of Maccabees since it was not part of the Torah. Interestingly, the Jewish religious leaders were warned not to read Ben Sirach as it was seen as a dangerous book! Wright would have avoided this error if he had followed his own reflections concerning the danger of making sweeping generalizations given to his readers in his *Faithfulness of God,* 108–9.

cryptic saying' about giving to Caesar what was due to him would be understood as a 'coded and subversive echo of Mattathias' last words'; that 'the words Jesus said would, prima facie, have been heard as revolutionary'; or that Jesus was advocating a different kind of revolution that 'subverted the blasphemous claims of Caesar and the compromises of the present temple hierarchy, and the dreams of the revolutionaries' proven.[198] If these books were not read during the feast of Hanukkah, as is evident from the Talmud, then it is entirely speculative to claim that Jesus was familiar with the books of the Maccabees. Wright has read an awful lot to into Jesus's saying about Caesar.

Another problem with this favoured model is the dating of the texts commonly known as 1, 2, 3 and 4 Maccabees.[199] This collection of accounts about the persecution of the Jews and the emergence of the Maccabean dynasty were written by different authors with different interests and at different times. The book known as 4 Maccabees is the most important text for establishing the Maccabean martyrdom theology and is widely accepted to be the last of the four documents to have been written. This text has been dated as written anywhere between 1st century B.C.E. and 135 C.E. So again, the evidence is far from conclusive that Jesus knew its content.[200]

---

[198] Wright, *Victory of God,* 504–7.

[199] 3 Maccabees doesn't have anything to do with the Maccabean revolt—it is about the persecution of the Jews under Ptolemy IV Philopator, decades before the Maccabee uprising.

[200]D. Campbell, 'The Rhetoric of Righteousness in Romans 3:21–26,' *Journal for the Study of the New Testament* 66 (Sheffield: Sheffield Academic Press. 1992), 102–30 [esp. 107], 130–37, 219–28. Cited by Jarvis J. Williams, *Maccabean Martyr Traditions in Paul's Theology of Atonement* (Eugene, OR: Wipf & Stock, 2010), 10. https://en.wikipedia.org/wiki/4_Maccabees claims that the book is generally dated between the 1st century B.C.E. and the 1st century ce, due to its reliance on 2 Maccabees and use by some of early Christians. It has been suggested that it was written before the persecution of the Jews under Caligula, and before the fall of Jerusalem in 70 C.E. Clearly there is too much disagreement to be confident on the book's composition and dating to make it a key text for interpreting such a key Pauline doctrine.

Theological Conflict

However, there are other reasons, apart from the dating problem (which we will return to in the next chapter), for suspecting that the wrong model has been chosen to explain the purpose and achievements of Jesus death. In his recent PhD research on the subject, Jarvis Williams, who supports the claims of the Maccabean influence, has noted that the doctrine of vicarious martyrdom is an eclectic doctrine as a result of merging Jewish traditions and Greco-Roman practices, some of which are about humans sacrificing themselves for the sake of others.[201] The significance of this observation needs to be carefully noted, for neither Williams nor Wright have appreciated it! Without the support of these extra- biblical sources in which Greco-Roman ideas are introduced into Jewish intertestamental literature, the idea that Jews could sacrifice themselves for the sins of others cannot be sustained. The doctrine depends on pagan practices of sacrifice which are found in the OT.[202] This is because the OT unequivocally condemns the practice of a humans offering themselves for others as a sin offering (Deut 12:31; 18:10; Lev 18:21; 2 Kgs 3:27; Jer 7:31; Ps 106:37–41; Hos 6:6; Mic 6:7). Could Jesus interpret his death in the light of a clearly pagan practice? Could the early (Jewish) Christian community really substitute the OT sacrificial models that had been ordained by their God with a model that was essentially pagan in its sacrificial understanding? It might be argued that Israel had yet again disobeyed the commandments that had been given for her good, but is it seriously going to be suggested that Jesus was taken up with this story of national heroism and driven by its example? Was Paul, a Hebrew of the Hebrews, who became a follower of Jesus, so easily able to step outside of the Torah's clear prohibitions? Such adaptation is beyond credibility, especially when there was a model available that was authoritative, clear and powerful— the Paschal New Exodus model, the model that we will consider in the next chapter.

Of course, it could be argued that the servant of Isaiah 53 is doing the very same thing. In the traditional understanding of this passage the servant is offering himself as a sacrifice of atonement for the sins of his people. However, this is not the problem it might first seem to be. In the OT, when

---

[201] A view endorsed by Wright, *The Resurrection of the Son of God,* 147.

[202] Jarvis J. Williams, *Traditions,* 34 says: 'However, the sacrificial death of a human for the benefit of others was not a novel concept to the writers of 2 and 4 Maccabees. In fact, the practice was ubiquitous in the Greco-Roman world.'

there was any suggestion of someone making atonement for another, it was always strictly limited to the family redeemer figure, and in the case of being a vicarious atonement, it was always the firstborn. Even with this clear designation of representation, Yahweh forbade actual human sacrifices and provided animals to take the place of the firstborn. In fact, the marvellous thing is that Yahweh himself had determined to be Israel's Redeemer (Gen 15:17–21; Isa 47:4; 49:7; 49:26; 54:5). There are other deep issues that need to be resolved about the content of Isaiah 53, but I will not raise them here as I have addressed the problems concerning the traditional reading in my book *Missing Lenses: Recovering Scripture's Radical Focus On Our Common Life In Christ* (London: Apiary Publishing, 2018).

Unworthy Examples

Another insurmountable problem with the Maccabean model lies in the supposedly high example it provided, in that their willingness to lay down their lives as martyrs is seen to have inspired Jesus. In reality, the Maccabees were a ruthless nationalistic group who murdered not only the Greeks they opposed but any Jew who got in the way of their understanding of national restoration. They were not only stained with the blood of many innocent people, but they also gloried in it. For them the kingdom of God would not be brought in through self-sacrifice for the sake of others, but through the willing self-sacrifice of warriors which was required to achieve military conquest. The kingdom which the Maccabees sought to establish and the manner through which they thought it would come was totally different from that which Christ explained and practised. 'Love your enemies, do good to those who persecute you.' How could such teaching and attitude come from such a perverse nationalistic theology? Maccabean martyr theology is simply not consistent with the doctrine of the suffering servant which Jesus identified with which is evidenced by the way he quoted key texts and applied them to himself as their fulfilment (Matt 11:2–6 cf. Isa 42:7; Luke 3:4–6 cf. Isa 40:3–5; Luke 4:18–21 cf. Isa 61:1–2). This is enforced by how the gospel writers applied the theme to him (Matt 12:15–21 cf. Isa 42:1–4; Mark 1:9–11 cf. Isa 40:3) and is shown in how he had taught his disciples to apply the servant theme to their own ministries (Matt 10:24, 26; Luke 6:20–23). The passages that he used to describe his role demonstrate that he saw his mission as that of the anticipated suffering servant of the Lord. With the Maccabean model supplanting the servant of the Lord understanding, as claimed by Wright,[203]

---

[203] Wright, *Victory of God,* 583–4.

we witness a tragedy, namely the loss of the key Old Testament theme that guided the church in her understanding of her Saviour's ministry as well as her own calling! It echoes the question of Pilate, 'Who do you want, Christ or Barabbas?'

To say that the Maccabean practice pleased God and influenced Jesus is worse than allowing David, who had slain the enemies of Israel, to build the temple of the Lord. He could not do this because his hands were stained with blood. The same principle surely applies to the Maccabees. Their hands were also stained with blood, often of innocent people, so how could they become an example to both Jesus and to Paul of how to turn the wrath of God away from Israel? The contrast between the two is that one was a ruthless warrior, who killed his enemies and was prepared to die as a sacrifice if necessary, but not voluntarily, and the one who went as a lamb to the slaughter and put himself into the hands of his enemies to die for his people. Again, the former hated his executioners, the latter prayed for their forgiveness. The former struggled as a wild animal to be released, the latter went as a lamb to the slaughter. There is absolutely no echo of the former in the latter at all, only its repudiation.

A further problem for the Maccabean model is that if it was guiding Jesus as he approached his death, why didn't he arrange his last meal with the disciples on the night of Hanukkah. If this is the key to understanding Jesus's mindset, then it has to be asked why this feast was not chosen by Jesus to illustrate the meaning of his coming death? Instead, he explained his death and its significance right in the centre of the Passover celebration. All of the Gospel writers, as well as Paul, saw this as the key detail for understanding how Jesus viewed what his coming death was for. To lose sight of this and replace it with a different construct, and one that had its origins in pagan atonement theory, is to give evidence of a breakdown in biblical understanding and therefore the loss of a proper understanding of the Bible's theology. The only support that the advocates have for appealing to Maccabean martyr theology is that Jonathan Maccabeus prayed that his death would be accepted as an atonement for the nation's sins. This was not a voluntary sin offering but an attempt to turn a violent life and now death into something useful; a sacrifice that could not be accepted because it was far from being without blemish. It is the use of the term hilasterion ('sacrifice of atonement'), so NIV, as a propitiation by his blood, so ESV, found in Romans 3:25 that is the link that supporters of influence of the Maccabean story on Jesus believe establishes their case. But the different contexts, not the similarity of a single word, are what prove decisive. They accept the exodus echoes in Romans 3:21–26 but reject its control over the hilasterion term as in their thinking there is no atonement in the Passover. However, I will show that this is a mistaken understanding as we look at the Roman passage in our next chapter.

There is simply no evidence that a Maccabean theme, never mind a Maccabean text, is present in the NT, nor is there even one example that shows Jesus intended to use it as a model for his death. The reasons for its absence are obvious. First, the scarcity of ITL in the NT is a clear indication of the early church's indifference to its content.[204] Second, it presented a doctrine of human sacrifice for atonement that was abhorrent to both the OT and NT Jewish authors. Third, it promoted a kingdom that was so utterly different from that proclaimed by Jesus. Fourth, it gloried in unashamed nationalism and promoted violence as a legitimate means of achieving its goals. And fifth, the availability of the book and therefore its claimed influence in the days of Jesus, is far from certain; it is quite possible that it was written decades after the life of Jesus had passed. For these reasons it should be rejected outright as a source of building our understanding of what influenced Jesus as he thought about what his mission was about.

The way that this model has been so uncritically accommodated into biblical theology as the source of Jesus's and Paul's understanding of the atonement presents a clear warning of the danger of utilizing sources from outside of the Christian community, as I warned in chapter six. What is surprising regarding this Maccabean martyr theology is that proponents of this view have assumed the actual historical or theological background of 4 Maccabees and have failed to test it before accepting it as evidence for the way the wider Jewish community viewed the achievements of the Maccabees. It is assumed that the tradition given in the four books, though different, are historically accurate and that they were read and celebrated so widely that evidence regarding their supposed influence has not needed to be thoroughly investigated and tested, a crucial failure that calls into

---

[204] The one apparent exception is Jude 14–15 citing Enoch (1 Enoch 1:9 or 1 Enoch 2:1 depending on the translation). Such an exception leads me to suggest that Jude is not citing the text of 1 Enoch but that both are citing a common or similar oral tradition. question the unsubstantiated claims made for its contribution to New Testament understanding of atonement theology.

Textual Concerns

But another problem for this solution is the fact that the Maccabean prayers, which contain the key hilasterion term, were not recorded until well after the event and possibly over two hundred years later.[205] The fact is widely accepted that its author was an unknown, but very gifted, Hellenized Jewish writer who lived outside of Palestine and who wrote the history without citing either his sources or any evidence to support his account. Thus, we have no independent record of what was actually said other than what is in 4 Maccabees, and this was compiled so late after the event that it cannot be trusted. Even if the earliest possible date for its writing is chosen, and the evidence of its widespread influence is very fragile, Wright's case still must be questioned.

As we have noted, there is evidence that the Jewish community was deeply divided over what the zealot movement achieved. What we do know is that at some undefined point the Maccabees became a model for the zealot movement to inspire its members to sacrifice themselves for their cause. The book appears to be addressed to those who appealed for peaceful coexistence with Rome, as it presents the Maccabees as true believers who were an inspiration to those who wanted to be faithful to their God. The zealot movement brought Israel into unbelievable suffering, since Rome took action against Israel as a whole rather than the specific zealot 'trouble makers', and this inevitably led to deep resentment.

As we have no clear evidence for the dating of 4 Maccabees, I would suggest that it is very reasonable to postulate that the document was written as part of a PR campaign that would put their actions in a favourable light with the Jewish community, in that God supposedly delighted in and validated their commitment. Such an account would have been written to inspire the zealots and silence their critics.

If this is the setting and the purpose behind the writing, then there is no need to insist on an early date for its composition. Supporting this proposal, H. Anderson notes that 4 Maccabees has a good deal of authorial licence as the account is clearly embellished to give the best impression.[206] Wright

---

[205] Campbell, *Rhetoric, appendix II,* who dates it circa 135 C.E.

[206] H. Anderson, '4 Maccabees', 531–564, in J. Charlesworth, ed. (1985) *The Old Testament Pseudepigrapha and the New Testament: Prolegomena for the Study of Christian Origins* (Harrisburg: Trinity, 1985; Second Edition 1998),

himself concedes the poor evidence to support an early dating and defends its relevance and value saying, 'What matters here is not so much what actually happened as the way in which the stories of martyrdom were written up retrospectively.'[207] In light of this we must ask why there has not been the required scrutiny concerning these documents and their contents.[208]

Why haven't the voices that opposed the zealot movement been considered? To build the NT doctrine of atonement on the evidence of these texts is a betrayal of the early churches commitment to the Old Testament as a testimony to Jesus and his work. Anderson is also uncertain over the accuracy of the accounts saying, 'Whether these stories have a genuine historical foundation in genuine historical fact is an open question.'[209] Indeed Anderson had earlier said, 'The possibility, therefore, that 4 Maccabees was in fact composed as a fictive discourse cannot be lightly dismissed.'[210] This admission is very significant for the discussion of Wright's construction because Anderson is a world recognized authority on 4 Maccabees. The date of a late composition for 4 Maccabees is supported by the fact that it was never used in any account of the celebration of Hanukkah, and just as significant, it was not found in the library of the Qumran community.[211] This

---

537: 'The basic materials for his martyrdom stories were most probably derived from the tradition embedded in 2 Maccabees, although our author has patently stretched them and adorned them at will to suit his own philosophical and theological purposes, particularly in the speeches he has placed on the lips of the dying martyrs'. Anderson goes on to say, 'Whether these stories have a foundation in genuine historical fact is an open question. If we have no means of approving their historicity, neither should we reject them out of hand as completely legendary.'

[207] Wright, *Victory of God,* 582.

[208] Wright, *Victory of God,* 582 refers to 4 Maccabees as 'more or less contemporary with the time of Jesus'. This is far too casual for such crucial evidence for something that has supposedly influenced both Jesus and Paul so deeply.

[209] Anderson, '4 Maccabees', 537.

[210] Anderson, '4 Maccabees', 536.

[211] Shira Lander, 'Martyrdom in Jewish Traditions,' A paper delivered to the Bishops Committee on Ecumenical and Interreligious Affairs and the National Council of Synagogues, December 11, 2003. In footnote 4 she says that there are 'Major problems with using Maccabees as "Jewish," not the least of which is no ancient versions found (e.g. at Qumran); although the references to the Maccabean shrine in Antioch as Jewish suggests otherwise

later fact is most significant for it suggests that the document was not available until after the community was dispersed as a result of their justified fear of the advancing Romans. Added to these factual details concerning dating of 4 Maccabeans is the that Flavius Josephus never cites from nor mentions the book once, something that is most surprising in the light of his enthusiasm for citing other Maccabean texts. This all challenges the early dating for the work which Wright's thesis requires if his claims are to be ratified as historically founded. Without the availability of 4 Maccabees for his sources, important areas of the theology of Wright simply crumble.

Thus, my proposal, that the book was written as part of a PR effort to win favour for the struggling zealot movement after the fall of Jerusalem has better evidence for its authenticity than anything that Wright has provided to support his own position. Indeed, he sees no need to defend his position because he does not see that it needs to be defended! Wright is far from being alone in being in this position and it is only because the hypothesis has not been properly tested that many New Testament scholarship embrace Maccabees as a key for reading the New Testament.

So, with all of these details considered, can we really have confidence in the claim that 4 Maccabees guided or influenced Jesus in his understanding of his mission to die? What we have here is the presumption of influence built on an early dating of 4 Maccabees that would support the existence of these teachings before the ministry of Jesus and so influence him, even though there is no unanimity over a correct dating. What has also been deliberately ignored is the historical trustworthiness of the crucial account of 4 Maccabees.[212]

This is a very similar situation to that of another famous and respected theologian, Rudolf Bultmann. He had decided that Mithraism, an ancient Roman religion, had preceded Christianity and that the teachers of the church had used their practices and teachings to explain the Christian message to people who were already familiar with their cult. The effect was that Mithraism dominated the interpretation of the New Testament and changed its meaning and significance drastically, leading to a devastating scepticism toward the Bible's authority and message. The church in the West has not recovered from this tearing down of biblical confidence to this day.

(Chrysostom/Augustine).' However, the two authorities Lander refers to are very late, Chrysostom c. 349–407 and Augustine 354–430, too late to overturn the late date hypothesis presented here

[212] For evidence supplied by the Patristic Fathers see pages 384-385.

Bultmann's scholarship dominated Europe and North America for decades until someone thought the claims he had built his understanding on needed to be examined more closely. This researcher found that Bultmann had made one fundamental mistake. He had presupposed Christianity followed Mithraism when in fact the evidence showed that it was the other way around. It was Mithraism that had borrowed and adapted the church's teaching rather than the church had borrowed theirs. Bultmann's arguments crumbled and few would give his conclusions much time today.

In a similar way, without the historic evidence, Maccabees is being foisted on the NT to control the meaning of one of its most important teachings, the significance and achievements of the death of Jesus. Wright treats the case he makes as established and is so confident in it that he ignores all other views when there are equally reputable scholars who disagree with the claim that Maccabees has influenced New Testament theology. Williams has surveyed the positions of 48 scholars[213] and found that 36 conclude that there is no influence,[214] he finds that 2 accept some influence but this does not extend to sacrificial language.[215] Finally, he finds 10 who accept that there is sacrificial language influence.[216] With such division in the scholarly community it is surely incumbent on Wright to establish his case for

---

[213] J. J. Williams, *Traditions,* 15–26.

[214] These include Ethelbert Stauffer, Leon Morris, Theofried Baumeister, Ralph P. Martin, Stanley E. Porter, Nico S. L. Fryer, Cilliers Breytenback, G. K. Beale, Bradley H. McLean, Wolfgang Kraus, Douglas A. Campbell, Margret E. Thrall, Peter Stuhlmacher, Stephen H. Stravis, Douglas J. Moo, Kenneth Grayston, Danile P. Bailey, Thomas Knöppler, Daniel Stökl Ben Ezra, Tom Holland, W. Sanday and A. C. Headlam, Hastings Rashdall, Jacques Dupont, C. E. B. Cranfield, I. Howard Marshall, Robert J. Daly, Otfied Hofus, Christopher A. Davis, Seyoon Kim, Paul Barnett, Thomas R. Schreiner, J. D. G. Dunn, Scot McKnight, L. Arik Greenberg and Robert Jewett. This list needs to be treated cautiously because while Williams gives them this listing he often goes on to qualify a degree of support for a contributory role of martyr theology. I take Sanday and Headlam as two scholars holding this position.

[215] Sam K Williams, David Seeley.

[216] David Hill, J. C. Beker, John S. Pober, Theofried Baumeister, Warren Joel Heard, Gerhard Barth, Joseph A. Fitzmyer, Stephen Anthony Cummins, Daniel G. Powers, N. T. Wright.

Maccabean influence beyond a sweeping assertion backed up with a deafening silence regarding the evidence.

There are other issues about the use of this literature and I shall return to it in the next chapter when I shall be discussing Paul's understanding of the death of Jesus.

An Alternative Reading

I want to suggest that by reading the evidence through the Paschal New Exodus prism the perspective and meaning of what Paul, and Jesus, were saying becomes much, much, clearer.[217] I have written extensively on how the early church saw Jesus to be the Passover sacrifice that took away their sins. Something of this idea is present in the opening of Matthew and Luke, where—in each nativity narrative—there are heavy hints concerning the destiny of the baby Jesus, and these hints are linked with the expectation of the fulfilment of Israel's long promised redemption, the Second Exodus.

Matthew 1:25 says, 'but knew her not until she had given birth to a son. And he called his name Jesus'. The mention of Jesus being the firstborn of Mary is sometimes overlooked; nevertheless, the passage stresses that Jesus was her first child. Because of this implied status, some modern translations have felt it is virtually repetitive and have dropped the word 'firstborn' entirely.

There is a solitary second century copy of the Gospel which omits the term probably because the scribe considered it redundant (the text had already made clear that Jesus was Mary's first child). This one omission has provided the only justification for the NIV, NET, and NAS, to remove this well-established reading. Such flimsy textual evidence would never normally be sufficient to overturn the testimony of so many reliable manuscripts. Fortunately, the parallel in Luke 2:7 NIV ('and she gave birth to her firstborn, a son') has no textual evidence to support its removal, and so firstborn stays in all modern translations.

So, what is the function of this term in the accounts of the two Gospels? In both openings, Jesus has been presented as the descendant of David, who would bring about Israel's salvation (Matt 1:17; 2:3–6; Luke 2:4; 3:31). Remembering that the Davidic king was called God's firstborn (Ps 89:27), the

---

[217] See Holland, Contours; and Romans: The Divine Marriage.

child is being presented as the one who would be at the centre of Yahweh's universal rule. It was this Davidic king who would provide the eschatological paschal sacrifices. The 'firstborn' would be Yahweh's King, his Son, who would redeem his people.

A very important fact that every Jew knew, but which is almost universally missed by Christian commentators, is that in the Old Testament, every firstborn male had to be redeemed. This fact was so well known because every Jewish couple was obliged to redeem their firstborn son, or he ceased to be theirs and he became the Lord's, and in turn, he became part of the priestly community. If the redemption was not enacted, they had to give their only son up to be trained for the priesthood in the temple. The omission of this crucial detail in Jesus's story is hugely significant.

The redemption of a firstborn did not require a visit to the temple; only the payment of half a shekel of silver to a rabbi was required.[218] This fact becomes significant in Luke's account of Jesus's presentation in the temple; for strangely, although Jesus was brought to the temple (which the law did not require), there is no explicit mention of him being redeemed.

This reading is supported by the Magnificat, Mary's song about Gabriel's announcement of her coming conception (Luke 1:46–55). Her song was based on the one that Hannah sang (1 Sam 2:1–11) after she had dedicated her firstborn, Samuel, to the Lord to become a priest in the Tabernacle (1 Sam 1:27–28).

This understanding of the text is supported by Luke's unfolding narrative, when at the age of twelve, Jesus was mystified by his parents' concerns about his presence in the temple. He asked them, 'Why were you looking for me? Did you not know that I must be in my Father's house?' (Luke 2:49). In other

---

[218] Following the arrangement for the first Passover these laws changed. From that time on there was not the requirement of a Levite to substitute for each firstborn, but he would have been redeemed like the sons who following the Passover were redeemed with a half shekel of silver, see S. Schechter, J.H. Greenstone, 'First-Born, Redemption Of:', *Jewish Encyclopaedia,* http://www.jewishencyclopedia.com/articles/6138-first- born-redemption-of, a practice that continues to this day, and Rabbi S. Simmons, 'Pidyon Ha'ben - Redemption of First Born,' *aish.com.* http://www.aish.com/jl/l/b/ Pidyon_Haben_-_Redemption_of_First_Born.html. Thus, it was a ritual Jesus as Mary's firstborn would have had to have shared in if he was to remain her son. His dedication in the temple, something not required in the law, suggests a special significance in what was taking place.

words, 'you know whom you have dedicated me to. Why are you surprised to find me here? Like Samuel, the other unredeemed firstborn, whose mother's song inspired you, my place is in the house of the Lord'.

The priestly status of the Lord's firstborn comes out again in Luke. He records, 'Now Jesus's mother and brothers came to see him, but they were not able to get near him because of the crowd. Someone told him, "Your mother and your brothers are standing outside, desiring to see you." But he answered them, "My mother and my brothers are those who hear the word of God and do it"' (Luke 8:20– 21). In other words, 'I do not adhere to natural family relationships. I was not redeemed at birth, and so I belong to the Lord'.

Added to these priestly themes in Luke is the fact that his relative, John, was born to an Aaronic priestly couple, Elizabeth and Zechariah. Elizabeth is Mary's kinswoman, suggesting that Jesus was, in some way, linked by blood to Aaron. This possibility is not raised in Luke's Gospel—perhaps because it would detract from the theme of Jesus's priesthood being in the order of Melchizedeck, a priesthood which is not dependent on lineage.

The Son of Man Theme

Jesus uses the Son of Man title to point to his ministry as the promised eschatological priest in Mark 2:23–28. Here, Jesus allows his disciples to pluck corn on the Sabbath day, and he is criticized by the Jewish leaders for allowing them to break the law. His response to this criticism was:

> Have you never read what David did, when he was in need and was hungry, he and those who were with him: how he entered the house of God, in the time of Abiathar the high priest, and ate the bread of the Presence, which it is not lawful for any but the priests to eat, and also gave it to those who were with him?" And he said to them, "The Sabbath was made for man, not man for the Sabbath. So the Son of Man is lord even of the Sabbath". (Mark 2:23–28)

What is significant is that, in claiming authority to let the disciples do something that the law prohibited (working on the Sabbath), Jesus is not appealing to the actions of David, as is often supposed, but to that of Abiathar, the high priest. Hence, he likens his authority to that of high priest, who permitted David and his men to eat the holy shew bread, in apparent contradiction to the law. If this reading is correct, then Jesus, in this particular passage, is not claiming to be the Davidic king but the high priest.[219] Of course, these offices of king and priest are combined in Melchizedek.

Wright rightly identifies the Son of Man motif as a key paradigm for Jesus's self-understanding. However, Wright's emphasis is that the Son of Man is the judge. This is, of course, true; but it is also true that the Son of Man is seen by the majority of Old Testament scholars to be a priestly figure, and that is why he stands before the throne of the Almighty (Dan 7:13), interceding for Yahweh's suffering people. So, here we find another link with the priestly theme that our examination of the nativity narratives has uncovered.

However, this is not the end of the matter, for an examination of how Jesus used the Son of Man designation reveals that it functions in some defined ways.

First, Jesus said that the Son of Man has no possessions; nowhere to lay his head, something even the foxes have (Matt 8:20). This corresponds to the fact that the Levites, the priestly community, were not allowed to possess an inheritance, 'Therefore Levi has no portion or inheritance with his brothers. The Lord is his inheritance, as the Lord your God said to him' (Deut 10:9).

Second, Jesus spoke of the Son of Man forgiving sins (Matt 9:6; Mark 2:10). The pronouncement of cleansing and absolution was—in the Old Testament—the role of the priest alone; here Jesus is claiming it for himself.

Third, another theme of Jesus's Son of Man sayings was that he would come with the angels in judgment (Matt 16:27). The priesthood was the community designated to act as Israel's judge in the Old Testament (Deut 17:8–13; 21:5; Ezek 44:24), and the function was still bound up with the priestly community in New Testament times. Jesus, for instance, was judged by the high priest, and the priests sat in judgment on the disciples (Acts 4:1, 6–7).

The fourth theme is that the Son of Man was to give his life as a ransom, 'For even the Son of Man came not to be served but to serve, and to give his

---

[219] This possible priestly theme is strengthened by the introduction to Mark 2 where Jesus repeatedly performs miracles which made people clean (Mark 1:21–28; 29–34; 40–45) and his pronouncement that he forgave sins (Mark 2:8–12). These are functions of the priest alone (Lev 14:1), no other person was given this authority, not even the Davidic King.

life as a ransom for many' (Mark 10:45). Here, Hooker's observation is that Mark 10:45 has associations with the Passover. She noted that, in the whole of biblical history, it is the only event where one life was substituted for another in an act of redemption. In other words, there had to be one Levite to represent one firstborn.[220]

When the number of firstborn was established to be greater than the number of Levites, each firstborn without a representative had to be redeemed by the payment of half a shekel of silver. The point is that, in contrast to the many individual substitutions required in the Old Testament Passover narrative, the Son of Man, as a priestly person, represents many in his death. This arrangement turns all who have been redeemed by the Son of Man into a priestly community.

The link between the Son of Man and the Passover event is more sharply defined in Matthew's account: 'You know that after two days the Passover is coming, and the Son of Man will be delivered up to be crucified' (Matt 26:2). This is a regular theme of John's gospel, too, where the Son of Man and Passover themes are intertwined throughout (Passover: John 2:13, 23; 6:4; 11:55; 12:1; 13:1; 18:28, 39; 19:14. Son of Man: John 1:51; 3:13, 14; 5:27; 6:27, 53, 62; 8:28; 9:35; 12:23, 34; 13:31).

Scholars have long been aware that the Son of Man sayings are only found in the Gospels and that they are always Jesus's self-description. In other words, no one ever addresses Jesus as the Son of Man. Even outside of the Gospels there is clear reluctance to call him this, suggesting that the church respected the term as a self-designation. Its use was, for some reason, a 'no go area' for the development of the community's growing awareness of who Jesus was.

However, there are four references which, while they do not directly call Jesus the Son of Man, have distinct echoes of the title. The first of these is in Acts 7:56, where Jesus is described as 'the Son of Man who stands before the throne of God'—a clear echo of Daniel 7:13. The statement is generally agreed not to be a direct messianic statement but merely a description of the exalted Jesus.

> But he, full of the Holy Spirit, gazed into heaven and saw the
> glory of God, and Jesus standing at the right hand of God. And he

---

[220] M. Hooker, Jesus and the Servant: The Influence of the Servant Concept of Deutero- Isaiah in the New Testament (London: SPCK, 1959), 77.

said, "Behold, I see the heavens opened, and the Son of Man standing at the right hand of God" (Acts 7:55–56).

The second text that reflects the Son of Man theme is:

For there is one God, and there is one mediator between God and men, the man Christ Jesus, who gave himself as a ransom for all, which is the testimony given at the proper time. (1 Tim 2:5–6)

The third passage that reflects this theme is Hebrews 2:6,

It has been testified somewhere, What is man, that you are mindful of him, or the son of man, that you care for him? You made him for a little while lower than the angels; you have crowned him with glory and honour, putting everything in subjection under his feet. Now in putting everything in subjection to him, he left nothing outside his control. At present, we do not yet see everything in subjection to him. But we see him who for a little while was made lower than the angels, namely Jesus, crowned with glory and honour because of the suffering of death, so that by the grace of God he might taste death for everyone. (Heb 2:6–9)

The final passage, outside of the Gospels, is Revelation 1:13. We shall cite the wider context of this description. It is set in imagery that is clearly a reflection of the Son of Man imagery from Daniel 7.

Reflections on the Evidence

The most significant common feature of these four passages is that Jesus is described in priestly terms. Most scholars agree that in Acts 7:56, because Jesus is standing before the throne of God and interceding, he is functioning as a priest. The passage has distinct echoes of Daniel 7:13, which is about Israel's priest interceding for the suffering people whom he represents. Here is a similar priestly person, also described as the Son of Man, who functions in the same way.

The passage in 1 Timothy 2:5 is widely acknowledged by scholars to echo Mark 10:45; indeed, the Timothy passage is considered to be a Hellenized confessional form of the passage in Mark. What is clear is that, in the Timothy passage, Jesus is a mediator between God and man, and is, therefore, functioning as a priest. Also, as we noted earlier, Hooker recognized the paschal background to Mark 10:45. She noted that, in the Passover, because the firstborn were spared the judgment they were designated to bear, they were taken by the Lord to be the priestly community.

However, rather than take Israel's firstborn from her families, the Lord substituted the tribe of Levi in their place. The replacement was precise; it was one Levite for one firstborn son. The Levites were counted and so were the delivered firstborn. The lack of the number of Levites to substitute on a one to one replacement had to be compensated for by the payment of half a shekel of silver (see Num 3:45–48). Here, in 1 Timothy 2:5, it is the death of this priest who has redeemed a new priestly community. Regardless of these supporting background details, what is clear is that the passage is describing Jesus as a mediator—a high priest, who has given his life as a ransom for many.

Hebrews 2 is not so straight forward because scholars point out that the statement is, in fact, a quotation of Psalm 8, and speaks of mankind as appointed to be God's representative. The title 'son of man', as used in the Psalm, is therefore not messianic; it is a generic statement describing humanity. This observation of the term's meaning in Psalm 8 is correct, but it does not consider its new context in the letter to the Hebrews. Clearly, the author is using the quote as an introduction to a passage explaining the role of Jesus as the one who has tasted death for all men in order to become their faithful high priest (Heb 2:17). The passage points out that while man is not ruling—as described in Psalm 8—Jesus, the eschatological Son of Man, is. He is the forerunner of those he calls brothers, and these will share in his glory (Heb 2:10–16). This imagery of the Son of Man prepares for a discussion about Jesus as the one who is the Melchizedek high priest (Heb 5:6–10). In this passage, the theme continues that of Hebrews 2:10–16. He is the one who dies in the place of his brothers; and this is repeated in Hebrews 5:6–10, where Jesus is the Melchizedek priest.

Thus, while the quote from Psalm 8 is a generic reference to man being the son of man, its application by the writer to the Hebrews has elevated it to function with a messianic significance. It is, of course, true that rabbinic tradition sees Adam as a priestly figure. But this specific use of Psalm 8 is Christ-centred in terms of what he, as the Saviour of his brothers, has achieved. All this is because he functions as a priest, and so the term Son of Man combined with the idea of a king who was crowned with glory and honour for achieving the work of the great high priest.

When we consider the use of Son of Man in Revelation 1, we first notice that the reference to 'one like the Son of Man' is made within a context that is heavily laden with exodus and paschal (Passover) terminology.

To him who loves us and has freed us from our sins by his blood;

> and made us a kingdom, priests to his God and Father, to him be glory and dominion forever and ever. Amen. Behold, he is coming with the clouds, and every eye will see him, even those who pierced him, and all tribes of the earth will wail on account of him. Even so. Amen. (Rev 1:5–7)

> And in the midst of the lampstands one like a son of man, clothed with a long robe and with a golden sash around his chest. (Rev 1:13)

This Son of Man is dressed in what are, very clearly, priestly garments, and he represents his people before God. The themes of Passover and firstborn are very similar to those found in the other non-gospel passages that we have considered, and this suggests that they were widely known and understood throughout the early church.

The significance of all this is that, while everyone notes the priestly theme in Hebrews, few, if any, have seen how widely it is found throughout the New Testament writings. I want to argue that this theme of the priesthood of Jesus is much more powerful than that of his prophetic role. It is in this theme that the provision of a sacrifice is embedded, for this is what the priestly theme is all about—it is about a cleansed people being represented before God.

What is important to note is that this theme was embedded in Jesus's self-designation as the Son of Man. The sense of his priestly calling goes back to, at least, Luke 2:49. This is the earliest record of Jesus's words, and they were focused on his priestly calling. It is here—contrary to Wright's view—that any attempt to understand what Jesus thought about himself must begin.

The songs of the early church were also focused on Jesus Christ. In his excellent book, Worship in the Early Church, Ralph Martin says, 'The Christ-centred nature of Christian worship is one of the most clearly attested facts of the New Testament literature'. Almost all the New Testament hymns refer directly or indirectly to who Christ was or to what he did. These songs preserve the very earliest confessions of the believers' faith in Jesus and hence they serve as the litmus paper for testing a correct understanding of the rest of New Testament Christology.

In other words, if we think that the Son of Man's priestly status was linked by the early church with his work as redeemer—the firstborn of his people—then we should be able to find support for this idea in the liturgical confessions of the early church.

The Testimony of Early Christian Hymns

It is important to note the content of the apostles' preaching in order to identify the themes that occupied their interests and concerns. But it is important to keep in mind that their worship summarized their teaching, for it expressed what they had come to know about Jesus, their Lord and Saviour.

There are four recognized hymns in the New Testament: the Colossian hymn (Col 1:13–20), the Philippian hymn (Phil 2:6–10), the Hebrew hymn (Heb 1:3–6), and the Apocalypse hymn (Rev 1:5–18). We will examine each of these hymns in turn.

The Colossian hymn says:

> He has delivered us from the domain of darkness and transferred us to the kingdom of his beloved Son, in whom we have redemption, the forgiveness of sins. He is the image of the invisible God, the firstborn of all creation. For by him all things were created, in heaven and on earth, visible and invisible, whether thrones or dominions or rulers or authorities—all things were created through him and for him. And he is before all things, and in him all things hold together. And he is the head of the body, the church. He is the beginning, the firstborn from the dead, that in everything he might be preeminent. For in him all the fullness of God was pleased to dwell, and through him to reconcile to himself all things, whether on earth or in heaven, making peace by the blood of his cross. (Col 1:13–20)

First, some initial observations. The first two verses are generally not seen to be part of the original hymn and appear to have been added by Paul. The theme of these two verses, which speak of rescue, redemption, and forgiveness are widely seen to pick up on the exodus event. For this reason, they are normally seen to be based on a 'New Exodus motif.

Many scholars see the reference to Jesus as the Creator, who is head over all things and to have been composed to show the gentile world that Jesus is superior to any of the gods that they worship.

The reference to Jesus being 'the head of the body, the church' is considered by many to indicate an advanced Christology that was not possible to formulate in the first century. This was because of the church's limited philosophical vocabulary and inability to think of Jesus in such cosmological terms.

The reference to Jesus being 'the firstborn from the dead' reflects the church's worship of him as the Messianic conqueror of all things, including the great enemy of death.

The reconciliation of 'all things' in the final stanza is, again, argued to be too high a Christology for the first century church to grasp, let alone to have developed.

Now, I am in agreement with almost all that Wright has said about this hymn. I applaud him for challenging the widely-held consensus that Paul never wrote the letter, saying that he saw no reason why it could not have been written by him. However, as I will show, I think the evidence for Pauline authorship is even stronger than he has described.

My central disagreement with Wright is over how he has interpreted the phrase 'firstborn over all creation'. Wright argues that the phrase is rooted in Jewish Hellenistic literature (another example of his commitment to these non-Christian texts). In the Wisdom of Solomon,[221] wisdom is described in lofty terms as a heavenly being, who was present with God in his act of creation and who has become personified, appearing among humans.

Now, undeniably, there are themes in the Wisdom of Solomon that could be identified with the wisdom theology of John's Gospel, except that there is one huge difference. In Greek thought, anything that is material is evil or sinful. Only spirit is pure and good. John says that the Logos (he does not actually call Jesus the wisdom of God) 'became flesh'. At this point, all the Greeks would have left the room!

The idea of spirit and flesh being combined is just not something that Greek thinkers could give their assent to, as witnessed when Paul preached the resurrection on Mars Hill (Acts 17:22–34). His hearers mocked him, as resurrection for a Greek is not salvation but a restoration to enslavement, returning the spirit to the corrupt human existence of the body. Wisdom could never become flesh in Greek thought.

However, the connection between 'firstborn' and 'wisdom' is not as clear as has been claimed. Philo called wisdom the protogonos (elder brother), whereas Paul calls Jesus the firstborn *prōtotokos*. Also, the Colossian hymn links the firstborn with redemption (1:13) and reconciliation (1:20), themes that have absolutely nothing to do with Greek wisdom in any shape or form.

---

[221] Wright, *Justification,* 132.

This raises a question: 'Why should we import meanings from Hellenism when the passage is so heavily impregnated with Old Testament sacrificial language and the two just do not correlate?' Wisdom and sacrifice have nothing in common. Because of their very strong antithesis, the wisdom meaning of firstborn must be questioned. However, if we do not accept this wisdom meaning for firstborn, where do we turn for a better understanding?

We have already noted the presence of the Passover theme in Paul's description of the death of Jesus (cf. our exegesis of Rom 3:21–26). We have also noted that the introduction to the Colossian hymn is based on a New Exodus theme. Also, we must remember that it is widely accepted that any introduction is intended to guide the reader in the understanding of the on-going argument. Also, the conclusion of any work serves as a summation of what the reader should have understood in the main body of the work. Thus, the introduction and conclusion to any work are crucially important for gaining a correct understanding.

So, what does this introduction to the Colossian hymn guide us to? It has to be the Passover and the role of the firstborn. Christian tradition has focused on Jesus being the Lamb of God, linking his death with the blood smeared on the doorposts and lintels on that momentous night. That is understandable as there are references that suggest this meaning elsewhere in the New Testament. However, the statement that Christ is the firstborn of (or over) all creation goes beyond the symbolism of the lamb. It points to the one the lamb represented—the firstborn.

It was the firstborn's death that was at the heart of the Passover. As we have seen, he was spared that sentence by the provision of a substitute, the lamb. If the lamb had not died; the firstborn would have died. Even though the lambs died for the Jewish families to protect their firstborn, Yahweh still claimed the firstborn as his own, and exchanged the tribe of Levi as their substitutes. So, there was an extended and ongoing substitution of the firstborn, and, most interestingly, their service in the tabernacle, was to make atonement for the people (Num 8:19).

And so, as Paul calls Jesus 'the firstborn of all creation', he is saying that Christ's death was not just for his family (see Rom 8:28; Heb 2:11–15; Rev 1:5–6).

Now, as the introduction tells us how to read the body of the text, so the conclusion tells us what we should have understood by reading it. The conclusion of the Colossian hymn fully supports the interpretation of the term 'firstborn of all creation' in the Passover context. Since this idea is preceded by a New Exodus theme, the text naturally links it to the Passover sacrifice and reveals that Jesus's death was not for his family alone but for the whole of creation. He is the firstborn of all creation because he reconciles all things to himself, 'whether things on earth or things in heaven, by making peace through his blood, shed on the cross' (Col 1:13 NIV). This is the inheritance man lost through Adam, which was cursed because of human sin and guilt. This lost inheritance has now been restored for Christ's death has reversed the tragedy of Adam's sin.

The Strange Case of the Missing Redeemer

This reading is upheld by the strange anomaly of the 'missing redeemer' in the New Testament. Throughout the Old Testament, Yahweh is presented as Israel's Redeemer. His work is described in terms of what the eldest son of the Jewish family (the *go'el*, the firstborn and redeemer), was to do on behalf of his family.

His first responsibility was securing revenge for the family. When a member was murdered, the redeemer's duty was to exact blood- vengeance on the guilty party—the law of retribution meant that the responsibility rested on his shoulders (Gen 4:14–15). I am claiming that this messianic redemptive concept is bound up with the title of firstborn (Gen 4:24; Num 35:16–21; Deut 19:4–7).

In the latter part of Isaiah, where Yahweh is often called the Redeemer, Yahweh promised to act as the avenger of his people (Isa 43:3–4, 14–15; 47:4; 49:25–26; 59:16–20). In the New Testament, Christ himself is presented as fulfilling this same role (Luke 1:68–79; 18:7; 2 Thess 1:6–9; Rev 6:9–11).

The second role of the firstborn/redeemer in the Old Testament was that of securing property, which had been lost to the family through debt. Hence in Ruth 4:4, Boaz requested Naomi's nearest kinsman to act as the redeemer to secure the family's field. In Leviticus 25:8–34, the principle of Jubilee is outlined. It fell to the 'nearest relative' to act, whenever possible, as the Redeemer, to recover the family's property (v. 25).

Once again, we find Yahweh promising to act as Israel's Redeemer; thereby securing for her the land she had lost (Isa 51:11; 52:8–10). In the New Testament, we find this role attributed to Christ, who recovers the kingdom of heaven for those who were deprived of it by sin (Col 1:13–14; Heb 9:15; Rev 21:1–4).

The third role of the redeemer was to fulfil the law of the levirate.[222] This law appointed the redeemer to act as the protector of the widow in the family. If a woman was widowed and childless, it was the responsibility of the redeemer to take her as his wife and raise up a family on behalf of his deceased brother (Deut 25:5–10; Ruth 3:13; 4:1–8).

Once again, an aspect of the redeemer's role is used to illustrate the salvation Yahweh promised his people: 'He will save Jerusalem from her widowhood and raise up children for her' (Isa 49:20–21; 50:1–2; 54:1–8; 62:4–5). This same role is applied to Christ, who takes the church to himself and acts as her husband. Note how this fits into the concept of a second marriage in Romans 7:1–4 (also 1 Cor 6:20; Eph 5:25; Rev 19:7–8).

Although we have clear continuity with the Old Testament models of redemption, there is one incredible omission in the New Testament. Jesus is never called 'the redeemer'. His work is certainly modelled on the work of the Old Testament redeemer figure, but he is never called the redeemer. What we do find is that, in those passages describing his redeeming work, he is called 'the firstborn'. Now why should this be?

It is because the redeemer was, strictly speaking, the firstborn. In other words, the firstborn was not only spared and allowed to live with his family, but he was also given the role of being its redeemer. If he did not want to be responsible for this duty, he could abdicate it and allow the next in line to fulfil the role. Even so, although he was allowed to abdicate his responsibilities in these social functions, the eldest son could not abdicate his role on the night of the Passover. He was the designated victim, and his death was certain unless, as in the case of Isaac, the Lord provided himself with a sacrifice.

So, the firstborn is the redeemer; but in social terms he was not obliged to function as such. However, he could not give his role to another on the night of the Passover, for on that night he was to die. All the New Testament's descriptions of Christ's work as redeemer are directly linked to his passion. In that paschal event, he bore his people's guilt, released them from slavery, secured their inheritance (heaven), and took them as his bride, producing children of righteousness through his church. Therefore, he is rightly called the firstborn, because the 'redeemer' is not precise enough a term and is not

---

[222] For further discussion, see E. W. Davies, 'Ruth IV.5 and the Duties of the go'el' *VT* 33 (1983): 231–234 [232ff.] and D. R. G. Beattie, 'The Book of Ruth as Evidence for Israelite Legal Practice' *VT* 24 (1974): 251–267.

as anchored in the Passover event. He is the firstborn of all creation—totally reversing the consequences of the fall of the first Adam.

I would argue that Wright has missed this rich Old Testament heritage, opting instead for a Hellenistic solution that fails to properly explain the introduction and conclusion of the Colossian hymn, leaving the church without an adequate understanding of the work of her redeemer and a confused picture of his person.

However, there is further evidence that supports this understanding of the term 'firstborn'. We find further evidence in the Christological hymn of Philippians 2. Wright has written a significant paper on this hymn, the main portion of which examines its Adamic theme.[223]

Other scholars have undertaken similar studies, and in general most agree about the significance of Adam within the hymn (presenting Christ as the last Adam). The hymn says:

> Have this mind among yourselves, which is yours in Christ Jesus, who, though he was in the form of God, did not count equality with God a thing to be grasped, but emptied himself, by taking the form of a servant, being born in the likeness of men. And being found in human form, he humbled himself by becoming obedient to the point of death, even death on a cross. Therefore God has highly exalted him and bestowed on him the name that is above every name, so that at the name of Jesus every knee should bow, in heaven and on earth and under the earth, and every tongue confess that Jesus Christ is Lord, to the glory of God the Father. (Phil 2:4–11)

The widely-accepted comparison of Jesus, the last Adam, with the first Adam is clearly in view here. The first Adam was grasping and wanting equality with God, and the outcome was his alienation from God. Jesus, the last Adam, behaved according to his nature as God. Because of this, he has been given a name that is above all names— one to which every knee will bow. This is a clear reference to Isaiah 45:23 where every knee is to bow before Yahweh, who will not share his glory with another.

In the hymn, there is a clear reference to the death of the last Adam, 'being found in appearance as a man, he humbled himself by becoming

---

[223] N. T. Wright, 'Jesus Christ is Lord: Philippians 2.5–11' in *N. T. Wright, The Climax of the Covenant: Christ and the Law in Pauline Theology* (Edinburgh: Clark, 1991), 56–98.

obedient to death—even death on a cross'. That this death inaugurates the pilgrimage of the believing community is confirmed in verse 15, where the language of Isaiah (speaking of Israel's role to be a light to the gentiles) is pulled across to express the Philippian community's similar calling. Paul says:

> That you may be blameless and innocent, children of God without blemish in the midst of a crooked and twisted generation, among whom you shine as lights in the world. (Phil 2:15)

This pilgrimage theme is returned to in the following chapter, where Paul describes his own sense of pilgrimage and encourages the Philippian church to be similarly committed (Phil 3:12–4:1). There is clear evidence that Paul understands a pilgrimage to be in progress, with the anticipation of entry into the heavenly Zion where their citizenship resides (Phil 3:20).

This clearly echoes the pilgrimage of Israel, which was made possible by the death of the firstborn before the Egyptian exodus. The suffering and death of the servant of the Lord has brought about a Second Exodus, and this servant has been identified as the Son of David (Jesus) by Isaiah 55:3 which identifies the one who suffered in Isaiah chapter 53 that he might justify many.[224]

The message of the pilgrim community is the message of the cross; Paul defines the enemies of God's people as those who promote circumcision, rather than faith and repentance. Those who claim that they can have salvation in Moses and physical circumcision are not in a right relationship with God. Although Paul himself had once valued circumcision as much as anyone else, he now came to see it as no more than 'mutilation'.

> Brothers, I do not consider that I have made it my own. But one thing I do: forgetting what lies behind and straining forward to what lies ahead, I press on toward the goal for the prize of the upward call of God in Christ Jesus. Let those of us who are mature think this way, and if in anything you think otherwise, God will reveal that also to you. Only let us hold true to what we have attained. Brothers, join in imitating me, and keep your eyes on those who walk according to the example you have in us. For many, of whom I have often told you and now tell you even with tears, walk as enemies of the cross of Christ. Their end is

---

[224] For further discussion, see Holland, *Missing Lenses: Recovering Scripture's Radical Focus On Our Common Life In Christ* (London: Apiary Publishing, 2018).

> destruction, their god is their belly, and they glory in their shame, with minds set on earthly things. But our citizenship is in heaven, and from it we await a Saviour, the Lord Jesus Christ, who will transform our lowly body to be like his glorious body, by the power that enables him even to subject all things to himself. (Phil 3:13–21)

Thus, the flow of the Philippian letter's themes supports the suggestion that the death of the last Adam, referred to in the hymn, is as his peoples' representative. Where the first Adam alienated his family from God, the death of the last Adam restores the relationship and creates a people who acknowledge their Saviour as God. The bowing of the knee is particularly significant as it has been shown that, in the Passover, the community knelt before its God in fulfilment of Isaiah 45:23.[225]

All of the above observations, taken together, suggest that although the term 'firstborn' is not used in the Philippian hymn, the identification of Jesus as the last Adam figure, who acts as his people's firstborn-redeemer, is essentially expressing the same theology as is found in the Colossian hymn.

The next New Testament hymn to be considered forms the basis of the first chapter of Hebrews. The writer says:

> Long ago, at many times and in many ways, God spoke to our fathers by the prophets, but in these last days he has spoken to us by his Son, whom he appointed the heir of all things, through whom also he created the world. He is the radiance of the glory of God and the exact imprint of his nature, and he upholds the universe by the word of his power. After making purification for sins, he sat down at the right hand of the Majesty on high, having become as much superior to angels as the name he has inherited is more excellent than theirs. For to which of the angels did God ever say, "You are my Son, today I have begotten you"? Or again, "I will be to him a father, and he shall be to me a son"? And again, when he brings the firstborn into the world, he says, "Let all God's angels worship him." Of the angels he says, "He makes his angels winds, and his ministers a flame of fire." But of the Son he says, "Your throne, O God, is forever and ever, the sceptre of uprightness is the sceptre of your kingdom. You have loved righteousness and hated wickedness; therefore God, your God, has anointed you with the oil of gladness beyond your companions." And, "You, Lord, laid the foundation of the earth in the beginning,

---

[225] See Wright, 'Jesus Christ is Lord', in *Wright, Climax of the Covenant,* 56–98.

and the heavens are the work of your hands; they will perish, but you remain; they will all wear out like a garment, like a robe you will roll them up, like a garment they will be changed. But you are the same, and your years will have no end." And to which of the angels has he ever said, "Sit at my right hand until I make your enemies a footstool for your feet"? Are they not all ministering spirits sent out to serve for the sake of those who are to inherit Salvation? (Heb 1:1–14)

Once again, the themes found in the Colossian hymn are present here. The Son is the exact image of God (Heb 1:3, c.f. Col 1:15). He made all things (Heb 1:2, c.f. Col 1:16). He sustains all things (Heb 1:3, c.f. Col 1:17). He has provided purification for sin (Heb 1:3, c.f. Col 1:14, 20). He is the Son of God, who is the King (Heb 1:4–5, c.f. Col 1:18). He is God's firstborn, who he has brought into the world (Heb 1:6, c.f. Col 1:15, 18). He purified sin (Heb 1:3; c.f. Col 1:22). He has been exalted to the highest place (Heb 1:3, c.f. Col 1:18), and his death will bring about the renewal of all creation (Heb 1:12, c.f. Col 1:15, 20). So once again, the paschal theology found in Colossians 1:13–20 is reflected in the hymn of Hebrews 1.

The final hymn to be considered takes up a large part of the first chapter of the Revelation.

> And from Jesus Christ the faithful witness, the firstborn of the dead, and the ruler of kings on earth. To him who loves us and has freed us from our sins by his blood, and from Jesus Christ the faithful witness, the firstborn of the dead, and the ruler of kings on earth. To him who loves us and has freed us from our sins by his blood and made us a kingdom, priests to his God and Father, to him be glory and dominion forever and ever. Amen. Behold, he is coming with the clouds, and every eye will see him, even those who pierced him, and all tribes of the earth will wail on account of him. Even so, Amen. "I am the Alpha and the Omega," says the Lord God, "who is and who was and who is to come, the Almighty." (Rev 1:5–9)

> Then I turned to see the voice that was speaking to me, and on turning I saw seven golden lampstands, and in the midst of the lampstands one like a son of man, clothed with a long robe and with a golden sash around his chest. (Rev 1:13)

> Fear not, I am the first and the last, and the living one. I died, and behold I am alive forevermore, and I have the keys of Death and Hades. (Rev 1:17–18)

Once again, the paschal theme is evident; the idea of being freed as a result of the shedding of blood especially (Rev 1:5; Col 1:13, 20) has clear paschal links. Also, the fact that this event has produced a kingdom of priests (Rev 1:6) correlates with Paul's unpacking of the Colossians' hymn in Colossians 1:22–27, where the gentiles are to fulfil the priestly role of Israel—and is a definite echo of the outcome of the Egyptian exodus, where Israel was set apart as a priestly community (Exod 19:6). Note also the citation from Zechariah which is included in Revelation 1:6, 'And I will pour out on the house of David and the inhabitants of Jerusalem a spirit of grace and pleas for mercy, so that, when they look on me, on him whom they have pierced, they shall mourn for him, as one mourns for an only child, and weep bitterly over him, as one weeps over a firstborn' (Zech 12:10). The citation skilfully places the theme of 'as one grieves for a firstborn son' into a paschal theme, which re-enforces the idea of the paschal nature of Jesus's death.

The claim that the title Alpha and Omega (Rev 1:7; Col 1:18) represents a statement of Christ's divinity is supported by the fact that the title is taken from Yahweh's self-proclamation as Israel's Redeemer, 'Thus says the Lord, the King of Israel and his Redeemer, the Lord of hosts: "I am the first and I am the last; besides me there is no god"' (Isa 44:6). Here again, Jesus is being portrayed as a high priest figure; his triumph over death and his everlasting reign are both asserted (Rev 1:18; Col 1:18). As we saw earlier, the mention of Jesus as the Son of Man is significant here for the priestly theme the term carries.

So then, the outcome of our examination of these New Testament hymns is as follows: the hymns share a common theme which focuses on a community's release from captivity and its reconciliation with God. The hymns represent the heart of the early church's worship and open the door which allows us to appreciate that church's theological understanding.

Conclusion: A Choice of Two Saviours

What I find concerning about Wright's presentation of Jesus is his attempt to keep anything that he considers 'confessional' out of his exegesis of the Gospels. I believe he has made a huge mistake in doing this, for he has denied Jesus the knowledge that, even at the human level, he ought to be 'allowed' to have had.

Wright understands that Jesus could not have known that his death would be for any nation other than Israel, to fulfil her return from exile. Wright recognizes the Old Testament predictions concerning a promised Second Exodus with its new covenant was not limited to the Jews but that it would be extended to gentiles also. The Jews would take this message to the nations and so fulfil its long-forgotten mission, of being a light to the nations. This reading does not require Jesus to understand that his death was an atonement for the wrongdoing of the gentiles. It seems that all he is concerned to show is that the Jews are set free from sin and death through the death of Jesus, and this benefits the gentiles. He has no problem in seeing that Paul has argued that Jesus has died for the whole of humanity and that the whole of Scripture recognizes that the gentiles are cut off from God because of sin. However, could it really be that Jesus failed to understand that the atonement/redemption he was about to achieve would be for the gentiles as well as for the Jews? Were the gentiles to be accepted in some other way, and if they were, what was that way?

Wright's claim that Jesus did not see his death as being for any other than his own people means that the church was guilty of assigning to his work something that he never did, the salvation of the gentiles.[226] But was Jesus really only dying for Israel? How could Jesus have gotten his mission so wrong? If he was dying to save Jerusalem as Wright claims, how could he have succeeded, for the Romans did destroy it?[227]

If Jesus has got these things so badly wrong, why could he not, in Wright's construction, also get his calling and identity wrong? Rather than being what his disciples later claimed him to be, was he simply a misguided enthusiast? After all, there have been plenty of those throughout history! A salvage job by some devoted followers does not give one confidence in taking Jesus seriously. Such a disconnection between the Jesus of history and the Christ of faith smacks of marketing by a set of well-meaning but unworthy followers of the Messiah.

Wright's methodology has left us with a well-meaning leader who led his followers to disaster. If we take the positive aspect of Wright's position, in that he believes in the resurrection, then we have a Jesus, who awoke on the resurrection morning to find he had achieved far more than he ever dreamt of

---

[226]Wright, *Victory of God,* 608 says that Jesus would die for Israel bearing her fate

[227] 'Jesus believed he would suffer the fate that was hanging over Jerusalem; indeed, that he would suffer so that she might avoid it'. Wright, *Victory of God,* 571.

before he took his last breath. I do not doubt that Wright seeks a robust scholarly solution to the thorny problems of Christology that commends Christ to a sceptic world. My problem is that I am not too comfortable with the sort of Saviour he has described.

A Ministry that No Mere Man Could Fulfil

All of these observations support the idea that the high-priesthood of Jesus was a major theme of the early church's understanding of his identity. This takes us somewhat further into the mindset of the early church than Wright has so far penetrated. Jesus and his biographers all seemed to be aware that he was the promised priest which Israel had been looking for.

Moreover, it may suggest a path by which we might gain insights into the self-understanding of Jesus. By observing not only Jesus's but also the Gospel writers' critical clues at crucial stages of his life, we have evidence that he was fully aware of belonging to a community other than that of his biological siblings (Matt 12:48–50; Mark 3:32–35; Luke 8:19–21; John 2:3–5). This theme is clearly important, as all four Gospel writers raise it. In the model we have discussed above, there is no need to suggest that Jesus woke up one day with the taste of a 'spiritual orange' in his intellectual/spiritual mouth. Instead, we have identified how Jesus may, from his early years, have understood his calling to be a priest for his people; a priest who was called to fulfil a unique function that no other person could fulfil.

None of this establishes that Jesus knew himself to be God. Perhaps it is fair to say that since it would be impossible for any human to enter into the mind and experience of the incarnate God, the only evidence we can legitimately weigh in seeking to grasp this subject involves the words which Jesus used about himself.

To dismiss the doctrine because it does not match human experience is saying, albeit in a different way, that we cannot accept God is greater than man with his finite experience. We would not be sharing the faith of the apostolic community but that of the first century equivalents of modern humanists.

Of course, liberal scholarship has rejected the authenticity of many references found in the Synoptic Gospels. Those statements which say that Jesus had a unique eternal relationship with the Father are frequently rejected because they were not articulated by him. Scholars reason instead that they were the creation of later communities in an attempt to give Jesus a greater status than he had ever recognized or claimed for himself.

In responding to this, I want to ask why unbelievers should be allowed to dictate and control which evidence is, or is not, acceptable within the believing community. This is especially so when it can be shown, as we have seen, that Jesus had a profound knowledge of his mission and that, at the very least, he understood himself to be the servant of the Lord. The fact that Jesus knew his death was the essential element of the New Exodus is most significant. Only he could fulfil the Isaianic promises concerning the New Exodus that the death of the suffering servant would redeem creation.

But, of course, this is not the complete story. We know that Jesus not only knew he would eventually die, but also that he would be raised from the dead, and that his death would bring about the establishment of the promised new covenant. In seeing his mission so clearly, he would have known what the new covenant would achieve and amongst these accomplishments was the transformation of the whole created order, the regeneration of all things.

This means that Jesus knew his death would achieve far more than a mere servant could achieve. Only the Creator can redeem his creation. There is no way of squaring this circle, other than by acknowledging that Jesus saw and embraced these connections.

If this is the script that Jesus was following—and this was the script that the Old Testament prophets had written and of which he was fully aware—then we get a glimpse into his expectations and therefore his self-understanding. Perhaps we are not able to follow this line of reasoning fully, for how can we, as mere creatures, understand the self-understanding of the Creator? Even so, we may observe that none of these ideas about Jesus's understanding of his unique status and role clash in any way with the plan outlined throughout the Scriptures of Israel and the early church.

Moreover, such a construction is supported by the hymns of the early church. The one they worshipped was the one who had given up his life for their salvation. He was not just their elder brother; he was the firstborn of all creation. In a hymn powerfully rooted in Israel's history, he was not only the firstborn sacrifice, dying to protect his people, but also the firstborn of all creation. His death was about the redemption of all creation—the regeneration of all things.

Thus, the Isaianic New Exodus, which Jesus knowingly fulfilled as the servant of the Lord whose death justified many, included within its scope the redemption of creation, with all things being made new—a salvation which only the Creator can achieve. Here, I would suggest, is a very narrow window through which we can see something of Jesus's own understanding and expectations. We cannot plumb the depths of his self-understanding, but even the little we can fathom shows us that he must have seen himself to have infinitely more significance than a mere prophet from Nazareth could possibly have had.

In this proposed construction of the early church's Christological understanding, we do not depend on an evolutionary model but on one that links the understanding and confessions of the early Christian community with what Jesus understood and said about himself. If this is a valid reconstruction, then it has shown that the Christology of the early church had no need to borrow from Hellenism as Wright has done.[228] Its understanding was founded entirely in the Scriptures of Israel and the witness Jesus gave to the fulfilment of its promises.

In the Christology of Wright, the incarnate Jesus was limited with regard to knowing future events. He had no understanding that his death was for the salvation of the gentiles. Instead, Wright sees Jesus's understanding as being limited, it was only for Israel, and that his death was so that the nation might avert the impending judgment of 70 C.E..[229]

Again, according to Wright, Jesus explains his death by reference to the Maccabean martyrs,[230] who saw their deaths as necessary to avert God's

---

[228] Wright suggests that the meaning of firstborn is to be found in the Wisdom of Solomon. See Wright, *Perspectives,* 85.

[229] Wright, *Victory of God,* 592: 'There was, then, no such thing as a pre-Christian Jewish version of (what we now think of as) Pauline atonement-theology. There was a variegated multifaceted story of how the present evil exilic age could be understood, and how indeed it could be brought to an end . . . Jesus, therefore was not offering an abstract atonement theology; he was identifying himself with the sufferings of Israel. We are faced once more with appropriate similarity and the dissimilarity. The symbolism and the story-telling of Jesus make sense only within this Jewish world, but they play their own strange and unique variation of their dark theme. What Jesus did and said stands out a mile from what early Christianity said about him and his execution, but early Christian atonement theology is only fully explicable as the post-Easter rethinking of Jesus essentially pre-Easter understanding.'

[230] Wright, *Victory of God,* 465.

wrath from his disobedient people. Also, Jesus did not have a fully-developed doctrine of atonement, not even in its limited Jewish focus; it was, according to Wright, a construction of his followers in the generation after him.[231]

While Wright is totally committed to orthodoxy, he has, in fact, followed a theological method that has enslaved the human Jesus in an experience that debars him from anything other than normal human understanding. While it may avoid the need to stand against proponents of the historical method, he has at the same time surrendered that which only faith can comprehend.

The Jesus who is left is inadequate to be the Jesus of the faith of the apostolic community. Of course, Wright claims that it is within this community that the person of Jesus is defined as being the Eternal Son, so he is confessing the very same faith as the apostles. However, the reality is that this reconstruction leaves a community knowing far more about the identity of Jesus than Jesus, before his resurrection, knew about himself, and such a Jesus does not engender the sort of faith that the apostles had.

How reasonable is the narrative suggested above? How likely is it that Jesus would have identified his calling and drawn from it saw the inevitability that, in order to fulfil it, he had to be much more than a man? Was he really so subjected to the message of the Law and the Prophets that they not only shaped his thinking and understanding but also persuaded him that he was the fulfilment of all that the Scriptures pointed to (Luke 24:44)?

The scope of Jesus's mission was made clear in his early days when prophecies were made concerning him. Zechariah prophesied about his son, John (Luke 1:67–79). It is clear that there were many witnesses to his outburst, which would mean that the future ministry of John would be common knowledge. Many would have looked on with the attitude of 'watch this space'!

John the Baptist would have known about his father's prophecy, and no doubt it served as a deep influence in his development and his eventual going into the wilderness in anticipation of his call to Israel to get ready for her Messiah's coming. It is more than likely that he would have shared this with his relative, Jesus, on occasions, such as festivals, when their families met up.

---

[231] 'Matthew is not suggesting that Jesus' death will accomplish an abstract atonement, but that it will be the means of rescuing YHWH's people from their exilic plight.' Wright, *Victory of God,* 561.

His father Zechariah was filled with the Holy Spirit and prophesied:

> 'Praise be to the Lord, the God of Israel, because he has come to his people and redeemed them. He has raised up a horn of salvation for us in the house of his servant David (as he said through his holy prophets of long ago), salvation from our enemies and from the hand of all who hate us—to show mercy to our ancestors and to remember his holy covenant, the oath he swore to our father Abraham: to rescue us from the hand of our enemies, and to enable us to serve him without fear in holiness and righteousness before him all our days. And you, my child, will be called a prophet of the Most High; for you will go on before the Lord to prepare the way for him, to give his people the knowledge of salvation through the forgiveness of their sins, because of the tender mercy of our God, by which the rising sun will come to us from heaven to shine on those living in darkness and in the shadow of death, to guide our feet into the path of peace.' And the child grew and became strong in spirit; and he lived in the wilderness until he appeared publicly to Israel. (Luke 1:67–80)

It is clear from the recorded words of Jesus that he saw the great enemy of his people to be Satan, and not Herod. This means that he saw his work to be about spiritual emancipation and not political redemption. To do this would require a figure far more significant than the anticipated son of David, great though his anticipated work was expected to be. Indeed, Jesus deliberately rejected this role and insisted that his work was to die in order to inaugurate God's kingdom.

So, the sort of things that Jesus said about his saving work for his people elevates his self-understanding far beyond that of what the greatest messianic figure could ever have achieved.

I shared my understanding of Jesus being the firstborn of all creation with Wright in a letter in early 1990. He kindly replied in the May of that year and responded saying that he preferred the wisdom origin offered by C. F. Burney. Interestingly, despite his identifying strong Hebraic themes in Paul's letters, he chose not to embrace them for the Colossian letter—even though he had identified the introductory verses as based on a New Exodus motif, and therefore thoroughly Hebraic. As the introduction is always intended to guide the reading of the main theme, it is all the more surprising that it pays no contribution either to his reading of the opening verse of the hymn or to any other part of it.

Interestingly, some years later I was visiting the Tyndale Library and at the morning refreshment break I joined the queue for coffee. One of the researchers kindly engaged me in conversation, asking me about the reason for my visit. I explained to him that I was researching the theme of Jesus being the firstborn of all creation and briefly explained where my thinking had got to. I did not know who this pleasant young scholar was, but he replied, 'Why have I not heard that before? I have studied all of the literature on the subject in English, French, and German, and no one has suggested that. Yet it is obviously correct!' I went on to find his name—Christian Stettler— and that his PhD on the Colossian Hymn had been published two years earlier by a leading academic publisher and it had received excellent reviews.[232]

Since then I. Howard Marshall reviewed the argument and kindly reported that it demonstrated that the Passover had an atoning element;[233] while Anthony Thiselton, in his review, said that scholars should read what I had written in order to correct widespread misunderstandings of Paul.[234] Clearly not all scholars think that either Burney or Wright have had the last word on this subject.

---

[232] Christian Stettler, *Der Kolosserhymnus: Untersuchungen zu Form, traditionsgeschichtlichem Hintergrund und Aussage von Kol 1,15–20. WUNT 2*, 131. (Tübingen: Mohr Siebeck, 2000), 132.

[233] I. Howard Marshall, review, 'Contours of Pauline Theology: A Radical New Survey of the Influences on Paul's Biblical Writings,' *EQ* 77.3 (2005): 270–272.

[234] A. Thiselton, review, 'Contours of Pauline Theology: A Radical New Survey of the Influences on Paul's Biblical Writings,' *ExpT*, vol. 116 (Sep 2005): 425–426.

Chapter 8:
Probing Paul's Doctrine of the Atonement

Tom Wright's scholarship has achieved much good for the Anglican Communion, to which he belongs, as well as for the wider Christian community. He has directed its leaders back to a far more serious engagement with Scripture and has challenged established ways of reading the text, causing many to reflect on previously held assumptions which have not been adequately evaluated.

However, because of his exceptional academic achievements, not to mention his superb persuasive writing, preaching, and inter-personal skills, many people are prepared to accept his statements as truth, whilst not appreciating that the required supporting evidence is sometimes lacking or weak. As a consequence, in some cases, Wright's arguments have not been adequately tested. In particular, I feel that especially in his earlier writings, Wright harmed the Reformed position by frequently misrepresenting it. His sweeping claims have weakened the heritage of the Reformers' doctrine of justification with the inevitable logical conclusion that, 'if they got things so wrong over the doctrine of justification, it must cast doubt whether they

can be trusted over other doctrines.' This uncertainty has resulted in growing numbers of once Reformed believers, and especially leaders, turning to either the Roman or the Orthodox churches.[235] Some have specifically cited the influence of the New Perspective for the loss of confidence in their previously held Reformed/Protestant faith. The loss of this unique heritage to future generations of the church is serious and deeply regrettable. I am not saying that Reformed scholarship has been all that one might want it to be, but its high view of Christ and the Scripture has anchored me personally in its tradition.

---

[235] T. Marshall, 'Does N.T. Wright lead to the Catholic Church?', *Taylor Marshall PhD: Stay Salty My Friends,*
http://taylormarshall.com/2008/03/does-nt-wright-lead-to-catholic-church.html. Also see Fr John Tanveer,' Why I Became Orthodox: Part Two,' November 29, 2015, *Journey to Orthodoxy,*
http//journeytoorthodoxy.com/2015/11/why-i-became-orthodox-part-two.

The theme I want to examine in this chapter is specifically Wright's understanding of Paul's doctrine of the atonement. As indicated in the previous chapter, I believe this is a topic that demonstrates how the texts of other Jewish communities have averted his gaze (and that of many others) from the texts of the Christian community. I suggest that this re-focusing was as a result of thinking that the scholarly study of the Old Testament was exhausted and that it was no longer providing answers to the problems that needed to be solved. However, rather than resolving these problems, the introduction of Jewish texts other than the Old Testament has, I contend, seriously distorted the apostles' intended meanings. I believe the vital topic of atonement provides a good example of the inadequacy of this 'historical method', which is so widely followed by many of today's academics.

So, what is my concern? Wright most definitely believes in the central importance of the death and resurrection of Jesus. This is not disputed. What I am concerned about is how he unpacks the way the apostles understood what was happening and what was being achieved through the death of Jesus.

Sacrificial Language and the Death of Jesus

From his writings, I have always sensed that Wright was losing his way on this subject. Because of this it was not entirely surprising to hear him say, at the Tyndale Conference (Cambridge, July 2014), that while he held to substitutionary atonement, he could not understand what the New Testament does with the sacrificial language used to describe Jesus's death.[236] This was an honest admission, which many other, if they were to be equally

---

[236] He has since published on this, see N. T. Wright, *The Day the Revolution Began* (London: SPCK, 2016). He fails to engage with critical texts such as Ezek 45:21–24. Even though he notes the importance of John 3:16, he cites the passage but does not discuss the Paschal context of the discussion with Nicodemus (John 2:25). This is very important omission for it links Jesus not with the lamb but the one who the death of the lamb spares, the beloved firstborn Son whom the Father does not withhold. Nor does Wright explain how the Son is the sacrifice of atonement. His interpretation can be read as nothing more than John giving a moral argument. I believe that the New Testament has a comprehensive Paschal Atonement Theology which even though Wright has increased in awareness of its presence (See Wright, Revolution), he has missed its comprehensive nature and significance.

transparent, would need to acknowledge. What was surprising, however, was to hear him say that he did not think that this lack of clarity was important.

In recent years, evangelical scholarship has been in a state of transition on this very subject of atonement. Even the distinguished New Testament conservative scholar Leon Morris moved from his previous conviction and for a time embraced the views which Wright was eventually to hold.[237] However, Morris had second thoughts and came back to the biblically based understanding that he had previously held. What is surprising is that he never tried to establish what the model was that Paul drew upon, not even mentioning Lev 16 (the Day of Atonement) once in his entire commentary. Just as surprising is that he did not once reference any intertestamental literature of any kind, something very different from his previous works.[238]

So, what caused Leon Morris to go on this journey? It was the growing recognition that a key text, which explains the purpose of Jesus's death, did not match the Old Testament text that was thought to have influenced it. It had long been assumed that the Jewish Day of Atonement, which is described in Leviticus 16, was the event that inspired the language of Romans 3:21–26. This key New Testament passage says:

> But now the righteousness of God has been manifested apart from the law, although the law and the Prophets bear witness to it—the righteousness of God through faith in Jesus Christ for all who believe. For there is no distinction: for all have sinned and fall short of the glory of God, and are justified by his grace as a gift, through the redemption that is in Christ Jesus, whom God put forward as a propitiation by his blood, to be received by faith. This was to show God's righteousness, because in his divine forbearance he had passed over former sins. It was to show his righteousness at the present time, so that he might be just and the justifier of the one who has faith in Jesus. (Rom 3:21–26)

Morris noted that the passage spoke of the sacrifice being προτίθημι ('presented'), the Greek word meaning 'publicly displayed' or 'set forth.' Such a description could not possibly apply to the presentation of the sacrifice on the Day of Atonement. This sacrifice was not offered in public, but in the Holy of Holies by the high priest with no one else present other than God—

---

[237] L. Morris, *The Atonement: Its Meaning and Significance* (Leicester: InterVarsity, 1988), 159, 168, 198 fn 4.

[238] L. Morris, *The Epistle to the Romans* (Leicester: InterVarsity, 1988), 172–183.

indeed the smoke from the burning incense concealed the atonement cover even from the high priest. Morris, for a time, left the traditional reading and argued that the correct background was from an event recalled in 4 Maccabees 6:29. Even though Morris was not completely satisfied with this, he thought it was the best theory to explain the background to Romans 3:21–25. Eventually, however, he came to be even more dissatisfied with this than with his previous position, and so returned to his earlier understanding.

The Significance of 4 Maccabees

So, what is the argument that Wright has stayed with, even though Leon Morris could not? The answer is that while he believes that Paul's teaching drew on the Old Testament sacrificial system and Isaiah 53, he says that Paul was not directly echoing any of the Jewish sacrifices offered in the temple. Wright sees that the key influence came from writings he thinks were written much later that than Old Testament Scriptures, to an event that took place about 200 years before the apostle wrote. As we have already noted Wright considers that the Maccabean traditions are the key to how Jesus understood his death. Wright also argues that the event is an important key to understand Paul's teaching about what Christ's death has accomplished.

4 Maccabees is a document that records the painful time in Israel's history following the return from exile. After the demise of the Persian Empire, Alexander the Great established the Greek Empire as a world power. He died at the very young age of thirty-one, and the Empire was split up amongst his four generals. The most ruthless of these was Antiochus, who established what was to become known as the Seleucid Dynasty (also known as the Syrian Greek or Seleucid Greek kingdom). It was that part of the original Greek Empire of Alexander which included Palestine. Antiochus asserted his authority by demanding that all of his subjects must cease following their religions and instead obey his edicts. He required the Jews to worship his gods and then demanded that they must run naked in the athletic games he had introduced into Jerusalem. This caused most Jewish men, afraid of displaying their covenant with Yahweh (indicated by their circumcision), to find ways of hiding their badge of covenant membership.

While there were many Jewish men who were prepared to do what Antiochus demanded, there were others, admittedly a minority, who were deeply offended. The last straw came when they were made to worship Antiochus as a god. An altar was set up in every community throughout the land, and the people were ordered to come to their altar where officials would verify that, by throwing incense on the altar, they had worshipped the Emperor.

The Emergence of a 'Royal Family'.

The Maccabean story begins with the heroism of a rural priest, known as Mattathias the Hasmonean, who was called to offer the sacrifice, but he refused. In an effort to protect him from the consequences, another Jew stepped forward to make the offering on his behalf. Mattathias, indignant that anyone would worship Antiochus on his behalf, struck out and killed him. He and his five sons fled into the wilderness of Judah where Mattathias died about a year later. His son, Judah Maccabee, became the leader of the group and led an army of Jewish dissidents. They engaged in guerrilla warfare against the Seleucid dynasty for many years. The story is a fascinating episode of Jewish history, with the Jews eventually being granted freedoms that marked them out from other nations. These freedoms continued— even with the change of masters and the eventual rule of Rome—until the fall of Jerusalem in 70 C.E.

A key event in this story was when Eleazar, one of the sons of Mattathias, was put to death as a martyr. The account of his death reads as follows:

> When Eleazar had in this manner answered the exhortations of the tyrant, the spear bearers came up, and rudely haled Eleazar to the instruments of torture. And first, they stripped the old man, adorned as he was with the comeliness of piety. Then tying back his arms and hands, they disdainfully used him with stripes; a herald opposite crying out, 'Obey the commands of the king'. But Eleazar, the high-minded and truly noble, as one tortured in a dream, regarded it not all. But raising his eyes on high to heaven, the old man's flesh was stripped off by the scourges, and his blood streamed down, and his sides were pierced through. And falling upon the ground, from his body having no power to support the pains, he yet kept his reasoning upright and unbending. Then one of the harsh spear bearers leaped upon his belly as he was falling, to force him upright. But he endured the pains, and despised the cruelty, and persevered through the indignities; and like a noble athlete, the old man, when struck, vanquished his torturers. His countenance sweating, and he panting for breath, he was admired by the very torturers for his courage. Wherefore, partly in pity for his old age, partly from the sympathy of acquaintance, and partly in admiration of his endurance, some of the attendants of the king

said, 'Why do you unreasonably destroy yourself, O Eleazar, with
these miseries? We will bring you some meat cooked by yourself,
and save yourself by pretending that you have eaten swine's
flesh.' And Eleazar, as though the advice more painfully tortured
him, cried out, 'Let not us who are children of Abraham be so evil
advised as by giving way to make use of an unbecoming pretence;
for it were irrational, if having lived up to old age in all truth, and
having scrupulously guarded our character for it, we should now
turn back, and ourselves should become a pattern of impiety to the
young, as being an example of pollution eating. It would be
disgraceful if we should live on some short time, and that scorned
by all men for cowardice, and be condemned by the tyrant for
unmanliness, by not contending to the death for our divine law.
Wherefore do you, O children of Abraham, die nobly for your
religion. Ye spear bearers of the tyrant, why do ye linger?'
Beholding him so high-minded against misery, and not changing
at their pity, they led him to the fire: then with their wickedly-
contrived instruments they burnt him on the fire, and poured
stinking fluids down into his nostrils.

It is in the final words of this narrative that the key term is found which
Wright and others rely on for interpreting Romans 3:21–25. The section in
Maccabees says:

And he being at length burnt down to the bones, and about to
expire, raised his eyes Godward, and said, 'Thou knowest, O God,
that when I might have been saved, I am slain for the sake of the
law by tortures of fire. Be merciful to thy people, and be satisfied
with the punishment of me on their account. Let my blood be a
purification for them, and take my life in recompense for theirs.'
Thus speaking, the holy man departed, noble in his torments, and
even to the agonies of death resisted.

It is the presence of this technical term *hilastērion* ('propitiation') found
in 4 Maccabees as well as Romans 3:25 that has led a growing number of
scholars to conclude that this account of Eleazer's death provides the
background to the key text about the significance of Jesus's death. Thus, it is
argued that Paul presents Jesus as the perfect martyr who gave his life as a
sacrifice for his people's sins, and it is through his sufferings that God's wrath
is averted.

What was the reason for adopting this Maccabean theme? The scholars
who have subscribed to this explanation have done so because they cannot see
any other source for or solution to the use of this key Greek term in Romans
3:25. Because Wright has adopted this solution, I believe he has closed the

door to a fuller and richer understanding of Paul's handling of the subject of atonement that we shall shortly consider.

In fairness to those who hold this position, they normally don't see 4 Maccabees 6:29 as the sole influence on Paul. They see links between the death of Eleazer and Old Testament texts such as the description of the suffering servant in Isaiah 53:6. However, these Old Testament texts are often made subservient to the influence of the Maccabean text and justification for their intended link with 4 Maccabees 6:29 is not convincing because hard evidence for their association is not given. The fact is that there is no evidence for the link; it is entirely speculative. I have earlier shown how Isaiah is part of the redeemer doctrine of the OT and Maccabean martyrdom has nothing to do with this for the Old Testament repeatedly forbad the offering of any human as a sin offering.

4 Maccabees forms part of an extensive rabbinical and theological structure of atonement. In this teaching, it was claimed that the 'offering' of Isaac in Genesis 22 had been accepted by Yahweh as atonement for Israel's sins, even though Isaac never died. The doctrine, known as the Aqedah, went so far as to argue that all of the sacrifices offered in the temple were mere remembrances of the 'offering' of Isaac, and it was his willingness to die for his offspring that gave these sacrifices their efficacy. Isaac's willingness to accept martyrdom was used by the zealot movement to inspire Jews to offer up their lives for the sake of God in much the same way as modern radical Muslims are urged to sacrifice themselves and so becomes martyrs. Maccabean martyrdom theology is taken as modelled on Isaac's willingness to offer his life for the sake of his offspring—an even greater act of faith for Abraham than the giving up of his life, for Isaac, was still a young man or a boy and certainly without offspring! Of course, this is a poor adaptation as Isaac did not actually die and Yahweh commanded that no human sacrifices should be made.[239]

But another problem with adopting the Aqedah doctrine as Paul's paradigm, is the ongoing controversy regarding the dating of the various rabbinic authorities. Claims that link Paul's teaching with this understanding are contested on the basis that there is no certainty that Paul ever knew these texts. The fact is that they were not written down until the third century ce and

---

[239] For details of this Jewish teaching see Holland, *Contours,* 253–273.

there is a debate as to how reliable they are as true records of the rabbinic teaching.

However, the books of Maccabees, three of which contain the story of the Maccabean martyrs' death, do not depend on rabbinical material, as most regard the four books existed pre-Paul. As indicated in chapter 7, this is debatable as the dating of 4 Maccabees has not been properly settled. However, even if the dating could be settled as pre-Paul, to what extent the traditions of the Maccabean martyrs were known in Rome at the time of Paul's letter cannot be established. This presents a problem for scholars, for without knowing the text to which Paul was (allegedly) alluding, the Roman church he was writing to could not be expected to make the supposed connection.

Wright claims that the death of Jonathan Maccabeus, when he prayed that his death would be an atonement for the sins of Israel, was a key event that informed Jesus and Paul about the purpose of his death. Wright claims that virtually every Jew in Jesus time would have known about the martyrdom of the Maccabees and the sacrificial atoning significance their deaths were said to have had, because the event was so widely known and celebrated. The Feast of Hanukkah marked the restoration of the temple and the great victory over the foes of Israel which secured the sanctuary. While it is understandable that this event became so significant for Jewish history, and that it is celebrated, what is wrong with Wright's construction is that he has built on this event when there is considerable debate concerning the book's dating and significance. Wright neither raises nor discusses this issue, presenting his view as something that is nonexchangeable. Because the text was written by a supporter of the zealot movement it inevitably presents a one-sided picture of the significance of the event. Any responsible reading should ask questions about the accuracy of the details of the text, are they reported objectively or was the author a reliable witness. There are many Jewish examples, and this is found in most if not all religions, where texts have been fabricated to give historical support when no such credence existed. What we must do is to also listen to those who were not swept along in the euphoria of the Maccabean conquest and hear their concerns about this event and its celebration. And who can give us this material? It is the community of the rabbis who have left us a wealth of ancient writings which records their concerns and alternative understanding.

We know that the rabbinic community was divided into two main strands, those who followed Shammai who advocated violence for defending

Jewish interests and those who followed Hillel who was a pacifist. Wright has made the case that Saul (Paul) belonged to the Shammaites and argues that this was the reason he sought to kill all who belonged to the Christian community. Wright has attempted to argue that while Saul studied under Gamaliel, a follower of Hillel who promoted peaceful coexistence, that as a student rabbi he could belong to both streams at the same time, so he could simultaneously follow his teacher Gamaliel as well as share the Shammite vision and follow its militant philosophy. To support this unusual claim Wright has appealed to the example of Akiba who practiced violence contrary to the teaching of his mentor, Nehunya. I have considered this example in chapter 2 and shown that it doesn't relate to Saul's situation. Akiba never disagreed with his pacifist teacher while he was in his school as a student. He changed his view many decades later when his own followers had to defend themselves against deadly Roman aggression. Because of the high loss of life, he changed from his pacifist position and supported their right to take up arms. This does not match Saul's situation, for he had put himself as a trainee rabbi under Gamaliel, who was a follower of Hillel. I have argued that Wright's claim that Saul was a zealot only survives if one ignores the claims that Paul makes concerning his status as a Roman citizen, and his willingness to act for the Sanhedrin, and if one does not question Wright's claims about the meaning of Paul's self-description as being 'zealous'. Investigation of the use Paul has made of this term is not compatible with the extremist kind of person that Wright has linked him with. Paul is saying no more than that he is zealous for the heritage and teaching of the Jewish people which he believed was God given. My contention is that Saul was a loyal follower of Gamaliel alone. In other words, he was no Machiavellian.

The zealots vigorously promoted the Maccabean story for it supported their claims that it was necessary to follow a violent path to overcome the forces they saw as threatening Israel. On the other hand, the school of Hillel saw the whole event from a very different angle. While they recognized the Maccabeans' military achievement and its benefits for the nation, they wrote their own version of the event, which was very different from the one promoted by those who followed Shammai, and it was this version that they celebrated on the feast of Hanukkah. This was the version that most Jews celebrated, and it lacked those elements of the story that Wright depends on for his construction of the theology of both Jesus and Paul.

The Search for Truth

Tracing Jewish History and its Consequences

The history of the consequences of the Maccabean revolt shows how the descendants of the Maccabean freedom fighters abandoned their original idealism and went on to undermine what was a notable victory in Israel's history.

Despite the defeat of the Seleucid armies and the rededication of the temple that followed, the Maccabean community was divided. Should they accept the gains they had made and content themselves with that, or should they fight on to turn a famous victory into a historic trouncing of the Seleucid armies that would lead to establishing an independent state that could assert its new-found military might?

The policy that was chosen of seeking to expand the Jewish borders was to eventually fuel the divide between the Pharisees and Sadducees under later Hasmonean monarchs such as Alexander Jannaeus. It was Judah Maccabee who led those who decided on the continuation of the war.

Judah died in battle in 160 B.C.E. and was succeeded as army commander by his younger brother, Jonathan, who was already high priest. Jonathan developed his influence by making treaties with various foreign states. This caused further division between those who desired no more than religious freedom and those who aspired to secure greater power through military conquests.

Johnathan ruled for eighteen years until 142 B.C.E. when he was assassinated by Diodotus Tryphon, a pretender to the Seleucid throne. Jonathan was succeeded by Simon Maccabee, the last remaining son of Mattathias. Simon gave support to Demetrius II Nicator, the Seleucid king, and in return Demetrius exempted the Maccabees from tribute. Simon, with this Seleucid acquiescence, conquered the port of Joppa where the gentile population were 'forcibly removed'. He took the fortress of Gezer and expelled the garrison from the Acra in Jerusalem. After only two years from taking the reins of power, he was recognised by an assembly of the priests, leaders and elders as high priest, military commander, and ruler of Israel. He was formally recognised as Israel's ruler in 140 B.C.E. The decree that elevated him became the basis of the Hasmonean kingdom. Shortly after, the Roman senate renewed its alliance with the Hasmonean kingdom and commanded its allies in the eastern Mediterranean to do so also. Although the Maccabees had won autonomy, the region remained a province of the Seleucid Empire and Simon was required to provide troops to Antiochus VII

Sidetes, the brother of Demetrius II. When Simon refused to give up the territories he had conquered, Antiochus took them by force.

Simon was murdered in 134 B.C.E by his son-in-law Ptolemy and was succeeded as high priest and king by his son John Hyrcanus I. Antiochus took advantage of the instability and conquered the entire district of Judea but decided that it was prudent not to attack the temple or challenge Jewish observances in any way. Judea was freed from Seleucid rule on the death of Antiochus in 129 B.C.E.

Independent Hasmonean rule lasted until 63 B.C.E. It ended when the Roman general Pompeius intervened in the Hasmonean civil war, making it a client kingdom of Rome. The Hasmonean dynasty finally ended in 37 B.C.E when the Idumean Herod the Great became King of Israel, designated 'King of the Jews' by the Roman Senate, effectively transforming the Hasmonean Kingdom into a Herodian Kingdom—a client kingdom of Rome.

Thus, the Hasmoneans descended into a pro-Hellenist party which became obsessed with achieving personal power and rule over all other Jewish groups, even daring to install themselves as priestly kings. The very dynasty that had liberated Judah from the rule Seleucid rule ended up surrendering to its culture and adopting its ruthless military aspirations.

It is little wonder that most Jews of the first century ce who celebrated the violent achievements of the Maccabeans were the zealots, the followers of Shammai. As we have seen, the Hillites had their own version of the overthrow of Seleucid rule. This version rejected any focus on military victory and promoted the event as the victory of truth over error. This was the feature of the celebrations held in the Hillite controlled synagogues throughout Judaism, a version that their Roman minders would have had no objection to.

Thus, the only way that Saul, the student rabbi, could imbibe the violent Maccabean model was if he was a zealot, a member of the Shammai community. Wright has attempted to argue that this was where his allegiance lay, but as I have noted, the evidence he has presented has failed to prove that Saul really was a zealot in any other sense than he was (as the entire nation was) zealous for the law and the traditions of the nation (Rom 10:2; Acts 22:3).

Given the incredibly chequered history of the Maccabean dynasty that we have noted above, their teachings would have been a very unstable foundation upon which to build a case for how Jesus and Paul understood the purpose of the cross. From the evidence available, most Jews despised their achievements rather than revered them. This is a fact that Wright ignores as he presents a united Israel celebrating the zealot version of Hanukkah. He mentions nothing of the fact that there were two versions of the event and promotes, indeed only mentions, the one he favours to establish the narrative of Jesus that he has created.

But there is a further issue that we have not yet properly considered, and this is that he has assumed that his preferred dating of the writing of 4 Maccabees is correct. This needs to be established by the available evidence.

But even if the dating of these documents could be shown to be early enough to have influenced Jesus and Paul as Wright has claimed they are, we have to further ask, 'how accurate are these accounts?' At least some of them rely on oral tradition, so we have to ask if these traditions are reliable and how do we know that these documents represent what really took place? Are they reliable records or were they written as raw uncollaborated propaganda to encourage support for the zealots?

We have no way of knowing how accurate they are, but we do know that fighting for the hearts and minds of communities and nations has been a part of warfare and uprisings throughout history. Why treat these documents as an accurate record of national sympathy and not submit them to the normal test required by historians, i.e. with at least a little suspicion as to the claims made and the purpose for which they were written? What are the factors that should be considered to get an accurate picture of this issue? While the first three books are generally accepted as preceding Jesus, there is no such consensus for 4 Maccabees, and it is this book that provides the key evidence for Wright's construction. The claim for the dating that Wright favours should be tested.

Such a challenge is reasonable as the dating of 4 Maccabees is heavily contested among scholars. H. Anderson is a contributor to the work edited by James H. Charlesworth, The Old Testament Pseudepigrapha, and he wrote the article on 4 Maccabees. Concerning the dating of 4 Maccabees, after a detailed analysis of all the evidence he suggests that they could fit into a time slot between 63 B.C.E–70 C.E. However, he acknowledges that:

> Two passages in the Annals of the Roman historian Tacitus (2.58; 13.8) point to approximately 19–54 C.E. as the period during which Syria-Silicia made up one region for Roman administrative purposes, and Bickermann's view that 4 Maccabees falls somewhere within this period must be deemed a very plausible

hypothesis.[240]

If we accept Bickermann's dating that Anderson is willing to allow as 'a very plausible hypothesis', it challenges Wright's claim that Jesus would have been aware of the theme of 4 Maccabees for it is giving no more than a maximum of ten years (giving Wright the advantage of accepting the earliest date) for it to be established as a part of the Hanukkah celebrations. Even more difficult for Wright's case, as we will see in a moment, is that the celebration of the death of the Maccabees was never part of the feast of Hanukkah.

The claim that 4 Maccabees exerted an important influence on Jesus and Paul is therefore deeply suspicious. It is stretching the evidence to its extreme to support the case that Wright wants to make, and so what is certain is that Wright cannot prove the early preferred date that his hypothesis requires. While Wright does not say that Paul was influenced directly by 4 Maccabees it still requires time for the tradition to become ubiquitous. In fact, Wright seems to be aware of the weakness of his argument at this point, for he wrote, 'What matters here is not so much what actually happened as the way in which the stories of martyrdom were written up retrospectively'.[241] This sort of reasoning easily slips into the attitude that the dating of 4 Maccabees is not too important either, as long as we have an account from which we can make our argument and that would support the case being made, as long as no one looks too closely!

But whatever the dating, more significant is that Anderson has rejected the possibility of the book being read in synagogues because of its contents— or better, the lack of its contents. Anything delivered in the synagogue would begin with a quotation from Scripture and there is not even one quotation in the entire book. The only way a message could be effectively delivered throughout Judaism was for it to be read to the gathered synagogue congregations, and that, according to Anderson, is excluded.

Anderson notes another detail that is often overlooked by those who advocate the influence of 4 Maccabees—it was not written to be read at the Hanukkah celebration as many have claimed. Anderson says:

> It has been maintained that 4 Maccabees was intended for oral delivery on a special occasion, and that occasion was in fact the

---

[240] Anderson, '4 Maccabees', 534.

[241] Wright, *Victory of God,* 582.

Jewish festival of Hanukkah. But the trouble with this assertion is, on the one hand, that if composed for Hanukkah, 4 Maccabees must assuredly have alluded to the heroes of the Maccabean war whom that feast celebrated, which it never does, and, on the other hand, that there is no Jewish tradition that associates the martyrs of 4 Maccabees, Eleazar and the mother and her seven sons, with Hanukkah. It is with such consideration that M. Hadas invites us to think of 4 Maccabees as a real address delivered at "an annual commemoration of the martyr's celebration at the site, actual or supposed, of their burial.[242]

Wright addresses none of these important issues raised by Anderson. Also, the events/story that Wright keeps saying are part of the celebration of Hanukkah are found to have no link whatsoever in Jewish tradition. The events are in 4 Maccabees but not found in any record of the celebration of Hanukkah. This is strange and is probably more than likely because they had never been linked. If this is so, then the book was written at a much later date when the zealots' actions had wreaked such havoc for the Jewish people. It is likely that a supporter living away from Palestine decided to write the book and link the two events in an attempt to make the feast into an event that was more supportive to the zealot cause.

A further problem for Wright's claim that Maccabees is important for Jesus's self-understanding is that Jesus had a clear model that guided which was not the Maccabean revolt, it was the Son of Man figure (Mark 10:45). While there is clear reference in the Gospels that links Jesus with the Son of Man, there is no clear reference, other than conjecture, to link Jesus with the Maccabees. This fact is underscored in that the term Son of Man is never once found in any of the Maccabean books. The absence of both themes in these books, rather than these motifs being joined, makes clear that there was a theological separation between the themes in the writings that record the history and the achievements of the Maccabees. Without clear evidence of the existence of this merger, Wright's claim for their dual importance must be questioned. The absence of a close identity between these themes in

---

[242] Anderson, '4 Maccabees', 535. This is a very different setting from what Wright, *Victory of God,* 582 promotes for he says 'We must remember, too, that the Maccabees were celebrated in the big annual feast of Hanukkah, causing their story to be widely known; and that some of Jesus' symbolic actions and explanatory riddles seem deliberately to have evoked Maccabean action.'

Maccabees and in the words of Jesus is an issue that needs to be addressed and satisfactorily explained before Wright's conjecture can be considered as a serious contribution to Christ's self-understanding.

And finally, the passage that Wright relies on to show how Jesus understood what his death was to achieve—the details of the death of the martyrs—is not historically reliable. Anderson is very clear that the account was creatively developed by the author of 4 Maccabees.[243] Whatever was taught in the earlier Maccabean tradition that circulated in Judaism, based on these details, it did not assert that the martyrs died to save Israel from wrath. That, if we follow Anderson, had been deliberately removed from the account, or it was added much later.

So, to sum up, the problems that we consider that those who advocate that Jesus was to some degree influenced by Maccabean martyrdom theology include:

1. The difference between the sort of kingdom the martyrs sought to establish and the one that Jesus established makes it very difficult to believe that their example inspired him. The contrast between the actions of the martyr warrior and the suffering servant is a major stumbling block for claiming Jesus was influenced by their example.[244]

---

[243] Anderson, '4 Maccabees', 536: 'The possibility, therefore, that 4 Maccabees was in fact composed as a fictive discourse cannot be lightly dismissed.'

[244] Wright, *Victory of God,* 607: 'And, despite all the overtones of the Maccabean martyrs which clustered around this event, as he went to his death he seems not to have responded to his pagan torturers in the time honoured manner. Instead of hurling insults and threats at them, he suffered either in silence or with words of forgiveness: a startling innovation into the martyr-tradition, which sent echoes across early Christianity in such a way as to be, I suggest, inexplicable unless they are substantially historical.' It is only a startling innovation if Jesus is modelling his death on the Maccabean model, it is far from innovative if he models his work on that of the Servant of Isaiah 53. This demonstrates how Wright has forced the passion narrative into the Maccabean account when there is a far more natural reading of the gospel account for they all show Jesus to be the Servant of the Lord and Isaiah 53 is at the centre of his work of redemption. This shows how Wright has allowed none of the canonical texts to control and override the canonical links which were unquestionable recognized by the entire Jewish population, both inside and outside of Palestine, with their much clearer explanations.

2. The book was written outside Palestine and incorporated Hellenistic pagan understanding of human sacrifice and what it achieved. Human sacrifice was expressly forbidden in the Old Testament.

3. There is no certainty over the dating of the important 4 Maccabees document, with some dating it as late as 135 C.E. which, if correct, clearly precludes the account from having any influence, either directly or indirectly, on Jesus or Paul.

4. A very sizable part of the Jewish community was under the leadership of the followers of Hillel and they forbad the celebration of the violent version of the Hanukkah celebration in which the account of the death of the martyrs was celebrated. The version of the majority Hillel school focused on a victory of truth over evil and not the military overthrow of the Seleucids.

5. There is no Jewish tradition that associates the martyrs of 4 Maccabees, Eleazar and the mother and her seven sons, with Hanukkah. The absence of this crucial evidence is a serious flaw in the argument Wright has made.

6. The possibility of 4 Maccabees being written later and it not recording history accurately has not been properly considered by Wright or any others who favour his reading. The purpose of the author of 4 Maccabees could have been to provide propaganda for the zealot movement which was struggling because of failing popular support, if in fact such support ever existed. This possibility is reasonable considering the absence of Eleazer and the mother and her seven sons from the traditions of the celebration of Hanukkah. It is also questionable as a result of the absence of the book from the Qumran library. Inclusion in this collection should be expected because the theme of the necessity of the temple's cleansing at the heart of 4 Maccabees is the theme at the heart of the Qumran's message. This absence is also found in Josephus and Philo, which are two sources we would naturally expect to cite 4 Maccabees as they have cited from earlier volumes of the 'series'. Their silence on this vital text is immensely significant and should alert us to the need to reflect on the claims of those who promote an early date for 4 Maccabees. Let me repeat this again, for it is crucially important. There is no evidence of the existence of 4 Maccabees even in the days of Paul so certainly not in the days of Jesus. If it had existed, we should have seen it in Philo, Josephus, and the Dead Sea Scrolls, and it is in none of these crucial historical sources, even though they all refer to 2 Maccabees.

7. Human sacrifice is absolutely forbidden in the law (Lev 18:21;

Deut 18:21). Its presence in 4 Maccabees is only possible because the book was written by someone who was a Jew of the Diaspora where, because of Greco-Roman practices, such understanding was possible. It is extremely unlikely that such a practice would have been adopted by an earlier generation because they did not need martyrs to atone, for they had the temple and its sacrifices until 70 C.E. This suggests that the teaching of the death of the martyr originated after the fall of Jerusalem. This makes sense of the absence of the details of the book's version of Hanukkah in earlier celebrations of the feast due to the need of an alternative source of atonement. Also, after this date it would be easier to introduce teaching that lacked strict compliance with Old Testament law as the means of following its instruction had been taken from them. This factor has not been part of any earlier discussions but in light of the above it must be considered.

8. Linking 4 Maccabees with the death of the servant in Isaiah 53 is to override OT teaching about the redeemer figure that the OT specified each family was to have and the promise that Yahweh alone would be Israel's Redeemer. This clear Old Testament teaching dispossesses the Maccabean model of its appeal and need.

9. We have seen that there is no link between the Son of Man and the Maccabean leaders that explains the significance of the martyr's death.

10. For Wright to fail to enter into any discussion on the issues considered above and to present his own views as though they are beyond being challenged suggests either failure to fully research the issue or a simple ignoring of the discussion led by Anderson. This is a serious failure which ought to cause concern; it demands an explanation.

These points should make us extremely suspicious of the value of the Maccabean model for interpreting the New Testament texts concerning Jesus' death and its achievements. The absence of historical support for the early existence of the book and the absence of key references in the book from the verifiable history of the celebration of Hanukkah is much firmer evidence for the proposed thesis that 4 Maccabees is a late document that has no bearing on the development of Jesus's understanding or the theology of Paul.

Wright also depends on the Maccabean model for his construction of Jesus' expectation of his coming resurrection after suffering at the hands of his enemies. We will consider this at the end of the present chapter once we have considered the Paschal New Exodus paradigm which I believe is the true setting of Jesus's thinking and achievements.

Solving the Enigma

The key term in Romans 3:21–26 is *apolutrōsis* ('redemption'). Now, there is only one cultic event in the entire Old Testament, and in Jewish literature generally, in which redemption is celebrated, and that is the Passover. That this is the model used by Paul becomes obvious when it is realised that this is also the only cultic event that could be celebrated away from the temple. So, Jews in every part of the Roman Empire could celebrate the Passover without having to make a pilgrimage to Jerusalem. Because of this it is reasonable to claim that all of his readers in Rome would have known of its details intimately, and therefore would have been able to grasp Paul's intended allusion.

This background for interpreting the atoning significance of the death of Jesus was probably overlooked because of the description of the offering as *hilastērion*. Most interpreters believe that there is no propitiatory value in the Passover; and although an atoning content could be supported by appealing to a range of authorities, such an exercise would merely illustrate the confusion which exists over the nature of the Passover. Even those who see propitiatory value in the Passover—either that practised in the Mosaic period or that which is intimated by the New Testament allusions to it—fail to see a connection between the Passover and Romans 3:21–25. However, there is evidence which has not been considered hitherto and which is very important to our study, but also as evidence of her relationship with God. When Yahweh made his covenant with Abraham, he said that Abraham's descendants would be slaves for 400 years but that he would rescue them from their sufferings (Gen 15: 12–15). So, the exodus from Egypt identified Israel as God's redeemed people.

There is something else about the exodus that is often overlooked. We can easily assume that the Passover was about the judgment of Egypt, but it was much more than that. Ezekiel 20 describes the condition of Israel in Egypt.

> Let them know the abominations of their fathers, and say to them,
> Thus says the Lord God: On the day when I chose Israel, I swore
> to the offspring of the house of Jacob, making myself known to
> them in the land of Egypt; I swore to them, saying, I am the Lord
> your God. On that day I swore to them that I would bring them out

of the land of Egypt into a land that I had searched out for them, a land flowing with milk and honey, the most glorious of all lands. And I said to them, Cast away the detestable things your eyes feast on, every one of you, and do not defile yourselves with the idols of Egypt; I am the Lord your God. But they rebelled against me and were not willing to listen to me. None of them cast away the detestable things their eyes feasted on, nor did they forsake the idols of Egypt. "Then I said I would pour out my wrath upon them and spend my anger against them in the midst of the land of Egypt. But I acted for the sake of my name, that it should not be profaned in the sight of the nations among whom they lived, in whose sight I made myself known to them in bringing them out of the land of Egypt. (Ezekiel 20:4–9)

We see here that Israel was not an unwilling resident; her only complaint was the oppression she was suffering. Ezekiel tells us that Israel had abandoned the right of circumcision, willingly worshipped the gods of Egypt and copied the lifestyle of her persecutors. The judgment was not only on Egypt, it was on the descendants of Abraham as well, for they had become as ungodly as their hosts! Because of this, Israel's firstborn would also die if they were not protected. On that momentous night, Israel deserved and was under judgment as well as Egypt.

Unravelling the Passover

So, the night of the Passover was massively significant. Israel was under what would eventually be defined as, the 'covenantal curse' because she had been unfaithful to her God. Her firstborn, who represented the families and collectively the nation, were to be judged. The only way of escaping death was by a substitutionary sacrifice, a propitiatory sacrifice, or hilasterion—and this is what the death of the Passover lambs achieved. They atoned for Israel's sin, which the firstborn would have borne. What needs to be noted is that the death of the firstborn functioned as atonement for their respective families, and they were only spared because substitutes had been provided. This, of course, was not the case for the Egyptian firstborn.

Now such an understanding will be challenged because scholarship sees the Passover to be about redemption and not atonement. It will be pointed out that sin is atoned for on the Day of Atonement and not at the time of the Passover.

I want to challenge this widespread understanding, for if the smearing of blood on the doorpost and lintel to turn away the Angel of Death is not an act of propitiation then, I confess, I do not know what is! Of course, it is also about redemption; but in the first Passover, I believe there is ample evidence to show that on that one occasion atonement and redemption were combined.

This combination did not continue in subsequent Passovers. The nation was instructed to celebrate an annual memorial. The ongoing need for atonement for the sin of Israel was not retained within the annual Passover but was transferred to the Day of Atonement. This undeniably atoning event was also to be inaugurated and celebrated annually as a separate feast. What has confused scholars is that redemption and atonement, achieved through the original Passover, were separated into two annual feasts. As a result, because there is no atonement in the Passover memorial, it has been concluded that it was not in the original Passover either.

To reiterate, if my analysis is correct, the original Passover combined atonement and redemption, but all subsequent celebrations had a different shape with the essentials of the original event located in two separate feasts. The mistake that has been made is to think that the content of the memorial was identical to the original Passover when it clearly was not.

Clarifying the Nature of the Passover

At the heart of the original Passover was the death of the firstborn. The death, or sacrifice, of the firstborn is spoken of throughout the Old Testament.[245] This was recognized by the rabbis, who argued that within their system of teaching, the enacted death of Isaac (Abraham's firstborn son of promise) was considered by Yahweh to atone for Israel's sins. Of course, if the tradition existed before Paul's 'conversion' then he, the 'converted' rabbi, could no longer assent to solution—it was only through the actual shedding of innocent blood that sin was atoned for. This is what won many Jews in those early heady days of the kingdom. They could see that the promise to deal with Israel's sin had been fulfilled, and it was through the death of the royal Son of God, the firstborn (Ps 89:27), the appointed king, who had died for his people's sin. This is what all of the gospels show; he died as Israel's king in the very feast of the Passover. Paul develops this understanding one step further (keeping to Jesus's teaching) in saying that Christ is the firstborn of all creation (Col 1:15). The king has died to restore his entire inheritance to its pre-cursed condition (Rom 8:18–25).

---

[245] See Holland, *Contours,* 241–254 for references and discussion.

Paul's Use of Ezekiel's Sacrificial Language

Amongst the flood of promises Israel was given by the prophets when in exile was one that Yahweh would raise up a descendant of David and that he would be the key figure in the nation's redemption from exile (Isa 11:1ff.; 55:3–4; Jer 23:1–8; 33:4–17). The Prince—Ezekiel's designation for the Son of David—would be the Shepherd King that Israel longed for (Ezek 34:23–31; 37:24–25). Ezekiel tells how this king would rebuild the temple once he had led the remnant back to the promised land (Ezek 40–48). However, he would not only restore the temple and its worship, he would also provide sin offerings to cleanse the temple and the nation so that she could worship her God as his new covenant people. The significant thing that is often overlooked is that this atonement would be made at the time of the Passover! This eschatological Passover, when Israel is put right with her God, would be an atoning event, just as the original Passover had been.

In Ezekiel 45:21–24, the prophet tells how, having built the eschatological temple, the Prince would provide an abundance of sin offerings for the sins of the people. The passage says:

> Thus says the Lord God: In the first month, on the first day of the month, you shall take a bull from the herd without blemish, and purify the sanctuary. The priest shall take some of the blood of the sin offering and put it on the doorposts of the temple, the four corners of the ledge of the altar, and the posts of the gate of the inner court. You shall do the same on the seventh day of the month for anyone who has sinned through error or ignorance; so you shall make atonement for the temple. In the first month, on the fourteenth day of the month, you shall celebrate the Feast of the Passover, and for seven days unleavened bread shall be eaten. On that day the prince shall provide for himself and all the people of the land a young bull for a sin offering. And on the seven days of the festival he shall provide as a burnt offering to the Lord seven young bulls and seven rams without blemish, on each of the seven days; and a male goat daily for a sin offering. (Ezek 45:18–24)

It is clearly significant that these sacrifices are not made on the Day of Atonement as would be expected. In fact, Ezekiel never mentions the Day of Atonement at all. What he does say is that these sacrifices (which would normally be offered on the Day of Atonement) were to be offered instead as part of the Passover celebration. Ezekiel even says that the ritual of putting blood on the door post was to be done on the temple door. This is of fundamental importance for our understanding of Paul. If Ezekiel, a priest who had preached against the sin of tampering with the laws of Yahweh, does the unthinkable by changing the law of Moses and the sacrificial system, then he can be doing only one thing—he is emphasising the importance of the Passover as a means of dealing with the sins of the people.

It is significant that Ezekiel had the Davidic Prince providing these paschal atoning sacrifices and that Paul introduced Jesus as the Davidic descendant at the opening of the letter to the Romans (Rom 1:3).[246] Furthermore, the expression 'spirit of holiness' (Rom 1:4) is also significant because it has been identified as an Old Testament term describing the criteria of acceptance for the animal sacrifices in the Jewish temple.[247] By his use of this cultic expression, Paul indicates that it is Jesus, the Son of David, the Son of God, who achieves redemption for his people through his death (Rom 3:21–26).

Obviously, the redemptive death of the Davidic Prince is not something that Ezekiel anticipated, but it is what all the Gospels bear witness to, and what Jesus clearly wanted his disciples to focus on. in their understanding of the achievements that his coming death would secure. There is much more evidence to support the influence of Ezekiel on Paul and the New Testament generally, but to deal with it here would take our focus off the passage under consideration. For a fuller understanding of the scale of Ezekiel's influence see chapter 8.

Further Paschal Themes in Romans 3:21–26

The presence of this Passover model is supported by the reference to πάρεσις (*paresis*, 'passing over') (Rom 3:25 BYZ): 'because in his divine forbearance he had passed over former sins' (Rom 3:25 ESV); 'because in the forbearance of God He passed over the sins previously committed' (Rom 3:25 NAS); 'God in his forbearance had passed over the sins previously committed' (Rom 3:25 NET). Here, there is a clear echo of Yahweh passing over the Jewish homes on the night of the Passover because of the presentation of the paschal lambs' blood but visiting Egyptian homes to strike their firstborn sons in judgment. In the eschatological Passover (1 Cor 5:7), God 'passed over' the family of humanity but visited his wrath upon his firstborn, who had no substitute and who, therefore, died as the paschal victim. According to John,

---

[246] As this has not been identified by Wright who looks for explanations elsewhere.

[247] E. Käsemann, *Romans* (Grand Rapids: Eerdmans, 1980), 11.

Jesus died at the time when the Passover lambs were slain— Yahweh striking his own beloved Son, his firstborn and our elder brother (Rom 8:17, 29). Jesus is the Redeemer (Rom 3:24)—the *gō'ēl* of his people. There is not only an allusion to the Passover in the use of paresis ('passing over') but also to the way it was used by the translators of Isaiah, who, in a Second Exodus context, used the same term to speak of Yahweh keeping back his anger from sinful Israel (Isa 64:10–12; 42:14; 63:15 [LXX]).

'Justification' (Rom 3:24) is also a New Exodus term and adds weight to the paschal setting of the passage. When Israel was brought out of exile in Babylon, she was said to have been justified (Isa 50:8; 53:11). The expression spoke of being removed from one kingdom and placed into another. While held in exile, Israel was defiled and shaped by the people who had taken her captive.[248] The return to her own land sanctified her, for she was cleansed from all that polluted her and enabled to live in the ways that God wanted.

The display of God's righteousness (Rom 3:21–22) links with justification (Rom 3:24, 26). This again is a motif of the New Exodus, especially as provided by Isaiah. Yahweh's act of redemption not only justified his people but also justified himself to the nations concerning his character as the covenant-keeping God. His righteousness refers to 'his right acts' in being faithful to his promises. Yahweh—who promised to act to secure deliverance for Israel through his servant David—had now fulfilled his promises (Gen 15:13–14; Isaiah 55:1–13). When his own Son was given up to death, his righteousness was universally displayed, and his covenant faithfulness was blazed abroad. The Davidic Prince was not merely to provide sacrifices for the eschatological Passover; he was the eschatological Passover. As the king was Yahweh's firstborn over the kings of the earth (Ps 89:27), so Jesus the promised descendent of David was 'put forward' (publicly displayed) to the whole of creation, and, as the King of the Jews (Rom 1:3), as

---

[248] G. Bornkamm, 'The Revelation of Christ to Paul on the Damascus Road and Paul's Doctrine of Justification and Reconciliation: A Study in Galatians 1', in R. Banks, ed., *Reconciliation and Hope: Old Testament Essays on Atonement and Eschatology Presented to L. L. Morris on His 60th Birthday* (Exeter: Paternoster, 1974), 90–103 [102]; J. Reumann, 'The Gospel of the Righteousness of God: Pauline Reinterpretation in Rom 3:21–31', *Int.* 20 (1966): 432–52 [445]; R. P. Casey, 'The Earliest Christologies,' *JTS ns 9* (1958): 253–277 [274]; Käsemann, *Romans,* 41; P. Stuhlmacher, *Reconciliation, Law, and Righteousness: Essays in Biblical Theology* (Philadelphia: Fortress Press, 1986), 81.

all four Gospels spell out, he suffered death for his people in the midst of the Passover.

In addition to the above themes of 'public display', 'passing over', 'justification' and 'God's righteousness', there is the undisputable paschal language of 'the redemption that came by Christ Jesus' (Rom 3:24). The language of redemption through blood is uniquely paschal and cannot be housed in any event other than the Passover. It is about how Yahweh delivered his people—the indisputable theme of the Passover. The mention of blood (Rom 3:25) reinforces this claim. The Passover was, therefore, about redemption, which was secured through the shedding of blood. Further support for the claim that the ideas of Romans 3:24–25 find their origin in the Passover is provided by exponents of form criticism who have attempted to identify the source of the text. They generally agree that the passage reflects a liturgical formula, which was used either as a baptismal or a Eucharistic confession. Whichever it may have been, both themes are strongly linked with the death of Christ and its setting in the context of the Passover.

Moreover, the claim that the passage has an Adamic content also fits well with the picture of the eschatological Passover. The redemption that Paul describes reverses the catastrophic effects of humanity's fall, bringing humankind out of the spiritual bondage in which they have been incarcerated since Adam violated the covenant with Yahweh (Rom 5:12–21). This salvation comes through faith in Christ Jesus. Paul concludes the section (Rom 3:26–28) by insisting that the law was fulfilled in the redemption which is in Christ. In other words, Paul understands that the Law and the Prophets—the whole of Scripture—had looked forward to this eschatological event of atonement and redemption.

As with the claims concerning Ezekiel's influence on Paul, there is much more evidence to support a paschal reading than has so far been presented, but to deal with it here would once again take the focus away from the passage under consideration. This extra relevant material for a fuller understanding is provided in chapter 8.

Comparing the Two Models

So, having considered the background material, we shall now consider the interpretation of this important text.

We find key terms in the passage that have nothing to do with the martyrdom theme suggested by Wright. Apart from the fact this imports a concept of human sacrifice, which is essentially pagan in its origin and totally speculative as to its influence, the Maccabean narrative is solely about a prayer that Eleazer made that his death would be accepted as an act of atonement. There is nothing in the Maccabean narrative of the other themes that are found in the Romans passage. In Romans 3:21–25, there's the mention of redemption, propitiation, the public display of the sacrifice, and (most importantly) the passing over of sin. In contrast, the only term in the Maccabean text found in Romans 3:21–26 is propitiation—it does not echo or cite any other term in the passage. However, all of these themes found in Romans 3:21–25 are present in the Passover narrative and the theology that emerges from it.

Not only does the presence of these unique terms point to the Passover as the source of Paul's model, but so also does the fact that the whole letter follows Exodus themes. Despite noting this,[249] Wright loses contact with this theme by introducing non-scriptural material, with little or no New Exodus associations, as the key to explaining a passage whose thematic context he has rightly identified by other means.

There is one very significant piece of evidence that shows that Paul did not use the Maccabean model. Paul always links the death of Christ with cosmic redemption (see Rom 3:21–26; 8:22–25; Eph 1:7, 21–23; Col 1:19–20; Phil 2:8–9; 3:20–21). Moreover, this link is not only found in Paul—other New Testament writers also share it (see Heb 1:3, 11; 1 Pet 1:2; 2 Pet 3:13; Rev 1:4–6; 21:15). In the light of this clear association it is totally inappropriate to appeal to the Maccabean texts for the early church's understanding of the significance of Christ's death, since there is not even a hint of the idea of cosmic redemption in those texts. Instead, Paul's understanding of the significance of Christ's death clearly comes from the prophecy of Isaiah with its clear Second Exodus/new creation themes, and its association with the death of the servant of the Lord. In turn, the background of Isaiah's message was the first exodus, rooted as it was in the death of the firstborn or the substituted lamb.

This setting of the Passover as the background for Paul's atonement theology is further supported by ancillary themes such as baptism into Christ, which is the typological fulfilment of Israel's baptism into Moses and is presented by Paul in 1 Corinthians 10:1–4. It was an exodus-based event, as is the deliverance from slavery (Rom 6:10–14). The gift of the Spirit (Rom 5:5,

---

[249] Wright, *Perspectives,* 85.

which fulfils the giving of the law at Sinai), and the leading of the Spirit (Rom 8:5–39, which matches the leading of the Shekinah through the wilderness) was also an exodus event. All of these themes are found in the exodus and Passover but are entirely absent from the Maccabean story.

Also, as we saw in chapter seven, Maccabean martyr theology is anything but Jewish. Williams has acknowledged that its origins are not in the Scriptures of Judaism but from the practices of Hellenism.[250] It is a thoroughly pagan practice which has, it is claimed, been adopted by the writer of 4 Maccabees. We have also discussed the false assumption that the history was widely known in a way which gave the whole of Judaism access to the incident as an interpretive lens through which to understand the death of Jesus. Also, we noted that the dating of this crucial document is possibly as late as 135 C.E. Hence the link between what Paul says about the death of Jesus and the Maccabean model is entirely speculative. Compared to the evidence that supports a Paschal New Exodus reading of the argument of Paul the model is massively flawed.

However, this is by no means the only problem for those wanting to use the Eleazer passage to interpret Romans 3:21–25; the motifs of righteousness, justification, and redemption found in it simply do not occur in martyrdom theology.[251] In contrast, they are all at home in the New Exodus model and the terms 'public display' and 'the passing over' certainly find no parallel in the Maccabean texts. This demonstrates to me that Wright has not understood how extensive and controlling the New Exodus model is, even though he promotes it. His confidence in the intertestamental literature as a source which Paul has drawn upon, or which he was influenced by, has led him away from those points of evidence which are undoubtedly within the text of the Passover event; evidence which undoubtedly leads to a far better understanding of Paul's meaning. Since Paul's repeated claim is that this redemption is borne witness to by the Law and the Prophets (Rom 1:2; 3:21), it would surely be sensible for us to focus on these writings to find Paul's model.

The Maccabean model demonstrates my concern over Wright's willingness to go outside the recognized Jewish canon. It has taken him (and many others who adopt the same approach) away from the Scriptures of the early church. These were the texts that the entire believing community had

---

[250] J. J. Williams, *Traditions,* 33.

[251] J. D. G. Dunn, *Romans 1–8* (Waco, TX: Word, 1988), 180.

access to, enabling them to identify important key terms within the context and detail of Paul's argument and to understand how they typologically fulfilled the old order. These were the texts that had been sealed by the testimony of Jesus, and these were also the texts that all the apostles cited or alluded to in their preaching and writings. Far too much time and energy have been expended in the search for exegetical keys to the New Testament outside the sacred text of the believing community. As a result, inadequate explanations have been too readily embraced, causing many to lose sight of the power of the biblical narrative and the confidence that the apostolic community had in the divine authority of its message.

Reflections on Wright's Doctrine of the Resurrection.

Wright has written an extensive study on the subject of the resurrection of Jesus which has received widespread praise. It is a very thorough work in which he surveys every possible source of the idea of a resurrection. His sources include those that come from the Greco-Roman world and beyond, including the teachings found within the Jewish world and especially the Old Testament Scriptures.

Wright has dismissed pagan ideas as a source and has argued that the Old Testament offers little if any material that established a belief in resurrection among Jews. He claims that there is little there that supported such teaching. He notes that there is an understanding of post mortem survival, but he recognizes that resurrection is a very different matter.

When Wright examined the often-claimed Old Testament texts used to support an Old Testament basis for the origin of the teaching he dismissed the claims saying that most texts had nothing to do with this crucial doctrine. In his opinion they spoke of post mortem survival but not resurrection. Nevertheless, he saw three possible seed texts that might have produced the initial ideas for a later doctrine of resurrection to have developed from but was clear that they lacked the required content that meant that they could be seen to have actually birthed this doctrine.

Three Key Old Testament Texts

In Ezekiel 37 we read of The Valley of Dry Bones.

> The hand of the Lord was upon me, and he brought me out in the
> Spirit of the Lord and set me down in the middle of the valley; it

was full of bones. And he led me around among them, and behold, there were very many on the surface of the valley, and behold, they were very dry. And he said to me, "Son of man, can these bones live?" And I answered, "O Lord God, you know." Then he said to me, "Prophesy over these bones, and say to them, O dry bones, hear the word of the Lord. Thus says the Lord God to these bones: Behold, I will cause breath to enter you, and you shall live. And I will lay sinews upon you, and will cause flesh to come upon you, and cover you with skin, and put breath in you, and you shall live, and you shall know that I am the Lord." (Ezek 37:1–6)

Then he said to me, "Son of man, these bones are the whole house of Israel. Behold, they say, 'Our bones are dried up, and our hope is lost; we are indeed cut off.' Therefore prophesy, and say to them, Thus says the Lord God: Behold, I will open your graves and raise you from your graves, O my people. And I will bring you into the land of Israel. And you shall know that I am the Lord, when I open your graves, and raise you from your graves, O my people. And I will put my Spirit within you, and you shall live, and I will place you in your own land. Then you shall know that I am the Lord; I have spoken, and I will do it, declares the Lord." (Ezek 37:11–14)

The passage is clearly about Israel. Her exile is described as a condition of death. She is assured by the prophet that Yahweh had not forgotten his promise and would bring his people out of exile to life in the coming kingdom. The imagery does not speak of physical resurrection but of national restoration to its own land, being the inheritance that Yahweh had promised to Abraham and his descendants. Wright does not suggest that there is anything here other than that it describes Israel's restoration to fellowship with Yahweh in national deliverance.

Wright is much more positive about the second relevant text, Isaiah 26:13–19 which says:

O Lord our God, other lords besides you have ruled over us, but your name alone we bring to remembrance. They are dead, they will not live; they are shades, they will not arise; to that end you have visited them with destruction and wiped out all remembrance of them. But you have increased the nation, O Lord, you have increased the nation; you are glorified; you have enlarged all the borders of the land. O Lord, in distress they sought you; they poured out a whispered prayer when your discipline was upon them. Like a pregnant woman who writhes and cries out in her pangs when she is near to giving birth, so were we because of you, O Lord; we were pregnant, we writhed, but we have given birth to wind. We have accomplished no deliverance in the earth, and the inhabitants of the world have not fallen. Your dead shall live; their bodies shall rise. You who dwell in the dust, awake and sing for joy! For your dew is a dew of light, and the earth will give birth to the dead.

Wright sees that there are similarities between Isaiah's description and that given by Ezekiel considered above. He says of the passage:

The context is a vivid payer of loyalty to YHWH in the midst of fierce and continuing persecution by pagans. Other lords have ruled over Israel, 'but we acknowledge your name alone'. Pagans, and those who follow their ways, have no future beyond death to look forward to. But those who seek YHWH in distress find themselves in pangs like a woman giving birth; and when birth comes it turns out to be the new birth of the dead themselves (26:16–19). In the original Hebrew this refers literally to bodily resurrection and this is certainly how the verse is taken in the LXX and at Qumran. It is still possible, of course, that here resurrection is, as we shall see in Ezekiel, a metaphor for national restoration; but the wider passage, in which God's renewal of the whole cosmos is in view, opens the way for us to propose that the reference to resurrection is intended to denote actual concrete events.[252]

These comments are interesting because Wright switches between metaphoric and literal understandings of resurrection on the basis that the passage refers to the recreation of the cosmos. That clearly fits with a Christian understanding, but it does not mean that the passage in its historic setting meant this. For Isaiah, the resurrection of the nation would usher in the renewal of creation, even the deserts turning into a source of food as an indication that the cosmic renewal was taking place. The citing of the Hebrew text, speaking of a literal resurrection, holds no force because that is what metaphor is all about, using actual things to speak of spiritual truths.

The third passage that Wright considers to speak of resurrection is Daniel 12:2–3, which says:

And many of those who sleep in the dust of the earth shall awake, some to everlasting life, and some to shame and everlasting contempt. And those who are wise shall shine like the brightness of the sky above; and those who turn many to righteousness, like the stars forever and ever

---

[252] Wright, *The Resurrection of the Son of God,* 117.

Wright says of this passage

> There is little doubt that this refers to concrete, bodily
> resurrection. The metaphor of 'sleep' for death was, as we have
> seen, already widespread; sleeping in the dust of the earth
> (literally, 'the earth of dust' or 'the land of dust') was a clear
> biblical way of referring to the dead. It was therefore natural to
> continue the metaphor by using 'awake' to denote bodily
> resurrection—not a different sort of sleep, but its abolition. This is
> not, of itself, an 'other worldly' idea, but a 'very worldly one'.[253]

Wright is not alone in claiming that Dan 12:2–3 is about the resurrection.
Despite it being widely assumed, there is no evidence to show that the Jews
had reached this understanding by Daniel's day. It is better to keep to the
same understanding that Ezekiel gives, that Israel's release from exile was her
resurrection. In fact, the story of the book of Daniel is about four young
Israelites in exile, and thus about the nation in exile, or death, waiting for her
deliverance, her resurrection. In other words, the imagery is metaphorical and
not literal as is obviously the case in Ezekiel 37 and I would claim is also in
Isaiah 26:14–19. There is no reason or evidence to claim that the terminology
was anything other than about national restoration, which for Israel was her
resurrection. Thus, I would argue that Wright is forcing the Christian doctrine
of resurrection into an Old Testament text. Wright acknowledges that the
Hebrew text of the Old Testament fails to provide evidence of a belief in the
resurrection of the Jews. But what he does recognize is that the doctrine
emerged as a result of the Hebrew text being translated into Greek. It was as
Hellenistic Jews read the Greek version of the Old Testament that they saw
linguistic parallels that while not there in the Hebrew were introduced by the
Greek translators and the translation created links to the doctrine of
resurrection that others, such as the Maccabeans, had come to hold. Clearly
this stream had come into Palestinian Judaism through Hellenistic Judaism.[254]

---

[253] Wright, *The Resurrection of the Son of God,* 109–110.

[254] Wright, *The Resurrection of the Son of God,* 147 says: 'It is impossible to
tell, at this remove, what overtones different Jewish readers of the Greek Old
Testament might have read in the different words. What is more, it is quite
impossible, at this stage of our knowledge of early text-forms, to be sure in
any given case that when we compare even the best modern editions of the
Hebrew and Greek Bibles we are in touch with either the Hebrew that the
original LXX translators used or the Greek that they first wrote. In many
cases it is quite possible that the LXX seems to represent a sharp move from

In other words, the Jews could not have reached this understanding without the Greeks and the translation they had so significantly influenced.

Such a reading of resurrection being held in the Old Testament clashes with the passage in 2 Timothy that says:

> Therefore do not be ashamed of the testimony about our Lord, nor of me his prisoner, but share in suffering for the gospel by the power of God, who saved us and called us to a holy calling, not because of our works but because of his own purpose and grace, which he gave us in Christ Jesus before the ages began and which now has been manifested through the appearing of our Saviour Christ Jesus, who abolished death and brought life and immortality to light through the gospel, for which I was appointed a preacher and apostle and teacher, which is why I suffer as I do. But I am not ashamed, for I know whom I have believed, and I am convinced that he is able to guard until that Day what has been entrusted to me. Follow the pattern of the sound words that you have heard from me, in the faith and love that are in Christ Jesus. By the Holy Spirit who dwells within us, guard the good deposit entrusted to you. (2 Tim 1:8–11).

This statement makes it clear that this knowledge of life and immortality had not been known before. It is totally different from the shadow that the Old Testament saints were limited to. The Christian doctrine of resurrection is not based on an obligation to reward for faithfulness but is of a totally different magnitude.

Old Testament Limitations

Because the Old Testament Scriptures offered nothing like the certainty that Christ was to give his people, Wright looked for the needed evidence to show that the Jews had a doctrine of resurrection and this he claims is found in Maccabean theology. Wright says that Jesus was inspired by the stories of the martyrs who believed that they would be rewarded for their devotion to God with resurrection in the last day. As we have seen, Wright thinks everyone was familiar with the martyr tradition, but as seen above this is seriously

---

the original.' This is a worrying argument. Wright has not even considered that the views of resurrection which he has listed may have in fact had no influence on Christian understanding at all. I will soon argue that the Christian view has nothing to do with the Hellenistic sources that Wright has listed, but that it came from a different stream, the typological exegesis of sacred redemption history alone.

challenged by the absence of the deeds of the martyrs from the celebration of Hanukkah which he says was the publicity machine of the zealot tradition. Wright argues that the confidence that these men had that they would share in the resurrection as they went to their death inspired Jesus to believe that after his own suffering, he would join the earlier generations of faithful witnesses. The major challenge to this hypothesis is that there is not a shred of evidence that Jesus ever engaged with these traditions, so the solution is speculative.

Wright's claim that the Maccabean tradition is the source of Jesus's belief that he will be raised from the dead means that Maccabees has made a unique contribution to this crucial Christian doctrine of the resurrection. He accepts that there is no firm Old Testament evidence to show that the Jews had a doctrine of physical resurrection. The implication is obvious if he is correct; the resurrection is not a biblical doctrine, it has come from Hellenism. Wright's problem is that he needs to establish that the Jews had arrived at this understanding before the New Testament era because clearly the Pharisees held to such a doctrine. His search for the seed of this doctrine took him once again to the Maccabean tradition and although he recognized that Maccabees introduced dualism into Judaism, he is willing to accept that a pagan doctrine fertilized one of the most important Christian doctrines. So welcoming is he to this understanding that under the heading 'Resurrection in the Bible', he has a subheading 'The more Greek the better'. This is a strange statement from one who has insisted that he has neither Hellenized Paul nor does he see that Paul Hellenized the Jewish tradition he was a part of.[255] Wright went on to defend this transfer saying, 'it was capable of being imported without necessarily bringing all its latent Platonic baggage with it.'[256] It is clear from the previous discussion that Wright relies heavily on the theology of the Maccabees for his reconstruction of his Christology, soteriology and now, also for his doctrine of resurrection. All of this has been built on a book, i.e. 4 Maccabees, which scholars have not been able to reach consent on regarding its date of authorship and which all recognize is essentially a Hellenistic document.

But even if we accept an unproven early date for the book so that it could have influenced Jesus's understanding of resurrection, there is something absent from this tradition that is repeatedly found in the details that Jesus gives about his anticipated death and resurrection which became central to the

---

[255] Wright, *The Resurrection of the Son of God,* 147.
[256] Ibid, 173.

proclamation of the early church and has stayed so throughout the centuries. And this is, that after three days, Jesus said, he would be raised from the dead (Matt 16:21; 17:23; 20:19; 27:63; Luke 9:22; 13:32; 24:7; 24:21; 24:46 and parallels. See also Acts 10:40; 1 Cor 15:4). This became the central fact of the apostolic gospel and the councils saw that the event was at the heart of the gospel of God and made it to be at the centre of the historic confessions.

But where did this conviction concerning his coming resurrection after three days come from come? There is not a whisper of it in the Maccabean tradition. They did not expect any sort of immediate resurrection, so it never came from them even if we allowed the book to have had some influence on Jesus. It is not a detail that can be treated as incidental for it was seen as so important that Jesus continually repeated it as did the church. The resurrection after three days was an essential part of her creed. The absence of this detail in the Maccabean tradition alone ought to give good reason for doubting Wright's suggested source of Jesus's understanding.

Paul's Own Account

So where is there a tradition in which atonement and a resurrection after three days are linked together? For this we can look to the earliest written tradition of the church's confession, 1 Corinthians 15:1–4.

> Now I would remind you, brothers, of the gospel I preached to you, which you received, in which you stand, and by which you are being saved, if you hold fast to the word I preached to you— unless you believed in vain. For I delivered to you as of first importance what I also received: that Christ died for our sins in accordance with the Scriptures, that he was buried, that he was raised on the third day in accordance with the Scriptures (1 Cor 15:1–4).

Paul then goes on to speak of the evidence for the resurrection in the witness of the 500 who had seen the risen Christ. He then says:

> But in fact Christ has been raised from the dead, the firstfruits of those who have fallen asleep. For as by a man came death, by a man has come also the resurrection of the dead. For as in Adam all die, so also in Christ shall all be made alive. But each in his own order: Christ the firstfruits, then at his coming those who belong to Christ. Then comes the end, when he delivers the kingdom to God the Father after destroying every rule and every authority and power. For he must reign until he has put all his enemies under his feet. The last enemy to be destroyed is death.

> For "God has put all things in subjection under his feet." But
> when it says, "all things are put in subjection," it is plain that he is
> excepted who put all things in subjection under him. When all
> things are subjected to him, then the Son himself will also be
> subjected to him who put all things in subjection under him, that
> God may be all in all. (1 Cor 15:20)

In these two passages, which are at the heart of Paul's presentation of the
gospel, we find important clues to the conundrum of the origin of the
resurrection and of it being after three days. Paul speaks of Jesus presenting
himself as the firstfruits three days after his death (1 Cor 15:3, 20). This is far
from a 'throw away comment'. It is immensely significant that the priests
presented the firstfruits of the harvest three days after the Passover (Lev
23:11).

> The Lord spoke to Moses: "Speak to the Israelites and tell them,
> 'When you enter the land that I am about to give to you and you
> gather in its harvest, then you must bring the sheaf of the first
> portion of your harvest to the priest, and he must wave the sheaf
> before the Lord to be accepted for your benefit—on the day after
> the Sabbath the priest is to wave it. On the day you wave the sheaf
> you must also offer a flawless yearling lamb for a burnt offering
> to the Lord, along with its grain offering, two tenths of an ephah
> of choice wheat flour mixed with olive oil, as a gift to the Lord, a
> soothing aroma, and its drink offering, one fourth of a hin of wine.
> You must not eat bread, roasted grain, or fresh grain until this
> very day, until you bring the offering of your God. This is a
> perpetual statute throughout your generations in all the places
> where you live. "'You must count for yourselves seven weeks
> from the day after the Sabbath, from the day you bring the wave
> offering sheaf; they must be complete weeks. You must count
> fifty days—until the day after the seventh Sabbath—and then you
> must present a new grain offering to the Lord.

It is very easy to miss the significance of what is going on and its
relevance to what Paul has said in 1 Corinthians 15:1–20. The passage
instructs the priest to offer the firstfruits three days after the Sabbath. It is
from this Sabbath that the people are to count fifty days when they are to
celebrate a second Sabbath, a day after which they are to present the grain
offering.

This makes it clear that the first Sabbath is the Passover; the second
Sabbath fifty days later is Pentecost. Three days after the Sabbath (Lev
23:11), the priest is to present the firstfruits to the Lord. This is hugely
significant, for Paul says that Christ died for our sins according to the

Scriptures and was raised three days later (1 Cor 15:3). And then he says (1 Cor 15:20) that Jesus is the firstfruits from the dead! Of course, it was three days after his paschal death that Jesus arose and presented himself as the firstfruits of the resurrection community that he is the head of.

What is going on in 1 Corinthians 15:3–20, and I would argue throughout the entire letter as well as in Paul's other letters to the churches, is a detailed typological exegesis of the Old Testament in the light of the Christ event. In this chapter the two Sabbaths centre on the Passover and Pentecost, the latter feast being typological concerning the ingathering of the church which the remainder of the chapter goes on to explain. The Passover is when Christ secured his people, described as the harvest which is the firstfruits of the dead. The great eschatological Pentecost is when the harvest is given up to the Father (15:42–49) after it has been rescued from death and decay (represented by the exile, typifying the eternal separation of humankind from its Creator), and presented to God (15:50–55). The victory (15:57) is the giving up of the kingdom to God that he might be all in all as explained earlier (15:20–28). It is quite possible that this model provided the background for Jesus' assertions that he would fulfil the type of Jonah (Matt 12:39) and the principle demonstrated by agriculture (John 12:24) that death is essential before life can be given.

This exegesis makes sense and provides the theological background for the resurrection after three days. This is when the firstfruits were presented to God. It links in perfectly with the fact that Jesus saw himself to be a priest as we saw earlier. He also knew himself to be the firstborn who had not been redeemed and as the promised son of David, i.e. of David's line he knew he had a kingly calling. But significantly, God had appointed Israel's king to be the firstborn over the kings of earth (Ps 87:29). So, his ministry has brought into existence a community of brothers redeemed by their firstborn. Paul makes this clear where he says:

> For I consider that the sufferings of this present time are not worth comparing with the glory that is to be revealed to us. For the creation waits with eager longing for the revealing of the sons of God. For the creation was subjected to futility, not willingly, but because of him who subjected it, in hope that the creation itself will be set free from its bondage to corruption and obtain the freedom of the glory of the children of God. For we know that the whole creation has been groaning together in the pains of childbirth until now. And not only the creation, but we ourselves, who have the firstfruits of the Spirit, groan inwardly as we wait

> eagerly for adoption as sons, the redemption of our bodies. For in this hope we were saved. Now hope that is seen is not hope. For who hopes for what he sees? But if we hope for what we do not see, we wait for it with patience.
>
> Likewise, the Spirit helps us in our weakness. For we do not know what to pray for as we ought, but the Spirit himself intercedes for us with groanings too deep for words. And he who searches hearts knows what is the mind of the Spirit, because the Spirit intercedes for the saints according to the will of God. And we know that for those who love God all things work together for good, for those who are called according to his purpose. For those whom he foreknew he also predestined to be conformed to the image of his Son, in order that he might be the firstborn among many brothers. And those whom he predestined he also called, and those whom he called he also justified, and those whom he justified he also glorified. (Rom 8:18–30)

This typological reading is also found in the prophecy of Isaiah. Israel in exile was rescued by her king, the Davidic prince. He brought her to the inheritance that she should have enjoyed with her God. All this had been lost until the prince who is her Redeemer delivered her by his death. The fact that Jesus linked into the redemptive promises of the Old Testament and saw his death as essential for his people's salvation. He saw that his death would produce a great harvest (John 12:20–26) suggesting that he was thinking in terms of Isaiah 53:10. It is significant that Jesus described himself as the seed that must die and this statement follows immediately after Jesus was hailed the king of the Jews in his triumphal entry into Jerusalem indicating again that he had come to die to produce a great harvest.

Another possible source for Jesus's understanding is the importance of the Passover in Jewish thinking. Rabbinic sources teach that the earth was created on the 14th Nissan, the date of the Passover. Abraham was about to sacrifice his son Isaac on the 14th of Nissan. The walls of Jericho fell on the 14th Nissan. From this we can see that the Passover had massive significance in the thinking of the Jewish community. That Isaac's intended offering was after three days' travel, he would therefore have returned to his home after another three days. Also, that he saw his death would be a sign like Jonah who was three days and nights in the fish (Luke 11:29). All of this point to additional endorsements of the Passover typology that we have noticed.

Paul taught that Jesus was the true promised seed. Did he come to this himself, or does it reflect a wider tradition that he expands on? As the true Isaac, the firstborn of his people, he is the one, if following a typological exegesis, who must return after 3 days. Christ's certainty of resurrection is echoed in Paul's exposition that Abraham must have believed that Isaac would be raised from the dead because all of God's covenant promises were focused on him and death could not thwart God's promises (Rom 4:18–24). This is yet another possibility, and dare I say, far more probable insight into the thinking of Jesus that keeps to the biblical narrative, rather than needing to seek a very poor solution in Hellenized sources that introduce pagan thought into the Christian narrative. In this model, we do not have Israel borrowing from pagan neighbours but being driven, like Abraham was, to theological conclusions as a result of direct revelation (i.e. Yahweh's command to Abraham to offer his only [firstborn] son); conclusions that human wisdom could never have discovered.

This proposed typological reading is not limited to 1 Corinthians 15. The whole letter is structured in the same way and Romans has also been written to show that Jesus is the typological fulfilment of all that the Old Testament foretold.[257]

There are a number of problems with Wright's proposal. Up until the resurrection he has argued that Old Testament language is metaphorical, and its fulfilment is of a different kind from what orthodoxy has concluded. So, the second coming is the fall of Jerusalem and the establishment of a different kind of kingdom. Yet here in his construction of the resurrection we have Old Testament language that everyone knew was metaphorical resurrection, which is changed to speak of a literal physical resurrection of the individual. Wright's methodology is seriously inconsistent. He argues this way because he knows where he has to end up, i.e. the Pharisees holding to a doctrine of resurrection and Jesus teaching that he would be raised from the dead.[258] But

---

[257] Holland, Contours, 145–147. See also Holland, Divine Marriage, which is a typologically based exposition of Romans in light of the Paschal New Exodus. Joel White, 'He was Raised on the Third Day According to the Scriptures (1 Cor 15:4): A Typological Interpretation Based on the Cultic Calendar in Leviticus 23' TynB 66 (2015), 103–119 suggests a similar argument to the one I had made earlier (Holland, Contours, 284), but White has not appreciated the breadth of Paul's typological exegesis which I have argued is fundamental to understand his exegetical method. White finishes his typological exegesis in the middle of the chapter but I see it goes to the very end of the chapter and indeed controls not only the entire first letter to the Corinthians but most other Pauline letters.

[258] Whether Saul of Tarsus held to this Maccabean version of resurrection we

the seed he borrows from the Maccabeans to grow his doctrine bears no resemblance to the doctrine that adorns Christian belief. Believers will not be raised because they gave their lives up to death for that will exclude the vast majority of believers from the hope of the resurrection. Christians will be raised in the last day because they have already been raised with Christ and seated with him at God's right hand. Christian resurrection is of grace from first to last; this is not what the Maccabees sought or taught.

And how did the Pharisees come to their understanding of resurrection? They were of course the descendants of the Maccabees, so that version is possible. But what they would have inherited would have been a resurrection based on works, of having been loyal to the Torah and keeping it in face of fearful opposition. A very commendable development in their theological journey, but it has come nowhere near to a Christian doctrine of resurrection. It is likely that Saul had travelled this way in his understanding until he met the resurrected Christ and discovered that Christian resurrection is very different from that accepted by the Pharisees. Jesus was not guided by the Maccabean model as argued by Wright. He had a full a bodily resurrection understanding which depended neither on reading Old Testament texts separately from their historic context, nor in making Maccabees into something it was not: a serious source for major Christian teaching. A huge difference between the Hellenized Jewish tradition and that taught by and brought about by Christ is that the former teaching was that resurrection was a reward for faithfulness. The Christian understanding is so very different; we look forward to the resurrection not on the grounds of our faithfulness but on the grounds of the faithfulness of Christ. His people do not rely on their own achievements but on the fact that they as a people were baptized into Christ in

---

do not know, it is possible that he did but it is dangerous to assume that there was only one version of the doctrine in pre-Christian Judaism. What is clear is that he never cites any Maccabean texts and so claims that it is the source of his teaching are ignoring the problems the claim entails as well as failing to consider the evidence of a far more certain source, the theology of the Old Testament and Jesus's actual death and resurrection. If Saul had held to the Maccabean version, it is clear that it became totally inadequate as a model to explain the biblical basis of this greatest of events. 'For I delivered to you as of first importance what I also received: that Christ died for our sins in accordance with the Scriptures, that he was buried, that he was raised on the third day in accordance with the Scriptures, and that he appeared to Cephas, then to the twelve. Then he appeared to more than five hundred brothers at one time, most of whom are still alive, though some have fallen asleep' (1 Cor 15:3–6 ESV).

his death and they have shared with him in his resurrection. This hope is absolutely certain, no one can take it away for nothing can separate us from the love of God that is in Christ Jesus our Lord.

Thus, Maccabees has nothing to do with Christ and his resurrection. Instead, the idea of resurrection is based on God being faithful to his covenant and bringing from the grave the redeemer he had appointed to deliver his people from the power of death.

Chapter 9:
Probing Wright's Doctrine of Justification

Tom Wright was catapulted into the centre of the theological bull ring when he announced that the Reformers had misunderstood Paul's doctrine of justification. In making this claim he effectively declared that the Reformation was a mistake.[259] Coming from someone who had once identified himself as a Reformed evangelical,[260] it shocked many and began a major shift in Christian understanding. He has effectively visited the church in Wittenberg and torn down the ninety-five theses from the door.[261] The effect of Wright's claim continues to reverberate throughout the Protestant churches.

However, the background to the New Perspective, which Wright has advocated, goes back to before Wright was born. A challenge to Reformed understanding from within the Protestant churches had been in progress for many decades with a growing number of scholars questioning the received understanding of 'being under the law'.

What made Wright's challenge different from those made earlier was that he not only questioned traditional understanding of key texts but that he additionally offered a change in basic assumptions about the way the Bible should be read. This focused on the narrative nature of the biblical books and this attracted many serious readers. Such a reading, which is a strand of biblical theology, was found by many to make better sense of a number of difficult passages.

This was an advance on earlier challenges to Reformed understanding because he could call on evidence from the relatively recently discovered

---

[259] See, for example, Wright, *What Saint Paul Really Said,* 98.

[260] As an Oxford undergraduate, Wright contributed a chapter to a volume published by the conservative Reformed publishing house Banner of Truth; see John Cheeseman, *The Grace of God in the Gospel* (Edinburgh: Banner of Truth, 1972), although listed as an author with John Cheeseman, Philip Gardner and Michael Sadgrove their individual contributions are not listed.

[261] There were of course very serious issues that Luther posted on the church door that, regardless of his view of justification, needed to be dealt with. At this stage, Luther was calling for reform, not a reformation.

Dead Sea Scrolls (DSS). He was also able to use the research results of E. P. Sanders, which had produced an intellectual earthquake as a result of his challenging the certainties of earlier theological understanding, especially in the way Jewish attitudes to the law were understood.[262] Sanders' work meant that it could no longer be claimed that first century Judaism was a legalistic religion; instead, it was one that stressed the grace of God in his dealings with Israel. Sanders' case was that the law had not been given to judge and condemn Israel, but rather to bless her, and that is how she viewed it. This research supported Wright's claim that the storyline of the Bible and the immediate narrative context of the passage being considered—along with its theological and historical contexts—are the crucial keys to a text's proper interpretation.

Wright argued that the Reformed understanding of law in Paul was flawed. He pointed out that Hebrew understanding did not come from the Roman legal system but was part of the OT teaching concerning covenant. The law (Torah) had been given to Israel to guide her in her relationship in the covenant she had been brought into by Yahweh. This covenant was about God promising to protect Israel, his people and to vindicate her as his elect in the last day. For Wright, it is this covenantal setting that provides one of the trio of truths that defines Paul's doctrine of justification. It was about being in a covenant relationship with God, a relationship which will be displayed to the nations on the final day when Yahweh puts all the wrong caused by sin right. For Wright, justification is not about how one was made right with God, but about being declared to be in the right with God because of being in the covenant. To this Wright claimed the court as another strand of the doctrine. Here the judge acquitted the guilty, not by bestowing his own righteousness but by declaring a legal status of having been found not guilty. The third strand to Wright's understanding of justification is the eschatological dimension, when Israel will be declared to be God's people before all the nations of the earth.2[263] Thus Wright challenged the Reformed understanding which focused on how people are made right with God through the death of Jesus. For him justification is a doctrine of ecclesiology and not soteriology. It is about who is in the church rather than how one comes into it. While in the Old Testament it is about how Israel was identified as the covenant people it developed into how the church is identified as the New Israel.

---

[262] E. Sanders, *Paul and Palestinian Judaism* (London: SCM Press, 1977).
[263] See Wright, *What Saint Paul Really Said,* 117.

Wright's appeal is not only to the biblical text and its history but also to the wider historical context. It is achieved by introducing non- biblical Jewish texts from the New Testament period as evidence for his preferred understanding.[264] He is anxious to show that the New Testament writers in general, and Paul particularly, were 'singing from the same hymn sheet' as other Jews of the same period. These intertestamental writings, Wright claims, are the crucial evidence which confirms how the New Testament texts should be read and interpreted.2[265] The accumulative changes to biblical exegesis produced by this method of reading created arguments that were novel and to some they were persuasive, with an increasing number of scholars and Christian leaders embracing them. As a result, the evangelical theological landscape has changed quite drastically in recent years. Wright's revisions have challenged the exegesis of many traditionally established interpretations of key passages that the Reformers had promoted, especially concerning their doctrine about justification. Before we can engage with Wright's view that the Reformers had got it wrong, we must first remind ourselves of their distinctive teaching and its origins.

The Reformers' Teaching on Justification

It is widely recognised that the Reformers based their understanding of justification on the metaphoric use of the Hebrew and Greek words for 'justified' *tsādek* (Hebrew) and *dedikaiōtai* (Greek).[266] Both words share the same semantic domain and have the same two meanings in both languages. First, 'justified' meant that something was credited to someone's account. It was thus a term taken from accountancy. A person might be in debt, but if someone puts money into this person's bank account, the payment changed his or her position from one of being in debt to one of being in credit. In theological terms, the justified were freed from the debt of sin and released from the burden they otherwise would have carried. God had credited

---

[264] The use of these sources is now standard for most scholars of New Testament studies.

[265] In doing this he followed the method that was being developed by among others James Dunn. See J. D. G. Dunn, Christology in *Making: A New Testament Inquiry into the Origins of the Doctrine of the Incarnation* (London: SCM Press, 1989).

[266] See J. V. Fesko, *Justification: Understanding the Classic Reformed Doctrine* (Phillipsburg: P&R Publishing, 2008).

(imputed) Christ's righteousness to the account of the believing sinner so that he or she was treated as being not guilty.

The second meaning the Reformers identified was that justification was about being acquitted from guilt. This imagery came from the criminal law court, where someone had been charged with an offence and tried. When the judge declared the defendant not guilty and released them from the threatened sentence, the accused was justified—found innocent of the charge. What the Reformers understood was that God declared the repentant sinner to be 'not guilty.' This was not because of the efforts of the sinner who had somehow atoned for his or her sins, but through the free mercy of God himself who, by the death of his Son, had atoned for the offending transgression. They understood that the guilty person was treated as innocent by God because Jesus had suffered their due penalty as the sin offering. Christ had died, 'the just for the unjust that he might bring us to God' (1 Pet 3:18). God's (Christ's) righteousness was imparted to the one who was acquitted.

Wright, being persuaded by the earlier work of Sanders, took exception to this understanding which he had earlier held.[267] Sanders had conducted detailed research of first century Jewish texts; a work made possible because of the discovery of the Dead Sea Scrolls (DSS)—a collection of 981 ancient texts discovered between 1946 and 1956 at Khirbet Qumran on the West Bank of the Dead Sea. These texts provided much needed documentary evidence concerning the way in which a particular group of first century Jews viewed a whole range of topics. Of special significance was how these Jews viewed the Mosaic law. Sanders, whose study was not limited to the DSS, claimed that his research demonstrated that the Jews did not live in fear of the law as the Reformers had believed. He persuaded many scholars that the Jews had a very positive and relaxed understanding of the role of the law, for rather than seeing the law as a threat, they viewed it as the greatest blessing Israel had ever been given. The law was understood to have been a wedding gift from God to his bride, Israel. It was given as a guide for their life together and to bless the nation.

This new way of understanding of the law was called 'covenantal nomism' (covenantal law) by Sanders. It is this revision that has changed the way many modern scholars now understand what Paul taught about the relationship that exists between the law and the believer in Christ. This new

---

[267] See his contribution in Cheeseman, *The Grace of God in the Gospel.*

understanding, heavily promoted by Wright, became the base for assessing all other views.[268] This, in turn, impacted on how Wright understood what Paul meant when he wrote about justification.[269]

Wright's stance (termed the 'New Perspective on Paul' or NPP) on this issue is not so much a fresh insight which serves to clarify and add richer layers of understanding to the Reformed position as it is a radical reinterpretation of justification, saying that the Reformers got Paul's teaching totally wrong.[270]

> If we use the language of the law court, it makes no sense
> whatsoever to say that the judge imputes, imparts, bequeaths,
> conveys or otherwise transfers his righteousness to either the
> plaintiff or the defendant. Righteousness is not an object, a
> substance or a gas which can be passed across the courtroom ....
> If we leave the notion of 'righteousness' as a law-court metaphor
> only, as so many have done in the past, this gives the impression

---

[268] N. T. Wright, *'The Paul of History and the Apostolic Faith'*, TynB 29 (1978), 61–88 [77]. Whilst using the research of Sanders where it suited his case, Wright has argued that Sanders never understood the implications of his own study for the doctrine of justification. Wright went on to say that Sanders read the texts of Intertestamental Judaism too woodenly, rejecting the method of Hay's intertexualisation. See also Wright, *Perspective,* 10.

[269] Wright says: 'Despite a long tradition to the contrary, the problem Paul addresses in Galatians is not the question of how precisely someone becomes a Christian or attains to a relationship with God. (I'm not even sure how Paul would express, in Greek, the notion of 'relationship with God', but we'll leave that aside.) The problem he addresses is: should ex-pagan converts be circumcised or not? Now this question is by no means obviously to do with the questions faced by Augustine and Pelagius, or by Luther and Erasmus. On anyone's reading, but especially within its first-century context, [the problem] has to do, quite obviously, with the question of how you define the people of God. Are they to be defined by the badges of the Jewish race, or in some other way?' Wright, *What Saint Paul Really Said,* 120.

[270] It needs to be noted that in the early years of the NPP there tended to be one common focus: Paul's understanding of the law. However, since then there have been many developments and some who share some of the conclusions of the Reformers also share insights from the NPP. Other NPP theologians do not necessarily agree with Wright on justification, even if they agree with him on the importance of Paul's Jewish background. For this reason, it is wise to speak of New Perspectives rather than on the singular, New Perspective.

of a legal transaction, a cold piece of business, almost a trick of thought performed by a God who is logical and correct but hardly one we would want to worship.[271]

Indeed, as noted earlier, Wright went so far as to say that the Reformers had made a far-reaching mistake in understanding what Paul meant when he spoke about justification.[272]

As Sanders' work has been scrutinized, it has been shown that he was far too optimistic in his conclusions. Even though Wright has acknowledged his mistake for relying too heavily on Sanders, he still continues to promote the essential revision he proposed in the early days before it was shown that the research of Sanders was flawed.[273]

That there are texts in which Paul clearly speaks in both positive and negative terms about the same law cannot be ignored, and Wright has not

---

[271] Wright, *What Saint Paul Really Said,* 98. 'This is where the so called "new perspective" has made one of its necessary points—that every time Paul discusses justification he seems simultaneously to be talking about Gentile inclusion—but has not, usually, shown how this integrates with the traditional view that he is talking about how sinners are put right with God. Once we frame the question within the overall narrative of creation and covenant, the way is clear and open to a fresh statement of Paul which will do far more exegetical justice to the passages concerned and which will show how these two emphases are in fact part of the same thing, both to be equally stressed.' Wright, *Perspectives,* 36 [emphasis added]. This claim can only be sustained by ignoring a range of texts that do not fit the claim, such texts as Rom 5:12–21 and Acts 13:32–43.

[272] This reflects Wright's commitment to the ecumenical movement and this commitment needs to be recognised in his exegetical work for it is a determining factor in his understanding of a range of texts. '"It cannot be right that the very doctrine which declares that all who believe in Jesus belong at the same table (Galatians 2) should be used as a way of saying that some, who define the doctrine of justification differently, belong at a different table. The doctrine of justification, in other words, is not merely a doctrine in which Catholic and Protestant might just be able to agree on, as a result of hard ecumenical endeavour. It is itself the ecumenical doctrine, the doctrine that rebukes all our petty and often culture- bound church groupings, and which declares that all who believe in Jesus belong together in the one family .... The doctrine of justification is in fact the great ecumenical doctrine.' Wright, *What Saint Paul Really Said,* 158.

[273] Wright, *Perspectives,* 109.

addressed this issue adequately. These tensions must be addressed before anyone can claim to have arrived at the apostles' understanding of the law and its associated theme of justification. Indeed, Wright's own position has become confusing, for while he continues to advocate a very positive Hebrew understanding concerning the law, he has claimed that the law was given with the purpose of controlling Israel's sinful behaviour, the very understanding many reformed scholars held was its purpose.[274]

Reviewing History

Clearly, at the time of the Reformation, the Reformers' argument was directed against the Church of Rome. They detested the doctrine of penance and the pressure it put on financially impoverished members of the church. These often desperately poor people were pressurised into paying money that they could ill afford to purchase indulgences for their deceased loved ones, having been promised that these payments would release them from the pains of purgatory. The practice drove many of these desperate people into ever deeper debt and further poverty as they purchased these heavily promoted ways out of post-mortem suffering. The money that was spent to secure these passages from purgatory went straight into the coffers of the church.

The Reformers saw that the Bible's teaching on justification completely cut across the legitimacy of this practice. They taught that being made right with God was not a status anyone could merit or purchase but an unmerited gift of God to the repentant sinner who puts his or her faith in Christ. Thus, at the heart of their doctrine of justification was the belief that no person could be justified by keeping the law (regarding the Reformer's understanding, by his or her own efforts to be righteous before God). They understood the law to be God's means by which sinners were pursued and brought to see their sinful condition, and they taught that it was powerless to save people because it served only to reveal humanity's condemnation.

---

[274] The Torah had a purpose all right; it was indeed God's holy law; but its purpose was to keep Israel in check, to stop God's wayward people going totally off track, until the time when, through the Messiah, the long-term ultimate promises could be fulfilled.' *N. T. Wright, Justification: God's Plan and Paul's Vision* (Downers Grove: IVP Academic, 2009), 107. This does not sound like the law that was given as a wedding gift that Wright elsewhere claims.

The Reformers were adamant that good works could not atone for sin, for sin taints all works of religion or righteousness. Because of such a clear understanding, the Reformers stood their ground against the Roman Church's teaching that salvation could be bought and preached and wrote passionately against the indulgence system. Their teaching challenged the Roman Church's authority and its ability to raise funds, and this led to the persecution of the Reformers and the communities that embraced their understanding.

It was not that Rome denied the need of faith. It acknowledged that faith was necessary for salvation, but it insisted that works were also an essential part of the salvific process. To this the Reformers strenuously responded that works played no part whatever in salvation—faith in the atoning death of Jesus alone made a person right with God.

Wright and the Impact of the New Perspective

The volume of Wright's publishing has been phenomenal; the same message being powerfully presented through different publications to different audiences. With the ever-increasing volume of books that he has published there can be traced some adjustments to his doctrine of justification. Inevitably, there have been some key texts along the way.[275] For example, when he reaffirmed his claim that justification was not about being made right with God, but that it is a statement made by God in which he declares someone to be in the covenant community. Rather than being made right with God, which was the Reformers' understanding, Wright continues to insist that being justified has nothing to do with being acquitted from sin—and even less does it mean that righteousness is credited to the believer. To put it another way, Wright denies the doctrine of the imputation of Christ's righteousness as taught by the Reformers, describing it as legal fiction.[276]

These repeated claims made by Wright have caused evangelical scholars to divide roughly into two camps. Whilst one group defends the traditional understanding of the Reformers, the other promotes Wright's New

---

[275] Wright, *What Saint Paul Really Said,* 113–133. Much time has been spent on defending this position. See especially his defence in Wright, *Justification,* 59–87 which is a reply to the charges made by John Piper in *The Future of Justification: A Response to N. T. Wright* (Wheaton: Crossway Books, 2007).

[276] N. T. Wright, *The Great Acquittal: Justification by Faith and Current Christian Thought,* Ed. Gavin Reid (London: Collins, 1980), 13ff.

Perspective understanding and has increasingly challenged the understanding of the Reformers on a range of subjects

Of course, Wright claims that he only wants to read the Scriptures properly, a wholly commendable motive, and he is entirely correct in saying that the Reformers are not exempt from being tested by the rule of faith that they themselves sought to uphold. The question to be considered, therefore, is; has Wright read the evidence correctly? We have seen earlier in our discussion of the identity of Saul being a zealot that Wright is not immune from making incorrect assessments. Could it be that the current scholarly confidence in the New Perspective is not as securely based on Scripture as Wright and many others have claimed? Wright has correctly argued the importance of taking the whole of the evidence into account and of not leaving passages off the table that are unfavourable for the preferred reading.[277] While this is a laudable appeal, I want to suggest that Wright has failed to respond to the challenge of submitting to the whole of the evidence himself.

The Protestant Doctrine of Justification

In my view, those who hold a New Perspective position on Paul have made some fundamental mistakes. Firstly, the early assessments made by New Perspective thinkers of the Reformers' doctrine of justification treated it as if it were monolithic. This assumption missed the fact that the Reformed position has always encompassed a wide spectrum of opinions. It is, therefore, dangerous to describe the Reformed position as being in any way monolithic, and then attack it. Using this approach is akin to attacking a straw man.

Even the Westminster Confession, which Wright takes aim at, should not be seen in this uniform way. For although this joint confession was agreed to provide a united bulwark against the false teachings that so deeply concerned them, the individual writings of the committee that compiled the Confession reveal that a much richer and more nuanced range of meanings lay behind

---

[277] 'All accounts involve "interpretation"; the question is whether this interpretation discloses the totality of the event, opening it up in all actuality and meaning, or whether it squashes it out of shape, closing down its actuality and meaning.' Wright, *People of God,* 92. Wright goes on to say: 'A Good Hypothesis includes all of the data; it must construct a basically simple and coherent overall picture,' 100.

their theological convictions than any one confession could succeed in conveying.[278]

By comparing two major confessions produced by the Reformers, we will find another example of the differences which existed in that movement. The first is the afore-mentioned Westminster Confession, which is forensic and legalistic in tone; and the other is the Augsburg Confession, which is decidedly covenantal in tone.

The Westminster Confession

The *Westminster Confession* (1647) defines justification as follows in Chapter 11 Of Justification:

> 1. Those whom God effectually calleth, he also freely justified: not by infusing righteousness into them, but by pardoning their sins, and by accounting and accepting their persons as righteous; not for anything wrought in them, or done by them, but for Christ's sake alone; not by imputing faith itself, the act of believing, or any other evangelical obedience to them, as their righteousness; but by imputing the obedience and satisfaction of Christ unto them, they receiving and resting on him and his righteousness by faith; which faith they have not of themselves, it is the gift of God.
>
> 2. Faith, thus receiving and resting on Christ and his righteousness, is the alone instrument of justification; yet is it not alone in the person justified, but is ever accompanied with all other saving graces, and is no dead faith, but worketh by love.
>
> 3. Christ, by his obedience and death, did fully discharge the debt of all those that are thus justified, and did make a proper, real, and full satisfaction of his Father's justice in their behalf. Yet inasmuch as he was given by the Father for them, and his obedience and satisfaction accepted in their stead, and both freely, not for anything in them, their justification is only of free grace, that both the exact justice and rich grace of God might be glorified in the justification of sinners.
>
> 4. God did, from all eternity, decree to justify the elect; and Christ did, in the fullness of time, die for their sins and rise again for their justification; nevertheless, they are not justified until the Holy Spirit doth, in due time, actually apply Christ unto them.

---

[278] For a range of meanings held by the reformers see Holland, *Contours,* 325–337.

5. God doth continue to forgive the sins of those that are justified; and although they can never fall from the state of justification, yet they may by their sins fall under God's Fatherly displeasure, and not have the light of his countenance restored unto them, until they humble themselves, confess their sins, beg pardon, and renew their faith and repentance.

6. The justification of believers under the Old Testament was, in all these respects, one and the same with the justification of believers under the New Testament.

The Augsburg Confession

In contrast to the Westminster Confession, The Apology of the Augsburg Confession (1531) 4:2 defines Justification by saying:

> That man enjoys that acceptance with God called 'justification', the beginning and end of salvation, not through his own moral effort even in the smallest and slightest degree but entirely and only through the loving mercy of God made available in the merits of Christ and of his saving death on the Cross. This was not a process of gradual ethical improvement but an instantaneous transaction, something like a marriage, in which Christ the bridegroom takes to himself an impoverished and wretched harlot and confers upon her all the riches which are his. The key to this transaction was faith, defined as a total and trustful commitment of the self to God, and is itself not a human achievement but the pure gift of God.[279]

Both these important confessions represent a collective 'compromise' through which those who ascribed to them provided a clear statement of those doctrines which united them; neither confession can, therefore, offer any clarity about the theological differences which existed between their respective signatories. In focusing on the Westminster Confession, Wright chose what he thought would best make his case and in doing so, has treated all other equally authentic confessions of Reformed theology as being of little relevance. Wright has more recently acknowledged the existence of this

---

[279] Apology of the Augsburg Confession (1531) 4.2, cited by Reumann in J. Reumann, J. A. Fitzmyer, and J. Quinn, Righteousness in *New Testament: Justification in the United States Lutheran-Roman Catholic Dialogue* (New York: Fortess Press; Philadelphia: Paulist Press, 1982), 3.

variation,[280] but nevertheless, he has not revised his position on justification.[281]

Methodological Concerns

There is a further reason why the claims of New Perspective scholars should be questioned. The evidence upon which the New Perspective has been built is not as secure as some scholars would like to assume, as is evident from the research Sanders undertook. It was this research that initially challenged the Reformed position, but on closer examination it was seen to have failed to provide the quality of evidence that the New Perspective theologians needed to make their case secure. This is exemplified in the way the leading New Perspective theologians split up the research of Sanders, using only what suited their agenda. This difference between Sanders, Wright, and Dunn (the theologian who first coined the term 'the New Perspective')[282] is not always appreciated. Sanders stated what he considered his research uncovered regarding Paul's theological understanding when he wrote: 'Paul does not have simply a "Jewish" or a "Hellenistic" or a Hellenistic Jewish conception of man's plight. It appears that Paul's thought was not simply taken over from any one scheme pre-existing in the ancient world.'[283]

---

[280] Wright, *Perspectives,* 109.

[281] Wright certainly improves on his earlier discussion when he says, 'Paul's understanding of justification must be interpreted resolutely in terms of OT affirmations of God's faithfulness to the covenant', Wright, *Justification,* 67. He went on to say: 'for Paul, "justification" whatever else it included, always had in mind God's declaration of membership, and that this always referred specifically to the coming together of Jews and Gentiles in faithful membership of the Christian family." Wright, *Justification,* 95. But his insistence that it is rooted in the issue of gentile acceptance without circumcision, while a crucial part of Paul's application of the doctrine of justification, is too narrow and ignores the abundance of NT evidence that he has excluded and which we shall soon consider. We will soon see that there are in fact nine distinct meanings within the semantic domain of 'justify'.

[282] For the claim that it was Wright who originated the term, see M. Colvin, 'Who Coined the Name "New Perspective on Paul"?', *Colvinism;* April 8, 2014, https://colvinism.wordpress.com/2014/04/08/who-coined-the-name-new-perspective-on-paul/

[283] Sanders, *Palestinian Judaism,* 555 says, 'Paul does not have simply a

So, in Sanders' view, it is fruitless to appeal to Judaism for an authoritative understanding of Paul's theology. Now this is the very thing that Wright and Dunn have done by engaging the Jewish intertestamental texts and using them as the key to reading Paul. These two leading exponents of the New Perspective claim that the way to properly understand Paul is to create a synthesis between him and the rest of Second Temple Judaism. This is especially true, they claim, regarding Paul's understanding of the function and purpose of the law.

Thus, while Sanders says that Paul moved from his traditional theological home of Pharisaic Judaism, Wright argues that Paul remained as a Jew who had discovered that Jesus fulfilled the promises given in Israel's Scriptures and that he must be read in that tradition. Many, of course, would agree with Wright's preferred location—and I certainly do—but the point is that Wright, having rejected the position that Sanders came to regarding Paul's intellectual and spiritual identity as a follower of Jesus, needs to explain why he regards Sanders as being so reliable in one field and so mistaken in another; especially when he is using the same method of research in both studies. The reason this problem is so critical is that if one accepts the conclusions of Sanders on covenantal nomism, but reject his conclusions concerning Paul's new Christian mindset, then we have arrived at conflicting conclusions while using the same method—not a situation we would wish to be in. Sanders' reading of Paul is very different from Wright's reading, and yet Wright has relied heavily on Sanders to support his interpretation of intertestamental Judaism. Could this be because he is attracted by a covenantal nomism understanding which serves his theological interests? Until Wright has vindicated his choice of Paul's post- conversion religious context and explains why he thinks Sanders can get things so right on covenantal nomism, but so wrong on the apostle's theological and cultural location, his reconstruction remains vulnerable. He lays himself open to the accusation of creating a Paul to his own liking, taking from Paul's letters the material he prefers rather than scrutinizing the whole of Scripture. In his more recent writings, Wright has accepted that his support of Sanders has been effectively challenged.[284]

Thus, like Sanders and Dunn, Wright has expanded the area of evidence to take into account the literature of Second Temple Judaism. I have already

---

"Jewish" or a "Hellenistic" or a Hellenistic Jewish concept of man's plight. It appears that Paul's thought was not simply taken over from any one scheme pre-existing in the ancient world.'

[284] See Wright, *Faithfulness of God,* 12–13.

dealt with the need for strict controls to be put in place to govern how these sources are used. Like Dunn, Wright offers no explanation of how he evaluates the relevance of the extra biblical material he appeals to, even though he says that it needs to be handled responsibly. My problem with his method is that he relies too heavily on this extended field of evidence, and I believe that some of his key arguments cannot survive once the misuse of these texts has been recognized.

I have absolutely no problem with claiming that Paul's understanding was derived from the Old Testament; after all, Paul repeatedly quotes from it and his theology owes so much to his interpretation of Israel's Scriptures, especially Isaiah.[285] In contrast, however, there is not one quote in Paul's letters that can be said to come from Second Temple sources. Frequently, all Wright can offer on this point is a poorly considered conjecture that a particular word reflects dependency on an intertestamental text.

The issue of method is very important; it deals with how evidence is gathered and interpreted, and what presumptions are being made to guide the selection of sources and their subsequent interpretation. These hidden factors have a controlling effect on the inevitable outcome of an argument. Wright has given a crucial insight into his own method under the heading of 'The Shape of Justification':

> How is one to display an argument like this to best advantage? As with all major Pauline topics, we face the choice of either working through all the relevant passages and then drawing conclusions, or setting out a working hypothesis and then showing how the key passages reflect it. For present purposes I choose the latter course[286]

In a footnote Wright expands on this chosen method saying:

> Of course either method takes its place on the larger hermeneutical spiral of many years of reflection, recorded in part in Perspectives and in commentaries etc.; the move from historical exegesis to thematic analysis and back again is never-ending. I am naturally aware of the major ongoing discussions of justification as a topic in historical and systematical theology, and what

---

[285] See Roger Nicole 'New Testament Use of the Old Testament' in Carl. F. H. Henry (ed.), *Revelation and the Bible* (Grand Rapids: Baker, 1958), 137–151 and Holland, *Contours,* 325–337.

[286] Wright, *Faithfulness of God,* 925.

follows will inevitably have considerable relevance to those
debates (since most debaters hold a high view of Scripture in
which what Paul actually says is supposed to be decisive and
determinative!). However, it will of course not be possible to
engage with details. For an important recent symposium see
McCormack 2006b.[287]

So, this is an important statement of Wright's method. He has chosen to
show how 'key passages' fit his hypothesis rather than trawl through all the
texts that could be considered. This is a reasonable decision to make, since it
saves time and effort, providing checks are put in place to deal with all those
texts that do not fit in with the stated hypothesis. Wright in his footnote flags
up that he is aware of the hermeneutical issues, but the fact is that by
following this method he has been able to ignore a number of equally 'key
texts'.

Key texts are of course defined by what the writer is seeking to prove;
another writer might select different texts that he or she considers to be 'key'.
Hence the key texts are the key texts to prove the preferred reading. A failure
to bring all relevant texts to the table means that Wright's method does not
have appropriate checks and balances in place. Such a failure to consider
conflicting evidence litters the pages of research papers.

It is not my intention to explore Paul's doctrine of law and sin here, but it
must be pointed out that to hold Paul's understanding of the law as being an
unconditionally qualified positive attitude (as Sanders has claimed
characterized Second Temple Judaism) is wholly unwise. The fact is that Paul

---

[287] Wright, *Faithfulness of God,* 925 fn 425 says that: 'All accounts involve
"interpretation"; the question is whether this interpretation discloses the
totality of the event, opening it up in all actuality and meaning, or whether it
squashes it out of shape, closing down its actuality and meaning.' Wright,
People of God, 92: 'A Good Hypothesis includes all of the data; it must
construct a basically simple and coherent overall picture.' Sanders's reading
of Paul is very different from Wright's reading, and yet Wright has relied
heavily on Sanders to support his interpretation of Intertestamental Judaism.
Could this be because he is attracted by a covenantal nomism understanding
which serves his own theological interests? Until Wright has vindicated his
choice of Paul's post-conversion religious context and explains why he thinks
Sanders can get things so right on covenantal nomism but so wrong on the
apostle's own theological and cultural location, his own reconstruction
remains vulnerable. He lays himself open to the accusation of creating a Paul
in his own liking, taking from Paul's letters the material he prefers rather than
scrutinizing the whole of scripture.

(and he, of course, is very much a Second Temple Jew) speaks of the giving of the law at Sinai as having been a 'ministry of death' (2 Cor 3:7). This suggests that he, whatever his pre-Christian understanding, came to see the law as threatening and judgemental. I shall give a possible solution to this conundrum later in the chapter.

A Positive Gain—Well Almost!

Despite what I have written so far, the fact remains that there have been crucial gains made as a result of the challenge of the New Perspective reading of Paul. It has led many scholars to undertake a detailed re-examination of texts in which Paul explains the role of the law in regard to believing gentiles. Wright (and Dunn) have in my view correctly highlighted that the discussions on justification and law-keeping in Galatians were not centred on how individual gentiles were made right with God; rather, they were about whether believing gentiles, as a community, needed to be part of Judaism to be right with God.[288] This clarifies the point that Paul's criticism of law-keeping was not about submitting to a code of ethics, which if followed would gain salvation; rather, Paul's teaching in Galatians was about submitting to circumcision, food laws, and the keeping of set holy days. In this letter, Paul dealt with the question of whether these practices were conditions of membership of the covenant community.

These practices were the identity markers of the Jewish nation, which the law required all Jews to submit to, thus marking the people of Israel out as Yahweh's people. Hence, it is true that Paul's ideas about 'keeping the law'— in Galatians at least—was not about a legalistic attempt to earn salvation as had been understood by the Reformers, but about what was necessary to be counted as a member of the covenant community. However, to accept these 'boundary markers' the gentiles would have become Jews; and so, would have had to accept the wider understanding of the law's requirements as understood by the Jewish community. In other words, the two issues of accepting the identity markers of Judaism and coming under the ethical demands of the law (as traditionally perceived by the Reformers) are inseparably linked. This is something that is often overlooked in this debate. It

---

[288] Even so, we still cannot escape that the debate was about entry into the covenant and not (as Wright claims) about being declared to be in the covenant. Wright, *Justification*, 96.

will be shown that this double meaning is reflected in the New Testament and Paul's writings particularly.

This larger corporate setting of the justification of believing gentiles helps us to understand the nature of Paul's argument and the importance of the believing gentiles not giving in to the demands of the Judaizers who sought to control the freedom of the gentile church.[289] Had the gentile believers submitted to their exhortations they would have converted to Judaism, and so would have had to do all the things required by Jewish law and tradition. The outcome would have totally emptied the promises of God of their power, for they would have rejected the apostolic message of God's free grace offered in the gospel.

Paul opposed this move, arguing elsewhere that Abram (Abraham) himself was not circumcised when God justified him in Genesis 15:6 (see Rom 2:28–29; 4:10–12 and clearly implied in Gal 3:18). At the heart of Paul's concern was that to demand that the gentiles should submit to circumcision as a condition of justification was to invent another religion. If Abram had been accepted without circumcision, and Israel was accepted into the covenant because of Abram, then Israel was also accepted without circumcision. This meant that the Judaizers' teaching that the gentiles must be circumcised was not an invitation into the faith of Abram at all—it was a demand to convert to a different faith, a works-based faith, where circumcision was the key to entrance. Clearly the Sinai covenant did require works as a condition of ongoing membership,[290] but Paul is not saying that the gentiles were ever thought to be a part of the community that was under the authority of Moses.

The Jews boasted that their covenant relationship with God was through Abraham. If the gentiles were converting to a works-based religion that Abraham was never a part of then, the gentiles would thus be excluded from God's free, undeserved grace forever! For this reason, Paul wanted them to understand that the true descendants of Abraham are those who are circumcised in the heart, not the flesh (Deut 30:6; Jer 31:31–34; Ezek 36:25–27; Rom 2:25–29; Gal 3:18 implied). Paul likens circumcision (as required by the Judaizers) to return to bondage under the weak and miserable principles

---

[289] It is quite possible that the Judaizers were not ethnic Jews but gentile converts, possibly who had previously professed faith in Christ but who now hold that they have found 'the truth' and urged the Galatian believers to join them as members of the Jewish community.

[290] Deut 31:29; Job 34:11; Heb 6:10.

which once controlled them (Gal 4:9; Col 2:20–23). In other words, they would be returning to the condition they were in before coming to Christ—like that which Israel had experienced in Egypt—a life without the Living God, who had been displaced by the god of this world.

I confess that for many years I could not understand why Paul did not use Isaiah 19 to settle the status of the gentile church in God's presence. This passage says:

> In that day there will be an altar to the Lord in the midst of the land of Egypt, and a pillar to the Lord at its border. It will be a sign and a witness to the Lord of hosts in the land of Egypt. When they cry to the Lord because of oppressors, he will send them a saviour and defender, and deliver them. And the Lord will make himself known to the Egyptians, and the Egyptians will know the Lord in that day and worship with sacrifice and offering, and they will make vows to the Lord and perform them. And the Lord will strike Egypt, striking and healing, and they will return to the Lord, and he will listen to their pleas for mercy and heal them. In that day there will be a highway from Egypt to Assyria, and Assyria will come into Egypt, and Egypt into Assyria, and the Egyptians will worship with the Assyrians. In that day Israel will be the third with Egypt and Assyria, a blessing in the midst of the earth, whom the Lord of hosts has blessed, saying, "Blessed be Egypt my people, and Assyria the work of my hands, and Israel my inheritance." (Isa 19:19–25)

Recently I have come to recognize that this incredible statement by Isaiah did not say enough to finally settle the issue. If Paul had used this text as his key evidence for the acceptance of the gentiles, it would allow the Jews to claim that the gentiles had come late to the party. They were an afterthought. Even with the incredibly honorific titles that they are given, they were not Abraham's true children but became recipients of God's acceptance by courtesy of the Jewish people. Thus, the gentile believers would be at the behest of the Jewish community.

Paul wanted to avoid the possibility of such an argument being made, and he did so by considering the case of Abram the gentile, whose acceptance by God meant the gentiles as well as Jews were together accepted. Moreover, by implication they were both accepted at the same time, when both were represented by the uncircumcised Abram. Thus, the gentiles are not 'late to the party'; rather their invitation to participate in God's kingdom had not arrived because the Jews had not yet delivered it as they had been commissioned to do!

Tom Wright's Understanding of Justification

Allow me to state at the outset of this section that I am completely in agreement with Wright in his reading of the debate concerning justification in Galatians; that it is about covenant membership. Where I disagree with Wright, however, is over his conclusion that this has nothing to do with the understanding of the Reformers concerning law righteousness. We will shortly see that there is clear evidence that at least some Jews kept the law in the belief that it was required to make them acceptable before God. What Paul could see was that whatever the reason for submitting to circumcision, it would ultimately lead to legalism, since conversion to Judaism inevitably meant an obligation to keep the whole law. If this was true for gentile converts then it exposed the flawed understanding of the Judaizers; for clearly some elements of Second Temple Judaism did have legalistic tendencies.[291] Apart from that, Paul could see that if the gospel was 'Christ plus circumcision' then it was not the gospel of Christ and it had to be resisted.

A major problem with Wright's approach to justification is that he takes the meaning that he has argued for Galatians and applies it to almost all occurrences of the term found elsewhere in Paul. This ubiquitous meaning is revealed in his response to Piper's critique where he says:

> . . . for Paul, 'justification', whatever else it included, always had in mind God's declaration of membership, and this always referred specifically to the coming together of Jews and gentiles in faithful membership of the Christian family[292]

This understanding is at the heart of another statement that Wright makes concerning his claims concerning Paul's teaching on justification when he says:

> The point is that the word 'justification' does not itself denote the process whereby, or the event in which, a person is brought by grace from unbelief, idolatry and sin into faith, true worship and renewal of life. Paul clearly and unambiguously, uses a different word for that, the word 'call'. The word 'justification', despite centuries of Christian misuse, is used by Paul to denote that which happened immediately after the 'call'; 'those god has called, he has also justified' (Rom 8:30). In other words, those who hear the

---

[291] Carson, *Variegated Nomism,* Vol. 1, 5.

[292] Wright, *Justification,* 96.

gospel and respond to it in faith are then declared by God to be his people, his elect, 'the circumcision', 'the Jews', the 'Israel of God'. They are given the status dikaios, 'righteous'. 'within the covenant'.[293]

This claim, that justification is always about being declared to be in the covenant and nothing more, is clearly overstating the case, for he is not considering the individual situations in which the term was used.[294] The needs in Rome, for instance, were far from being the same as those in Galatia. There is no evidence of proselytising by Judaizers taking place in Rome as was the case in Galatia, and therefore, one is not surprised to find Paul tackling the subject of justification from a different perspective.[295]

Not only this, but Wright sometimes loses sight of the corporate element of Paul's argument in Galatians and applies the terminology to individuals—without giving any rationale for this transfer from the corporate to the individual.[296] As I have argued elsewhere,[297] the entire New Testament (apart from the private correspondence) should be read in a corporate context, for the letters do not relate so much to an individual experience as to the

---

[293] Wright, *Perspectives*, 121–2.

[294] This is not denying that Wright has moved on from his earlier very restricted view of claiming that justification means being declared to be in the covenant and he now sees variation within the word, but it is always anchored in this fundamental meaning, so: 'The righteousness of God' in Phil 3: is not quite the same as in Gal 2, Phil 2 has more of a forward look, sharing the Messiah's suffering: Wright, Perspectives, 16. See also 'Everywhere Paul discusses justification he seems simultaneously to be talking about Gentile inclusion'. Wright, *Justification*, 36.

[295] Wright, *Perspectives,* 20 says: 'My own acquaintance with Paul leads me to suspect that he would have been puzzled by such distinctions. Of course, he would say, all the letters were written to particular churches with particular needs. Even Romans—perhaps especially Romans—has that characteristic. But that doesn't mean for a moment that he would not claim to be expounding a consistent message throughout, even though it needs nuancing now this way and now that.' I will show that the case for justification in Romans had a much greater eschatological dimension and related to the legitimacy of the unfolding divine marriage.

[296] Seen in his acknowledgment that Rom 6:1–6 is based on Israel's baptism unto Moses which was a corporate event yet interpreting Christian baptism individualistically, see Wright, *Faithfulness of God,* 1373.

[297] See Holland, *Romans: The Divine Marriage,* 18–20.

corporate experience of the community that is in Christ. This corporate reading, so natural to the New Testament world, neither robs the individual believer of personal blessings nor does it remove any personal responsibilities. What such a reading does, however, is recognize that the gospel message cannot be removed from the believing community which it has created, and which holds to it as its rule of life and faith. This was the original apostolic understanding, which stands counter to the obsessive individualism of so much Christian understanding today. While Wright has on occasion appealed for a corporate reading, I sense that he has not grasped the extent of such a task; for he only occasionally brings this hermeneutical requirement to bear, and only on certain sections of the New Testament.

Wright's neglect of the corporate reading can be seen in his exegesis of the following texts. Like others, he understands 1 Corinthians 6:19 to be a reference to the Spirit dwelling in the individual believer's body—yet the Greek text is explicit that it is ὑμῶν ('your'—plural) σῶμα ('body'—singular) where the Spirit dwells.[298]

In other words, the Spirit dwells in all of his fullness in the church but not in the individual (albeit the individual shares in that fullness of the Spirit as a member of Christ's body). The same oversight may be observed in Wright's reading of Romans 12:1–2,[299] for again it is not the individual bodies of believers that are to be offered as living sacrifices, but ὑμᾶς σώματα ('your'—plural; body—plural); one offering made by the entire community. They offer themselves individually, but it is one sacrifice that is made, not many individual offerings. Furthermore, in his reading of Romans 7:1–6, Wright says that the believer is married to Christ when, in fact, this understanding cannot be upheld; it is always the church that is married to Christ.[300] This lack of clarity along with his wider exegesis persuades me that Wright does not fully appreciate the extent to which the theology of the New Testament letters is controlled by Paul's Semitic corporate perspective. If he had done so, then he would have applied the corporate understanding of justification (which he found in Galatians) to other texts. By so doing he might have found an

---

[298] 'In 1 Corinthians we find the church, and individual Christians, described as, among other things, the renewed Temple.' Wright, *Perspectives,* 45.

[299] 'These sacrifices are "holy".' Emphasis added. Wright, 'Romans' *NIB,* 704.

[300] Rom 7:1–4; 2 Cor 11:2; Eph 5:25–28; Rev 18–19.

alternative explanation of 'justified' as in the Romans 6:7 text,[301] for as the context is corporate, so is the significance of the use of the term 'justify' here.

This failure by Wright to keep to the corporate setting of Paul's theological construction is an important clue for detecting the fragmentary nature of his argument. Wright repeats these mistakes despite his repeated affirmations concerning the importance of the corporate. Having argued for the corporate understanding of justification found in some parts of the letter to the Galatians he imposes the same meaning onto the word *dedikaiwtai* (justification) wherever he finds it in other Pauline letters. But often, when he does this, he has abandoned the corporate setting that he says is essential for the meaning and treats the texts as describing individual justification. In this matter, he surprisingly follows the Reformers whom he criticizes (applying the term to the individual) and fails to be consistent to his own claim for the meaning he has derived from the Galatian letter!

Thus, it is my contention that despite his repeated urgings to read the New Testament corporately, Wright does not do so himself.[302] The fact is that

---

[301] Interestingly, Wright argues for the corporate reading of chapters 1–5 and 7–11 but stays with an individualistic reading of chapter 6. He is forced into this as a result of failing to challenge his ecclesiastical heritage concerning the meaning of this passage and mocks those who are unable to accept the implications of his reading, that water baptism actually secures salvation for the one baptized, see N. T. Wright, 'New Exodus, New Inheritance: The Narrative Substructure of Romans 3—8' in Sven K. Soderlund & N. T. Wright (eds.), *Romans and the People of God: Essays in Honour of Gordon D. Fee on the Occasion of His 65th Birthday* (Grand Rapids: Eerdmans, 1999), 35: 'It was always dubious, in view of the combination of the same themes in Galatians 3–4, especially 3:23–4:7, to set apart faith and justification on the one hand, and baptism and the Spirit on the other, and to suppose that they belonged, in Paul's mind, to distinct universes of discourse. As John the Baptist would no doubt have agreed, baptism and Spirit speak of new covenant, a Second Exodus, and thereby of the renewal, however unexpected, of the people of Abraham. And the Exodus is itself the action whereby God justifies as well as liberates.' However, this logic falls apart as soon as the chapter is read corporately, the passage does not mention water, but it does echo the connection he correctly identifies which is the type Paul builds on (1 Cor 10:1–4). This corporate salvation is far bigger and more glorious than water baptism can ever be! For how the ontological baptism justifies, see Holland, *Contours,* 141–154.

[302] Wright, *Perspectives,* 45.

the letters were not generally written to individuals but to communities. They do not speak of individual salvation but the salvation of the community. Indeed, they do more than this. While the application is normally to the community, and sometimes applied to groups within the community, such as parents, slaves, wives, and so on, yet the theology of salvation goes far beyond the specific community to whom the letter was written and speaks of the people of God as a whole. The letters of Paul therefore are about the creation of a universal community and what God has done for it and the teaching should be read in the same vein as when we read what Paul has to say about Adam's representative role when he acted for all humankind.

Reading the letters as addressed to individuals—as if they were written to tell each believer what God has done for him or her—has resulted in the distortion of the grandeur of the gospel message. It has created an individualism that Wright (surprisingly) at times endorses by his own exegesis[303]—but this is simply not biblical. The apostle does not focus on multiple covenants that God had made with millions of individual believers but on the one covenant that all of his people have come into. Only when individuals are brought into the community through repentance and faith, do they receive all the blessings that the covenant community as a whole, as Christ's bride, has been bequeathed, including the imputation of his righteousness.

In other words, Paul's justification language is essentially corporate, but not necessarily in the sense that Wright has argued. We will find examples of Paul applying these great truths to both individuals and unbelievers in the record of his preaching. For example, in Acts 13:38–41 and Acts 15:7–11, which is where we notice the correct individually applied understanding of the Reformers. This failure to read the letters corporately affects not only justification but also other important doctrines such as adoption, the work of the Spirit, election, the new creation, sin, and so on. Such a reading does not challenge Reformed understanding other than bringing greater clarity to the truths they proclaimed.

Thus, while Wright's understanding of the meaning of 'justify' in Galatians is correct, he has assumed that it always has this meaning, and then

---

[303] As when he interprets Rom 6:1–6 to be about baptismal initiation when it is locked between two chapters that he acknowledges are universal and corporate in their content.

drops the corporate element he rightly claims it normally has in Galatians as he applies it elsewhere to individuals! He has assumed that the meaning that he has found in Galatians is the only meaning and has imposed this on all other uses of the term justify and these readings have not been vindicated.[304] Also, despite claiming the importance of reading the New Testament corporately, Wright fails to do this, as he comes 'in and out' of individual/corporate reading strategies seemingly without realizing it.

If Wright's argument had been: 'while the Reformers missed the corporate dimension of certain texts, their understanding of other texts correctly identify an important thread of Paul's doctrine of justification', that would have been helpful. However, he does not follow this. He insists that the meaning he has identified is the only meaning and declares that the Reformers were wrong in their understanding of Paul's doctrine of justification for not grasping his (i.e. Wright's) meaning. Interestingly, James Dunn, who once held the same position that Wright continues to hold, eventually modified his view and accepted that there are New Testament texts that support the Reformers understanding of justification.[305] This is a modification Wright has not been willing to make. This revised modification recognizes that Second Temple Judaism held to legal and ethical requirements concerning keeping the law and if not fulfilled they excluded Jews from salvation. This is the position Sanders himself is reportedly now embracing.[306] Thus, Wright continues to hold to this original NPP meaning even though he has admitted that the contributors of Justification and Variegated Nomism have demonstrated that Sanders had claimed too much in his from his original research.[307] He has accepted that there are clear exceptions to the claim that

---

[304] Wright, 'Romans', *NIB*, 473 sometimes strays from his own definition, and when he does, he comes very close to the argument that I am making in this chapter, that justification includes the creation of or entrance into a covenant relationship with God. On page 465 he says: '"justification" in its Pauline contexts, regularly includes both aspects: the rescuing of sinners from their sins, and the creation of worldwide family of forgiven sinners.' Such a statement is not necessarily specifically about the status of gentiles.

[305] J. D. G. Dunn, *The Theology of Paul the Apostle* (Edinburgh: T&T Clark, 1998), 367.

[306] Guy Prentiss Waters, *Justification and the New Perspectives on Paul,* 167, notes 'Sanders has conceded to me that Ephesians 2:9 teaches the traditional view'.

[307] Wright, *Perspectives,* 109 says that 'Recent attempts to suggest a more

Sanders had originally made that first century Judaism was not a religion of law keeping.[308] However, even this admission that Sanders was not accurate in his understanding of the role of the law, has not caused Wright to revise his claim that the Reformers were wrong in their understanding.

Wright, Justification, and the Dead Sea Scrolls

Far more has been brought to the 'justification' table than that which we have considered so far. Wright has not only appealed to a range of passages in the letters of Paul for his understanding but has argued that a document found amongst the DSS (known as 4QMMT) provides the key support for the correctness of his understanding of Paul's doctrine of justification. He claims that this text shows that for the Jews 'justification' was never about being made right with God but about being declared to be right with God; that is, in covenant relationship with him.

Before considering the evidence presented in Wright's latest presentation, i.e. *Paul and the Faithfulness of God,* we need to consider what he had written in an article in 2006 in which he discussed the value of 4QMMT for supporting his argument concerning Paul's meaning of justification. Wright's current position leaves me somewhat surprised, as in the article he had identified many of the issues I had concerns over as I read his reasoning for using this text.310[309] He had acknowledged in the 2006 article that the

---

variegated attitude to the law than was allowed for by E. P. Sanders in Paul and Palestinian Judaism are undoubtedly right to stress variety, and undoubtedly wrong to use that as a way of smuggling back an anachronistic vision of a Pelagian (or semi-Pelagian) or medieval works- righteousness. I shall be in implicit debate, in the details of the exegesis and in the structure of thought, both with the so-called "new perspective" and with its opponents; but I shall not have space for any hand-to-hand exchanges. My aim is a more strategic outflanking.'

[308] D. A. Carson, P. T. O'Brien, and M. A. Seifrid (eds.), *Justification and Variegated Nomism, Volume I: The Complexities of Second Temple Judaism* (Grand Rapids: Baker, 2001)

[309] N. T. Wright, '4QMMT and Paul: Justification, Works, and Eschatology', in Sang- Won (Aaron) Son (ed.), *History and Exegesis: New Testament Essays in Honor of Dr E. Earle Ellis for His 80th Birthday* (London: T&T Clark, 2006), 104–132. says: 'However, a caveat must be entered at this point. We do not know if the Pharisees held any form of inaugurated eschatology corresponding to that which MMT assumes for Qumran. We do not know, in other words, if the Pharisees believed that they themselves were the already

theological context of 4QMMT is not equivalent to that which lay in the background of Paul's epistles and that all that the fragment gives is evidence that the language of justification took place in a covenant context.

The latter claim is not a problem for most Reformed scholars, it is what Wright seeks to claim from this, that justification is solely about being in the covenant; therein is the problem. In this earlier article, he also acknowledged the vast difference between the covenant that the writer(s) of 4QMMT defended and that which Paul proclaimed. The former was very much about the exclusion of anything that has had gentile contact whereas that which Paul proclaims welcomes gentiles themselves as full members of the covenant. What I cannot understand is why, having identified these important weaknesses for establishing his argument, he fails to mention them in his recent work, which is written for a wider audience and is clearly intended to be his definitive work on Paul. These important observations should have been noted in his recent book, but instead, he introduces the reader to the Dead Sea Scrolls as though there were no issues relating to their use that needed to be considered. To my mind, this failure to disclose the problems he has elsewhere acknowledged is a weakness. It fails to help the readers consider all the related evidence. Indeed, elsewhere he has said, 'A glance at

---

inaugurated new covenant people of Israel's God, or, if so, what defining event (corresponding to the founding of the Qumran community, or at least its refounding by the Teacher of Righteousness) had brought such a movement into being. It may be that the Pharisees believed that adhering to their interpretation of Torah constituted them as such a renewed community, but we have no clear evidence for saying so. Neither Hillel nor Shammai was regarded in Paul's day as having brought a new age into being, even secretly or partially. The fact that Paul the Christian, with his own form of inaugurated eschatology, rejects his former self-understanding and that of the agitators in Galatia (who we have no reason to think held views identical or even similar to Paul's own pre-Christian ones), does not mean that either he (before his conversion) or the "agitators" held an inaugurated eschatology.' He goes on to say (page 129): 'The problem Paul meets in Galatia is not that a particular extra-biblical halakhah is being taught, to which he objects as one sectarian Jewish group might object against another ('your halakhah says this, my halakhah says that'). Nor is it that he regards the "agitators" as teaching a moralistic "self-help" soteriology, or a reliance on religious ritual rather than inner spirituality (the classic protestant view of what Paul's protest was about). The fundamental issue is Paul's eschatological claim that Israel's God has now acted in Jesus, demonstrating him through the resurrection to be Israel's Messiah (Rom 1:4).'

4QMMT may help us here. There remains quite a bit of confusion as to exactly what that text is saying and how it relates to Paul.'[310]

4QMMT and Justification

Wright's claim in Paul and the Faithfulness of God that 4QMMT is the only text that speaks of justification in the ITL is strange.[311] In his 2006 article, he had already referred to a range of texts that he saw as supporting his views about 4QMMT; he lists 1QS 11.2–3; 12; 13–15, and he says that the 'The Qumran hymns (1QH, etc.) are full of similar sentiments'. The fact that he discards this discussion in is magnus opus of his theology of Paul, Paul and the Faithfulness of God, is difficult to explain because it is crucial evidence for the discussion.

Wright's appeal to 4QMMT as evidence that supports his understanding of Paul's meaning of justification is such an important support for his understanding that it needs to be considered separately in order to establish whether his claim for its significance is correct.

Wright asserts in Paul and the Faithfulness of God that 4QMMT 'is the only pre-Christian Jewish text we possess that uses the phrase "works of the Torah"', in complete contradiction to what he had written in 2006. He goes on to give his translation of 4QMMT where the author says to the priest in Jerusalem, 'We have indeed sent you this selection of works of the Torah according to our decision for your welfare and the welfare of your people.'[312] Clearly this short text is crucially important, for it is the one text that Wright uses to support his proposed meaning for justification given by Paul in his letter to the Galatians. This is because the same term found in 4QMMT 'the works of the law' is also found in Galatians: 'because by works of the law no one will be justified' (Gal 2:16). It is the presence of the term in both texts that persuades Wright that 4QMMT is the key to understanding justification in Galatians 2:16.

We will come back to considering the implications of 4QMMT in a moment. First, I want to note that I have already discussed the danger of misusing intertestamental literature. Indeed, Wright has also given similar

---

[310] Wright, *Justification,* 123.

[311] Wright, *Faithfulness of God,* 167.

[312] Wright, 'Romans' *NIB,* 460.

warnings.[313] However, while he has shown that he is aware of the need to exercise caution, he has walked right into the trap he has warned others away from, a point I will now explore.

First, we will note that Wright claims that justification was rare in Judaism, suggesting it is only found in 4QMMT, saying: 'justification is not a major topic in Second Temple Judaism, this is rare, with Qumran providing (in 4QMMT) the only example.'[314] Now this claim of Wright is simply not correct, for we have other clear statements in Qumran which, whilst not using the 'works of the covenant' expression, certainly refer to justification, and one of them says:

> As for me, in God is my judgment (משפט). In his hand is the perfection of my path and the uprightness of my heart, and by his righteous acts (ובצדקות) he will cancel my transgression. From the fountain of his righteousness is my judgment (וממקור צדקתקו משפטי) .... And if I stumble, the mercies of God are my salvation for ever (חסדי אל ישוצתי לצד), and if I fall in guilt of the flesh, my judgment is by the righteousness of God (בצדקת א ל) which endures eternally (IQS 11:2–3, 5, 12).[315]

While clearly this is not the same as the traditional Reformed understanding of justification, which is based on the significance of Christ's saving death, the writer has understood his own experience of justification in terms very familiar to the Reformers—that justification is the result of Yahweh's kindness and righteousness, which makes the believer clean. What is important about this, as in the 1QS 11:11–15 text, is that it gives a very different meaning of 'justification' than that which is claimed by Wright to exist in 4QMMT. It is not being declared to be in the covenant, for here it is not his status in the covenant that is referred to, but the way he is made

---

[313] Wright, *New Testament,* 38–46.

[314] Clearly, if Wright had said that that 4QMMT is the only reference to the works of the law in the DSS he would have been correct. But he goes beyond this and makes the clam that it is the only reference to justification. In this he is clearly mistaken. Below we will look at some of the texts that refer to justification.

[315] See Bockmuehl, '1QS and Salvation at Qumran', in D. A. Carson, P. T. O'Brien, and M. A. Seifrid (eds.), *Justification and Variegated Nomism, Volume I: The Complexities of Second Temple Judaism* (Grand Rapids: Baker, 2001), 381–414. Pages 398–9 refer to other texts that speak of righteousness and being made acceptable to God.

acceptable before God. At the very least we can see from the above text that there is more than one meaning for 'justification' in Qumran.

Bockmuehl gives another example of justification language in Qumran, he says of 1QS 10–11:

> Perhaps the clearest account of what one might call "Qumran's doctrine of justification" appears in 1 QS 10–11, which is partly paralleled in 4QS. It is remarkable to note how this passage presumes a consistently forensic context with an emphasis on the individual—i.e. perhaps the Maskil in the first instance, although the language seems clearly intended to be read in paradigmatic fashion. Here, then, the individual offers a forthright confession of his own sinfulness and inadequacy— qualities that he accepts as characteristic of the human condition and altogether outside his power to change" Man cannot establish his own steps, for to God belong judgment (מ שפט) and perfect of way" (1QS 9:10; cf. 1QH 7[=15]:16), "no one is righteous in your judgement, or innocent at your trial" (1QH 17[=9]:14f).[316]

Falk also notices relevant facts about justification language in the DSS when he says:

> . . . a number of passages in the Hodayot make clear that the community already experiences a significant release from the problems of human frailty through the impartation of divine knowledge to enjoy communion with the heavenly congregation (1QHP 19[=11]:10–14; 9[=1]; 31–33; 11[=3];19–22; 14[=6]; 7–8; 15[=8]: 19–20). "For the sake of your glory you have purified man (אנוש) ..." (1QH 11[=3]: 10–14) does not merely mean the pardoning of particular acts of sin but cleansing of impurity associated with being human (cf. 1QS 11:14–15). It is not possible to dismiss all such passages as concerning eschatological redemption because these are often in the context of asserting the union with the heavenly congregation that is an important part of the community's present experience.[317]

From these observations of Bockmuehl and Falk (who provide many more similar examples), it is hard to see how Wright can claim that there was no interest in justification in the DSS and that the meaning of justification,

---

[316] Bockmuehl, '1QS and Salvation', 398.

[317] Daniel Falk, 'Psalms and Prayers', in D. A. Carson, P. T. O'Brien, and M. A. Seifrid (eds.), *Justification and Variegated Nomism, Volume I: The Complexities of Second Temple Judaism* (Grand Rapids: Baker, 2001), 7–56 [31].

when the term was used, referred to people being in the community. Also, Bockmuehl and Falk's findings support the traditional Reformed understanding of being made right with God. These findings suggest that Wright is mistaken.

Furthermore, it is widely recognized that (in addition to the DSS) there were vast quantities of highly valued 'religious' texts produced by dozens (and possibly much more) of different communities across Palestine before the Roman war. Scholars accept that these were destroyed in that ruthless sweep of Roman military might across Palestine which led up to 70 ce and the destruction of Jerusalem. As a result, we cannot say that Judaism was not interested in the subject of justification. If Wright's claim is true, that there is only this one text (4QMMT) that speaks of justification (which, as we have seen, is a claim that is contradicted in other statements that he has made), then all this demonstrates is that it was of limited interest to one small community; a community which was not representative of Judaism. Because of the massive destruction of texts before 70 ce the fuller testimony concerning the Jewish understanding of 'justification' in the first century will never be heard. Because of this loss, we simply cannot claim that there was only the one understanding of 'justification' in Judaism (as Wright claims); nor can we assert that it was a doctrine very few were interested in.

4QMMT and its Theological Value

We need to consider further the value of the document that Wright has highlighted as his prime supporting evidence for challenging Reformed understanding. 4QMMT is a fragment of a manuscript found amongst the DSS. There is no unanimous scholarly consent as to who its author was, or what grouping the writer belonged to. Because of this, we cannot read the text against the writer's theological heritage and understanding. There is also disagreement about who it was written to. Most scholars see the author to have been either a Sadducee or a Pharisee, and that he wrote to a priest who served in the temple in Jerusalem. Obviously, if this is correct, then it was written sometime before 70 ce when the temple was destroyed. This places the text between early first century B.C.E. and early first century C.E.

The situation is further complicated by the fact that a leading DSS scholar has suggested that 4QMMT is the result of a merger of six individual manuscripts.[318] Wright accepts this evidence, so the document is not the work of one author but of an editor. Coming from the amalgamation of a range of texts it could possibly combine several theological traditions and hence make the task of interpreting it much more difficult. It seems to me that in the absence of other intertestamental manuscripts that use the term 'works of the law', it is irresponsible of Wright to rely on the use of this term to support his claims for the meaning of justification within the New Testament. His case rests on this single, eclectic, and limited intertestamental textual fragment.

As we have seen, most Reformed scholars hold two meanings for the word. The first is the meaning that comes from the traditional forensic or legal background and speaks of legal acquittal, of being found not guilty, of being justified. The second is the meaning that comes from the accounting world and carries the meaning of having no debt to pay. These are undisputable meanings that the word had in both Hebrew and Greek ancient society. The question, of course, is whether this secular meaning conveys the meaning used in Scripture. Does God pay the debt of people, and does he declare guilty people innocent when in fact they are guilty?

In the original Old Testament Hebrew text, as well as in the Greek translation (the LXX), the meanings outlined above are clearly found and refer to how God deals with people and their sins. Thus, these meanings became used metaphorically to express Christian truth regarding justification.

However, there is a second question to be considered, and it is whether these two meanings are sufficient to define the limit of the word's semantic range. Wright has rejected these two well-attested meanings, putting in their place what he believes 'justify' means in Galatians, supporting his claim by appealing to what he thinks the word means in 4QMMT: being declared to be in the covenant community. He claims this despite his acknowledgement that:

> We are bound to find it frustrating that we have almost no texts
> from this period that do what we would like, speak from a clearly
> Pharisaic point of view about what Paul the apostle calls
> 'justification by works of the law'. The closest we get, as is well
> known, is the Essene document 4QMMT. Though this document
> arguably criticizes the Pharisees, it appears to share, so far as we
> can tell, a sense of the shape of how eschatology works in relation
> to election and thus to present justification enabling us to make

---

[318] Which Wright acknowledges in Wright, '4QMMT' in Sang-Won, *New Testament Essays,* 104–132.

substitution of Pharisaic elements for Essene one in the hope that we will thereby come close to the answer.[319]

So, we are to take a document that criticizes the Pharisees' position, which Paul 'appears to share, so far as we can tell' and which Wright admits is being used 'in the hope' of finding Paul's meaning.[320] Wright is asking us to believe that Paul—raised as a Pharisee and continuing to identify with his earlier training—turned to texts written by someone who opposed his view, both as a Pharisee and as a follower of Jesus! Since Wright cannot find a clear Pharisaic text, he looks for evidence in the texts of opposing groups. I believe this methodology is being pushed too far.

Also, we need to note that Wright has said that 4QMMT is the only DSS text that mentions justification. We have seen that this is not strictly the case, for the text does not mention 'justification' as such; it refers only to 'the works of the law' and Wright has read justification into 4QMMT because of the link between the phrase 'the works of the law' and the justification argument in the Galatian text. Making this connection needs a lot more support than Wright has given. Indeed, he has given none!

However, the 4QMMT text that he has chosen to lever into the Galatian text (2:16) to provide the support he needs for his exegesis does not settle the meaning in Galatians, as 2:16 as it is not the only text in Galatians that uses the term 'works of the law', and in these other texts the meaning is very clear. I will list them all for the sake of clarity.

> yet we know that a person is not justified by works of the law but through faith in Jesus Christ, so we also have believed in Christ Jesus, in order to be justified by faith in Christ and not by works of the law, because by works of the law no one will be justified. (Gal 2:16)

> O foolish Galatians! Who has bewitched you? It was before your eyes that Jesus Christ was publicly portrayed as crucified. Let me ask you only this: Did you receive the Spirit by works of the law or by hearing with faith? Are you so foolish? Having begun by the Spirit, are you now being perfected by the flesh? (Gal 3:1–3)

> Does he who supplies the Spirit to you and works miracles among you do so by works of the law, or by hearing with faith—just as Abraham "believed God, and it was counted to him as

---

[319] Wright, *Faithfulness of God,* 184.

[320] Ibid.

righteousness"? (Gal 3:5–6)

So, what is the justification for using Galatians 2:16 and not Galatians 3:1–6 to interpret 4QMMT? The text of chapter three is much clearer in its meaning, and I would argue that it does not contradict what is said in 2:16 but rather supports and builds on it.

The opening of Galatians 3 is a challenge to those who had turned to the law for salvation. Paul argues that the gift of the Spirt was evidence that God had accepted them and made them the local expression of his kingdom, his church. Paul asks the Galatians whether this decisive evidence of acceptance was conveyed through a valiant surge of law-keeping, and the answer, of course, was no. The Spirit was given as a result of Galatians exercising faith in the one who is the centre of the gospel, Jesus Christ. This, for Paul, was decisive evidence that they could not gain salvation by keeping the law. To attempt to gain acceptance via the law would be to deny the gospel, and this would rob them of their status in Christ for they would be substituting Christ with another, the law!

Paul is not saying that they must not keep the moral law, but rather that the law must not substitute Christ as a means of salvation. He would agree, no doubt, with the writer of 4QMMT that keeping the law was good for their safety and wellbeing, but even that writer was not saying that by keeping the law they would be justified. He was only saying that by living by the works of the law, their lives would be blessed.

4QMMT and Common Contexts

Wright has defended his use of 4QMMT to interpret Galatians 2:22 and Romans 10:5–8 because in 4QMMT the mention of 'works of the law' is in the context of Deut 32, the passage which speaks of covenantal renewal. This connection, i.e. Deut 32 and the term 'works of the law', says Wright, is found in Galatians for the background to Paul's discussion on justification. These facts, says Wright, are the grounds for bringing the 4QMMT passage into Paul's discussion on justification.

However, this sort of transfer is based on assumptions that need to be carefully examined. Tentative links alone cannot justify such a transfer. Take for example, two texts which both belong to two distinct Christian traditions that are speaking of Easter. In both of these two distinct texts, there is the mention of baptism. It would be most unwise to say that they both mean the same when they refer to baptism because the discussions are both in the context of the Easter event. The wider Christian church has a range of understandings to do with the meaning and significance of Easter as well as the mode of administration concerning baptism and many understandings at to what baptism signifies and what it achieves. To impose one meaning onto the other text because they both share an Easter context would not lead to a clearer understanding of a particular text, but rather to confusion. So it is with using 4QMMT to interpret Paul. This is especially true in the light of Wright's acknowledgment, noted above that the meaning of justified in 4QMMT is distinctly different from Paul's understanding.

Elsewhere Wright has explained why the claim that higher Christology was the product of the Hellenistic church had been wrong. He wrote: 'The assumption that a high Christology must mean later, and non-Pauline, authorship has been brought to the material, not discovered within it'. [321]In describing what others believe to have happened in the development in Christology, he has objected to the importation of inappropriate external evidence to make his protagonists' case. Yet he has done the very thing that he has rejected, for in the way he appeals to 4QMMT he brings material to the NT rather than finding it within, and he has equally failed to make a convincing case.

Straining the Evidence

The seriousness of the flaw in this method has to be carefully noted for it appears to have gone undetected by most, if not all, scholars. No lecturer worth his or her salt would ever allow even a freshman student to interpret Paul from a text written by John or Peter, even though they belonged to the same community and shared in its leadership as recognized teachers. The mantra that 'only the writer can safely interpret what he is saying' needs to be respected and applied in the study of Paul. We are careful to follow this same principle when we interpret the Gospels, for we never mix the Johannine account with that of the Synoptics because we know they are different in kind even though the same in subject matter.[322] In the light of these controls, how can we possibly admit the views of a group who were opposed to the

---

[321] Wright, *Justification*, 19.

[322] So supported by Wright, *New Testament,* 119 when he says: 'We have learned that we must not glibly pass over differences of setting and time, imaging continuity of thought between documents of different provenances', but failing to apply the principle is a much more serious case of cross contamination.

Christian message as crucial evidence for our understanding of Paul? If the teaching of another apostle is not allowed to influence the voice of a fellow apostle, how much less should the writings of his opponents.

This demonstrates the scale of the confusion that arises as a result of the method Wright has chosen—a method that gives the text of an opposing community the authority to control our understanding of what Paul is teaching. We know who wrote both Romans and Galatians. We know who the recipients were, and we know the theological presuppositions of Paul in detail from the letters he wrote to the churches. We have a huge amount of material to provide us with the correct context to detect how Paul understood the terms which he used.

On the other hand, we know so little about the circumstances of the writing of 4QMMT that the likelihood of our obtaining the writer's understanding is seriously weakened. It is possible, for example, that the word he used for 'justify' may have carried a range of meanings for him, and that this fragment and perhaps others like it, have only preserved one of them.[323]

Moreover, since 4QMMT is supposed to have been appealing to Jewish priests, not Christian churches, we have to challenge the assumption that there is a correlation between this text and what Paul taught at all. Indeed, we cannot find any definite theological equivalence between the two communities; and yet the 4 QMMT text continues to be presented as the vital evidence that establishes the meaning of 'justify' or 'made righteous' in Paul

Even if we could discover the theological stable of the writer of 4QMMT, this is not likely to help us, for he is an opponent of the Jesus community and is much more likely to clash with their views, if he knew them at all. Hence, it is far more likely—if not certain—that by taking the writer of 4QMMT as our guide to understand Paul, we will miss what Paul is saying by miles.

Compared to the New Testament's collection of Christian texts, 4QMMT has absolutely nothing to commend its elevation to a position of autonomy and authority. We cannot compare this text with any other that the author has written or from the community he represents; and even if we could, the fact

---

[323] Wright has identified similar texts in support of his reading in 1QS 11.2–3; 12; 13–15 the Qumran hymns (1QH, etc.) to show that these ideas were widespread, although he omits this argument from Paul and the Faithfulness of God. Yet the fact that a word was used more than once in a particular text does not imply that it held the same meaning in every context. See M. Bockmuehl, '1QS and Salvation at Qumran,' 381–414.

remains that not all texts found at Qumran represent the community's views—for it is recognised that there are texts in the collection that reflect theological conflict. The collection of documents that we know as the Dead Sea Scrolls do not speak with a common voice and have no united theological position.

Because of this, we cannot be certain that 4QMMT is an official view of the Qumran community. 4QMMT could be the product of another community that we have no details of, but which like others we know of are represented by entries in the library at Qumran. We do not know if the author held to the single meaning expressed in the text or whether he understood the term 'justify' to have a greater semantic range. It is entirely possible that other texts which may have shed light on this conundrum (if any ever existed) were destroyed in the Roman war. Surrounded by such a degree of uncertainty it is most unwise to appeal to 4QMMT as key evidence for determining the way in which 'justify' was understood in Paul; but this is precisely how Wright uses the text.

Assuming that the writer(s) of 4QMMT (and those of other Qumran texts) knew of more than one meaning for 'justification' (and it would be very surprising if such were not the case, considering the frequency—in most languages—of a diversity of meanings in semantic domain of most words), what confidence can we have in Wright's decision to make this one meaning that he has constructed control the New Testament meaning of every use of the term? Were the New Testament authors limited to this one meaning? Even if they were (which is most unlikely), how can any assertion that they were be proved? At this point, the argument in favour of a 4QMMT reading for justification in the New Testament is so weak due to the lack of evidence that it is highly improbable.[324]

It seems that Wright is engaging in a very high-risk strategy for establishing such an important doctrine.[325] Indeed, in the light of the earlier

---

[324] Nevertheless, Wright has used this same method in his construction of his argument for the person of Christ and in his construction of the meaning of atonement.

[325] When Wright is challenged, he simply says that his questioner is asking the wrong question, insisting that they do not understand the meaning of 'justification' in the New Testament. So he says: 'When people say, "what did Paul say on the topic of how people are converted, saved and assured of a safe passage to heaven?" These questions, when properly reframed, are of course

discussion in chapter 6 there are no formulated rules for calling on intertestamental texts as aids for interpreting meaning in the New Testament. This field of study remains a free-for-all in which every man does that which is right in his own eyes. This use of the intertestamental literature has been followed by many New Testament theologians; the picking up of texts and even individual words to 'prove' particular points[326] without carefully providing justification as to the correctness of doing so is not a method which characterizes careful scholarship.

Important Differences

One must not overlook the different backgrounds that lie behind 4QMMT and the writings of Paul. 4QMMT is a document concerned with the Qumran community's legal purity,[327] while the argument made by Paul is about the status of the new covenant community—a status which Paul—for the sake of

---

important, but they are not exactly what Paul meant by the word "justification" itself. All this means that much of Carson, O'Brien and Seifrid is beside the point, despite the high quality of the essays.' Wright, Faithfulness of God, 929 fn 498. In saying that it is not what Paul meant by the word 'justification', Wright assumes that Paul meant what Wright believes 4QMMT says! Such a circular response to the question has not entered into a meaningful debate of any kind.

[326] Wright himself (Wright, *Justification,* 38) has written concerning the documentation of second Temple Judaism: 'Judaism was richly varied, right across the period from the last two or three centuries B.C. to the second century ad, so much so that many have understandably wanted to speak of 'Judaisms', plural. There are many different theologies, many different expressions, many different ways of standing within, or on the edge of, or in tension with, the great ancestral traditions of Israel. There is what has, perhaps unhappily, been called "Variegated Nomism", a rich panoply of ways of understanding Israel's law and trying to obey it. Not only is it too simple to say, as some versions of the new perspective have said, that all first-century Jews believed in grace; they meant many different things by "grace" and responded to those meanings in a rich variety of ways. Yes. All this I grant.' With such an admission Wright has made my case for me, but he does not seem to appreciate its consequences!

[327] Assuming that the writer was one of the community, but we have no evidence that makes this assumption sure.

his gentile converts—is at pains to argue is not defined by any ideas of legalistic purity.

Indeed, the 4QMMT fragment is not about 'covenantal nomism' as Sanders has defined it, but about proving that covenantal acceptance is on the grounds of having kept the law. This is the very understanding that the Reformers believed Paul was encountering. So rather than 4QMMT supporting covenantal nomism, its message is that keeping the law was essential for God's acceptance on the last day. Such an understanding means that there can be no certainty about final acceptance because we can never know if we have kept the law to the necessary requirement and, therefore, the doctrine of assurance has been blown apart.[328] It is difficult to see how such implications can be missed but this is what Wright has managed to do. He justifies this reading by appealing to Romans 2:3–8 which we will consider shortly. It is here that I find Wright confusing, for he claims that the final declaration has been brought into the present (which is what Reformed understanding holds), but then he appeals to Romans 2:3–8 to show that Paul's understanding is the same as that of the writer of 4QMMT. There is a lack of consistency in these explanations.

Finally, we note that to support his claims concerning the meaning of 'justify', Wright has had to deconstruct the Reformed understanding of NT texts that appear to be negative towards the law and then reconstruct their meaning to favour his meaning of justification which is found in covenantal nomism—i.e. the law did not threaten the people. He has to do this to make his case stick. However, does he succeed in these reconstructions? We shall consider how unconvincing they are shortly.

Here, then, is why I consider that Wright's understanding of justification, supposedly supported from 4QMMT, should be rejected. A possible meaning of a word, found in a fragment of no established provenance, has been transferred across community boundaries—indeed, across theological boundaries. It has been imposed on a wealth of texts by an identifiable author, who wrote to identifiable communities, about identifiable theological issues.

---

[328] Wright elsewhere is emphatic to the point that I rejoice with what he says about the certainty of the declaration of justification, as he understands it, as being ratified with certainty on the last day, Wright, *Faithfulness of God,* 949; and *Justification,* 128, but he then comes out with this attack on the certainty of salvation unless works are maintained. There is a clear tension that admittedly others have been caught up in throughout the centuries of Christian exegesis.

The theological issues that Paul was addressing were the outcome of the new covenant, which welcomed believing Jews and gentiles on the basis of their faith in the Messiah. For Paul, these members of 'the new man' entirely replaced the priesthood that the writer of 4QMMT was referring to.

The parallels which would be required in order to even begin allowing such a transfer of linguistic meaning do not exist. Furthermore, rules to establish the legitimacy of such a transfer do not exist either. Whatever 'justification' meant to the Christian community, it is extremely unlikely to have held the same meaning as it did for the Qumran community, the horizons of the two being so very different. In transferring linguistic meaning so thoughtlessly, a major transgression of hermeneutic practice has been committed.

Final Comments on Wright's Case for Justification

Wright has appealed to the work of Alister McGrath to show that there has been a progressive change in the meaning of justification in Western Christianity and claims that when the Reformers became engaged in the debate, they were not arguing for the same doctrine that the apostles had taught, but one that had been changed by the languages and cultures that it passed through. He claims that by the 15th century the doctrine was about acquittal from sin, and that this was not at all the original New Testament understanding. The misunderstanding, he thought, was particularly due to the church's use of Latin as its official vehicle of communication and the forensic meaning that the Latin term 'justified' carried.[329] This gave Wright the evidence that he needed to support his claim that the Reformers had got this doctrine wrong and he made it his mission to put it right. He argued from Galatians that the doctrine meant nothing more than being declared to be in the covenant.

Like McGrath,[330] Wright sees that the apostles' own understanding of the term is found in the Hebrew and the loss of this context is an important factor in the church's distortion of this vital doctrine.

---

[329] Wright cites M. Bockmuehl, '1QS and Salvation at Qumran,' in Carson et al., *Justification and Variegated Nomism,* 381– 414 to support that fact these ideas were widespread.

[330] McGrath, *Iustitia Dei*:5.

Now it is abundantly clear that doctrines are transformed by cultures and that they are moulded by prior understanding of words and the concepts they carry. But did the Reformers have the medieval understanding through Latin as Wright claims? Luther particularly wrestled with the medieval judicial understanding that he was under the sentence of God's wrath because of his violation of the law, but that is not where he remained. It is not his pre-Christian understanding that should judge him but how his understanding grew. There is evidence of Wright himself changing his position on a range of doctrines throughout his career so far, so are we to hold him to his first insights and not to let him reflect and grow? Wright is much more appreciative of Calvin's union with Christ doctrine and lays the blame on the need to recover the doctrine of justification on Luther, who stressed the legal nature of Paul's doctrine of being under the law. He says that the New Perspective would not have been necessary if the Reformed view had dominated scholarship instead of the Lutheran.[331] But such an assertion does not absolve Wright himself, for as we are about to see, Luther held to the doctrine of union with Christ even though it did not have the same prominence for him as it did for Calvin. It could quite legitimately be claimed that if Wright had known his historical theology better, he might not have run with the claims of the New Perspective in the first place.

A Poor Case Against Luther

The claim that Luther uncritically followed the doctrine of the scholastics is false. Luther was so aware of the failure of the Latin understanding to satisfy his deep spiritual hunger that he committed himself to study Greek and Hebrew and then taught as a professor of theology before becoming the leader of the Protestant Reformation.

Luther's mature position cannot be better expressed than by the Augsburg Confession, which we have already noted. This does not represent a man crushed by the law but one who is filled with thankfulness for the grace that he had come to receive in Christ. This is not to say Luther got everything right, but then who has? Yet to argue that Luther saw justification solely in terms of deliverance from wrath is clearly wrong. He saw it much more positively, as about being saved and totally accepted by God for no other reason than that God freely loves the undeserving. The terror of the law that Luther experienced was neutralised. Luther came to a clear understanding of

---

[331] Wright, *Justification,* 53.

union with Christ as the basis of receiving all of God's grace and not on some form of revised medieval doctrine that had changed the gospel from what it had once been to become a distortion of the apostles' teaching.

Moreover, Luther was as clear concerning the 'union with Christ' aspect of justification as Calvin was. It is true that the term justified is not used in the following passage, but its teaching is clearly present. It is also true that Luther does not give union with Christ the same key position that Calvin gave it. But is equally true to say that he was not ignorant of it, and that he embraced it as a gospel truth. A quick comparison between this passage and the earlier cited Apology of the Augsburg Confession will show that one text is dependent on the other and that the Apology is quite definitely speaking of justification, for is it is headed in the Confession as being such. Luther says:

> The third incomparable grace of faith is this: that it unites the soul to Christ, as the wife to the husband, by which mystery, as the Apostle teaches, Christ and the soul are made one flesh. Now if they are one flesh, and if a true marriage—nay, by far the most perfect of all marriages—is accomplished between them (for human marriages are but feeble types of this one great marriage), then it follows that all they have becomes theirs in common, as well good things as evil things; so that whatsoever Christ possesses, that the believing soul may take to itself and boast of as its own, and whatever belongs to the soul, that Christ claims as His. If we compare these possessions, we shall see how inestimable is the gain. Christ is full of grace, life, and salvation; the soul is full of sin, death, and condemnation. Let faith step in, and then sin, death, and hell will belong to Christ, and grace, life, and salvation to the soul. For, if He is a Husband, He must needs take to Himself that which is His wife's, and at the same time, impart to His wife that which is His. For, in giving her His own body and Himself, how can He but give her all that is His? And, in taking to Himself the body of His wife, how can He but take to Himself all that is hers? In this is displayed the delightful sight, not only of communion, but of a prosperous warfare, of victory, salvation, and redemption. For, since Christ is God and man, and is such a Person as neither has sinned, nor dies, nor is condemned, nay, cannot sin, die, or be condemned, and since His righteousness, life, and salvation are invincible, eternal, and almighty—when I say, such a Person, by the wedding-ring of faith, takes a share in the sins, death, and hell of His wife, nay, makes them His own, and deals with them no otherwise than as if they were His, and as if He Himself had sinned; and when He suffers, dies, and descends to hell, that He may overcome all

things, and since sin, death, and hell cannot swallow Him up, they must needs be swallowed up by Him in stupendous conflict. For His righteousness rises above the sins of all men; His life is more powerful than all death; His salvation is more unconquerable than all hell. Thus the believing soul, by the pledge of its faith in Christ, becomes free from all sin, fearless of death, safe from hell, and endowed with the eternal righteousness, life, and salvation of its Husband by Christ. Thus He presents to Himself a glorious bride, without spot or wrinkle, cleansing her with the washing of water by the word; that is, by faith in the word of life, righteousness, and salvation. Thus He betroths her unto Himself "in faithfulness, in righteousness, and in judgment, and in lovingkindness, and in mercies" (Hos 2:19, 20). Who then can value highly enough these royal nuptials? Who can comprehend the riches of the glory of this grace? Christ, that rich and pious Husband, takes as a wife a needy and impious harlot, redeeming her from all her evils and supplying her with all His good things. It is impossible now that her sins should destroy her, since they have been laid upon Christ and swallowed up in Him, and since she has in her Husband Christ a righteousness which she may claim as her own, and which she can set up with confidence against all her sins, against death and hell, saying, "If I have sinned, my Christ, in whom I believe, has not sinned; all mine is His, and all His is mine," as it is written, "My beloved is mine, and I am His" (Cant. ii. 16).[332]

The only thing that needs to be added to this statement by Luther is that what he says of the bridegroom and bride is about Christ and the church, and not immediately about the individual believer. Scripture, contra Wright,[333] nowhere calls the believer the bride of Christ. It is a description of the relationship between Christ and his church.[334] As a member of the New Israel, the believer in the moment of conversion inherits all that the covenant community has been historically blessed with. This follows that pattern of the

---

[332] Luther, *Liberty,* 353–97.

[333] Wright, *'Romans'*, NIB, 415.

[334] Wright, *Justification,* 56 says, 'The key question facing Judaism as a whole was not about individual salvation, but about God's purpose for Israel and the world.' If Wright had kept this in mind, he would have avoided the individualising of texts that are clearly corporate. While I agree with his observation of the Jewish view of justification prior to Christ's coming, it does not account for a much wider use of the justification language found in the New Testament.

Old Testament where all who were circumcised entered into all that the covenant had bestowed on the descendants of Abraham.

However, this is not the limit of Luther's insights into union with Christ. As Carl Trueman has noted:

> ... there is no doubt that in, say, The Freedom of the Christian Man, Luther's preferred analogy for justification is not so much the courtroom but that of the marriage union of bride and groom. While it is true that the analogy does involve a certain legal dimension—for example, the "joyful exchange" of property which takes place within marriage occurs partly because of the legal framework which defines the union—we should not overplay this. Union with Christ is indisputably part and parcel of Luther's approach to justification, and this has a variety of roots and connections, not all of them by any means legal.[335]

Apart from these important texts from Luther, some scholars have recently argued that participation theology in Luther's works has been overlooked. Members of the Helsinki School of Lutheran Theology have made the case that Luther taught a doctrine of participation in Christ which his doctrine of justification was an expression of. The claims made by these scholars are being carefully scrutinized.[336]

So, let us not misrepresent the Reformers. After all, what characterized their theology was not dependence on the Latin, as argued by McGrath and followed by Wright.[337] They had recognized that this Latin translation had produced something which they felt seriously hindered the true intention of the NT authors. To overcome this difficulty, they craved access to the Hebrew and Greek texts and learned these languages to recover what the Scriptures actually taught and so better understand their message. This is a crucial fact

---

[335] Carl R. Trueman, 'Is the Finnish Line a New Beginning? A Critical Assessment of the Reading of Luther Offered by the Helsinki Circle', *WJT* 65 (2003), 231–44 [235]. Trueman references the essay by Oberman, 'Gemitus et Ratus: Luther and Mysticism' in idem, *The Dawn of the Reformation,* 126–54.

[336] Tuomo Mannermaa and Kirsi Irmeli Stjerna, Christ Present In Faith: Luther's View Of Justification (Minneapolis: Fortress, 2005). For reflections on this claim see Carl E. Braaten and Robert W. Jenson (eds.), Union with Christ: The New Finnish Interpretation of Luther (Grand Rapids: Eerdmans, 1998).

[337] Wright, ibid, 5; Wright, *Justification,* 59.

which both McGrath and Wright surprisingly overlook, choosing instead to anchor the Reformers' understanding in the limitations of medieval thought-form which they had in fact to a large extent been liberated from. And so, with this context of the Reformers' theological understanding firmly identified, we can see that they were not dependent on their cultural/theological inheritance. Rather, it was this inheritance which they deliberately rejected, returning to the Hebrew and Greek texts so as to secure a clear understanding of the gospel.

I have written elsewhere about the Reformers' teaching of justification.[338] What I found was a very different picture from that described by Wright. They had such an incredible grasp of biblical theology that to suggest they were bound to creeds that they did not understand is an unwarranted assault on their competence. Their understanding of biblical theology was of the highest calibre and they should neither be charged with the ignorance of earlier generations nor with the unfaithfulness of later ones. Yet this is not the evidence that I want to appeal to, for all men have their flaws, and it is not what these giants of the Christian faith taught that is the final deciding matter. What is decisive is what the Old and New Testament authors have said and what they intended by the terms which they used. It is to these texts that we will now turn.

---

[338] See Holland, *Contours,* 325–337

Chapter 10:
Probing Paul's Doctrine of Justification in Romans and Galatians

While there can be debate over the meaning of a particular text in the epistles, the meaning that Paul intended to convey can often be established from the way he used these key terms in his preaching. Here the terms were employed more directly than in the epistles where the term often formed part of a more complex argument. In the context of his sermons, we can see how the terms were used in evangelistic work, and this provides crucial evidence that helps to establish what Paul wanted his recipients to understand. Because of this, we will now consider the justification language in the preaching recorded in the Acts of the Apostles.

In Acts 14 we find Paul preaching to Jews in a synagogue. These worshippers were clearly in the covenant—the men were circumcised and knew themselves to be Abraham's children. It was to such men that Paul preached what was eventually to be at the heart of the Reformers' message. Paul says to the very people whom Sanders claims were comfortable with the law:

> Let it be known to you therefore, brothers, that through this man forgiveness of sins is proclaimed to you, and by him everyone who believes is freed from everything from which you could not be freed by the law of Moses. Beware, therefore, lest what is said in the Prophets should come about: 'Look, you scoffers, be astounded and perish; for I am doing a work in your days, a work that you will not believe, even if one tells it to you.' (Acts 13:38–41)

It is unfortunate in the above rendering that the translators of the ESV have opted for 'freed from' when the Greek is δικαιοῦται ('justify').

Such preaching cannot possibly fit the original model presented by New Perspective theologians, which is still claimed to be the correct understanding by Wright. Paul's reference to 'everything from which you could not be justified by the works of the law' cannot refer to circumcision, Sabbath-keeping, food law observation, and the like; for few, if any, of the Jews in the synagogue are likely to have been failing in such fundamental Jewish requirements. Then, as now, religious works (rituals, identity makers, legal observances) cannot produce justification, and though these Jews sought to do these works, they remained condemned.

Hence, the meaning of 'justification' in this passage is clear: Paul was saying that because the Jews had not fulfilled the requirements of the law (and from the context this must refer to the moral demands that it made), they must believe, repent, and be forgiven in order to be justified (get right with God). Wright makes no mention of this passage anywhere in his book *Paul and the Faithfulness of God*, and so the implications it carries against his argument are completely ignored.[339]

We find a similar understanding of justification in the account of the apostolic council in Jerusalem. Its very purpose was to discuss the status of the believing gentiles, making the deliberations especially important to our discussion. Were the believing gentiles to be recognized as having an intrinsically equal status with the Jews, or would they only be accepted by God once they accepted circumcision?

> And after there had been much debate, Peter stood up and said to them, "Brothers, you know that in the early days God made a choice among you, that by my mouth the gentiles should hear the word of the gospel and believe. And God, who knows the heart, bore witness to them, by giving them the Holy Spirit just as he did to us, and he made no distinction between us and them, having cleansed their hearts by faith. Now, therefore, why are you putting God to the test by placing a yoke on the neck of the disciples that neither our fathers nor we have been able to bear? But we believe that we will be saved through the grace of the Lord Jesus, just as they will. (Acts 15:7–11)

Instead of giving a homily that eulogizes the apostles' appreciation of the law, Peter does the very opposite. He declared that the law had put a yoke on the Jews that they had not been able to bear. He urged the council not to put this same burden on the shoulders of the growing gentile believing community. This does not sound like the joy that New Perspective theologians claim characterized first century Judaism! Once again, Wright

---

[339] Similarly, in his major work Justification (a response to John Piper, *The Future of Justification*) Wright does not refer to Acts once. This same important omission is made in his Paul and the Faithfulness of God. This is crucial evidence that Wright has put to one side and this seriously challenges his hypothesis.

makes no mention of this passage in *Paul and the Faithfulness of God*. Once again, its implications against his argument are completely ignored and thereby he has failed to put the checks and balances in place for his preferred methodology.

Wright charges earlier generations with the very charge I am making against him, of failing to deal with all the relevant materials. He says:

All theologians and exegetes are involved in the same kind of hermeneutical circle. However, in coming to grips with the particular formulations that have been adopted down the centuries, we must always ask: Why did they emphasize that point in that way? Moreover, in particular, which Scriptures did they appeal to, and which ones did they seem to ignore? Which bits of the jigsaw did they accidentally-on-purpose knock on the floor? In the passages they have highlighted, did they introduce distortions? Were they paying attention to what the writers were actually talking about and if not, what difference did that make?[340]

So, he perfectly sums up the charge I am making against his research.

The 'Greater' Doctrine of Justification

There are many statements referring to justification in both the Old and New Testaments. Most of these were given against the background of the fulfilment of the Second Exodus promises made by the prophets, especially Isaiah. If we fail to appreciate the development of this theme and how the New Testament writers built on it, then we will miss important markers that would help us in our exegesis. For this reason, I will briefly lay out the material relating to the Second Exodus.

Second Exodus Theology

Israel was warned of coming judgment because she had broken her covenant with God and refused to repent and return to him. Despite this threat and its eventual fulfilment through Judah's exile in Babylon, the prophets promised that Yahweh would again act to redeem Israel from her captivity which fulfilled the covenantal promise made to Abraham (Gen 15:12–21) and the warning of the covenantal curses given to Israel (Deut 28–32). This was

---

[340] Wright, *Justification*, 29.

called a Second Exodus, and it would revolve around a Son of David, who would be the instrument of Israel's return from exile.[341]

There are many additional promises that accompany this specific Second Exodus promise. For example, the people would be led through the wilderness, the Davidic prince, on returning to Zion, would build a temple to replace that built by David's descendant Solomon. This experience would parallel the pilgrimage their ancestors experienced when delivered from Egypt, and the nation would be brought into a new covenant with God, who would circumcise not their foreskins but their hearts. They would love God and take joy in serving him. The gentiles would recognize what God had done for his people, and they would turn to the Lord. There would be a great celebration of God's love and the divine marriage would take place in which Israel became God's bride.

However, rather than these promises being fulfilled, the return was a dismal failure as far as the expectations of those who returned was concerned. There was no Davidic king, there was no glorious temple, and there was no recognition by the gentiles that God had blessed her.

New Exodus Theology

Most scholars who work in this field of intertextual studies recognize a core element to the NT's use of the OT. It concerns the promises and covenants Yahweh made with Abraham, David, and then Israel who, because of her disobedience over hundreds of years, had been given over to the Babylonians and taken into exile. The eighth century prophets onwards proclaimed that, though Israel had suffered what seemed a fatal blow from the hand of her God, he had not cast her off. He would still, in a marvellous way, bring together all the promises that had been given to her ancestors. In addition, in an incredible act of salvation, he would bring repentant Israel out of her captivity and back to her homeland to be established as 'the planting of the Lord.' This act of salvation was going to be like their deliverance from Egypt (Isa 50:1–23) and, because of this, it was seen to be a Second Exodus.[342]

Before falling under this judgment, the people of Judah believed that the prophets were wrong in their warnings because, having been faithful to the Davidic throne, God would not allow this to happen to them. Once the predicted judgment fell, they came to accept that the exile was punishment for

---

[341] For a fuller description see Holland, *The Divine Marriage*, 10–14.

[342] The term developed in both biblical and theological understanding.

their sins and found great difficulty in thinking that there could be a new start. However, this was the very thing the prophets had promised them. Despite the destruction of Jerusalem, the deportation of her people and the collapse of the royal family, the prophets predicted that a descendant of David would be raised up (Isa 11:1; 55:3–4; Jer 33:14–17). It was he who would lead the people from their captivity back to the Promised Land (Isa 11:11; 48:20–21; 52:1–12; Ezek 36:24). He would be anointed with the Spirit of the Lord for this task (Isa 61:1–2) and would lead the people through the wilderness (Hos 2:14; 12:9).

This pilgrimage through the desert would be under the protection of the Holy Spirit (Isa 44:3; 59:21; 61:1–3; Ezek 36:24–28; 37:1–4), just as the pilgrimage from Egypt had been. There would be miracles (Mic 7:15), just as there were when they came out of Egypt, and the desert would be transformed as nature shared in the re-creation of the nation (Isa 55:13). The exiles would return, telling of the salvation of God (Isa 52:7–10), and a new covenant would be established, which would centre on the Davidic prince (Isa 9:6–7; 11:1, 55:3–4; Jer 33:14–17). Unlike the exodus from Egypt when flesh was circumcised, the hearts of the people would be circumcised (Jer 31:31–34; Ezek 36:26–27).

It was predicted that, once the people arrived back in Jerusalem, they would build a magnificent temple, which the descendant of David would dedicate (Ezek 44–45). Into this temple, all the nations, without converting to Judaism, would come to worship Israel's God (Isa 2:1–5; 9:1–7; 19:23–25; 49:6–7, 22–23; 56:3; 60:3, 10). The believing peoples of the earth would become one holy nation, the Lord would come into His temple (Mal 3:1) and the marriage between God and his people would be celebrated with a great cosmic banquet (Isa 54:1–8; 61:10; 62:4–5; Hos 2:16,19).

So, these predictions and promises are at the heart of what God said he would do for Israel. They are the Second Exodus promises and give shape and substance as to what the promised new covenant would secure for Israel.

We find the history of the return of the Jews from exile in Babylon in the books of Ezra, Nehemiah, and the Minor Prophets such as Haggai, Zechariah, and Malachi. What these books show is that, while the people attempted to rebuild a temple in Jerusalem (Ezra 3:7ff.; Neh 4:1ff.), it was pathetic compared to the one that had been destroyed by the Babylonians (Hag 2:3–9). They constantly looked for the coming of the descendant of King David (Hag 1:13–14; Zech 3:8–9) to fulfil the Second Exodus promises, but he did not appear. For four hundred years they groaned in their sense of failure, guilt and disappointment.

As the years passed, there was no significant change. Though the Jews returned to their homeland, they were always under the control of another nation. Their exile seemed to continue, and they longed for its end. They had returned to their own land but were as far from God as they had ever been, for, despite a brief period during the days of the Maccabees, they never had their own independence. For them, God had not yet fulfilled his promises. Not until they had complete freedom could they accept that their punishment was over. The literature of the Jews during this period—known as the intertestamental or Second Temple period—shows the faith they continued to have. They clung to the hope that God would fulfil the promises he had made through the prophets. The Scriptures surveyed above were their light through the long, dark years of shame under the domination of Rome. They longed for the promised deliverance from their helplessness and enslavement. These promises, though interpreted differently by different Jewish groups, seem to have been the source of hope for them all.

This brief survey indicates the degree to which the expectation of a fulfilment of the promised Second Exodus had saturated the nation at the time of the Baptist's ministry. While there were different opinions on how the promises would be fulfilled, the evidence shows that these promises provided the core of the teaching of many groups of Jews throughout Palestine in the time of Jesus. To ignore this expectation, in any attempt to understand the development of the Christian message, would be folly. What is abundantly clear is that the hope that these promises would one day be fulfilled did not die. It is on these promises (which spoke of the sons of Abraham being inclusive of believing gentiles) Paul focuses when he writes that all the promises of God are 'Yes and Amen' in Christ Jesus.

These features need to be recognised in New Exodus theology:

1. Exodus theology tends to be about identifying types in the original exodus from Egypt.

2. Second Exodus theology is about the promises Yahweh made to Israel concerning her redemption from captivity. The prophets saw the exodus from Egypt as a type of the forthcoming Second Exodus. The promises were primarily nationalistic and geographically focused, about being returned to the promised land to become the most blessed people on earth. In this promised

Second Exodus the descendant of David, the prince of Ezekiel, replaces Moses as the great redeemer.

3. New Exodus theology is about the typological fulfilment of both the Egyptian exodus and the Second Exodus theology based on the promises given through the prophets. In the New Testament, these are explored and often merged and shown to be fulfilled in the person and work of Jesus. What the work of Moses and David pointed to was all fulfilled in Jesus.

In the light of this, it is important to recognize that the term 'justified' will have different nuances depending on what act of salvation is being referred to. Outside these specific exodus contexts there are other references to justification, and their meanings must be determined by their contexts. Not all references to justification are directly related to the exodus themes, but I will argue that the theme of the exodus is lurking in the background, influencing the particular use of the term to some degree.

I shall propose nine meanings of justification and will refer to them as sublevels. This is to highlight the fact that they have either not been previously recognised or given proper attention.

Investigating Sublevels of Justification

The doctrine of justification tends to be almost exclusively interpreted by Reformed scholarship at an individual level. Despite Reformed theology having a very strong corporate appreciation of the Old Testament covenants, and a keen appreciation of how these are embedded in New Testament soteriology and ecclesiology, the corporate nature of the New Testament documents themselves has frequently been overlooked. As a consequence, the glorious themes explored within the New Testament are applied exclusively to the individual. While there is, of course, a vitally important personal application of the New Testament's teaching—in that the individual must respond in faith to the grace that God offers in Christ—that is not the total picture of justification. The New Testament passage that has most references to being justified is Romans 5:12–21, a passage that is clearly corporate—all who are in Adam die, and all who are in Christ are 'justified'.

The Corporate Nature of Justification

In this way, the corporate understanding of the Old Testament shines through in Paul's writings. Israel was baptised into Moses at one decisive moment and, through this vital participation (1 Cor 10:1–5), became the covenant community. Every Jew throughout history, even those yet to be born, was counted as being present and so shared in this historic moment, as they did in the exodus from Egypt (see Exod 13:14). Even so, they still had to be individually circumcised to become experientially a member of that community. It was in that community that all of God's blessings resided, and to share in these blessings, each male child had to be circumcised. It was only by being part of the community that everything promised to Abraham became the possession of the individual. It was not exclusively his, nor did he receive it in isolation from the believing community—God was not dealing with the individual in some unique way. Being in Moses, or in Abraham, he receives everything, including the promises, because he is in the covenant community.

This is the background Paul uses to describe the work of justification and the New Testament people of God. They were all justified together (Rom 5:16; 1 Cor 6:11) in the same decisive moment of Christ's death. The Messiah's circumcision (Col 2:10–12) was also theirs through having been baptised into his death. So, in his death, Christ saved his people and justified them. Likewise, as people have faith in Christ as Saviour and submit to the Spirit, so the Spirit circumcises their hearts (individually, at different times, and in different locations), and they, like Jewish children, are brought into the justified community. It is by their being in the covenant community, which has been united with Christ (Rom 6:1–5), that they are justified and enjoy all the spiritual blessings that go with their new status.

If Wright had kept his eye on this corporate dimension of justification and given proper attention to Romans 5:12–21 where the imputation of Christ's obedience is repeatedly referred to (vv. 16, 19 'gift of righteousness' and in vv. 17–18 'imputed'), then he would not have been so eager to attack the doctrine of imputed righteousness.[343] This chapter speaks of the imputation of righteousness several times, and it is contrasted with the imputation of Adam's disobedience to his offspring (Rom 5:18–19). Thus, to deny that imputation of righteousness is present in Romans 5 would be to deny the doctrine of 'original sin'; the whole biblical doctrine of salvation would fall apart.

It is not that Wright fails to stress the importance of a corporate reading of the texts Romans 6:1–7 of the New Testament, but rather that he is not

---

[343] As with other texts, Wright avoids Rom 5:12–21 and its clear teaching on justification on entry into the community because it challenges his model of justification being about those who are already in the community.

consistent in doing so. This lack of consistency in reading the text corporately shows itself in the way he exegetes Romans 6:1–7. From a passage that is clearly corporate (Rom 5:12–21), with no indication from Paul that he is doing something different, Wright has Paul arguing about individual initiation through baptism in the opening of Romans 6. He then comes to Romans 7:8–24 and this, in Wright's interpretation, swings into a corporate description of the power of sin. However, before he begins to exegete this passage, he claims from the illustration in 7:1–4 that individual believers are brides of Christ—an idea totally out of sync with the rest of the Christian Bible, where the bride of Christ is always the church. Wright had already linked the baptism of Rom 6:1–4 with 1 Cor 10:1–4, but what he did not note was that the baptism of 1 Cor 10 is not about the individual Jew or Christian being baptised but the community. Had he been guided by that fact he would have avoided his claim for baptismal regeneration.[344] While Wright reads Romans 7 as a corporate description of the experience of Israel, I believe he has missed the larger picture of the Fall. The sin is not about the transgression of the Torah but the disobedience of Adam which the transgression of Israel is manifested through her covenantal disobedience.[345]

Once he has worked through chapter 7, Wright brings the same corporate reading into chapter 8 and this corporate reading is then followed through to the end of Romans 11. I am not against these passages being interpreted corporately—I have done it myself,[346] though with some differences from the reading that Wright has offered. What I am asking is: why does he not keep to this method when he reads the openings of Romans 6 and 7? Moreover, why, despite identifying the exodus echoes in Romans 6 does he fail to keep to the corporate reading that should flow out not only from chapter 5 but also 1 Corinthians 10:1–4 which he has identified as important for interpreting Romans 6:1–4? Such indiscipline leaves the text floating around with no

---

[344] 'When Paul speaks of baptism in Romans 6, he has in mind the crossing of the Red Sea at the Exodus. He makes exactly this connection of course, in 1 Cor 10:2.' Wright, *New Exodus, New Inheritance*, 28.

[345] 'In Romans 7, Paul expounds what happened when the Torah arrived in Israel, and what happens still as Israel lives under the Torah. Israel actually recapitulates the sin of Adam and the sinful human life which follows from it'. Wright, *Perspectives*, 3.

[346] See Holland, *The Divine Marriage* for a detailed corporate exegesis of the letter to Romans.

historic or exegetical controls, allowing Wright to appeal to the passage as teaching a sacramental theology of baptism. Like many others, he has introduced the idea of water baptism into a passage that has nothing to say about water, giving the act of water baptism significance that Paul (judging from his letters) never saw it as having.[347] For Paul, water baptism was nothing more than an outward confession of repentance and identifying with Jesus's saving work, as achieved through his death and resurrection. What it symbolised, therefore, had happened long before the baptized person made their individual confession.[348]

Thus, Wright further loses the trail of Paul's narrative by supposing that Romans 6:1–4 is about baptismal initiation and regeneration. It is not. It is a corporate event, and it is expanding on the arguments made concerning two communities, one in Adam and the other in Christ. The passage speaks of a corporate event of deliverance and is the antitype of Israel's deliverance from both Egypt and Babylon when they were brought out of one kingdom and established in another. On each occasion, the language of justification was

---

[347] Wright, *Faithfulness of God*, 422 correctly identifies the passage as developing the theme of the New Exodus, but in my opinion, he confuses what was achieved in the actual death of Jesus when the corporate baptism took place, with what takes place in water baptism. I see no reason why the act of water baptism is intended to be anything other than a confession of repentance and faith in the crucified and risen Christ which the act of baptism eventually came to be seen to symbolize. Wright, *Romans*, 534 says, 'There is every reason to suppose that Jesus himself saw John's baptism as the starting point for his own work, not just chronologically but thematically, and the earliest church likewise looked back not just to Jesus but to Jesus as the leader of a movement that had begun with John's baptism.' I would claim that the only reason that the baptism Jesus commanded became different from that which he inherited from John is that the significance of the historical baptism into Christ was confused with what was achieved in water baptism and the two were merged. With that, water baptism was given a significance it never had for the early church, and so the church lost sight of the great doctrine of union with Christ. Some of this doctrine was rediscovered in the reformation but its focus was that of 'the individual and Christ' through water baptism and not 'the church and Christ' through direct entry into his death.

[348] I wonder if Wright fails to follow through on Paul's doctrine of the resurrection because he sees it as the Maccabean expectation of resurrection that motivates Christian witness and martyrdom, so Wright, *Perspectives*, 72 'resurrection which marked out the martyrs in particular. This is, it seems, what he was saying the Philippians to imitate.'

used to describe what Yahweh achieved for the community of his people. The opening of chapter 6 explains how this 'community in Christ' came into existence; it is a historical and single event never to be repeated, being an experience shared by the whole community. Interpreting it individualistically means ignoring the corporate nature of the passage (indicated by Paul's selection of grammar and tenses) and tears the text away from the corporate narrative that Wright elsewhere promotes.

If Wright had stayed with the corporate nature of the narrative, then he would not have needed to argue that Paul did not mean 'justified' in Romans 6:7—for he clearly does. Paul never means anything else whenever he uses the term, as he does 17 times in his letters. I have shown elsewhere that this term 'justified' in Romans 6:7 follows on from the justification of the community that is argued for in Romans 5.[349] Wright misses this and so, I believe, overlooks an important sublevel of meaning for the term 'justification.' This leads him, as it does many others, to ride roughshod over the Greek text to keep a degree of consistency in his exegesis. From this distortion of what Paul is actually saying, Wright then argues for a sacramental reading that, despite his mocking the position of others who cannot accept his claims,[350] serves to betray the faults of his own exegesis far more than the faults of those he mocks.

Now having established the nature of corporate justification, we can consider aspects of this vitally important work of God.

Covenant Making

Another 'sublevel' of meaning is found on a closer examination of Genesis 15:6, the foundational text for the doctrine of justification which Paul cites in both Romans 4:3 and Galatians 3:6. Traditionally, it has been understood that when Abraham was counted righteous, he was acquitted of his sin by Yahweh. The difficulty with this understanding is that there is no mention of sin in either the immediate or the wider context of Genesis 15. In the previous chapter, Abram acted as an exemplary God-fearer. He delivered Lot from King Chedorlaomer and the kings allied with him (Gen 14:17). These kings had been at war with the King of Sodom and his allies when Abram's nephew had been captured. Abram recovered the plunder they had taken as well as the

---

[349] See Holland, *Contours*, 207–234.

[350] Wright, *Faithfulness of God*, 421.

captives. After he returned from the rescue mission, he met the grateful King of Sodom and Melchizedeck who was the King of Salem and priest of God Most High.[351] Abram paid a tithe of everything to Melchizedeck and was blessed by him, but to the King of Sodom he returned the spoils, saying that he did not want anyone to say that the King of Sodom had made him rich. Following these encounters, Abram returned to his camp and to Sarai, his wife.

Throughout this narrative there has been no mention of sin. Indeed, as noted, Abram had behaved in an entirely godly way. Now, obviously, from a New Testament perspective we can say that Abram was a sinner and needed to be forgiven; but if we do that sort of exegesis, with no interest in context, we play the dangerous game of irresponsibly transposing meaning from one part of the Bible to another without vindicating the legitimacy of the transfer of meaning. If it is forbidden to do this, how much more to irresponsibly transfer second temple literature into New Testament passages as discussed in chapter 6. This, alas, is often done with disastrous consequences for the meaning of the text. If Abram were being justified in the way normally understood, then the context would surely support the proposed meaning.

We must ask, therefore, why has the meaning of acquittal been chosen for this particular use of 'justification'? I would suggest it is because this meaning is found in the statement made about David in Romans 4:6. Scholars have assumed that the same meaning is found in 4:3 (which speaks of Abraham's saving faith) as in 4:6 (a statement about David's acquittal) because of the proximity of the ideas in Paul's argument; but this is not necessarily the case. While acquittal provides one aspect of the experience of justification, I believe that Genesis 15:6 helps us understand another of the meanings of 'justify' in Paul's theology of salvation.

In fact, the key to this meaning is found in the Psalms. In Psalm 106:31 we read that when Phinehas slew the Midianite and her Jewish lover, the Lord counted Phinehas righteous on account of what he had done. The confusion over the meaning of 'justified' as used here is so widespread that the Reformed scholar John Murray felt forced to say that Phinehas was justified by works whereas Abraham was justified by faith.[352] Murray was accepting by this statement that there are other ways of being justified than through

---

[351] Gen 14:18.

[352] Murray, *Romans*, 151–52. One hardly needs to expand on how this interpretation undermines the doctrine of justification by faith!

Christ; humanity is capable, in Murray's statement, to be justified by works and not just theoretically for he says that Phinehas was justified by works! What Murray missed, however, was that the solution to this conundrum might be found by looking at the original narrative in which the account of the slaying of the Midianite and her lover took place. It reads:

> And the Lord said to Moses, "Phinehas the son of Eleazar, son of Aaron the priest, has turned back my wrath from the people of Israel, in that he was jealous with my jealousy among them, so that I did not consume the people of Israel in my jealousy. Therefore say, 'Behold, I give to him my covenant of peace, and it shall be to him and to his descendants after him the covenant of a perpetual priesthood, because he was jealous for his God and made atonement for the people of Israel.'" (Num 25:10)

So, the Psalmist describes the same event as the occasion when Phinehas was justified, whereas the source-text says that Yahweh made a covenant with Phinehas in response to his obedience. The Psalmist explains Yahweh's action of 'creating a covenant' with Phinehas as Yahweh 'counting him righteous'. Thus, this creation of the covenant is the same as being justified; the declaration concerned Phinehas and his family being appointed as the Lord's priests. In this context, it could be thought that it has nothing to do with justification by faith, but that would be a wrong conclusion, for faith(fullness) motivated his action

Here we see evidence for the 'covenant making' sublevel of the meaning of 'justification'. It means 'to make a covenant with'—and that is exactly what was happening in Genesis 15:3, where Yahweh made a covenant with Abram and promised that his descendants would become a mighty nation that would bring Yahweh's blessing to all other nations.

Now, interestingly, this is the very issue Paul was battling with in his letter to the Galatians. Had God really made a covenant with the Jews alone? If the gentiles wanted to enter, did they have to embrace Judaism? Paul's answer is that no one is justified (brought into the Abrahamic covenant) by the works of the law. Outside of Christ, everyone is equally under the authority of sin and Satan, and so condemned to eternal separation from God. However, in Christ, everyone who believes—Jews and Greeks, males and females, bond slaves and free—are all members of the one community that has been made right with God (Gal 3:26–29; Col 3:9–11). In this community, there is no preferred ethnicity and no requirement to adopt the circumcision which characterised the old covenant.

The original text of Genesis 15:6 has links to the exodus in that the formal inauguration of the covenant (Gen 15:12–19) promised redemption from slavery. This promise was clearly fulfilled in the exodus from Egypt. I would suggest it is this sublevel of meaning that brings clarity to a range of uses of the term 'to justify' or to 'declare righteous' in Paul and, as a consequence, it brings greater clarity to the biblical doctrine of justification.

Covenant Ratification

A fact which has often been overlooked by scholarship is that covenant ratification shares the language of justification. The end of Romans 4 initially appears to be problematic, for in it Paul could be taken as saying that, as a result of Sarah conceiving Isaac, Abraham was declared righteous. He writes:

> In hope he believed against hope, that he should become the father of many nations, as he had been told, "So shall your offspring be." He did not weaken in faith when he considered his own body, which was as good as dead (since he was about a hundred years old), or when he considered the barrenness of Sarah's womb. No unbelief made him waver concerning the promise of God, but he grew strong in his faith as he gave glory to God, fully convinced that God was able to do what he had promised. That is why his faith was "counted to him as righteousness." But the words "it was counted to him" were not written for his sake alone, but for ours also. It will be counted to us who believe in him who raised from the dead Jesus our Lord, who was delivered up for our trespasses and raised for our justification. (Rom 4:18–25)

The problem with this widely-followed interpretation is that in order to understand Abraham as being justified by the conception of Isaac, we must ignore the fact that Abraham was living anything but a life of faith at this time; yet Paul presents him in Romans 4:19–20 as someone who lived by faith. He presented Sarah as his sister on at least two occasions to save his own skin, and not once in these passages is anything said that commends him. The prevailing reading exists solely because there is a reference to Sarah's womb being 'as good as dead'.

The logic behind this interpretation that Isaac's birth was the occasion of justification is so removed from reality that John Murray resorted to saying that Abraham received faith to copulate with Sarah despite his body being weak through his extreme age. This, for Murray, was the reason for his justification, for it was in his weakness that he acted out his faith! The fact that Abraham went on to have six children with Keturah,[353] after the death of Sarah, is not considered in this argument, nor is the fact that there is nothing essentially miraculous in the birth of a child to a woman in extreme old age; such 'miracles' seemed to occur rather regularly in the lives of the patriarchs!

Paul's point here could be not that Isaac was born as a result of Abraham's miraculous faith but as a result the incredible faithfulness of God who kept his promise. In one sense, it is God himself who is justified in the birth of Isaac; not Abraham. Looked at from such a perspective, the conception of Isaac is not the occasion when Abraham was counted righteous; that happened when he obediently offered Isaac, believing in a miraculous God who can raise the dead.

The only event in which Abraham's faith becomes a model for believer's faith according to Paul in Romans 4:24–25 was when he believed that Yahweh would keep his promise even though he asked Abraham to sacrifice Isaac. The appropriateness of identifying Moriah as the event of Abraham's justification is that if Sarah's womb was as good as dead when she conceived Isaac, which is the normal interpretation, how much truer was it when Abraham was challenged to sacrifice him years later?

Thus, the reference to Sarah's body being as good as dead fits in with what Paul was saying concerning the offering of Isaac. The assurance that this is the true location that Paul takes us to (the event on Moriah) is clear from the statement made in the closing verses (Rom 4:24–25). It was this event that demonstrated Abraham's faith; by reading the passage as a whole we see that the occurrence of Abraham's justification was when he showed his faith in God by obediently offering Isaac. For Paul, this corresponds to the Father (God) offering his only Son (Jesus) whom he raised from the dead: 'But the words "it was counted to him" were not written for his sake alone, but for ours also. It will be counted to us who believe in him who raised from the dead Jesus our Lord, who was delivered up for our trespasses and raised for our justification' (Rom 4:23–25).

Thus, this statement concerning justification is clearly linked with the theme of the resurrection. Abraham's faith was demonstrated by his belief that, despite his intent to obey God and offer Isaac as a burnt offering, God would raise Isaac from the dead. This had to be so, for God had promised to make Isaac the father of a mighty nation. So, in this passage Paul is not

---

[353] Gen 25:1–4.

reflecting on the birth of Isaac, which is not mentioned at all, but on the offering of Isaac. Indeed, in the Genesis account, there is no mention of Abraham being justified in the conception narrative (despite New Testament readers regularly assuming that there is).[354] The construction I have given is more likely to be Paul's intended meaning.

A benefit of the interpretation offered above is that it respects the text of Genesis. It shows that Paul is not glossing over Abraham's failures and that he identifies the setting for the comment on Sarah's womb being as good as dead as being the Moriah incident. In this incident, Isaac is used as a type of Christ, and interestingly Paul immediately follows his argument with a discussion of Adam as a further type of Christ (Rom 5:12–21), linking this discussion once again back into the final statement of the earlier section. The interpretation also has the distinct advantage of resolving the tension between James and Paul. They both refer to Moriah as evidence of Abraham's faith, and so they are both singing from the same hymn sheet. Thus, Abraham was justified by faith in Genesis 15:3, and his faith was ratified in Genesis 22 as faith in the living God who raises the dead. The ratification of faith in Genesis 22 did not add to the act of justification in chapter 15, but it did justify God for accepting Abraham's commitment and demonstrated to Abraham's family that he was committed to the God who had called him.

Another very significant plus for the proposed reading is that it shows that Paul was a most careful Old Testament exegete, for he stays closely to the text of the Genesis narrative and does not add to it. He has not introduced 'justification' into the conception or birth of Isaac as most assume, although commentators, not appreciating its absence in the Genesis passage, have not questioned the traditional reading of Romans 4 in regard to Abraham being justified when Sarah conceived despite her womb being as good as dead. From this explanation, we can see that Paul never mentions the conception of Isaac, only Abraham's obedience in offering him as a sacrifice.

The Justification of Israel

The theme of righteousness or justification is very much part of the prophets' understanding of Yahweh's dealings with Israel. Put away in exile; Israel was assured that Yahweh had not forsaken her. He promised his people that he would redeem them from their enemies and bring them to their inheritance.

---

[354] Wright, Faithfulness of God, 1200.

This would be achieved by the creation of a new covenant which indicated the end of the Mosaic institution.

It is within this new covenant context that we must read Romans 4. It is only by being focused on this development that we keep in mind that 'righteousness' has specific covenantal roots and associations. To remove what Paul says from this background is to lose the key contextual setting that has been part of Paul's thinking and essential to understanding the term 'justified' in the theology of the apostle. We need to note that Romans 4 not only summarizes the earlier chapter 3, with its strong deliverance theme (Rom 3:21–26), but also anticipates chapter 6 with its strong exodus theme.[355] This New Exodus is essential because man in Adam is exiled in the realm of sin and death (Rom 5:12–21). As Wright has noted (although at the same time he overlooks some key issues), the Isaianic Second Exodus reverberates throughout the section, and with it the justification of God as he does his marvellous work of salvation.

So here we find, in this use of the term 'to be justified' (contrary to Wright), the creation of a covenant, for that is what was happening when Yahweh redeemed Israel. He promised he would make a new covenant with her, not like the former one which was based on the circumcision of the flesh but on the circumcision of the hearts of the people (Jer 31:31–34; Ezek 36:24–32).

The term 'to justify' is found in the prophets, particularly in the book of Isaiah, where Israel is promised a Second Exodus through which she would be justified (vindicated) in regard to her claim of being in relationship to the God who had promised to honour and give her the justice she had been denied because of her disobedience (Isa 29:17–24; 51:12–16; 65:9–10).

Thus, so far, we have identified the five possible meanings of justification: 1) The acquittal of sin; 2) The imputation of righteousness; 3) The declaration that one is in the covenant; 4) The creation of a covenant; 5) Justification ratification; 6) The deliverance and justification of Israel. Yet three more require our further attention.

The Justification of the Gentiles

The unrestricted inclusion of the gentiles in the new covenant community is particularly the language of Isaiah, but it is not confined to him. It is a

---

[355] Correctly noted by Wright, *Faithfulness of God*, 1333–1338.

common theme that links the classical prophets together (Hos 2:16, 19; Isa
54:1–8; 61:10; 62:4–5; Ezek 16:59–63). Israel's redemption is an aspect of
her justification and will be completed only when all of the promises Yahweh
has made to her are finally fulfilled. Justification, therefore, covers the whole
scope of salvation history, from Israel's election to her being perfected as the
bride of Yahweh.[356] Israel's justification is, moreover, linked with the
justification of the gentiles, for they are promised a part in this newly created
covenant community through the same promise given to Abraham.

We saw earlier that 'counted righteous' in Genesis 15:6 refers to Abram
being brought into covenant with Yahweh. This understanding is followed by
Paul when he cites Genesis 15:6 in Galatians 3:6, where he says: 'Consider
Abraham: He believed God, and it was credited to him as righteousness.' The
passage which precedes this statement speaks of how believing gentiles in
Galatia were leaving the true gospel. Paul warned how dangerous it is to be
inconsistent, telling of how he had been forced to rebuke Peter publicly for
withdrawing from table fellowship with the gentiles because some Judaizers
had arrived in Antioch (Gal 2:11–14).

Paul says in Galatians 2:15–16 that Jewish believers know that
justification is only by faith in Jesus Christ. He then asks that if Jewish
believers discovered the reality of sin through their faith in Christ, does this
make Christ responsible for promoting sin. The implication is that, if this is
true of the significance of the revelation of Christ, it is equally true of the
revelation that the law brings. Because it makes us aware of sin, it therefore
does not follow that the law is the cause of sin any more than the revelation of
Jesus is the cause of sin.

Thus, we see that the argument Paul uses here is a condensed version of
the one used in Romans 6–7. When Paul speaks of 'death', he refers to the
death of Christ in which he says all believers have shared. In that death, Christ
has fully satisfied the demands of the law. Thus, Paul argues that the new

---

[356] Wright fails to identify the divine marriage context for some key texts and
as a result builds a different picture from what Paul is presenting. P.
Stuhlmacher, *Reconciliation Law and Righteousness: Essays in Biblical
Theology* (Philadelphia: Fortress, 1986), 57 notes: 'As in 2 Corinthians 5:16–
21 and Romans 3:24–26; 4:25; 5:1–11 show, justification, atonement,
reconciliation and new creation have the most intimate connection for Paul. In
fact, these motifs begin to overlap as early as Isaiah (cf. Isa 43:3–4; 18–19;
50:8; 53:10–12; 65:17), and the same thing occurs in the Qumran texts.'

Chapter 9: Probing Wright's Doctrine of Justification

covenant centres on the death of Jesus, which has brought believers into a relationship with God that the law was unable to secure (because it was never intended to).

To drive this point home, Paul asks the Galatians in chapter 3 how they came into the covenant: was it by works or by faith? What is significant is that he is not asking if they were forgiven by keeping the law. Surprisingly, he asked if they received the Spirit by observing the law or by faith.[357] This is the very question that introduces the statement regarding Abram being justified by faith. The statement is, therefore, nothing less than their being asked how they came into the covenant. It was the very point raised by Peter at the council of Jerusalem in Acts when he said:

> And after there had been much debate, Peter stood up and said to them, "Brothers, you know that in the early days God made a choice among you, that by my mouth the gentiles should hear the word of the gospel and believe. And God, who knows the heart, bore witness to them, by giving them the Holy Spirit just as he did to us, and he made no distinction between us and them, having cleansed their hearts by faith. Now, therefore, why are you putting God to the test by placing a yoke on the neck of the disciples that neither our fathers nor we have been able to bear? But we believe that we will be saved through the grace of the Lord Jesus, just as they will.[358]

The point of these passages is that they focus on the justification of the gentile believing community. They did not have the covenants of the Old Testament, nor did they inherit the promises that Israel boasted of, and yet God in his kindness had not excluded them. Indeed, his calling and blessing of Israel was not for her own sake but so that she should take the message of Yahweh's love to all people that they might believe and be justified. Paul says the same thing to the Ephesians:

> Therefore, remember that at one time you gentiles in the flesh, called "the uncircumcision" by what is called the circumcision, which is made in the flesh by hands—remember that you were at that time separated from Christ, alienated from the commonwealth of Israel and strangers to the covenants of promise, having no hope and without God in the world. But now in Christ Jesus you who once were far off have been brought near by the blood of Christ. For he himself is our peace, who has made us both one and

---

[357] Gal 3:1–5.

[358] Ibid.

299

> has broken down in his flesh the dividing wall of hostility by
> abolishing the law of commandments expressed in ordinances,
> that he might create in himself one new man in place of the two,
> so making peace. (Eph 2:11–15)

The justification of the gentiles (their inclusion into the new covenant community), was not an afterthought of God. It had always been his intention, yet it had temporarily been thwarted by Israel through her disobedience. Even so, as Paul explains to the Romans, those who were not previously thought of as a people were now the people of God (Rom 9:25).[359]

What Paul insists is that *this* justification is *the* justification that matters in salvation history. He insists that all Jews must accept this and exercise faith in the same way that the gentiles are now doing. This was an incredible obstacle for all Jews, for they had rightly understood that their release from Babylon was the occasion of their justification.[360] What they are called to recognize is that they are in a far more serious bondage, as members of the kingdom of darkness together with the gentiles and that they have no hope of freedom if it is not secured for them by Christ. Thus, justification is at the heart of the Christian gospel, and the gift of the Holy Spirit is the evidence of acceptance with God.

The Justification of God

Only a just God can morally and legally justify the sinner. This is axiomatic, as no one would want to be judged by someone whose judgment was capricious or unsound. The judgment of such a person is bound to be called into question. It is for this reason that the justification of God to act as man's judge, and his ability to devise a moral and legal way of acquitting him although guilty, needs to be considered carefully. Will God's judgments be sound, or will they be challenged?

In his penitent Psalm, David said:

> Against you, you only, have I sinned and done what is evil in your
> sight so that you may be justified in your words and blameless in
> your judgment. (Ps 51:4)

David is asserting that God's judgments are always true, and that he is justified by them. God is shown to be righteous in that he deals with sin and

---

[359] See 1 Pet 2:10 for a similar understanding.

[360] See Holland, *Contours*, 207–208.

judges those who rebel against him, even when they are his appointed representatives. When they repent, as David did (the Psalm is about his experience of forgiveness), God is not compromised because he deals properly with the offence. To use Paul's language: 'It was to show his righteousness at the present time so that he might be just and the justifier of the one who has faith in Jesus' (Rom 3:26).

Earlier, I identified the use of the term 'justified' in relation to the justification of God as the one who 'keeps covenant faithfulness'; but we must not overlook the fact that the same term is also used to speak of Yahweh's status as being 'innocent.' God judges impartially, never showing favouritism. This was Israel's mistake. Being the people of the covenant, they thought they had special protection from Yahweh who would never allow them to come under judgment. Israel was to learn that God would never overlook their sins; he would never be found to be unjust. God's warning was, 'you only have I known of all the families of the earth; therefore, I will punish you for all your iniquities' (Amos 3:2). The same vindication of God as he is declared to be justified is given by Paul in Romans 3:4 when he writes: 'By no means! Let God be true though everyone were a liar, as it is written, "That you may be justified in your words, and prevail when you are judged"'. The fulfilment of the Second Exodus promises resulted not only in Israel's justification but also in Yahweh's justification (Isa 45:22–23; 46:8–13; 51:9–11; 52:6).

The justification of God is a topic to which Paul gives a whole section of Romans. There are some who see the statement in Romans 9:14–18 to be about God demonstrating his right to choose individuals to suffer eternal damnation. Their argument is that the beginning of the chapter has Paul praying for his countrymen that God would save them, setting the scene for God's judgment on Pharaoh, which they see as a statement that Pharaoh was denied salvation and sentenced to perdition. Those who hold this view believe that this absolute authority of God, which cannot be questioned by any person, displays his glory to all of humankind.

Even those who embrace this interpretation feel a degree of discomfort, for they recognize the harsh image of God which it creates. The argument suggests that God is simply not concerned about humanity and does what he chooses. Of course, he has every right to do this, for he is God and has absolute authority over the whole of his creation. But is that what Paul intends to say? Such a position has not justified God before a fallen world but has instead suggested that they are vindicated in holding out against the rule of such an absolute despot. The relevant text is Romans 9:1–33. I have provided a detailed exegesis of this elsewhere,[361] and so here I will highlight the salient points.

Claiming that the opening verses should control how vv. 14–18 should be read is a valid argument, the only issue is whether the opening verses are about the salvation of individual Jews, as most have taken, or the salvation of the nation in a broader sense. Only a few decades earlier, Jesus had warned the Jewish people of impending judgment, just as judgment came whenever Israel hardened her heart to the word of the Lord. Is it reasonable to think that this warning had been lost to the church so that its leaders considered that Israel was not under the threat of a divine judgment?

It makes sense to me that Paul is expressing his longing, as did Moses (whom Paul is widely thought to be imitating), that Israel, though deserving judgment, should be spared it. If this is correct, then the term 'saved' is not limited to eschatological salvation, but to the typically Old Testament use of the word which is picked up elsewhere in the New Testament. There is no reason why Paul should not be expressing his concern at this level and praying for the safety of Israel and her protection from impending judgment. Any attempt to maintain the traditional double jeopardy doctrine must answer this possibility which for most has so far been overlooked and make a case why it could not be Paul's intended meaning.

The argument has been made that in vv. 14–18 Paul says that God hardened Pharaoh's heart. From this is argued that Pharaoh's fate had nothing to do with his character or potential but God's sovereign decision. Since there was no history before this announcement, the hardening appears to be totally the result of God's elective choice and had nothing to do with Pharaoh as a man.

The problem with such an argument, however, is that it ignores the fact that Pharaoh (a term used to speak of the dynasty rather than as a title for an individual man), had been setting himself against God's will and his call to repent for generations. Moses's own life was at stake because of the oppression of the Pharaoh in his day. So, when Moses spoke these words to Pharaoh, addressing him as the last of a dynasty that had abused Israel, there was plenty of history for God to judge. It just is not good enough to say this judgment came out of the blue, and that God was not making his decision

---

[361] See Holland, *The Divine Marriage,* 295–336.

based on previous acts. This is as far from the truth as it is possible to be and simply ignores the historical context of the event referred to.

The others who are referred to in the passage—Abraham, Isaac, Jacob, and Esau—whilst individuals, are nevertheless representative figures in redemptive history. Each of them represents the community of descendants that came from them and so are corporate figures. This is important, for the election of these men was not at the level of 'election to eternal life', but election to service as the instruments God would use to promote and fulfil his purposes. This is a very different kind of election from that which guides the double jeopardy understanding, which is about the election to eternal salvation. This understanding of election matches what the Old Testament is familiar with and which must control the meaning of 'election' in the exodus narrative. Salvation as revealed in the New Testament, of deliverance from judgment through the death and resurrection of Christ, had not been made known and so to argue in such a category would be to read the text anachronistically.

Paul responds to the complaint of someone whom he imagines might not agree with his argument by saying that the potter has the right to choose what he does with his clay. Paul tells his protagonist that the potter has the absolute right to make pots that have noble uses, and he equally has the same right to make pots for menial uses. It would be ridiculous to think that the clay could dictate what it should be turned into. The danger of reading this statement out of its historical theological context is that it can be made to say something that the history of interpreting the original allegory it stems from would never support.

Paul is drawing from the prophecy of Isaiah as he does throughout the letter and there are two passages that qualify for being his source. The first is Isaiah 29:15–16 which says:

> Ah, you who hide deep from the Lord your counsel, whose deeds are in the dark, and who say, 'Who sees us? Who knows us?' You turn things upside down! Shall the potter be regarded as the clay, that the thing made should say of its maker, 'He did not make me'; or the thing formed say of him who formed it, 'He has no understanding'? (Isa 29:15–16)

And the second is Isaiah 45:9 which says:

> Woe to him who strives with him who formed him, a pot among earthen pots! Does the clay say to him who forms it, 'What are you making?' or 'Your work has no handles'? (Isa 45:9)

The Isaiah 29:15–16 passage is a rebuke to Israel for boasting in her achievements; she is reminded that there is nothing to boast about because she is nothing but the clay which the divine potter has moulded to fulfil his purpose.[362] The Isaiah 45:9 passage is far more significant since it comes after Yahweh has called Cyrus his servant. Cyrus has been raised up to achieve God's will for the nations, opening doors for freedom or closing doors for slavery. Israel, hearing this, wonders why a pagan king should be given such an honorific status, querying why she has been bypassed when she is the true servant. Yahweh silences her complaint saying:

> Woe to him who strives with him who formed him, a pot among earthen pots! Does the clay say to him who forms it, 'What are you making?' or 'Your work has no handles'? Woe to him who says to a father, 'What are you begetting?' or to a woman, 'With what are you in labour?' (Isa 45:9–10)

In other words, Israel as a nation, not an individual, is being addressed for her complaint that she has been by-passed in favour of Cyrus. The complaint is not about being judged and sent to eternal perdition, but about being judged for not functioning as a servant of the Lord should. She had failed to fulfil the role for which she had been elected, and so she cannot complain that God has used his sovereign prerogative to bypass her to give the role to another who would fulfil it.

The important thing to notice is that the passage Paul draws from is not about Israel's eternal destiny, but about her being replaced as God's servant by Cyrus, the gentile. This has been the focus from the beginning of Romans 9. Israel, God's chosen servant, had rebelled and deserved God's judgment. However, just as God was patient and merciful with Pharaoh, so he was with Israel. He has the right to bypass the natural order of things (as he did when he gave Jacob the privileges of the primogeniture that really should have fallen on Esau according to the laws of inheritance).

It is also important to notice that all Old Testament references to Yahweh being the potter are all focused on Israel as being the clay. In other words, the imagery is never used of God's dealings with individuals. To interpret Romans 9:21 as an exception to this rule, and deem it to be about individual

---

[362] Another Old Testament reference to Israel being likened to clay is found in Jer 18:6. Because Paul regularly cites Isaiah the clay sources are likely to be those of Isaiah also.

salvation, would require the kind of robust support which has not been—nor can it ever be—offered.

The flow of the argument that Paul makes and the way in which he has used texts from Isaiah 45 to support that argument matches the reading I am here suggesting. Paul has carefully selected his evidence from texts in which the context and theology discuss the nation of Israel and Yahweh's right to displace nations when they resist his will, no matter how exalted they have been.

The claim that the double jeopardy interpretation honours God and declares his character and righteousness find no support whatever in any other passage of Scripture. Even Piper acknowledges this, and so to support his own position he has had to turn to intertestamental literature—even then he is forced to acknowledge that the text he called upon for support does not say quite what he claims for the Romans 9:19–22 text. This is another example, this time from a conservative scholar, of abandoning best methodological practice (see chapter 6) to find support outside the early community's own Scriptures to support an otherwise unsustainable argument.

Instead of seeking such questionable support, there is a crucial passage in the Old Testament that challenges the double jeopardy reading of Romans 9. This passage is Exodus 33:4–9 which says:

> The Lord descended in the cloud and stood with him there and proclaimed the name of the Lord. The Lord passed before him and proclaimed, 'The Lord, the Lord, a God merciful and gracious, slow to anger, and abounding in steadfast love and faithfulness, keeping steadfast love for thousands, forgiving iniquity and transgression and sin, but who will by no means clear the guilty, visiting the iniquity of the fathers on the children and the children's children, to the third and the fourth generation.' And Moses quickly bowed his head toward the earth and worshiped. And he said, 'If now I have found favour in your sight, O Lord, please let the Lord go in the midst of us, for it is a stiff-necked people, and pardon our iniquity and our sin, and take us for your inheritance.' (Exod 33:4–9)

This passage, which tells of God's revelation of himself to Moses, shows that God does not want to be known as the God of judgment. This is not his primary characteristic. He reveals himself and wants to be known as the God who is merciful and gracious, slow to anger and abounding in steadfast love. He will judge, but this is not what he delights in. He only acts in this way because people have so abused his mercy and blessing that there remains no other way to deal with them but to judge. Judgment is always the last option, for his concern is to bring people and nations to repentance and blessing.

The double jeopardy interpretation of Romans 9:19–22 cannot stand up before the light of such a glorious truth. As I have claimed that the first eight chapters must be read corporately, so the text of Romans 9 should be read corporately. There is no special reason this section of the letter should be read differently. It is to be exposed to the same reading method as established in the preceding chapters, and if any individualistic reading were to be allowed to control the passage, it would require robust support. Only when read corporately do we see that the argument cannot possibly be about a God who exalts himself by deliberately sending unsuspecting victims to hell by decisions that are totally arbitrary. Such an argument challenges the evidence of Exodus 34, for that is not the sort of thing that God wants to be known for, and this is because he is not such a God.

These considerations bring us to the conclusion that the justification of God is not about his right to damn people because he chooses to damn them. Rather, it is about his right to transfer privilege and responsibility to other peoples who had not previously been selected for the honour of being called to the servant of the Living God. God is fully just when his judgment falls on nations and their representatives who have hardened their hearts to his word. If they do not repent, choosing instead to abuse the honour and privileges that they have been so richly blessed with, and using their status as an opportunity to serve self-interests and abuse the power they have been given, they will be judged. This was not only true of Israel and Egypt; it was also true of other nations that God raised up to serve him. Indeed, in this case, it was Cyrus, King of Assyria, as Israel protested against him being called Yahweh's servant. This elevation to serve God's purposes applies not only to ancient empires but modern ones as well.

Thus, the God of the whole earth is vindicated, justified, as being the God of truth and justice, whose judgments magnify his character and call all the people of all nations to turn to him to be saved. If they refuse to do this, they will be judged by using the words of Peter; there is no other name given among men whereby we can be saved.

Justification and the Divine Marriage

As argued earlier, the context is crucial if we are to catch the meaning of any particular word usage. Without it, we will be vulnerable to introducing meaning that has not been in the mind of the writer. This applies not only to Scripture but also to the meaning of any word in any text or oral narrative.

By the eighth century B.C.E., Israel had become so degenerate that her behaviour was the same as the surrounding nations. This was inevitable as they had long forsaken Yahweh, choosing to make covenants with pagan gods (Isa 28:15; Hos 12:1–2).

The latter part of the prophecy of Isaiah is set against the background of Israel's exile in Babylon. This followed the dreadful slaughter of many of the population and the destruction of the capital city and its sacred temple. Those taken into exile were warned by the prophets of the oncoming disaster resulting from Yahweh's setting his face against them because of their sins (Ps 102:2; Isa 54:11). Despite their experience, the prophets also proclaimed that God had not cast Israel off forever and that he would act as her Redeemer.

Moreover, now the years were passing by, and the exile seemed permanent. Most of the people adjusted to this new situation and many sought to take advantage of the things which their new location offered them. However, there were those who could not see their exile as an opportunity. These were the people of true faith whose hearts were circumcised (Jer 9:25). The pain of guilt, shame, and humiliation was not easing. The prophets, who had warned them of this disaster, were now promising hope. They were saying that Yahweh was going to raise up a leader from the family of David and that this man would come with God's word and lead them back to their homeland. Isaiah spoke of this event as being Israel's justification, when Yahweh would betroth Israel in righteousness (See Isa 46:13 and Isa 51:6–11. Related themes of justification which imply that Israel is justified are found in Isa 29:22; 42:6, 10–12; 44:21–22; 45:17, 23–25; 46:12–13; 51:4–6, 12–16; 53:10–12; 60:21; 62:1–2; 65:16). In fact, it was not only Israel's justification it was also Yahweh's justification. He was vindicated as the covenant keeping God before all the nations of the earth (Isa 45:22–23; 46:8–13; 51:9–11; 52:6).

However, the Passover and exodus were not just about deliverance; it was about the making of a covenant with the family of Abraham—that covenant was specifically described in marital language. Tragically, it was a marriage that was to encounter serious problems before it was ever consummated! Israel moved on from Sinai as an adulteress; having worshipped the golden calf she had broken her marriage vows with Yahweh. She should have been cast out, separated from the God whose people she had just become. In response to Moses's intercession for mercy, he spared them but told him that he would return to deal with the issue of Israel's unfaithfulness later (Exod 32:30–34).

Eventually, Israel was exiled. It was the final display of Yahweh's abhorrence of his people's repeated unfaithfulness. The exile suggested to everyone—especially the gentile nations—that Yahweh wanted nothing more to do with Israel and had disowned the nation. However, the prophets predicted that Yahweh would keep his promise, not only to redeem her but to take her again as his bride (Jer 3:14–18).

So, the seventh meaning of 'justified' can be determined from this Second Exodus setting, which was not only about Israel's elect believing community being restored to the land, but also to Yahweh in a new marriage relationship. A new marriage relationship can be established because the community had gone through death in the exile. This is a new relationship in the context of the new covenant that the prophets had promised. Wright completely misses the divine marriage theme and exegetes texts that reflect this motif outside of their originally intended theological context. Because of this, his exegesis is often far from satisfying.

The problem with Yahweh's marrying the newly-recreated Israel was that she belonged to other gods, and this relationship barred the way for the marriage that God sought to enter with her. Yahweh had experienced this same problem when he rescued Israel from Egypt, for she belonged to another god to whom she had sworn herself (see Ezek 20 for the prophet's accusation concerning Israel's condition in Egypt). She was no innocent victim; she was a willing worshipper of Egypt's gods, as was evidenced when she made gods on the night Moses received the law on Sinai (Exod 32:1–4). Yahweh could only take her because of the representative deaths of the firstborn (spared through the death of lambs in their place). This brought Israel's covenantal relationship with her lovers to an end through the covenantal annulling effects of death, even of a representative death. This aspect of Israel's history was re-enacted in the tragic experience of Hosea and his adulterous wife Gomer.

While the legal issue had been dealt with, the desires of the people had not. The law needed to be written on Israel's heart so that she would desire no one else other than Yahweh. The death of Israel in the person of the representative royal servant who justifies many (Isa 53:11) acts out this same theme of marriage. Israel's sin not only has to be forgiven but her covenant relationship with her chosen gods has to be brought to an end.

Israel being sent into exile in Babylon symbolized her death—it severed the relationship with her former pagan god husband and allowed a remarriage to Yahweh to take place. This change of status, being released from her lovers' hold would be the basis of a new relationship with the God of Abraham, for she was to be brought back from the dead to marry her Redeemer (Isa 25:8;[363] Hos 13:14[364] which is used by Paul in 1 Cor 15:55–56, when discussing the theme of resurrection).[365] Without this covenant-cancelling death, the new marriage would be illegitimate, and Yahweh would share in his people's sin.

Interestingly, on returning to the reference to the servant in Isaiah 53 whose death justifies many, the chapter's theme continues until we come to chapter 61 which speaks of the many who have been justified as being delivered. The chapter starts by saying:

> The Spirit of the Lord God is upon me, because the Lord has anointed me to bring good news to the poor; he has sent me to bind up the broken-hearted, to proclaim liberty to the captives, and the opening of the prison to those who are bound; to proclaim

---

[363] The text is being linked with a great feast, which in Isaiah is part of the divine marriage.

[364] The whole of the book is about the divine marriage, and the text deals with the overcoming of that which prevents its achievement.

[365] The passage in 1 Cor 15:54–55 says: 'When the perishable puts on the imperishable, and the mortal puts on immortality, then shall come to pass the saying that is written: "Death is swallowed up in victory." "O death, where is your victory? O death, where is your sting?"' The reference to the death being swallowed up in victory is from Isa 25:8 and follows on from vs. 6–7 which says: 'On this mountain the LORD of hosts will make for all peoples a feast of rich food, a feast of well-aged wine, of rich food full of marrow, of aged wine well refined. And he will swallow up on this mountain the covering that is cast over all peoples, the veil that is spread over all nations.' In other words, death is vanquished, and the marriage banquet is set out for the guests. The entire passage develops Paul's statement that Christ died for our sins according to the scriptures and was raised the third day (1 Cor 15:3–4). The significance of this is that the wave offering was offered three days after Passover when the firstfruits were presented to the Lord (Lev 23:11). Paul calls Christ the firstfruits of those who sleep, so the whole passage is rooted in Paschal imagery. In Jewish thought, the Passover was the occasion of the divine marriage. Thus, we have a montage of crucial Passover/divine marriage themes. Wright misses all of these Old Testament links because he too easily looks for solutions in intertestamental/Greco Roman literature.

> the year of the Lord's favour, and the day of vengeance of our
> God; to comfort all who mourn; to grant to those who mourn in
> Zion—to give them a beautiful headdress instead of ashes, the oil
> of gladness instead of mourning, the garment of praise instead of a
> faint spirit; that they may be called oaks of righteousness, the
> planting of the Lord, that he may be glorified. They shall build up
> the ancient ruins; they shall raise up the former devastations; they
> shall repair the ruined cities, the devastations of many generations.
> (Isa 61:1–4)

The passage continues describing the experience of the comforted community, and then the remnant says:

> I will greatly rejoice in the Lord; my soul shall exult in my God,
> for he has clothed me with the garments of salvation; he has
> covered me with the robe of righteousness, as a bridegroom decks
> himself like a priest with a beautiful headdress. (Isa 61:10)

Thus, the justified, comforted community was destined to be the bride whom Yahweh had promised his troth.

What is also interesting is that these are the very words Jesus chose to use to declare himself as the promised Messiah in the synagogue. We find this in Luke 4 where it says:

> And he came to Nazareth, where he had been brought up. And as
> was his custom, he went to the synagogue on the Sabbath day, and
> he stood up to read. And the scroll of the prophet Isaiah was given
> to him. He unrolled the scroll and found the place where it was
> written, 'The Spirit of the Lord is upon me, because he has
> anointed me to proclaim good news to the poor. He has sent me to
> proclaim liberty to the captives and recovering of sight to the
> blind, to set at liberty those who are oppressed, to proclaim the
> year of the Lord's favour.' And he rolled up the scroll and gave it
> back to the attendant and sat down. And the eyes of all in the
> synagogue were fixed on him. And he began to say to them,
> 'Today this Scripture has been fulfilled in your hearing.' And all
> spoke well of him and marvelled at the gracious words that were
> coming from his mouth. (Luke 4:16–22)

What is interesting is that Jesus announces soon after the above statement:

> Truly, I say to you, no prophet is acceptable in his hometown. But
> in truth, I tell you, there were many widows in Israel in the days
> of Elijah, when the heavens were shut up three years and six
> months, and a great famine came over all the land, and Elijah was

310

sent to none of them but only to Zarephath, in the land of Sidon, to a woman who was a widow. (Luke 4:24–26)

In other words, Jesus was announcing that he had come to comfort Israel in her widowhood. The desolate widow who had suffered through exile was to be a widow no longer; she was being visited by Yahweh's promised redeemer. These themes are not accidental; it has been shown that Mark wrote his Gospel so that it followed the pattern of the predicted Isaianic Second Exodus.[366]

The same themes of exodus and divine marriage are found in John's Gospel. Jesus is introduced via exodus imagery, the one who has come to tabernacle amongst his people (John 1:14 'dwelt/tabernacled among us'). He is the one who was to die as the Passover sacrifice (John 1:29), and he is the promised king (John 1:41). He is the one who is the guest at the wedding in Cana when in fact he is the one who transforms the occasion in such a way that it points to his own future ministry as the bridegroom who has come for his people (John 3:28–30). It is Jesus who in chapter 4 meets with the woman of Samaria who had been married five times before and who lived with a man who was not her husband (John 4:17–18), and now the true longed-for redeemer who cares for all who have been abandoned has come.

These divine marriage themes are found throughout Paul's letters. Christ died for the church to make her his pure bride (Eph 5:25–27). He has told the elders of the same church that Christ had redeemed them with his own blood (Acts 20:28) and had used similar language in 1 Corinthians 6:20 which concludes a passage that is saturated with divine marriage imagery (see vv. 15–17). He has said that Christ our Passover has been sacrificed for us (1 Cor 5:7), and it was during the Passover that Israel was betrothed to Yahweh in Egypt. In 2 Corinthians 11:2–3 Paul wrote: 'For I feel a divine jealousy for you, since I betrothed you to one husband, to present you as a pure virgin to Christ. But I am afraid that as the serpent deceived Eve by his cunning, your thoughts will be led astray from a sincere and pure devotion to Christ'.

In light of the above, when we turn to Romans 6:7, we have the New Testament application of this understanding of justification. The church's

---

[366] Note the difference between this term and that of the book by R. Watts, *Isaiah's New Exodus and Mark*, Wissenschaftliche Untersuchungen zum Neuen Testament, 2 Reihe, WUNT II (Tübingen: Mohr, 1997), 88. Strictly speaking, there is a big difference between the predicted Second Exodus and its fulfilment in the New Exodus.

justification follows from its sharing in Christ's covenant-annulling death. Romans 6:1–7 explains how the new community was brought into existence through the ending of the remnant's relationship with sin, in which she dies to her former husband (sin) so that she can marry her Lord, Master, and Creator. Previously, as part of the body of sin, she (the 'wretched person' of 7:21–25) had been united to Satan. He held an authority over her that she could not break. Only death, as Romans 7:1–6 makes clear could end the covenant relationship with the former husband.[367]

Because she had died with her redeemer, she was not only freed but able to marry another; she would be justified, for no charge of adultery could be brought against her for entering into this new relationship (Rom 7:1–4). Hence, the one who dies is justified from sin (that is 'sin', as distinct from 'sins') which speaks of Satan, so also Wright,[368] who does not see its deeper marital significance. Satan cannot bring any charge against Christ's bride for she has died with her redeemer who, as the true redeemer, has fulfilled his Levirate role and bound himself to her forever.[369]

The Significance of the Divine Marriage

The importance of the divine marriage metaphor has been overlooked by New Testament scholarship. Wright sees the return to the land to be the climax of the New Exodus theme, but as I have argued elsewhere, this approach does

---

[367] The illustration is not about the individual being married to Christ, as Wright, 'Romans', *NIB*, 559 claims. Nowhere in the Bible is an individual described as being the bride of Christ or being married to Christ. The imagery is used exclusively to describe the community's relationship with Christ (so Rom 7:1–4; Eph 5:25–27; 2 Cor 11:2; Rev 21:1–3).

[368] Wright, 'Romans', *NIB*, 539.

[369] The redeemer, who ideally should have been the firstborn, was to fulfil the law of the levirate. This law appointed the redeemer to act as the protector of the widow in the family (Deut 25:5–10; Ruth 3:13; 4:1–8). If a woman was widowed and childless it was the responsibility of the family's redeemer to take her as his wife and raise up a family on behalf of the deceased brother. This aspect of the redeemer's role is used to illustrate the salvation Yahweh promised his people. 'He will save Jerusalem from her widowhood and raise up children for her' (Isa 49:20–21; 50:1–2; 54:1–8; 62:4–5). This same role is applied to Christ, who takes the church to himself (Eph 5:25–27), note the citation from Isaiah just verses prior to this statement (Eph 5:14), and he acts as/became her husband. Note how this fits into the concept of a second marriage in Rom 7:1–4, see also 2 Cor 11:1–2 and John 2:27–30.

not take sufficient account of the vitally important theme of the restoration of believing Israel to be Yahweh's bride—something far bigger than her physical inheritance and a theme carried into the New Testament in a greater way than is sometimes recognised (Rev 21:1–3). It is this theme that is embedded in Romans 5–8, as Paul describes the severing of man's relationship with God through Adam and its restoration through the covenant-annulling death of Christ. Whatever else is going on, Romans 7:1–6 makes it clear that it is about a remarriage which cannot take place because the present husband's status, despite his causing the original marriage failure, is lawful and legitimate. Death must first happen to release the wife so that she can become the bride of her Redeemer.

Wright's failure to engage with the divine marriage theme has caused him to allocate texts to the wrong part of the narrative when they really belong to this incredibly important climax of eschatology. Like reading a novel after first reading the concluding chapter, the shape of the solution enables the reader to hear the scattered clues throughout the manuscript with a volume that the author did not want his reader to observe until after his plan had been revealed, and the wonder of his creativity had been recognised. However, if the last chapter is lost, one is left reading the book with an incomplete script and the unfolding of the story will not reach its intended climax nor will the narrative be properly understood. It will appear to be a failure of the author to hold his reader to the end or that the author has not really given as convincing a case as should have been given. This is the case with Wright's narrative. He is reading crucial clues without that final revelation and is forced to guess at the placing of the clues he instinctively feels are crucial. As a result, his argument is not as convincing as he might hope. There is still something missing, something that is vitally important.

The absence of this divine marriage final chapter is not the only problem with Wright's approach to Romans. Two other vitally important hermeneutic principles are also at play. First is the failure to preserve the essentially Semitic nature of the letter by importing Hellenistic themes and ideas that are incompatible with the Semitic mindset. The other is Wright's failure to read the entire letter corporately. These three factors—the missing 'last chapter', the Hellenization of the letter by soaking it in Greco-Roman culture and intertestamental texts, and the failure to read the letter corporately in its entirety are the crucial missing elements in Wright's view of the theology of Romans. This divine marriage theme, I would argue, is behind what Paul says in Romans 6:

> For if we have been united with him in a death like his, we shall certainly be united with him in a resurrection like his. We know that our old self was crucified with him in order that the body of sin might be brought to nothing, so that we would no longer be enslaved to sin. For one who has died has been set free from sin. Now if we have died with Christ, we believe that we will also live with him. (Rom 6:5–8)

While Wright has correctly noted the exodus connections with the passage, he does not make the connection that the purpose of the exodus was the divine marriage, so he fails to give this important theme a mention, not only here but in any of his exegetical works.

This oversight of the wider theological context of Romans 6:1–4 results in Wright's missing a whole layer of meaning concerning his use of *dedikaiōtai* ('justified') in v. 7. This is normally translated as 'freed', and so the theological significance of 'justified' is lost. Paul, it is commonly argued, could not possibly mean 'justify' in this verse, as it would contradict his doctrine of justification as described elsewhere in his letters. If this text is left as 'justified' rather than 'freed' then it is argued that justification would be the result of the experience of dying with Christ. This challenges the universally accepted view of Paul's doctrine of justification, resulting in virtually unanimous agreement to change the meaning. This suggests that interpreters of Paul still need to ask whether they are committed to following Paul's text or to whether they are fitting Paul into a system that has been created for him.

One must be wary of a model which necessitates changing the vocabulary that Paul has actually used; for this fact alone suggests that the model is wrong.[370] When we recognize that the semantic domain of *dedikaiōtai* contains other meanings than those traditionally identified and accepted—one of them being the creation of the covenant, as we have seen above—we find the key to unlock what Paul is saying, namely, that through the death of Christ, his people can become his bride (Rom 7:1–6). Thus, 'justified' here is a statement of innocence regarding the new relationship. It is not adulterous, for death terminated that relationship which denied Christ his bride. The

---

[370] The exception to this is when the context is so different from the normal meaning assigned to the Greek term. Language does evolve, and careful analysis must explore if this has happened in a particular place. In the case of Rom 6:7 no such evolution/change is evident.

partners in this new union are justified, that is, found 'not guilty' of an adulterous relationship (Rom 8:31–39).

Thus we have identified nine distinct meanings for the term justify: 1) The acquittal of sin; 2) The imputation of righteousness; 3) The declaration that one is in the covenant; 4) The creation of a covenant; 5) Justification ratification; 6) The deliverance and justification of Israel; 7) The justification of the gentiles; 8) The justification of God; 9) The justification of the divine marriage. These last three will require some further attention.

These nine meanings of justification not only demonstrate that Wright's one meaning of being declared to be in the covenant is inadequate to cover the diversity of meaning contained in the expression, but also, and far more importantly, it shows the glorious richness of the salvation that God has secured out of his grace for his people.

One of the difficulties in describing Wright's doctrine of justification is that it has evolved over the years. He seems to change his position and then reasserts earlier claims which then conflict with what appeared to be his later revision(s). The latest statement that he has made is found in his recently published *Paul and the Faithfulness of God*. In this publication he says of justification:

> There is, however, not much evidence that pre-Christian Jews spoke of that kind of "advanced marking out" in terms of "justification". This already presents us with an apparent oddity: might it be the case that not only Paul's particular view of justification, but also the idea of any "doctrine of justification", let alone it's apparent central importance, is itself a Christian innovation, like some of the others we have seen? Did Paul introduce the category out of nothing? Why then would he speak, looking back to his former self, of "justification by works of the law"? Was that whole idea a Christian back projection? Here we are once more, clearly, faced with the question of "plight and solution". And again, the answer is more subtle than a simple either or will allow.[371]

Wright's suggestion that the doctrine has emerged without any earlier precedence is telling, as is his analysis of the case. He has redefined justification and then gone looking for his redefinition and not found it. Because he cannot find it, he concludes that the Jews were not really

---

[371] Wright, *Faithfulness of God*, 929.

interested in the doctrine.[372] This reads the evidence from the perspective that Wright has created and has given the answer to. I would suggest that our review of Old Testament references to justification has firmly established a powerful and influential doctrine of justification that has many facets. These insights existed long before Paul was born, and it is these truths that Paul's doctrine of justification is the faithful presentation of the many aspects of the doctrine as found in the Old Testament. Indeed, Paul's statement that 'What no eye has seen, nor ear has heard, nor the heart of man imagined, what God has prepared for those who love him' (1 Cor 2:9) which is a citation of Isaiah 64:4 which is in a wider context of God's saving work of Israel. This sums up perfectly the enormity of the doctrine of justification that both Old Testament and New Testament writers rejoice in. Wright's singular lens supplied by Galatians locks the door to this truly marvellous work of salvation that Paul as well as the prophets proclaimed. We shall examine what we have found in the Old Testament to see how Paul stays faithful to it and how he unpacks and applies it.

---

[372] 'Since "justification" is not a major topic of second Temple Judaism, this is rare, with Qumran providing (in 4QMMT) the only solid example'. Wright, *Faithfulness of God*, 929.

Chapter 11:
Probing the Doctrine of Justification in the Romans and Galatians

In this section I shall examine the language of justification as found throughout the letters of Paul. By working through this material and noting how and where the language of justification occurs, I believe we will see that Wright has ignored some of the textual evidence in making his case for how he believes Paul understood justification. Even in texts where justification is not specifically mentioned, the presence of related themes alerts us that the matter of justification underlines much of Paul's argument. We will read the texts in the context of a corporate theology as argued for earlier. We will not look solely for the specific term, but also those themes that were very clearly part of justification found throughout the Old Testament: terms such as reconciliation, return, covenant, and redemption. Using these as markers of a similar understanding to the texts of the Old Testament which Paul was saturated in, we will seek to look behind the use of these specific terms in order to understand the much greater theological context of justification that we have identified throughout the Old Testament. Because many of the claims I have made in the earlier chapters need to be put together as part of the exegesis of the letters we are now going to consider, there will of necessity be some repetition. I have chosen to risk the reader's frustration, or possibly even wrath, to make sure that the points I have been trying to make in the context of particular arguments become clear as to how they all dovetail together in a way that I find utterly compelling.

I am going to limit this chapter to Justification in Galatians and Romans to keep the reading experience manageable. The following chapter will consider the remainder of the Pauline letters.

Galatians

I start with the letter to the Galatians, as it was the focus of the studies regarding the works of the law which impacted the doctrine of justification. Clearly, from what has been noted, there is an important corporate element to the subject of justification in Galatians. The issue Paul deals with is whether the gentiles have to be circumcised—as argued by the Judaizers—to be in the covenant. This being so, we have to ask whether every reference Paul makes to being 'justified' is part of the same corporate argument, or whether the apostle at times speaks of the justification of the individual as has been traditionally understood. Also, we have to ask whether Wright is consistent in his claims concerning justification being corporate. Why does he depart from this model in his treatment of the letter to the Galatians, by transferring his understanding about justification into the passages that he believes address individuals without explaining why Paul might take such a sudden change of perspective from corporate to the individual?

Whatever we decide are the answers to these questions, what is clear is that the discussion in Galatians was not only about the gentiles being declared righteous in the sense that Wright claims (that is, being declared to be in the covenant). In this letter, the discussion is also about how the gentile believers, if they are not in the covenant, are to come into the community. The Judaizers were denying that the gentile believers were really in the community. To come in, they insisted, the gentiles had to subject themselves to circumcision and Sabbath-keeping, along with feast days and food laws. These are the 'works of the law' that Paul refers to when he says that no one is justified by 'the works of the law' (Gal 2:16). In this particular case, it is claimed, it did not refer to keeping the moral law but the initiatory requirements of the law and the life that flowed from identification with Israel.

There is debate over the dating of the Galatian letter, with some scholars saying it was written before the Jerusalem Council and others that it came later. If the Council had met before the letter was written, then we are left asking why Paul did not refer to it as crucial evidence to settle the circumcision issue. The fact that this was not suggested infers that the earlier dating is probably correct.

What Paul certainly knew was that the gentile church had received the gift of the Spirit. The first outpouring of the Spirit on a gentile community had taken place when Peter preached to the gentile household of Cornelius (Acts 10:44–11:18). The Galatian church clearly had a similar experience (Gal 3:1–3). When Peter saw that the gift of the Holy Spirit been given to the household of Cornelius, he was persuaded that God had accepted them as gentiles, without them first being circumcised. This event and its evidence of gentile acceptance were the crucial circumstances for the Council to decide in favour of gentiles not requiring circumcision (Acts 15:1–21).

Thus, in the letter to the Galatians, Paul's discussion on the works of the law was not about whether the gentiles had been accepted by God. The issue was whether they had to add 'the works of the law' to saving grace to receive full citizenship and not to have second-class status. The Judaizers' case was, therefore, not likely to be about denying gentiles some sort of covenant membership, but that it was of a form that had to be upgraded to full membership by submitting to circumcision. Paul was determined that this should not be the status of believing gentiles, and he saw that for the Jewish church to treat them as such was a fundamental denial of the gospel.

Thus, the claim of the Judaizers was most likely that full membership could only be established by submitting to the 'works of the law.' We will find that this is very close to the issues being dealt with in Romans, although the two letters are not dealing with identical problems.

In Galatians the issue is not so much about national pride or self-righteousness, but about who holds the decisive veto. By demanding that the gentiles submit to circumcision, the Jewish church—unofficially represented by the Judaizers—was taking for herself the right to judge whether or not a particular gentile was fit for the community. To pass this test the gentiles had to show complete deference, as required by the Judaizers, to Israel's law. When we examine the letter to the Romans, we will find that the tone is decisively different and the objectives of the two Jewish believing communities are not the same.

As we consider the relevant passages in Galatians, we find Paul in his salutation welcoming believing gentiles as recipients of God's grace, sharing the very same status as believing Jews enjoyed.

> Grace to you and peace from God our Father and the Lord Jesus
> Christ, who gave himself for our sins to deliver us from the
> present evil age, according to the will of our God and Father, to
> whom be the glory forever and ever. Amen. (Gal 1:3–5)

Paul links himself (a Jew), with the same experience that the gentile Galatian church had shared, that of being delivered from sin according to God's will. The decisive 'who gave himself for our sins' makes this common experience explicit. Such a statement clearly recognises that Jews as well as gentiles need to experience the same saving grace of God in Christ that the gentiles need.

The same observation made on Galatians 1:3–5 is appropriate for what Paul says in 2:15–21 where he says:

> We ourselves are Jews by birth and not gentile sinners; yet we
> know that a person is not justified by works of the law but through

> faith in Jesus Christ, so we also have believed in Christ Jesus, in order to be justified by faith in Christ and not by works of the law, because by works of the law no one will be justified. But if, in our endeavour to be justified in Christ, we too were found to be sinners, is Christ then a servant of sin? Certainly not! For if I rebuild what I tore down, I prove myself to be a transgressor. For through the law I died to the law, so that I might live to God. I have been crucified with Christ. It is no longer I who live, but Christ who lives in me. And the life I now live in the flesh I live by faith in the Son of God, who loved me and gave himself for me. I do not nullify the grace of God, for if righteousness were through the law, then Christ died for no purpose. (Gal 2:15–21)

Paul is once again crystal clear. Even though the Jews had once enjoyed a privileged status above the gentiles, they did not have a right to a different salvation from that which the gentiles were called to. They could not be justified by works because the law was never intended to serve such a purpose. Only through faith in the person and work of Christ could Jews come to salvation. Paul is emphatic, 'by works of the law no one will be justified'.

Speaking of their endeavours to be justified, Paul highlights Jewish confidence to achieve justification. Such endeavour, however, cannot achieve the desired goal; it serves only to show the law's inability to save. Paul asks if such a discovery means that Christ is the servant of sin (this presupposes that the link has been made that the law serves Christ's purposes). Paul corrects this misunderstanding by pointing out that rather than being attached to the law as an instrument of salvation, Christ has delivered his people from the condemning power of the law which the Judaizers claim is essential for salvation.

Thus, by his death for his people, Christ has ended the law's power to condemn those who now belong to him. The law was not the servant of Christ in the way that the Jews perceived it to be. Israel's God never intended the law to function in the way it eventually had to. It was given to bless the covenant community—but they violated its commandments, and so instead of being blessed by it, they became the object of its judgment.

Paul is emphatic that the relationship with God which his Jewish kinsmen aspire to cannot be found through keeping the law. His message was that only by accepting in faith the achievements of Christ in his death and resurrection could God forgive and welcome his people.

In chapter 3 Paul challenges those gentile believers who were tempted to embrace Judaism as a result of the claims being made by the Judaizers. He reminds them that they know very well how they came into the covenant. They knew that their acceptance had been verified by the gift of the Spirit, and because of this, Paul could confidently appeal to a common event in which the community had all shared. Of course, they all went on to experience the inner work of the Spirit in their individual lives, but what Paul is referring to here is that corporate sealing that marked them out as the people of God.

> Let me ask you only this: Did you receive the Spirit by works of the law or by hearing with faith? Are you so foolish? Having begun by the Spirit, are you now being perfected by the flesh? Did you suffer so many things in vain—if indeed it was in vain? Does he who supplies the Spirit to you and works miracles among you do so by works of the law, or by hearing with faith— just as Abraham "believed God, and it was counted to him as righteousness"? Know then that it is those of faith who are the sons of Abraham. And the Scripture, foreseeing that God would justify the gentiles by faith, preached the gospel beforehand to Abraham, saying, "In you shall all the nations be blessed." So then, those who are of faith are blessed along with Abraham, the man of faith. (Gal 3:2–9)

The unexpected content of the question about how they received the Spirit is insightful. Most Christians would ask 'how were you saved?' But this is not the question Paul asks. He does not question their status before God, but he does challenge their understanding of the significance of this crucial inaugural event. Without it the community was illegitimate, they simply could not be the sons and daughters of God. Their reception of the Spirit, as a community, was for Paul the crucial evidence that they had been accepted. Because they had received the Spirit as a community, they had the required evidence that they were Abraham's true sons and daughters; any rituals added later to satisfy any doubts in the Jewish community could add nothing to their status before God.

> Now it is evident that no one is justified before God by the law, for "The righteous shall live by faith." But the law is not of faith, rather "The one who does them shall live by them." Christ redeemed us from the curse of the law by becoming a curse for us—for it is written, "Cursed is everyone who is hanged on a tree"— so that in Christ Jesus the blessing of Abraham might come to the gentiles, so that we might receive the promised Spirit through faith. (Gal 3:11–14)

The Search for Truth

Paul uses the same verse he cited in Romans 1:17, that the just would live by faith (Hab 2:4). The prophet's reference is about the remnant that was in exile and who were tempted to search for a way that they could return to the promised land. Habakkuk warns them not to try to bring this about themselves, for such an attempt would end in disaster. Instead, they were to wait for Yahweh's salvation—their release from captivity. Paul extracts the same message from the prophet's exhortation: attempting to secure your deliverance will not lead to the desired freedom but greater sorrow and frustration. The blessing of the promises made to Abraham had been secured through the death of Christ for all who believed and could not be obtained by any other means but by faith in him.

> Now before faith came, we were held captive under the law, imprisoned until the coming faith would be revealed. So then, the law was our guardian until Christ came, in order that we might be justified by faith. But now that faith has come, we are no longer under a guardian, for in Christ Jesus you are all sons of God, through faith. For as many of you as were baptized into Christ have put on Christ. There is neither Jew nor Greek, there is neither slave nor free, there is neither male nor female, for you are all one in Christ Jesus. And if you are Christ's, then you are Abraham's offspring, heirs according to promise. (Gal 3:23–29)

Paul returns to the Abrahamic narrative to establish the nature of Abraham's acceptance by God. While it was on the grounds of faith, the nature of that faith had been lost in later Jewish understanding, for Paul speaks of the law imprisoning them until faith should come. It is the reverse of Old Testament understanding, where faith precedes law.

However, the law had a task to fulfil. It was not about establishing righteousness but preparing for the coming Messiah. In fact, Paul described the law functioning as a *pedagogue*. While in Greek this often referred to a supervisor of the heir who ensured that he had completed the assignment given him by his teachers, it could refer to other roles. Wright sees it as a nursery nurse, but I prefer to see it as the best man who accompanies and protects the bride of his friend until they meet for their forthcoming marriage.[373]

---

[373] For details of this see my forthcoming book, *Squaring the Circle*, due 2018.

The reference to baptism is not about the confession of faith through water whereby the baptised receives the Spirit, so Wright and many others. Rather, it speaks of the great ontological event when all believers of all generations—together as one—were united by the Spirit and baptized into union with Christ as the bridal community.[374] It is the entire membership of this community, corporately, even before they came to faith, who were united with Christ in his death, and that is the basis of being a true descendant of Abraham.

> Look: I, Paul, say to you that if you accept circumcision, Christ will be of no advantage to you. I testify again to every man who accepts circumcision that he is obligated to keep the whole law. You are severed from Christ, you who would be justified by the law; you have fallen away from grace. For through the Spirit, by faith, we ourselves eagerly wait for the hope of righteousness. For in Christ Jesus neither circumcision nor uncircumcision counts for anything, but only faith working through love. (Gal 5:2–6)

Here Paul gives his final warning and appeal. If they submit to circumcision, they are not adding something to Christian experience, they are invalidating it. They have made a choice that challenges the completeness of Christ's saving work and they are choosing the law as a way of salvation. There can be no mixing of the ways; they can either accept salvation through the crucified Messiah or strive to obtain salvation through keeping the law, but the fact is that only the former of these ways will lead them truly to salvation. Clearly Paul is saying that the boundary markers can never save and to accept them as essential to salvation leads to the inevitable next step of having to obey the entire law. This cannot mean anything else other than the obligation to live under the laws and regulations of the Torah; and this is the very understanding that the Reformers held to.

---

[374] Wright, 'New Exodus, New Inheritance', in Soderlund & Wright (eds.), *Romans and the People of God,* 28 acknowledges this Exodus connection when he says, 'When Paul speaks of baptism in Romans 6 he has in mind the crossing of the Red Sea at the Exodus. He makes exactly this connection of course, in 1 Cor 10:2.' Despite observing this link which was about the baptism of the entire nation in one historic event, Wright reverts to an individual reading of Rom 6:1–4 and loses the narrative reading that he is so anxious to promote. For a full discussion on this see Holland, *Contours*, 141–154.

Romans

The discussion concerning justification in the letter to the Romans has nothing at all to do with proselytization. In Romans 2 the issue Paul raises is Israel's claim to be the privileged people when in fact she did not live her claimed status out before the world. At the heart of this debate that he sets up as a diatribe, he accuses Israel of self-righteousness and insists that there is a serious disconnect between what she thinks she is and what she really is.

Preliminary Overview and Comments

The notorious statement about being given eternal life as a reward for diligence and perseverance is made in Romans 2:9–10. We will shortly look into this passage in detail. Paul chides the Jewish people that there are gentiles who live lives that are more conforming to the law than many Jews. Wright claims that these law keepers must have been converted gentiles (because they alone had the Spirit who enabled them to keep the law) presses the case too much. This assertion ignores the repeated statements about 'godly gentiles' found throughout Scripture who had yet to become believers because they had not heard the truth of the gospel. These people are commended as models of moral uprightness and include Cornelius (Acts 10:31), Lydia (Acts 16:14), and the centurion (Matt 8:5–13). It is because some gentiles keep the law better than many circumcised Jews, Paul concludes that their circumcision has no significance (Rom 2:25–29). Wright's insistence that Paul would not consider gentiles to be able to keep the law because they do not have the Spirit is not consistently held. Wright argues that Romans 7 has an element of appeal to the moral pagan who keeps the law but knows that it still lacks completion which he says Paul states is the Christ dimension.[375]

It is not until we come to the end of chapter 3 (Rom 3:21) that the subject of justification is raised. Here Paul makes it clear that it is one of the achievements of the crucified King when he says that they are 'justified by his grace as a gift, through the redemption that is in Christ Jesus' (Rom 3:24). Following the statement of 'for all have sinned and fall short of the glory of God' (Rom 3:23), it is clear that this justification is of a corporate nature. The reasoning anticipates what will be detailed in Romans 5:12–21. Clearly justification is a status and relationship that is an important part of the gospel

---

[375] Wright, *Faithfulness of God*, 1377.

message, contra Wright.[376] Paul also makes it clear that it is not fundamentally a future event, as argued by Wright.[377] Justification belongs to the church now—as the use of the verb's participle present passive nominative masculine plural form shows in δικαιούμενοι δωρεὰν τῇ αὐτοῦ χάριτι, ('and are justified by his grace'—see Rom 3:24). Because the church was brought into union with Christ in his death and resurrection, she is the justified people of God.

In chapter 4 Paul returns to the theme of justification. Again, the issue is not whether the believing gentiles are in the covenant, but how the Jews came to be in it. Paul is dealing with the tendency, even of believing Jews, to think that in some way they are superior to the gentile believers, who do not have the same status. Their perceived superiority does not lead to an attempt to persuade the gentiles to receive circumcision, as in Galatians. The sense in Romans is that the Jewish believers are happy to have this distinction for it gives them a zone of their own in which they felt superior to the gentile church. It was this self-congratulatory tone that Paul rebuked at the end of chapter 3 (Rom 3:27–31).

To correct this superior spirit, Paul argues that the Jews must recognize the gentiles are equal members of the new covenant community. He lays out in Romans 4 the fact that they were exactly like gentiles when God accepted them. Their status was bound up with God's acceptance of their ancestor Abraham when he was uncircumcised (when he was a gentile), and in this condition God made the covenant with him. The proof that Abraham was truly in the covenant and was justified was that he obeyed God and was prepared to honour him with the ultimate sacrifice, the offering of his only son Isaac (Rom 4:19–25). The challenge is, 'does your faith match that of Abraham'? Not, 'are you circumcised like Abraham was'?

In chapter 5 Paul explains how justification is intrinsic to the work of Christ in his dying, for his act of obedience made many righteous. The whole discussion in vv. 12–21 is what Adam did for his people and what Christ has done for his, the argument being thoroughly Semitic and corporate in character. If they are not part of this justified group which belongs to Christ, they belong to the people who do not have righteousness and justification and so inherit the curse and sin-state that Adam's work bequeathed.

---

[376] Wright, *Justification*, 126.
[377] Ibid.

Chapter 6 is about the work of Christ which delivered his people from the sin-state in Adam. To achieve this, Christ had to die as the representative of his people. This death had the significance of breaking the former relationship with sin (Satan) that had existed because of Adam's disobedience. As the disobedience of the first Adam severed the relationship with God, so the death of the last Adam severed the relationship with sin because death terminates all marriages (Rom 7:1–3) and allows a new relationship to occur. It is against this background that Paul can say that the one who has died has been freed from sin (Satan).

It is in this section particularly that Wright shows his eclectic tendency. He abandons the corporate background of chapter 5 and, without any justification, exegetes the passage to be about the experience of the individual believer in water baptism. This is despite the corporate language of the opening verse, where Paul speaks of them all having been baptised into Christ's death; the tense suggesting that this was a historic event which all of his readers had together shared in. It is surprising that Wright misses this because he has correctly pointed out that Paul has used the baptism of the Jewish nation into Moses (1 Cor 10:1–4) as the type of Christian baptism, and that was certainly a corporate event.[378]

Wright further demonstrates that he has not sorted out Paul's anthropology because he assigns a Hellenistic dualistic meaning to the term 'the body of sin'. Had he followed the corporate terminology and argument of chapter 5, he would not have done so.

Paul in fact does not say 'freed', as most translations and commentators, including Wright translate it. He says *dedikaiwtai* ('justified') from sin. The correct reading has been almost universally rejected because it has been thought to compromise the doctrine of justification. In most Reformed understanding, union with Christ is a consequence of being justified and not its foundation. Surprisingly Wright follows this Reformed reading, not seeing the full force of the argument that is going on. The proposal I am making does not challenge Reformed understanding, but it does challenge the practice of correcting the text on doctrinal grounds without any textual support.[379]

---

[378] Wright, *Faithfulness of God,* 1334.

[379] I am not saying the Greek text was physically corrected but that a meaning was given to the word used that is not supported by any of Paul's letters, he always uses *dedikaiwtai* for justification, never for freed.

As Wright has noted, the baptism teaching reading of the in the opening verses (Rom 6:1–6) is exodus based and reflects the deliverance of Israel from Egypt.[380] However, Wright fails to follow up his observation that Israel was brought out of Egypt to be Yahweh's bride, and that it was a corporate event that involved the entire nation. In this Wright displays his weakness in understanding the importance of the divine marriage theme in the Bible. He has no reference to it in any of his indexes, but does occasionally catch its presence, without realizing its significance (so in Rom 8:31–39).[381] Before Israel could marry Yahweh, her relationship with the Egyptian gods had to be brought to an end. This was a major reason for the Passover when Israel, through her firstborn, who was substituted by the paschal lamb, died to the gods that had owned her as their bride through her blatant adulteress activity. This sort of imagery[382] is widespread throughout the Old Testament and is in abundance throughout the ancient world. People belonged to their gods as their bride.

---

[380] Wright, 'New Exodus, New Inheritance', 28.

[381] Wright comes close to seeing the divine marriage theme but does not appreciate how it is integrated as a grand theme in Paul's theology. Even though he does not recognize the power of the divine marriage motif in Romans, Wright, 'Theology', 55, says: 'Rom 8:31–39, like a musical coda, picks up the theme of the entire letter thus far and celebrates them in good rhetorical style. The divine love, which has been under the argument since 5:6–10, re-emerges as the real major theme of the entire gospel message. This is covenant love, promised to Abraham and his family, a family now seen to be the worldwide people who benefit from Jesus' death. Since this love is precisely the Creator's love, it remains sovereign even though the powers of earth and heaven may seem to be ranged against it. Since it is the love of the covenant god, it rests on his unbreakable promise. The language of the law court and the language of the marriage contract thus merge (8:33–34, 35–39), with both of them now revealed as vital metaphorical aspects of the one more fundamental truth, which can be expressed both as δικαιοσύνη γὰρ θεοῦ ('righteousness of god') and as ἀγάπη θεοῦ ('love of God'): the covenant faithfulness of the Creator god, revealed in the death and resurrection of Jesus the Messiah and the gift of the Spirit.'

[382] The tension of this relationship is described by Hosea who shared in the pain of his wife rejecting his love and seeking other lovers. Just like Yahweh, Hosea could not give her up even though in law she had broken the relationship.

Thus, the significance of the declaration of being justified through the Messiah's death is that there is no guilt in the new marriage relationship that the newly redeemed people have entered into. The new covenant people of God are legally innocent for having entered into this new relationship. They are justified from the claims and accusations of Satan (Rom 6:7; cf. Rom 7:1–6; 8:33–34), for they died to sin through taking a real part in the death of Christ.

Thus, the circumcision and justification language in the letter to the Galatians is of a completely different order from that found in Romans. Wright has not recognized this, and so drives his single chosen meaning, derived from Galatians, into all uses of the term throughout Paul's letters— missing as he does so other rich covenantal themes. This eschatological description of man's final destiny has been hidden by Wright's incomplete eschatological focus, as he sees the return to the land as the climax of the 'return from exile.' This misreading of the narrative results in an understanding of the text which Paul never intended.

In Romans 7:1–7 Paul explains how the law functioned in the matter of the divine marriage relationship.[383] Using human marriage as a metaphor, he opens out a discussion on the role of the law and relationships. We will see that the chapter has many stories within it, not least the story of Israel's failed marriage to Yahweh.

> Having explained the way in which the death of Christ brought freedom for his people, by meeting all of the law's demands, a freedom that Paul had described as having been justified in Romans 6:7. Paul concludes this section of the letter by explaining how the law, which had forbidden a new relationship, has been satisfied by the representative death of Christ. The end of the old

---

[383] John K. Goodrich, 'Sold Under Sin: Echoes of Exile in Romans 7. 14–25', *NTS* 59.4 (2013), 476–95. The article builds on Philonenko's work on the allusion to Isa 50:1 in the phrase 'sold under sin' (Rom 7:14) and seeks to identify echoes from LXX Isa 49:24–50:2 in Rom 7:14–25. Goodrich suggests that this link upholds Paul's use of Israel's sin/exile history. From this, 'the story of ἐγώ by connecting the allusions to Israel's early history in Rom 7:7–13 to images of the nation's later history in 7:14–25, thus showing the speaker's plight under sin to be analogous to Israel's own experiences of deception, death, and exile.' While Goodrich brings helpful insights to the exile theme in Romans 7, he does not pick up on the fact that Israel had bound herself to other gods and this relationship had to be ended before she could be redeemed from exile and restored to her status as the bride of Yahweh.

relationship with sin and death has opened the door to a new relationship with Christ who has died to make this relationship possible. He not only died to end the old relationship, but he also died to make the church completely clean and perfect so that she could stand before the Father in perfect innocence (Eph 5:25–27). The justification that the death of Christ has secured for his bride begins to transform her so that she has new desires which were not possible under the old relationship with sin-Satan (Rom 7:24–25).

In Romans 8, Paul refers to an act of justification when he says:

> There is therefore now no condemnation for those who are in Christ Jesus. For the law of the Spirit of life has set you free in Christ Jesus from the law of sin and death. For God has done what the law, weakened by the flesh, could not do. By sending his own Son in the likeness of sinful flesh and for sin, he condemned sin in the flesh. (Rom 8:1–3)

The acquittal that the people of God experience is far more than a legal transfer, it is a totally new way of life that is characterised by the presence of the Spirit, under whose law the community now lives. The removal of condemnation remains a vital component of justification regardless of the particular context. None of the other aspects of justification—covenant making, imputation of righteousness, covenant membership, deliverance from exile, or acceptance as the bride—can be possible without the discharge from guilt which caused the problem that required justification in the first place.

Because they are a justified community, the Spirit can now reside with them in the way Yahweh had longed for throughout the Old Testament, when Israel repeatedly trampled underfoot the significance of the provided sacrifices and did despite to the Spirit of grace. This is the same understanding found in the letter to the Hebrews where the writer says:

> How much worse punishment, do you think, will be deserved by the one who has trampled underfoot the Son of God, and has profaned the blood of the covenant by which he was sanctified, and has outraged the Spirit of grace? (Heb 10:29)

However, under the old covenant, they had no idea that in trampling underfoot the provided sacrifices, they were doing the same to the blood of the one who would be provided as the great offering for sin once and for all. Now there is no further forbearing, and if they continue to do this when the truth of what they had done is made apparent, 'how shall we escape if we neglect such a great salvation? It was declared at first by the Lord, and it was attested to us by those who heard' (Heb 2:3).

In Romans, Paul explains how this deliverance is not the completion of the work of salvation, but the beginning of a life lived under the Spirit's authority. The Spirit leads the bride toward the great event where she shall be presented faultless before the throne, and on that day her marriage to her Saviour—regardless of Satan's wildest protestations—will be declared justified. Paul says:

> Who shall bring any charge against God's elect? It is God who justifies. Who is to condemn? Christ Jesus is the one who died— more than that, who was raised—who is at the right hand of God, who indeed is interceding for us. Who shall separate us from the love of Christ? Shall tribulation, or distress, or persecution, or famine, or nakedness, or danger, or sword? As it is written. "For your sakes we are being killed all the daylong; We are regarded as sheep to be slaughtered." (Rom 8:33–36)

As we found in chapter 5, so we find here, a concentration of 'justification' terms that naturally flow with the narrative. We have found repeated references and echoes of the Passover (Rom 3:21–25; 5:7) and again we see it surfacing here with words such as 'firstborn,' 'predestined,' 'called', and 'not sparing his own Son.' The terminology is reminiscent of the Passover when Israel was called into a unique relationship with her God. In that covenant, he took full responsibility for his bride and challenged all accusations against the legitimacy of the marriage. The reference to Christ being the 'firstborn of many brothers' relates to his work of redeeming creation (Rom 8:18–27) which was marred by the fall of the first Adam, and as the last Adam he returned it to his brothers as their inheritance.

Then the passage breaks forth with even stronger paschal language that demands the death of the firstborn; he must be given up to death to secure the bride. It is because of this representative paschal death that the marriage is established on secure legal terms, for the redeemer's representative death has delivered the community from all claims that Satan might make. Through his death, the covenant with sin has been terminated so that now Satan can make no charge, he has no claims on Christ's redeemed people. The church is justified, cleansed, presented without spot or blemish—to borrow the terminology of Ephesians 5:25–27.

In other words, Paul is expanding on what he had already said in chapter 5 about the work of the last Adam. Wright himself has noted the marital language in this passage but misses the paschal setting as he has in most other places where the same theme throbs and lends its vibrant significance to the narrative. The pilgrimage of the new covenant community will be possible because they are led by the Spirit (8:5–17). Failure to identify the paschal marital language in the letter has caused Wright's exegesis to not reach the full extent of what Paul intended for his readers as they dwelt on the fullness of God's love for his people.

While neither the themes of circumcision nor justification are explicitly mentioned in chapters 9–11, they are implicitly present. The problem Paul is seeking to alleviate in Rome is one which threatened to destroy the oneness of the believing Jewish and the gentile community. The gentiles had gained numerical control of the gathering due to their evangelistic zeal and the fact that the Jews had been expelled from the city for some years under the edict of Claudius. This absence of the founding members and key teachers of the community must have given the gentiles the sense that the Jewish believers are no longer needed. On their return, the former founders would have sensed their loss of importance and status. These demoralised Jews who had been the community's teachers before being exiled would naturally seek to assert their importance as the natural inheritors of the promises. They would understandably claim that the gentiles must recognise that if it had not been for their faithfulness through the centuries there would be no gospel message in which to believe for there would not have been a Messiah.

In reply to this, the gentiles responded that God did not need Jews any longer, and they had been cut off from the kingdom. Paul was only too aware of the consequences of these attitudes and so in chapters 9–11 he seeks to correct them. The unity that he pleaded for was important at another level, for Paul wanted to take with him a mixed team of believing Jews and gentiles from Rome to Spain (Rom 15:28–33). He knew that the greatest demonstration of the power of God is when people who are enemies are made friends and partners in the gospel. If what was happening in the Roman church continued, their testimony would be almost worthless!

That is the reason chapter 12 begins with a call for everyone to present their bodies as a single living sacrifice (Rom 12:1–2), the singular 'sacrifice' making it clear that such an act of service cannot be done in isolation. As far as the text is concerned, it is not hundreds of sacrifices that Paul calls for, but hundreds of believers offering themselves to present to God one sacrifice to God (a truth Wright misses as he interprets the call to be for individuals to offer themselves individually as separate sacrifices to God). Paul urges the community to accept one another in love and demonstrate to the world the power of God in Christ. Failure to recognize and practise this intrinsic oneness in the gospel has been a source of much damage to the church's witness.

Romans 2:6–13

One of Wright's key texts for his understanding of justification is Romans 2:6–13. He claims that this passage cannot fit the Reformed understanding of justification, and so argues that the rest of the teaching by the Reformers on justification should be dismissed.

I want to challenge Wright's reading of this difficult text which has defied repeated attempts to make it fit comfortably with justification by faith alone. I offer the following exegesis of the passage as a way to resolve this problem.[384] I will work through the passage verse by verse in order to show that the passage does not represent a denial of the doctrine of justification by faith alone; indeed, it shows that works fail to bring even a basic 'Old Testament level' of justification.

- He will render to each one according to his works. (Rom 2:6)

Although Paul is reasoning at the corporate level, he cannot avoid making this categorical statement about the responsibility of the individual before God. The Jews of Jeremiah's day had tried to argue that they could not be held responsible for the things that their fathers had done and for which they were being threatened with punishment. Their favourite excuse was to recite the proverb: 'the fathers had eaten sour grapes, and the children's teeth are set on edge' (Jer 31:30). Jeremiah told his contemporaries that they were not being punished for the sins of others but for their own (Jer 31:29). In the same way, Paul is not prepared to allow anyone in Rome to think he or she can avoid responsibility by appealing to their circumstances or heritage. Individuals will not be punished for the sins of others—but will be held accountable for their own.

- To those who by persistence in doing good seek glory, honour and immortality, he will give eternal life. (Rom 2:7)

From the case of individual responsibility in the previous verse, Paul takes his argument to the corporate level by saying 'to those.' This statement may seem to imply that man can achieve acceptance by God through good

---

[384] For a more detailed exegesis see Holland, *Divine Marriage*, 54–64.

works, but the Greek makes it clear that it is not about people seeking 'eternal life'. The key to understanding this verse is to appreciate what is being sought. These people are seeking God's glory and honour. They are seeking the God, who alone grants immortality (1 Tim 6:16; Tit 2:11–14). They are not seeking their own righteousness but for the God, who can make them righteous. The present active participle, 'seeking', is marked out by its commitment and carries the idea of pursuance or continuance in seeking. The word, 'persistence', comes from the Greek *hypomonē* and means 'continuance' or 'endurance,' conveying the idea of consistency.[385]

The statement reflects what Paul has said in Romans 1:5, where he speaks of 'the obedience that comes of faith.' Such seeking is an expression of faith in God though of itself it is not the source of salvation. Paul does not suggest that men seek God through personal contemplation, but through works which reflect his character. Of course, such works can never save, but they can be evidence that a person is sincerely seeking and should not be despised (Luke 7:1–10; John 3:1–2; Acts 10:17–23; 16:14–15). Such seeking marks a community out as godly; they desire God's presence among them or rather they desire to be in his presence.

Paul's use of 'eternal life' in this verse is often interpreted in the light of John's use (e.g. John 3:16, 36; 5:24; 6:40; 10:28; 17:3). The terms that Paul normally uses for being right with God are 'reconciled' (Rom 5:10; 2 Cor 5:18, 20; Col 1:22) and 'justified' (e.g. Rom 3:24; 5:9; 8:30; Gal 3:24), terms not found in John's writings. Since this is Paul's only use of the term 'eternal life', we need to ask if Paul uses the term with the same meaning as found in John.

In John, eternal life is very much about being presently in the kingdom of God (John 3:1–8). So, in Romans 2:7 Paul, in debating with his Jewish representative, keeps to the language of the Old Testament. He is not using any developed Christian understanding of the term but wisely stays within the heritage and limited understanding of his opponent.

The Old Testament Jews clearly anticipated an earthly Messianic kingdom, where Israel would return from exile as the restored covenant community. This return was seen as her resurrection to eternal life (Ezek 37;

---

[385] Morris, *Romans,* 116, says that *hypomonē* denotes an active manly fortitude. He says it is used of the soldier who, 'in the thick of a hard battle, gives as much as he gets; he is not dismayed by the blows he receives, but fights on to the end.' Ibid., 257.

Dan 12:3). Paul keeps strictly to the Old Testament use of the term which
Jewish participants in the debate would identify with, in that they were still
expecting—or hoping—to receive eternal life after this manner—in being
members of the restored Messianic kingdom. However, this was not the
'eternal life' of the New Testament, for the 'kingdoms' in the Old and New
Testaments were very different.

We can see the distinctively Pauline use of 'kingdom' language in Acts
14:22, where the apostle encourages the believers in Antioch to remain true to
the faith. He tells them that he and they 'must go through many hardships to
enter the kingdom of God.' In Ephesians 5:5, Paul writes about the kingdom
'of Christ and of God.' Further, in 1 Corinthians 15:24–25 he explains: 'Then
comes the end, when he delivers the kingdom to God the Father after
destroying every rule and every authority and power. For he must reign until
he has put all his enemies under his feet.'

These texts suggest that Paul understood there to be two distinct stages of
entering the kingdom. Believers are already members of the kingdom of
Christ, and here they will suffer as they make their pilgrimage to the heavenly
Zion. They will enter the kingdom of God at 'the end' when Christ will
deliver the kingdom to God the Father.

John does not seem to know of such a progression. He views eternal life
as the eschatological gift that is enjoyed here and now. He uses the term
'kingdom of God' to describe the present and future inheritance of the
believer. There is no fundamental difference between the understanding of
John and Paul. John's use of 'kingdom' language reflects 'realized
eschatology' where the future is already present. Because of this John gives
very little teaching on the perseverance of the believer or church for they have
already taken possession of their inheritance.

The question posed by the rich young ruler: 'what must I do to inherit
eternal life?' (Luke 18:18) is chiefly concerned with the kingdom of the
Messiah. Most likely, he was not referring to 'heaven' but to the limited
kingdom meaning as used by Daniel. This Old Testament understanding is the
setting for Paul's statement in this verse. This becomes clear when it is
appreciated that Paul is explaining to his Jewish readers that God has always
left the door open for those who strive to enter the Messianic kingdom. His
use of Old Testament language would have resonated immediately in every
Jewish mind.

If the question is asked as to whether Paul's readers could be expected to differentiate between these two meanings of 'eternal life,' the answer must be an unreserved 'yes!' In Romans 1:3–4 Paul used the term 'Son of God' with its Old Testament echo of the descendant of David, the appointed king. Because the Messiah had been raised something could now be declared that was previously unknown about him, that he was ontologically the Son of God in the distinctively Christian meaning 'declared to be the Son of God in power.'

I prefer this reading to that of Wright, who sees it to be about the disclosing of Jesus's Messianic kingship. Such recognition was unnecessary, for it had already been revealed by the Spirit (Matt 16:13–20), and even the Jewish mob mocked Jesus as the promised king; it was clearly a claim that they were aware of. Indeed, Jesus, by riding into Jerusalem on a donkey, had made his own claim to such status. So, if the two meanings for Son of God are present in Romans 1:3 then such evidence demonstrates that the New Testament church had no difficulty in discerning the various shades of a word's meaning.

In doing this, they were not displaying exceptional ability but exhibiting a universal basic characteristic of the human brain to process linguistic information. Another example of the early church's ability to differentiate between Old Testament meaning and Hellenistic meaning is the way they could separate the secular meaning of flesh from the Hebraically rooted meaning when describing the condition of humanity in Adam. The Hebraic meaning is completely the opposite of the Hellenistic meaning with its emphasis on the duality of the spiritual and physical, a fact not lost on the early church.

It is important to note this development of key theological vocabulary from the Old Testament, for following the death and resurrection of Jesus it was infused with great meaning and significance; terms such as reconciliation, adoption, redemption, and judgment all came to have much greater meaning and significance than before, even though they retained their Old Testament roots. This is certainly true concerning the terms eternal life and the kingdom of God. If we do not recognize this fact, we will find it extremely difficult to make sense of some very important New Testament passages, and Romans 2:6–13 is one of them.

This observation gains further support from reflecting on Paul's use of the word 'flesh'. To understand Paul's use of the term one must recognize that this word has a very wide semantic range and care has to be taken to select the appropriate meaning intended by Paul. Failure to do this confuses Paul's teaching and leads into unhealthy views of human anthropology and his doctrine of sin.

The above discussion on the possibility of two kingdom stages found in Paul would seem to go against the teaching of the Gospels which speak of only one kingdom—the kingdom of God. However, the traditional understanding of this has recently come under scrutiny. Previously, most argued that the 'kingdom of heaven' in Matthew's Gospel was another way of saying the 'kingdom of God' as used by the other Gospel writers.[386] It was argued that Matthew chose the term 'heaven' to avoid using the name of God in a way that would offend the Jews for whom his Gospel was written, for the name of God was seen to be so sacred that they avoided using it through fear that they might defile it.

However, this explanation was never fully satisfactory as it did not explain why Matthew, having avoided 'kingdom of God' in the parallel passages found in Luke and Mark, still occasionally used the term he is supposed to have abandoned.[387] Some scholars have researched this anomaly and have challenged the traditional understanding of Matthew's use of the term 'kingdom of heaven'.[388] They have concluded that for Matthew, the

---

[386] It has recently been argued that Matthew's Gospel was widely known among the churches. See S. E. Lauer, 'Traces of a Gospel Writing in 1 Corinthians: Rediscovering and Development of Origen's Understanding of 1 Corinthians 4:6b' (PhD Thesis, Lampeter: Trinity St. David, 2010).

[387] See Matt 12:28; 21:31; 43.

[388] M. Pamment, 'Kingdom of Heaven according to the First Gospel', *NTS* 27 (1981), 211–232 [232], argues that the kingdom of God is a present reality, preparing individuals for the kingdom of heaven, which, in Matthew, refers to an eschatological and futuristic kingdom. She describes this future kingdom as a 'wholly future reality which is imminent but other-worldly in the sense that the world as it is experienced now will no longer exist.' This is a similar conclusion to that reached by W. E. Albright and C. S. Mann, *Matthew* (New York: Doubleday, 1984), 155, 233. However, Albright and Mann argue that the kingdom of heaven exists with Jesus *until* the final judgment, whereas the kingdom of God will be established *at* the final judgment. Whilst Pamment reverses the significance of the two kingdoms as seen by Albright and Mann, the point is that they both see a distinction between the two kingdoms. For a summary of the evidence relating to the use of the term 'kingdom' in the Gospels, see E. A. Udoeyop, 'The New People of God and Kingdom

'kingdom of heaven' and 'kingdom of God' are two stages of the same kingdom—God's kingdom. Gospel studies have moved towards the explanation of the kingdoms of Christ and of God given above for Paul's understanding, lending weight to the argument being made. So, in the Synoptic usage of 'kingdom of God,' the focus is the Old Testament meaning of the anticipated kingdom in Zion. Paul in fact augments his use of kingdom language with the language of adoption (Rom 8:15, 23; 9:4; Gal 4:5; Eph 1:5) and being reconciled (Rom 5:11; 11:5, 12; 2 Cor 5:18–20; Col 1:20), language which corresponds with this immediate state of kingdom membership.

The ultimate completion of salvation is when the pilgrim community enters the kingdom of God, and the community is secure in God's presence. John says that the believer's presence in the kingdom of God is an immediate reality and not one that has to be waited for.

- But for those who are self-seeking and do not obey the truth, but obey unrighteousness, there will be wrath and fury. (Rom 2:8)

The term Paul uses here for 'unrighteousness' is *adikia*, the same word he used in Romans 1:18 to contrast with God's righteousness. Rejection of God's truth exhibits itself in *eritheia* ('self-seeking' or 'selfishness'). Paul explained in Romans 1:18ff. that such behaviour led to wrath and anger. The shocking message of Paul for his fellow countrymen is that their failure to love God repeatedly demonstrated in the nation's history of idolatry, meant that Israel came under his wrath and was threatened by his judgment. Only the intervention of God can reverse this state of affairs.

- There will be trouble and distress for every human being who does evil: first for the Jew, then for the gentile. (Rom 2:9)

The Greek *thlipsis* ('trouble') can also mean 'pressure to the point of breaking.' The term is used to describe the force put on grapes when they are pressed. It speaks of acute suffering. Similarly, the term *stenochōri* ('distress') conveys the idea of being cramped for space, from which comes the idea of extreme affliction. Together, the two terms emphasize the anguish that will fall upon the ungodly.

Fruitfulness: An Exegetical and Theological Study of the Parable of the Wicked Tenants in Matthew 21:33–46 and its Significance for a Corporate Hermeneutic' (PhD Thesis, Belfast: Queen's University, 2006), 109–12.

Paul stresses that this judgment is not only for gentiles but also for Jews who reject God's salvation. This was very difficult for Jews to come to terms with. They saw themselves as different from the gentiles, who, they thought, deserved God's judgment for their obvious sins. The Jews were religious and considered themselves to be devout. They had a religious tradition that united them to their ancestor Abraham to whom God had made unique promises. They could point back to the exodus and say: 'this was when God saved us.' As a result, the Jews saw themselves as being in a right relationship with God.

However, Paul says this is not the case. Wrath and anger will be experienced in trouble and distress, and the Jews will be the first to be brought to judgment: 'first for the Jew, then for the gentile'. Because the Jews had religious privileges above the gentiles, they have no excuse before God for their disobedience. They were appointed to be the first who heard (Rom 1:17); now they are appointed the first to be judged (Amos 3:2).

> - But glory, honour and peace for everyone who does good: first
>   for the Jew, then for the gentile. (Rom 2:10)

For those who seek God, the end is so very different than for those who reject him. For the true seeker, there is glory, honour, and peace. When Paul speaks of glory, he is not speaking of the glory of success but about a dimension familiar to the Jew. Man had been created for the glory (praise) of God, having been given a dignity in creation that made him unique. He was made in the image of God, with characteristics that set him apart from the rest of creation. Being endowed with such unique qualities meant that he reflected the very qualities of God.

However, this glory was lost when Adam sinned (Rom 3:23). He was deprived of his position as one stripped of rank in the army and put out of service. From then on, man ceased to rule on God's behalf and ruled with his own interests on the agenda. Paul's reference to 'honour' reflects this background and the status that was lost through the fall.

Paul writes that peace will be granted to those who seek God. How different for those who disobey and experience wrath, trouble, and distress (Rom 2:5, 9). There is no exemption from this judgment—not even the Jews can escape it. Indeed, Paul repeats that it is the Jews who are the first to come under God's judgment, for they have had the greatest privileges of all the nations. This is not a new notion. The prophet Amos spoke God's word to Israel, saying: 'you only have I known of all the peoples of the earth, therefore I will punish you' (Amos 3:2). Paul drives home the truth of God's impartiality in judgment in the following verse.

- For God does not show favouritism. (Rom 2:11)

This statement lies at the heart of the Mosaic law. The judges of Israel were not allowed to show favouritism or accept bribes (Exod 23:1–9) because they represented God in their solemn work. For them to pervert the course of justice would be to implicate God in unrighteousness and corruption.

The Jews perceived that they were objects of God's favour, but Paul insisted this perception was founded on a wrong reading of the Old Testament. They were, indeed, a privileged people—called and blessed by God (Rom 9:1–5). However, these blessings were not so much signs of God's unique favour for Israel as a statement that Israel would be the means by which Yahweh's grace would be made known to the nations.

This understanding of the reason for Israel's blessing is found in many of the parables of Jesus. Often, they are read as if they are teaching for the church, but while there is obviously instruction in them, they were not intended or delivered in that way. The parables were essentially critical assessments of Israel's failure to be the true servant of Yahweh (see chapter 3). So, for example, the 'talents' of Jesus's parable recorded in Matthew 25:14–15 are not natural abilities but money or treasure. They were symbolic of the treasure of the knowledge of God that Israel was to share with the gentiles. The severity of God's judgment is the measure of how signally Israel failed in her task. The treasure was to be taken from Israel and given to another, the church, for her to share with the world. The application for the church is that when any Christian community sees itself in the light of its blessings and not in the light of its responsibilities, it is in grave danger of discovering that the blessings have been withdrawn. What was true of Israel can also be true of a local or even national church.

This Old Testament teaching on God's impartiality in his dealings with man is found throughout the New Testament. Jesus warned of the danger of being over-impressed with the rich and the powerful (Luke 6:24–26), and his message was regularly repeated to warn of the danger of respecting status (James 2:1–7; 1 John 3:17).

The church should not be a community in which the wealthy and successful are adulated and men are elevated to positions of responsibility only because of their natural abilities. The church's values should cause her to identify the grace of God at work in the lives of all people and to be concerned equally for those who have not succeeded materially as well as those who have. To close the door of leadership to people of faith and gifting simply because they do not have social standing is a denial of the work of Christ.

> - All who sin apart from the law will also perish apart from the law, and all who sin under the law will be judged by the law. (Rom 2:12)

Paul now turns to consider the condition of the gentiles. They have not had the same privileges as the Jews so that they will be judged against a different standard. Because they have not had the law, the law will not judge them. All who have sinned under the law (the Jews), will be judged by the law.[389] In stating this, Paul repeats his argument of v. 10, thereby closing off any way of escape for those who think they can avoid the issue of guilt.

The statement, in so far as it refers to those not under the law, was not unique to Paul.[390] The judgment he refers to is the Day of Judgment, when all Jews and gentiles, Christian and non-Christians, will be judged. In the case of the Christians who have put their trust in the atonement/redemption that Christ has secured and have accepted his lordship, their eternal destiny is secure. Christ has already taken the due penalty for their sin (Rom 3:21–26; Gal 3:13; 2 Cor 5:21). However, they will be judged on their work as believers, so 1 Corinthians 3:8—which refers particularly to apostolic labours, and 2 Corinthians 5:10.

> - For it is not those who hear the law who are righteous in God's sight, but it is those who obey the law who will be declared righteous. (Rom 2:13)

Paul here expounds the issue of the Jews' culpability, quite possibly because he was acutely aware of how he had excused himself before becoming a follower of Christ. He had been comfortably satisfied with his own religious achievements (Phil 3:4–6), even though he knew that he had not kept the whole law. In taking this attitude, he had been like most Jews. While he was aware of God's holiness and perfect standards, he saw himself as belonging to a nation that had been graciously chosen by God and forgiven.

---

[389] For a discussion on the meaning of 'under the law', see Morris, *Romans*, 143 ff., and, more importantly, W. Wilder, *Echoes of the Exodus Narrative in the Context and Background of Galatians 5:18* (New York: Peter Lang, 2001), 75–107.

[390] E.g. 2 Bar 48:40, 70.

This forgiveness was secured by the death of sacrificial animals, the means God had appointed to remove the defilement of sin and make Israel acceptable.

With such a solution to sin in place, Paul, like most of his fellow Jews, saw the problem of Israel's sin as having been dealt with. In his mind, it was only the gentiles who were outside of this special relationship with God and who needed to fear his judgment. However, Paul now attacks this Jewish concept of spiritual security. It is not those who know the law who are saved, but those who obey it. This obedience was about keeping all of the law's demands (Gal 5:3).

Thus, the passage should not be read as part of the traditional justification debate, as it so commonly is. Paul is dealing with the status of the Jews and their expectation of entering the Messianic kingdom which is what the term 'eternal life' refers to. Paul is saying that even in this limited sense of acceptance by God the Jewish people fall short, for they had not kept the law. Their sin of being a repeatedly adulterous people, leaving their God to respond to the enticements of other gods, means that they are excluded from the kingdom which those in exile had hoped for. Paul goes on to say that they need the same way of acceptance that is offered to the gentiles; not through the works of the law but faith in Christ Jesus. The passage is therefore not challenging the Reformed understanding of justification; rather it endorses it; for the law was not able to save Israel but grace is.

Thus, this often-misunderstood passage is not, as Wright (with many others) argues, dealing with justification by faith—it is dealing with what makes justification by faith necessary. The explanation normally followed has taken the passage out of its Old Testament context and its specifically Jewish eschatological vocabulary (points which Wright is normally so good in identifying). The debate in Romans 2 does not have the later Christian richness that came with the gospel. It is, therefore, wrong to argue that it challenged the Reformers understanding when it does the very opposite; it makes their understanding necessary.

This, in my judgement, is one of the most serious issues in Wright's doctrine of justification. He is saying that only on the Day of Judgment is justification finally given and that declaration depends on the life lived since an earlier declaration of being justified—not when the individual was converted—for he challenges this understanding of justification. This explanation leaves the true believer uncertain whether they have really been saved and are true 'citizens of Zion', for this will only be confirmed on the last day, and that judgment will be based on works, the life lived since becoming a Christian.

This introduces keeping of the law as a requirement for salvation. No one would deny it is evidence of true faith, but to make its keeping as the grounds of salvation robs the assurance which is one of the jewels of Christian truth and experience. Can anyone know that he or she has sufficiently kept the law as to anticipate justification? This sounds like a surrender of the doctrine of grace to a doctrine of justification by works; yet as Wright has commented so often on in the letter to Galatians, it is not Christ plus works, it is Christ alone. Wright's proposal is the result of faulty readings of passages. To support this reading, he appeals to Rom 2:5–11 (which we have considered), Rom 14:10–12 and 2 Cor 5:10.[391] Wright is not the only professing evangelical who has finished in this cul-de-sac, but in my judgment, it is a very serious surrender of the Christian hope.

Having already considered Wright's interpretation of Rom 2:5–11 and found it wanting, we shall consider the other two passages.

First in Rom 14:10–12 Paul says:

> Why do you pass judgment on your brother? Or you, why do you despise your brother? For we will all stand before the judgment seat of God; for it is written, "As I live, says the Lord, every knee shall bow to me, and every tongue shall confess to God." So, then each of us will give an account of himself to God.

The wider context makes it clear that the subject is Christian liberty and the right of all Christians to make their own decisions regarding what they eat or drink. Paul urges the congregation not to sit in judgement on such issues and he reminds them that they will all appear before the judgement seat of God when His Lordship will be proclaimed by all bowing before him.[392] The statement about giving an account must not have more put into it than the context allows and this is about whether they have insisted on their Christian freedom, lived thoughtlessly, and offended other believers unnecessarily. This is not a salvation issue; it is about their preferring one another above themselves and the honour that God promises to those who love and serve him. This understanding is evidently correct for Paul went on to say:

---

[391] See Wright, *1 Corinthians for Everyone*, 38–39.

[392] Of course, Paul has adapted the text to be a statement concerning the Lordship of Christ as a result of his resurrection.

> Therefore, let us not pass judgment on one another any longer, but rather decide never to put a stumbling block or hindrance in the way of a brother. I know and am persuaded in the Lord Jesus that nothing is unclean in itself, but it is unclean for anyone who thinks it unclean. For if your brother is grieved by what you eat, you are no longer walking in love. By what you eat, do not destroy the one for whom Christ died. So do not let what you regard as good be spoken of as evil. For the kingdom of God is not a matter of eating and drinking but of righteousness and peace and joy in the Holy Spirit. Whoever thus serves Christ is acceptable to God and approved by men. (Rom 14:13–18)

The other passage cited by Wright to support his claim that only the final judgement will justification be declared is 2 Cor 5:2–10 which says:

> For in this tent we groan, longing to put on our heavenly dwelling, if indeed by putting it on we may not be found naked. For while we are still in this tent, we groan, being burdened—not that we would be unclothed, but that we would be further clothed, so that what is mortal may be swallowed up by life. He who has prepared us for this very thing is God, who has given us the Spirit as a guarantee. So, we are always of good courage. We know that while we are at home in the body we are away from the Lord, for we walk by faith, not by sight. Yes, we are of good courage, and we would rather be away from the body and at home with the Lord. So whether we are at home or away, we make it our aim to please him. For we must all appear before the judgment seat of Christ, so that each one may receive what is due for what he has done in the body, whether good or evil. (2 Cor 5:2–10)

Once again, the context of the statement about being judged is crucial. The passage refers to the pilgrim community and its corporate weakness which causes them to long for Christ's presence when they will be tested. We note that the appearance is before the judgement seat of Christ rather than of God as in Rom 14:10–12. The contrast is between those who make it their ambition to please him and those who do not. Again, this does not focus on whether they are Christians, and so welcomed into heaven, but whether they lived the faith they professed and gave all for their Redeemer's glory. It is about their reward and if needed judgment concerning their spiritual walk. Murray summarizes his exegesis of the passage saying:

> . . . for Paul, this φανερωθῆναι[393] involved the appearance and examination before Christ's tribunal of every Christian without

---

[393] I.e. resurrection.

exception for the purpose of receiving an exact and impartial recompense (including the receipt or deprivation of commendations) which would be based on deeds, both good and bad, performed through the earthly body. The fear inspired by this expectation (v. 11) doubtless intensified Paul's ambition that his life should meet with Christ's approval both during and at the βῆμα (v. 9).[394]

Thus, Wright is incorrect in using this text to support a teaching that salvation can be lost on the Day of Judgment, for Paul is not speaking of salvation but of the examination of a life of service, which if not rendered, will deny the believer the joy that should have been through having whole heartedly served his crucified Lord. This is not speaking about a judgment concerning our being fit for salvation but a judgment about the reward that shall be given to those faithful servants who strove to do the will of their master.

Romans 3:24

Paul says that justification is about being delivered from sin: 'for all have sinned and fall short of the glory of God, and are justified by his grace as a gift, through the redemption that is in Christ Jesus' (Rom 3:23–24).

Paul is clearly speaking of the fall of the entire human race in Adam; none have escaped the disastrous consequences of this event. The act of justification would make no sense (in this context) if it did not explain how God has reversed this dreadful condition. Justification is about the removal of the guilt that all humanity shares in Adam, and the removal of the divine sentence of wrath—separation from God.

The contrast could not be clearer. In the 'all have sinned' of v. 23, the 'have sinned' uses the verb form indicative aorist active third person plural; it, therefore, speaks of an event that took place in history and involved many. In the case of those who are 'justified', Paul uses the verbal participle present passive nominative masculine plural from δικαιόω. In other words, they are now justified. This is not a condition that has to be confirmed on the Day of Judgement, it is a present status and received as a gift from God. The means of achieving this state of justification is clear; it is 'by his grace as a gift, through the redemption that is in Christ Jesus'. The death of Jesus is at the heart of justification and is the source of the new status which God bestows

---

[394] M. J. Harris, *The Second Epistle to the Corinthians*, 409.

on those who turn from their reliance on 'dead works' (Heb 6:1) to have faith in Christ.

As we have seen, Romans 3:21–26 is modelled on the Passover.[395] The redemption of the Jewish community took place when, through the Passover, Yahweh took them to be his bride. This was not about Israel being pronounced to be in the covenant (as Wright suggests), but rather it spoke of how she was brought into that covenant. As the type, so the antitype—and this will be found to control much of what Paul means when he speaks of the justification of God's people. They have been brought by their Redeemer King to be his bride and in this act, all charges against her have been satisfied before Yahweh's own justice. God has bestowed on her not only a 'righteous' status but also of being 'in' his Son, with all the privileges this involves.

Romans 4:1–10

Paul focuses on the justification of Abraham recorded in Genesis 15:6 and the testimony of David in Psalm 32:1–2 when he writes in Romans 4:1–10:

> What then shall we say was gained by Abraham, our forefather according to the flesh? For if Abraham was justified by works, he has something to boast about, but not before God. For what does the Scripture say? "Abraham believed God, and it was counted to him as righteousness." Now to the one who works, his wages are not counted as a gift but as his due. And to the one who does not work but believes in him who justifies the ungodly, his faith is counted as righteousness, just as David also speaks of the blessing of the one to whom God counts righteousness apart from works: "Blessed are those whose lawless deeds are forgiven, and whose sins are covered; blessed is the man against whom the Lord will not count his sin." Is this blessing then only for the circumcised, or also for the uncircumcised? For we say that faith was counted to Abraham as righteousness. How then was it counted to him? Was it before or after he had been circumcised? It was not after, but before he was circumcised. (Rom 4:1–10)

The fact that Paul cites the experiences of both Abraham and David concerning justification might be more significant than a casual reading might suggest. In the closing verses of chapter 3 he writes:

> Then what becomes of our boasting? It is excluded. By what kind of law? By a law of works? No, but by the law of faith. For we hold that one is justified by faith apart from works of the law. Or

---

[395] See pages 261–285.

> is God the God of Jews only? Is he not the God of gentiles also?
> Yes, of gentiles also, since God is one—who will justify the
> circumcised by faith and the uncircumcised through faith. Do we
> then overthrow the law by this faith? By no means! On the
> contrary, we uphold the law. (Rom 3:27–31)

In other words, Paul has argued that both Jews (circumcised—
represented by David) and gentiles (uncircumcised—represented by
Abraham) need the same justification. The point for our argument is that
David, a circumcised king, needed to be justified because he had sinned. Jews
need the same justification that gentiles need. There is no assurance for Jews
that their special relation status protects them from the need of repentance and
justification. David's need for justification did not focus on a final
eschatological outcome, but on his immediate need to be made right with God
as understood in Reformed theology. David was judged despite being loaded
with status and privileges. Such things would mean nothing when standing
before God.

Romans 4:11–25

I have deliberately divided chapter 4 into two sections so as to emphasize
what is going on in the later part of the chapter. Most see the reference to the
deadness of Sara's womb to date the event of Abraham's justification with the
conception or birth of Isaac. This seems to be a natural reading of the text
until it is examined more closely. The key verses say:

> That is why it depends on faith, in order that the promise may rest
> on grace and be guaranteed to all his offspring—not only to the
> adherent of the law but also to the one who shares the faith of
> Abraham, who is the father of us all, as it is written, "I have made
> you the father of many nations"—in the presence of the God in
> whom he believed, who gives life to the dead and calls into
> existence the things that do not exist. In hope he believed against
> hope, that he should become the father of many nations, as he had
> been told, "So shall your offspring be." He did not weaken in faith
> when he considered his own body, which was as good as dead
> (since he was about a hundred years old), or when he considered
> the barrenness of Sarah's womb. No unbelief made him waver
> concerning the promise of God, but he grew strong in his faith as
> he gave glory to God, fully convinced that God was able to do
> what he had promised. That is why his faith was "counted to him
> as righteousness." (Rom 4:16–25)

The usual reading cannot stand examination for a number of reasons.[396] Firstly, Abraham's life at this time was far from being a life of faith, twice claiming Sarah was his sister to save his skin (Gen 12:13; 20:10)—could Abraham truly be described, at this point, as a man of faith? Secondly, and most importantly, the Genesis account records nothing at all about faith and justification in the narrative of Isaac's birth. The emphasis of both the OT and Paul is not on Abraham's faith, and certainly not Sarah's faith, but on God's faithfulness. Confusing the event of Isaac's birth with Abraham's justification led John Murray to write the incredible statement that Abraham's faith gave him the strength to copulate with Sarah so that Isaac could be born![397] That Abraham went on to father more children through Keturah (Gen 25:1) after the death of Sarah proves the inaptness of this interpretation.

What has been missing in most attempts to exegete the passage is that the event that really demonstrated Abraham's faith was his obedience in offering up Isaac in response to the command given by Yahweh. It was then, when both their bodies were considerably older than when Isaac was born, that faith was needed. Abraham knew that the promise of the covenant that Isaac would become the father of a mighty nation, and through his offspring all of the nations of the earth would be blessed, was seriously at risk if Isaac was offered as a sacrifice. It is in this situation that Abraham believed in the God of resurrection; for he knew that if God did not raise Isaac from the dead the covenant promises could never be fulfilled, and it was all over. This is why Paul finishes the section in the way he does:

> No unbelief made him waver concerning the promise of God, but he grew strong in his faith as he gave glory to God, fully convinced that God was able to do what he had promised. That is why his faith was "counted to him as righteousness." But the words "it was counted to him" were not written for his sake alone, but for ours also. It will be counted to us who believe in him who raised from the dead Jesus our Lord, who was delivered up for our trespasses and raised for our justification. (Rom 4:20–24)

This is when Abraham demonstrated that faith which was the foundation of the covenant in Genesis 15:6. It was a true and living faith in the God who called and promised him, and so it is appropriate that Paul saw the two events as two aspects of the same true saving faith. As a bonus, this approach removes any tension that many have claimed to have existed in the

---

[396] Here I return to the point I raised earlier in the chapter.

[397] Murray, *Romans*, Vol. 1, 1.150–2.

understanding of Paul and James over faith and works. It also shows that Abraham was justified as a gentile, and then later, in the offering of Isaac, he was justified as a Jew.

Romans 5:1

> Therefore, since we have been justified by faith, we have peace with God through our Lord Jesus Christ. Through him we have also obtained access by faith into this grace in which we stand, and we rejoice in hope of the glory of God. (Rom 5:1–2)

There can be no doubt here that Paul is not speaking of a future justification, for he says that his readers have this blessing now. They have been justified, past tense; this justification is linked to the death and resurrection of Jesus as the end of chapter 4 (v. 25, the previous verse) made clear. The source of this justification is repeated in v. 9, they were 'justified by his blood'. This is not a future hope but a present reality, founded on the shed blood of Jesus and his resurrection. The result of this justification is not merely peace, for Paul says being 'justified by his blood, much more, we shall we be saved by him from the wrath of God' (Rom 5:9).

This passage draws heavily on the earlier paschal language (Rom 3:21–25). We noted that Paul emphasised that it is 'through his blood' that God supplies the answer to the need of forgiveness for all humanity and restoration to Himself, as illustrated by the life of David (Rom 4:6–8). Significantly, although this chapter has the highest concentration of references to justification in the entire Bible, Wright makes no reference to it.

Romans 5:6–10

> For while we were still weak, at the right time Christ died for the ungodly. For one will scarcely die for a righteous person—though perhaps for a good person one would dare even to die— but God shows his love for us in that while we were still sinners, Christ died for us. Since, therefore, we have now been justified by his blood, much more shall we be saved by him from the wrath of God. For if while we were enemies we were reconciled to God by the death of his Son, much more, now that we are reconciled, shall we be saved by his life. (Rom 5:6–10)

Justification is the result of Christ's death for his people. It is because of the Christ event that the righteous God can justify his people and deliver them from wrath. It was the love of God that motivated the giving of Christ and it is through the shedding of Christ's blood and his resurrection that people can be justified and reconciled to the one against whom they had offended. Such explicit teaching on the need, cause, and consequences of justification could not be clearer—it is the antithesis of what Wright claims the doctrine is about.

Romans 5:12–21

In addition, Paul discusses the role of the law in Romans five, where he says: 'Now the law came in to increase the trespass, but where sin increased, grace abounded all the more' (Rom 5:20), and 'for sin indeed was in the world before the law was given, but sin is not counted where there is no law' (Rom 5:13).

The law referred to is clearly the Mosaic law, given to Israel at Sinai. Again, these concepts of the law's function in condemning Israel cannot fit the New Perspective model which sees the law as a blessing to Israel. Paul's argument is corporate; its focus is on what the law does to the community that is in Adam, not to the individual in Adam; albeit the individual shares in its significance and consequences as a member of that community. It speaks of a law that did not bring the peace and well-being that New Perspective theologians claim. Instead, according to this key Pauline text, the law brought condemnation and terror to the covenant community itself. Although it was intended for Israel's blessing, the law clarified the nature of her rebellion and became a curse by putting her under the covenantal curses for being unfaithful (Gal 3:10–13).

The corporate nature of this discussion in Romans 5 controls the way we should read the statement:

> Therefore, as one trespass led to condemnation for all men, so one act of righteousness leads to justification and life for all men. For as by the one man's disobedience the many were made sinners, so by the one man's obedience the many will be made righteous. (Rom 5:18–19)

Wright challenges the doctrine of imputed righteousness, calling it legal fiction. Here we have humanity in Adam being credited with his disobedience and being declared unrighteous (imputed with Adam's guilt), and therefore, all are sinners. Here, then, is a clear case of the imputation of unrighteousness. The passage refers to the community of which Adam is the head. The members clearly share in the status of their federal head whose guilt they have endorsed as their own by their own disobedience. The individual receives this sinful status at birth when he or she comes into that community; it is not about personal sin or failing, but about a fundamentally imputed ungodliness or state of alienation. In other words, the imputation of unrighteousness is not an individual transfer of guilt; it is covenantal, and it is corporate—all who are in Adam share in it as members of the condemned community.

Since the new covenant community is the bride of Christ and her union with him through his death being the foundation of her justification, it is perfectly correct to talk of an imputation of Christ's righteousness to that community. His people have become what he is. His status has been in every sense transferred, imparted, or in other words imputed to his people. When a person becomes a believer, he or she shares in every blessing given to the justified community. To use the words of the Augsburg Confession (which unfortunately focuses on the individual without recognizing that the church alone is the bride of Christ):

> That man enjoys that acceptance with God called 'justification,' the beginning and end of salvation, not through his own moral effort even in the smallest and slightest degree but entirely and only through the loving mercy of God made available in the merits of Christ and of his saving death on the Cross. This was not a process of gradual ethical improvement but an instantaneous transaction, something like a marriage, in which Christ the bridegroom takes to himself an impoverished and wretched harlot and confers upon her all the riches which are his. The key to this transaction was faith, defined as a total and trustful commitment of the self to God, and is itself not a human achievement but the pure gift of God.[398]

Wright's criticism of the doctrine of imputation carries some weight if one focuses on the individual; but, as I have argued elsewhere,[399] that is not the focus of Paul's teaching. His focus is always on the justification of the collective people of God. Just as in the Old Testament, circumcision was linked with justification for it was a requirement of entry into the covenant community, so Paul brings the same two themes together here. In Colossians 2:11–13 he speaks of the community having been circumcised with the circumcision which Christ underwent in his death on the cross. Repeatedly he links the theme of the death of Christ (always in a Passover context) to the need for a circumcision of the heart. Clearly, he sees that these themes relate to the New Testament community's experience of salvation just as they were for his people in the Old Testament.

---

[398] Ibid.

[399] See Holland, *Divine Marriage,* 73–104.

Wright's mistake is that he has continued to focus on the salvation of the individual, contrary to what he has claimed about the corporate nature of justification in Galatians. This leads to an inconsistent exegesis, as Wright dances in and out of corporate and individual readings like dancers at a Scottish ceilidh. He misses the fact that Paul's argument is much bigger and more glorious. In this understanding, which makes better sense of Paul, the individual receives what has been given to the community as he or she enters it through faith in Christ. In this way, the individual becomes an inheritor of that imputed righteousness which has been bestowed on the community.

Under this understanding the Ordo Salutis becomes call (election), faith imparted by the Spirit, circumcision of the heart, and entrance into the new covenant community where the individual believer instantly becomes a recipient of everything bestowed on the community in Christ. The individual believer's experience is in this way similar to that of an immigrant who, on being granted citizenship, immediately receives all that the wider community has experienced for as long as the state and its laws have existed. As a member of the community that is the bride of Christ, all believers are justified and share the status of the heavenly husband, who has given all that he has to his betrothed people, the church. It is not only his righteousness that has been imputed to his beloved, but also everything that he is and which he has achieved.

Romans 6:7

> We know that our old self was crucified with him in order that the body of sin might be brought to nothing, so that we would no longer be enslaved to sin. For one who has died has been set free from sin. (Rom 6:6–7)[400]

Paul uses the term 'justify' in Romans 6:7 and this has led to continual debate, with most scholars, including Wright, suggesting that the term simply means 'freed.' This reading once again displays a clear disrespect for the integrity of the text. Paul never uses this term to speak of freedom, and it certainly cannot be used to denote a declaration of being in covenant as Wright claims. The term as used here has nothing to do with the individual being made righteous, but the community. Here sin is Satan (as Wright recognizes) and it is this union with Satan that Paul is explaining has come to a legitimate end, thus allowing the new union with Christ to be established. Because death has taken place there is no guilt in the new relationship

---

[400] Instead of 'been set free' the Greek text should be read 'been justified'.

between Christ and his church; both parties are justified in its creation. This is the only interpretation that respects the text and its context and upholds the terminology and its grammatical form that Paul has chosen. This is hugely significant, for it opens up vistas of meaning that Paul held regarding the work of Christ and the community he died to make his own. Here we see that something previously not understood is at the very heart of Paul's gospel. Rather than commentators questioning their own understanding they have challenged Paul's ability to say what he meant to say!

Romans 7:1–6

> Or do you not know, brothers—for I am speaking to those who know the law—that the law is binding on a person only as long as he lives? For a married woman is bound by law to her husband while he lives, but if her husband dies, she is released from the law of marriage. Accordingly, she will be called an adulteress if she lives with another man while her husband is alive. But if her husband dies, she is free from that law, and if she marries another man she is not an adulteress. Likewise, my brothers, you also have died to the law through the body of Christ, so that you may belong to another, to him who has been raised from the dead, in order that we may bear fruit for God. For while we were living in the flesh, our sinful passions, aroused by the law, were at work in our members to bear fruit for death. But now we are released from the law, having died to that which held us captive, so that we serve in the new way of the Spirit and not in the old way of the written code. (Rom 7:1–6)

Paul here returns to the theme of justification through participation in Christ's death which he raised in Romans 6:7. There he referred to the topic in concluding a passage that spoke of the church's death with her Saviour—a passage with clear exodus overtones. The death of the last Adam (for that is what Romans 5:12–21 has explained was necessary to undo the work of the first Adam), must speak of a paschal sacrifice which atones and brings liberation. At the original Passover, Yahweh took Israel to be his bride, and so it is natural that the theme of the eschatological divine marriage should be explained further in this context, for the community had belonged to another.

The 'legitimate' claims of the former husband can now be answered, for death ends all former covenant relationships, freeing a widow to marry another if she wished without violating the law or being called an adulteress.

Paul shows how God justifies his people from every possible charge that can be made against her. In the death of Jesus, a work of deliverance far more wonderful than most appreciate has been achieved. It has answered all, ended all previous relationships, and brought an end to all charges against her so that Christ can present his bride faultless to himself (Eph 5:25–27). In this way, the people of God are a justified community. This truth is especially powerful for people and communities who have entered into relationships with Satan and his dominions. In believing, they are not only freed, but they are also completely free from any pact that they had made. It is also a truth that is equally relevant to all who long to be right with God but have not seen how radical and complete his salvation is. To use Wesley's words, 'my chains fell off, my heart was free, I arose went forth and followed Thee!'

Romans 8:1–4

There is therefore now no condemnation for those who are in Christ Jesus. For the law of the Spirit of life has set you free in Christ Jesus from the law of sin and death. For God has done what the law, weakened by the flesh, could not do. By sending his own Son in the likeness of sinful flesh and for sin, he condemned sin in the flesh, in order that the righteous requirement of the law might be fulfilled in us, who walk not according to the flesh but according to the Spirit. (Rom 8:1–4)

Paul concludes his explanation of the role of the law in chapter 7 and the opening verses of chapter 8 assert that condemnation has come to an end. The judgment is ended because the law has been satisfied; the new relationship is legitimate and atonement for sin made, since the Son of God has been offered as the eschatological paschal (sin) offering (Rom 8:3). Sin's domination over man has ended, and the righteous requirements of the law have been met. No condemnation means that God's people are justified. They have a new relationship with God that centres on the death of his Son.

Romans 8:28–39

And we know that for those who love God all things work together for good, for those who are called according to his purpose. For those whom he foreknew he also predestined to be conformed to the image of his Son, in order that he might be the firstborn among many brothers. And those whom he predestined he also called, and those whom he called he also justified, and those whom he justified he also glorified. What then shall we say to these things? If God is for us, who can be against us? He who did not spare his own Son but gave him up for us all, how will he not also with him graciously give us all things? Who shall bring any charge against God's elect? It is God who justifies. Who is to

> condemn? Christ Jesus is the one who died—more than that, who
> was raised—who is at the right hand of God, who indeed is
> interceding for us. Who shall separate us from the love of Christ?
> Shall tribulation, or distress, or persecution, or famine, or
> nakedness, or danger, or sword? As it is written, "For your sake
> we are being killed all the day long; we are regarded as sheep to
> be slaughtered." No, in all these things we are more than
> conquerors through him who loved us. For I am sure that neither
> death nor life, nor angels nor rulers, nor things present nor things
> to come, nor powers, nor height nor depth, nor anything else in all
> creation, will be able to separate us from the love of God in Christ
> Jesus our Lord. (Rom 8:28–39)

This passage throbs with allusions to the New Exodus and the pilgrimage that
brought Israel to her inheritance. Inaugurated through the death of the
firstborn, this eschatological fulfilment centres on one specific firstborn who
has many brothers. His death brought justification to the people whom he had
called and who are destined to be glorified. These themes echo the story of
Israel but are now filled with greater significance as the story is brought to a
conclusion that the Old Testament writers could never have expected.

The final chapter of this story of redemption centres on the Father's
gracious giving of his Son to death, echoing the story of Abraham's offering
of Isaac, as well as that of the Passover where the firstborn sons of Israel were
protected by a substitutionary sacrifice, the paschal lamb. The scale and
significance of this final sacrifice is so vast that there is no possibility of the
community ever again being separated from God's love. She will be brought
safely to her inheritance, for justification carries the note of an inevitable
triumph for the bridal community; she will never be separated from the love
of her redeemer-husband.

Romans 9:30–33

> What shall we say, then? That gentiles who did not pursue
> righteousness have attained it, that is, a righteousness that is by
> faith; but that Israel who pursued a law that would lead to
> righteousness did not succeed in reaching that law. Why? Because
> they did not pursue it by faith, but as if it were based on works.
> They have stumbled over the stumbling stone, as it is written,
> (Rom 9:30–33)

Paul makes the incredible claim that the gentiles have come into the covenant
(attained righteousness) without works. This would not be quite as
devastating a claim but for the fact that Paul also says that Israel is excluded

from that covenant—despite her claims that her works of righteousness, through the law, entitle her to a place in God's covenant community. Such an analysis of the condition of Israel makes it clear that she did in some way rely on the works of the law for acceptance, and so the claims of full-blooded covenant nomism cannot be upheld. In recognizing this, we have to disagree with Wright's doctrine of justification.

Romans 10:1–4

> Brothers, my heart's desire and prayers to God for them is that
> they may be saved. For I bear them witness that they have a zeal
> for God, but not according to knowledge. For, being ignorant of
> the righteousness of God, and seeking to establish their own, they
> did not submit to God's righteousness. For Christ is the end of the
> law for righteousness to everyone who believes. (Rom 10:1–4)

It is surprising, having placed so much stress on the fall of Jerusalem for interpreting Jesus in the Gospels, that Wright follows most scholars in understanding this statement to show Paul's concern for the salvation of individual Jews. I have no doubt that Paul had exactly such a concern, but is that what he is writing about here in chapter 10?

I would suggest that the chapter is not about individual Jews, but about Israel losing her special status as the people called to represent Yahweh and in her place the church was called, the community of believing Jews and gentiles.[401] The Jews who became part of the church were those who had turned from any attempt to buy favour through keeping the law and had relied on the same grace that the gentile church had been brought into. Whatever the passage says about the Jewish-gentile relationships in the church, it is abundantly clear that Israel, by persisting in a law-based righteousness, had missed the very blessings she considered herself to be endowed with. Submitting to God's righteousness is clearly the act of being justified. Again, we find that this intertextual interpretation conflicts with Wright's interpretation of justification.

---

[401] For a full exposition of the passage see Holland, *Romans. The Divine Marriage*, 297–336.

Chapter 12:
Probing Justification in the Remainder of Paul's Letters

1 Corinthians

> And because of him you are in Christ Jesus, who became to us
> wisdom from God, righteousness and sanctification and
> redemption (1 Cor 1:30)

It has been thought that when Paul speaks of justification in this passage, he is
referring to God's imputation of Christ's righteousness to sinners. Wright has
challenged this by saying that if such is the case then Christ's wisdom,
redemption, and sanctification would also have to be imputed to his people—
and since this is unlikely to be Paul's meaning, then the idea of the imputation
of righteousness must also be wrong.

However, it should be noted that immediately after this statement (1 Cor
1:31) Paul quotes from Jeremiah 9:24 'let the one who boasts, boast in the
Lord.' This statement is part of Jeremiah's encouragement of those in exile
that Yahweh would fulfil his promises and redeem Israel from exile. Indeed, it
is Israel's exiled condition that 1 Corinthians 1:30 depends on, for Israel was
polluted, needing to be sanctified; was guilty, needing to be justified; in exile,
needing redemption; and in darkness, so needing understanding and wisdom.

As Wright acknowledges elsewhere, Israel's condition was a type of the
condition of all humankind; her exile in Babylon represents the exile of
humanity from God in the kingdom of darkness. What Israel needed to
complete her experience of salvation, the Corinthian believers had needed
before responding to the gospel. They have experienced the promised
salvation, fulfilled in a far more glorious way than the prophets could ever
have predicted, for it has all happened in Christ. He has become all of these
needed things for his people and because of this he has become their wisdom,
righteousness, justification, and redemption.

Paul has not used imputation language in this statement but guided by the
Old Testament type (cf. 1 Cor 5:7; 10:1–10, 12–14; 15:3), it would suggest
that the understanding of the Reformers was not far off Paul's intended

meaning. Indeed, if we explore further, we see that it is the servant who fulfils God's purpose regarding 'righteousness, justification, and redemption'. The servant's great work was to die for his people so that he could justify many (Isa 53:11). If this connection with Paul's thought is valid, and I believe that it is, then we will find the Reformed understanding of Christ as our justification lurking very near the surface of this Corinthian passage.

It is the failure to follow this Old Testament understanding that has led Wright to his mistaken conclusions. Like the way that the 'body, soul, and spirit' reference of 1 Thessalonians 5:23 was seen by earlier generations to speak of humanity's tri-partite nature, so Wright has treated the terms 'wisdom, righteousness, sanctification, and redemption' as separate acts or events. However, we have found that the way that the prophets use these terms shows that they are all aspects of the one saving act of Yahweh: his deliverance of his people from exile in Babylon. In other words, they are about the promised Second Exodus. In forgetting this, Wright has treated the terms independently of one another and given a faulty exegesis as a result of neglecting Paul's Hebraic mind and its Semitic framework. The reading I am proposing endorses the understanding of the Reformers as being essentially correct.

However, can the proposed exegesis be further supported to enhance the probability that it is Paul's intended meaning? I believe that it can, and the support comes from the flow of the arguments that proceed out of the statements.

In chapter two Paul describes his ministry as being that of a servant; it lacks all those qualities of assertiveness, self-confidence and self-promotion that might have impressed the unbelieving Corinthians. These qualities are the very opposite of those found in a true servant of the Lord whose task is to proclaim the year of the Lord's favour. Paul says in chapter 2:

> And I, when I came to you, brothers, did not come proclaiming to you the testimony of God with lofty speech or wisdom. For I decided to know nothing among you except Jesus Christ and him crucified. And I was with you in weakness and in fear and much trembling, and my speech and my message were not in plausible words of wisdom, but in demonstration of the Spirit and of power, so that your faith might not rest in the wisdom of men but in the power of God. (1 Cor 2:1–5)

Here we find Paul developing his theme about the wisdom of God which leads people to salvation. In this sense wisdom is attributed to those who believe because it is this same wisdom that has brought them the understanding that has led to faith. Without this impartation of wisdom there could be no salvation. Paul goes on to make clear that the wisdom he speaks about is not that of this world; it is the wisdom of God that relates to God's saving activity. He says:

> Yet among the mature we do impart wisdom, although it is not a wisdom of this age or of the rulers of this age, who are doomed to pass away. But we impart a secret and hidden wisdom of God, which God decreed before the ages for our glory. None of the rulers of this age understood this, for if they had, they would not have crucified the Lord of glory. But, as it is written, "What no eye has seen, nor ear heard, nor the heart of man imagined, what God has prepared for those who love him" (1 Cor 2:8–9)

Paul goes on to speak of this wisdom further, explaining its utter disparity with the kind of wisdom which the world values. He says:

> Let no one deceive himself. If anyone among you thinks that he is wise in this age, let him become a fool that he may become wise. For the wisdom of this world is folly with God. For it is written, "He catches the wise in their craftiness," and again, "The Lord knows the thoughts of the wise, that they are futile." So let no one boast in men. For all things are yours, whether Paul or Apollos or Cephas or the world or life or death or the present or the future— all are yours, and you are Christ's, and Christ is God's. (1 Cor 3:18–23)

By comparing the differences between the world's wisdom and that of God, Paul explains that while the former promotes in the eyes of men and gives them worldly advantages, the latter is despised by men. Nevertheless, for those who have received it, to whom it has been imparted or imputed, it transforms them, and they become true servants of God. Paul says:

> Already you have all you want! Already you have become rich! Without us you have become kings! And would that you did reign, so that we might share the rule with you! For I think that God has exhibited us apostles as last of all, like men sentenced to death, because we have become a spectacle to the world, to angels, and to men. We are fools for Christ's sake, but you are wise in Christ. We are weak, but you are strong. You are held in honour, but we in disrepute. To the present hour we hunger and thirst, we are poorly dressed and buffeted and homeless, and we labour, working with our own hands. When reviled, we bless; when persecuted, we endure; when slandered, we entreat. We have become, and are still, like the scum of the world, the refuse

of all things. (1 Cor 4:8–13)

The wisdom of the world leads to haughtiness and a disregard for the life that God calls his people to live. When they defended the incestuous relationship of one of their number, Paul has to remind the Corinthians where their lives are rooted—in the redemptive activity of their Saviour. Paul again says:

> Your boasting is not good. Do you not know that a little leaven leavens the whole lump? Cleanse out the old leaven that you may be a new lump, as you really are unleavened. For Christ, our Passover lamb, has been sacrificed. Let us therefore celebrate the festival, not with the old leaven, the leaven of malice and evil, but with the unleavened bread of sincerity and truth. (1 Cor 5:6–8)

Thus, a pure life, even as professing Christians, has been abandoned by their support of the incestuous brother. It is because of this sinfulness that the salvation that Christ has brought to his people has to be again embraced. Paul uses typology to draw out the significance of the leaven in the Passover. They are to get rid of the leaven of sin, because Christ their Passover sacrifice has died for them. If they do not do this, as Paul goes on to warn them (1 Cor 10:1–10) they could come under God's judgment as Israel did.

The One Act of Justification in 1 Corinthians 6:11

Paul makes the necessity of this purity absolutely clear when he says:

> Or do you not know that the unrighteous will not inherit the kingdom of God? Do not be deceived: neither the sexually immoral, nor idolaters, nor adulterers, nor men who practice homosexuality, nor thieves, nor the greedy, nor drunkards, nor revilers, nor swindlers will inherit the kingdom of God. And such were some of you. But you were washed, you were sanctified, you were justified in the name of the Lord Jesus Christ and by the Spirit of our God. (1 Cor 6:9–11)

This statement (which Wright completely misses out in his discussion on justification, saying that the only reference to justification in 1 Corinthians is found in 1:30) must be read in its wider context. 1 Corinthians 5:7 Paul has said that Christ our Passover has been sacrificed for us. This exodus setting controls the ongoing theological narrative that Paul follows in the letter.[402] When the Greek is examined it becomes clear that justification of members of

---

[402] For justification of this claim see Holland, *Squaring the Circle*, forthcoming.

the community is spoken of; Paul is speaking of a single event when they were all washed, justified, and sanctified. Such corporate language linked with a single event is the backbone of all that Paul says in Romans 5 and 6. Not only does this statement link in with his statement in the first letter (1 Cor 1:30) but Paul will speak about the Jewish nation's baptism into Moses which is a type of the church's baptism into Christ (1 Cor 10:1–7). This was a single event when the entire church came into existence just like the Jewish nation did in its exodus from Egypt. Thus, again we find exodus imagery controlling the meaning of this otherwise difficult to interpret statement.

Paul is saying that they, as a church, are part of a much greater community that was united with Christ in his death. They and all other believers of the oecumenical[403] church, the church of all generations and all nations were washed, justified (ἐδικαιώθητε—the verb δικαιόω in the indicative aorist passive second person plural), and sanctified. This was done even before they heard the gospel which they have since responded to. Indeed, this justification took place even before there was a church in Corinth, for it took place in the very death and resurrection of Jesus when he experienced his exodus (Luke 9:31 the word translated 'departure' carries the same meaning as 'exodus' in Greek) and his people were united with him by the work of the Spirit who brought them out of darkness, defilement, and death. This understanding of justified and sanctified confirms our reading of 1 Corinthians 1:30 considered earlier to be correct.

2 Corinthians

There is yet another Pauline text that challenges Wright's claim for the New Perspective understanding of justification. Paul writes:

> Now if the ministry of death, carved in letters on stone, came with such glory that the Israelites could not gaze at Moses' face because of its glory, which was being brought to an end, will not the ministry of the Spirit have even more glory? For if there was glory in the ministry of condemnation, the ministry of righteousness must far exceed it in glory. Indeed, in this case, what once had glory has come to have no glory at all, because of

---

[403] A term meaning much more than ecumenical for it includes believer of all generations, past, present and future. It speaks therefore of the creation of the universal community in Christ in his death. All believers, no matter what time in history they were born, were present in this event, as all had been present in Adam's act of disobedience.

the glory that surpasses it. For if what was being brought to an end came with glory, much more will what is permanent have glory. (2 Cor 3:7–11)

The passage closely mirrors the argument Paul has made in Romans 5:15–21 where the role of Adam, whose disobedience brought judgment and death, is compared to the role of Christ, whose obedience brought righteousness and life. This term is abbreviated by Paul to 'made righteous' in Romans 5:19. The terms are interchanged with the expressions 'ministry of condemnation' and 'ministry of righteousness'. By observing this parallel, we see that justification is the event that puts right the disobedience of Adam.

The New Perspective model cannot possibly accommodate this statement. Paul describes the actual giving of the law as a 'ministry of death', which brings 'condemnation.' This clearly creates a problem for Philippians 3:3–6, which suggests that Paul was once a contented member of the covenant community, living under a non-threatening law (Phil 3:6). I will deal with this tension later, but here in 2 Corinthians 3:7–11, Paul says that this law, since its appearing, has condemned Israel to death! Again, as with Acts 13:38–41 and Acts 15:7–11 (noted above), Wright makes no mention of this vital 2 Corinthians 3 passage in his justification arguments in *Paul and the Faithfulness of God*, he uses it only to support his Christology.[404] Its significance is a serious challenge to his claim that Paul's attitude to the law can be explained regarding covenantal nomism—and yet this important text is not even mentioned.

Wright further challenges the Reformed reading that Paul's words convey the idea of being imputed with the righteousness of God in his treatment of 2 Corinthians 5:21, which he recognizes as a text that, as the Reformers understood its meaning, challenges his view. To deconstruct the Reformed teaching, Wright points out that Paul has been describing his ministry as a servant of the new covenant. Hence, becoming the 'righteousness' of God is not, Wright contends, about imputation of righteousness, but about the role of one who is appointed to bring righteousness to the peoples of the earth.

Although I agree that the theme of the servant is fundamental to this passage, this does not mean that we can use it to control the key statements which Paul makes along the way. Paul has stated in the preceding verse that 'in Christ God was reconciling the world to himself, not counting their trespasses against them, and entrusting to us the message of reconciliation' (2

---

[404] Wright, *Faithfulness of God*, 726.

Cor 5:19). These two verses should not be separated, for together they explain what becoming the righteousness of God means. It is about 'not counting their trespasses against them'. The imperfect tense reflects events in the past. This reconciliation took place during a past event, which is clearly the death of Christ, as Romans 5:19 and 2 Corinthians 5:21 make clear.

The servant of the Lord theme is certainly present, as Wright has noted, but it is not about spiritual, social, nor political reform as he suggests. The servant is called to proclaim the way in which God has made it possible for the sentence of death—which the law placed on humanity (2 Cor 3:6–7)—to be removed. Paul explains that the crucial event for removing that judgment was the death of Christ and says:

> . . in Christ God was reconciling the world to himself, not counting their trespasses against them, and entrusting to us the message of reconciliation. Therefore, we are ambassadors for Christ, God making his appeal through us. We implore you on behalf of Christ, be reconciled to God. For our sake he made him to be sin who knew no sin, so that in him we might become the righteousness of God. (2 Cor 5:19–21)

It is more natural to read the statement 'become the righteousness of God' in the light of the sin-judged condition that Paul has been speaking about (2 Cor 3:7–11)—with Christ being made sin (that is, a sin-offering) for his people. This is a better reading than what Wright proposes in which ministry of the servant refers to Paul's apostolic ministry embodying God's faithfulness to the covenant.[405]

Indeed, Paul can only see himself as fulfilling such a role because he is proclaiming the message of the crucified Christ (2 Cor 5:19). It is his death that has somehow paid the penalty of sin or better, dealt with the issue of sin, for paying the penalty is only one part of Christ's achievement. To remove the message of the crucified Messiah dying for his people from Paul's argument is to do violence to the text. The passage is not at all about how sin has damaged humanity and creation (although, of course, Paul does deal with these themes elsewhere), but about man's condemnation as a result of rejecting his God and breaking the covenant (2 Cor 3:7–11). This has brought humankind into a relationship with sin and Satan that it was never made for,

---

[405] See Wright, *Faithfulness of God*, 881–884.

and which can only be annulled by the acceptance of what God has done through Christ.

This line of interpretation is supported by the Colossian hymn to which Wright has given close attention.[406] He has rightly identified that the letter is a genuinely Pauline letter and that the introduction to the hymn (Col 1:13–14) makes use of the New Exodus theme. However, in failing to recognize that the hymn, not just the introduction as he acknowledges, reflects on the paschal content of the exodus, he misses some keys in the text. Paul says:

> He has delivered us from the domain of darkness and transferred us to the Kingdom of his beloved Son, in whom we have redemption, the forgiveness of sins. He is the image of the invisible God, the firstborn of all creation. For by him all things were created, in heaven and on earth, visible and invisible, whether thrones or dominions or rulers or authorities—all things were created through him and for him. And he is before all things, and in him all things hold together. And he is the head of the body, the church. He is the beginning, the firstborn from the dead, that in everything he might be preeminent. For in him all the fullness of God was pleased to dwell, and through him to reconcile to himself all things, whether on earth or in heaven, making peace by the blood of his cross. (Col 1:13–20)

While recognizing the New Exodus introduction, Wright misses how it controls the reading of the hymn, mainly because of his understanding that Jewish Hellenism is the key to the hymn.[407] Wright holds to an ontological content in which Christ, as the Wisdom of God, is praised. However, I would argue that Paul's focus is not on Wisdom but Christ as the firstborn of all creation, the one whose death has brought about the reconciliation of all things. The Messiah is never linked with pre-incarnate Wisdom in any Jewish literature.[408]

Moreover, the conclusion of the hymn is most significant, for it says that the reconciliation of the whole of creation was achieved through Christ's making 'peace by the blood of his cross' (Col 1:20). It is, of course, the gospel of reconciliation that brings this state about, the preaching of the achievements of the death of Christ to a lost world. Because Christ by his paschal death has reconciled the whole of creation, he is rightly worshiped as

---

[406] Wright, *Climax of the Covenant*, 99–119.

[407] Ibid, 109–110.

[408] W. D. Davies, *Paul and Rabbinic Judaism,* 155.

the firstborn of all creation (Heb 1:1–6; Rev 1:5–6); that is to say, as its redeemer as well as its Creator.

Here in this crucial hymn, Paul makes it clear that reconciliation is not something he achieves by his service as a servant; his message concerns what Christ's blood, shed on the cross, has achieved. This is how 2 Corinthians 5:21 must be read. Indeed, these two passages (2 Cor 3–5 and Col 1:15–20) are thematically linked; both deal with the new creation and how it has been brought into existence. Hence, since the texts are clearly complementary, examining them together should clarify our understanding.

I would claim that these passages provide clear evidence that the New Perspective view of the function of the law, upon which Wright has built his understanding of justification, should be revisited. I am not saying that there is no merit in any New Perspective understanding, but that the work is far from complete and that in its current form it lacks credibility when attacking the Reformers' understanding. Evaluations of Sanders' claims have identified that works-based righteousness does exist in the intertestamental literature. Furthermore, the New Testament texts considered above have as much right to stand as evidence of how intertestamental Judaism understood justification as any DSS text has, and together they show Wright's understanding to be seriously flawed.

Ephesians

> Blessed be the God and Father of our Lord Jesus Christ, who has blessed us in Christ with every spiritual blessing in the heavenly places, even as he chose us in him before the foundation of the world, that we should be holy and blameless before him. In love he predestined us for adoption as sons through Jesus Christ, according to the purpose of his will, to the praise of his glorious grace, with which he has blessed us in the Beloved. In him we have redemption through his blood, the forgiveness of our trespasses, according to the riches of his grace, which he lavished upon us, in all wisdom and insight making known to us the mystery of his will, according to his purpose, which he set forth in Christ as a plan for the fullness of time, to unite all things in him, things in heaven and things on earth. (Eph 1:3–10)

The passage echoes the story of Israel who had been blessed with all of God's blessings.[409] Paul has taken a widely-recited confession of the Jewish community and adapted it to Christian worship by centring it on Christ and his work.[410] The themes of election, purification (sanctification), adoption, sacrifice, and forgiveness are all mentioned. Paul refers to 'us' who have been blessed, intentionally referring to both Jews and gentiles[411] as equal members of the new covenant community which had been promised not only by the prophets but also in the writings of the Pentateuch.

This entrance into a covenant relationship with Christ was possible only because of the redemption that has been secured through Christ's blood (death). As we have seen in Romans 3:21–26, justification has as its natural home the language that Paul uses concerning the death of Jesus.[412]

The prophets had predicted the transformation of the status of the gentiles which now has been marvellously fulfilled. This is what the display of the 'mystery of his will' means, for God had always desired the blessing of the gentiles as well as the Jews. This amazing transformation of status is what the Old Testament refers to when it speaks of the nations being brought into the Abrahamic covenant as equal partners with the Jews, just as Yahweh made clear when he made the covenant with Abraham and his descendants (Gen 12:3). Thus, the scriptural idea of justification is much bigger than that of an individual being made right with God; it speaks of a community prepared by

---

[409] See R. M. Cozart, *This Present Triumph* (Oregon: Wipf, 2013) who argues that the letter is heavily influenced by the theme of Isaiah's Second Exodus theology.

[410] P. O'Brien, *The Letter to the Ephesians* (Leicester: Apollos, 1999), 89.

[411] Indicated by the fact that Paul speaks of God who has blessed 'us' which is intended to emphasise Gentile inclusion, something missed by most exegetes, so O'Brien, *Ephesians,* 91; C. Mitton, *The Epistle to the Ephesians: Its Authorship, Origin, and Purpose* (Oxford: Clarendon, 1951), 46; Muddiman, *Ephesians, 63*; A. Lincoln, *Ephesians* (Dallas: Word Books, 1990), 88 rejects the writers intention was for the term to be inclusive of Jews and gentiles while Cozart, *This Present Triumph,* 118 affirms this understanding. Elsewhere Paul makes it clear that he is speaking of Jewish privileges or priority, so in Eph 1:12–13 which Lincoln reluctantly acknowledges.

[412] Lincoln, *Ephesians,* 28 says that 'Forgiveness is implicit in two of Paul's major themes, justification and reconciliation'. From this we may say that justification is implicit in two of Paul's major themes, forgiveness and reconciliation.

God be the true children of Abraham. It was this state of acceptance that God, through Christ, had brought the gentiles to experience.

> In him we have obtained an inheritance, having been predestined according to the purpose of him who works all things according to the counsel of his will, so that we who were the first to hope in Christ might be to the praise of his glory. In him you also, when you heard the word of truth, the gospel of your salvation, and believed in him, were sealed with the promised Holy Spirit, who is the guarantee of our inheritance until we acquire possession of it, to the praise of his glory. (Eph 1:11–14)

Paul's use of 'we' in v. 12 is to identify the believing Jewish community, who were first to believe in Christ; the gentile believing community came into existence through Jewish evangelism.[413] The church's inheritance is not based on its becoming part of Israel, fulfilling her demands so that they could be considered for acceptance. Rather, it is based on the relationship with the divine king himself who welcomes all believers, gentiles included.

The sealing with the Holy Spirit is not a future promise but a past action that God has fulfilled. It refers to the gift of the Spirit poured out on every believing community as they welcome the gospel and become part of the universal church of Christ. It was, and still is, the inheritance of every community that welcomes Christ as its Saviour. It is the Spirit (according to Ezekiel 37) who has given the elect, despite their disobedience and separation, life and power to return to God and receive their inheritance. The term 'sealed' was regularly used to speak of the engagement ring and here it is used to describe the betrothal of the community to her Redeemer-Messiah. The imagery is thoroughly corporate—it is the church, not the individual believer who is the bride (Eph 5:25)—but as Paul has demonstrated in Ephesians 5:1–21, the relationship has to be personally embraced and lived out.

The passage echoes Israel's experience of being brought out of the death of exile into a renewed covenant with her God.[414] In the fulfilment of this

---

[413] So Mitton, *Ephesians*, 57; Muddiman, *Ephesians*, 77. It could refer to the Jewish nation, so Lincoln and Cozart, but it is hardly right to say that they believed in Christ, it was applicable only to Jewish believers. Lincoln, *Ephesians*, 37, claims it refers to the entire Christian community, but it is hard to see how the whole community could have been the first to have trusted in Christ.

[414] So Cozart, *Present Triumph*, 118.

promise, God includes the gentiles, allowing them to share in the same justification that the prophets had announced for those Jews who obeyed and returned, not only from Babylon but from spiritual exile.

> And you were dead in the trespasses and sins in which you once walked, following the course of this world, following the prince of the power of the air the spirit that is now at work in the sons of disobedience— among whom we all once lived in the passions of our flesh, carrying out the desires of the body and the mind, and were by nature children of wrath, like the rest of mankind. But God, being rich in mercy, because of the great love with which he loved us, even when we were dead in our trespasses, made us alive together with Christ—by grace you have been saved— and raised us up with him and seated us with him in the heavenly places in Christ Jesus, so that in the coming ages he might show the immeasurable riches of his grace in kindness toward us in Christ Jesus. For by grace you have been saved through faith. And this is not your own doing; it is the gift of God, not a result of works, so that no one may boast. For we are his workmanship, created in Christ Jesus for good works, which God prepared beforehand, that we should walk in them. (Eph 2:1–10)

The description Paul gives of the human condition is reminiscent of Israel's condition in exile because of her disobedience to God.[415] Living according to the passions of the flesh was not a uniquely gentile sin, the Jews had also shared in this rebellious behaviour as 1 Corinthians 10:1–10 makes clear. Ezekiel 20 presents God's indictment against Israel, his covenant people, for she had turned from the true God and followed the behaviour of the Egyptians. Israel's sin meant that unless God acted to forgive and deliver her to bring her into a new covenant, she would be eternally separated from him. In other words, God had to justify her, and this is what he has done for the new covenant community.

> Therefore, remember that at one time you gentiles in the flesh, called "the uncircumcision" by what is called the circumcision, which is made in the flesh by hands—remember that you were at that time separated from Christ, alienated from the commonwealth

---

[415] Most focus on the believer's death with Christ when discussing this passage, so Muddiman, *Ephesians*, 102; Mitton, *Ephesians*, 81; O'Brien, *Ephesians*, 156. But this misses the point that the description is of their condition before they were united with Christ when they died to sin rather than when they lived in it. Babylon was called the land of sin and so to live in sin was to live in exile.

of Israel and strangers to the covenants of promise, having no
hope and without God in the world. But now in Christ Jesus you
who once were far off have been brought near by the blood of
Christ. For he himself is our peace, who has made us both one and
has broken down in his flesh the dividing wall of hostility by
abolishing the law of commandments expressed in ordinances,
that he might create in himself one new man in place of the two,
so making peace, and might reconcile us both to God in one body
through the cross, thereby killing the hostility. (Eph 2:11–16)

Paul explains that the promises made concerning the acceptance of the
gentiles, which was an aspect of the Second Exodus promises, have been
fulfilled. But the manner of their fulfilment is nothing like what even the most
devout Jew might have anticipated. The gentiles, even though still
uncircumcised, now share the same inheritance that the descendants of
Abraham were promised. This has not happened by God abandoning his
people nor by his being unfaithful to his character; God has remained true to
himself and to his promises, ending all hostility through the death of his Son.
Through his shed blood (his sacrificial death), he has brought peace and
reconciliation between humanity and God, and between Jew and gentile. In
Christ, the believing community has been accepted, is justified, and is the
'new man' made up of believing Jews and believing gentiles. The
terminology and the ideas that Paul employs here are thoroughly Old
Testament and speak of the eschatological fulfilment of all that was promised
to Abraham.

Of this gospel I was made a minister according to the gift of
God's grace, which was given me by the working of his power.
To me, though I am the very least of all the saints, this grace was
given, to preach to the gentiles the unsearchable riches of Christ,
and to bring to light for everyone what is the plan of the mystery
hidden for ages in God who created all things, so that through the
church the manifold wisdom of God might now be made known to
the rulers and authorities in the heavenly places. This was
according to the eternal purpose that he has realized in Christ
Jesus our Lord, in whom we have boldness and access with
confidence through our faith in him. So I ask you not to lose heart
over what I am suffering for you, which is your glory. (Eph 3:7–
13)

Paul understands his calling to be a servant of Christ, and this calling
defines his mission. In chapter 4 we saw that Paul never viewed himself as a
slave but as a servant figure as found throughout the Old Testament. His
calling was to bring the light of the knowledge of God to the nations so that

they could believe and be blessed by sharing in the unsearchable riches of Christ. The church's calling is not primarily about her blessing but about her service to God of bearing witness to all who are in darkness so that they too might believe.

The unsearchable riches of Christ and the manifold wisdom of God are part of the mystery that Paul had spoken of earlier. They refer to the bringing into the new covenant believing gentiles, whom the Jews had supposed were excluded from the covenants of promise despite Scripture affirming otherwise. Yahweh had always intended that the nations should participate in the grace that he showed to Israel.

> Take no part in the unfruitful works of darkness, but instead expose them. For it is shameful even to speak of the things that they do in secret. But when anything is exposed by the light, it becomes visible, for anything that becomes visible is light. Therefore it says, "Awake, O sleeper, and arise from the dead, and Christ will shine on you." Look carefully then how you walk, not as unwise but as wise, making the best use of the time, because the days are evil. Therefore do not be foolish, but understand what the will of the Lord is. And do not get drunk with wine, for that is debauchery, but be filled with the Spirit, addressing one another in psalms and hymns and spiritual songs, singing and making melody to the Lord with your heart, giving thanks always and for everything to God the Father in the name of our Lord Jesus Christ, submitting to one another out of reverence for Christ. Wives, submit to your own husbands, as to the Lord. For the husband is the head of the wife even as Christ is the head of the church, his body, and is himself its Saviour. Now as the church submits to Christ, so also wives should submit in everything to their husbands. Husbands, love your wives, as Christ loved the church and gave himself up for her, that he might sanctify her, having cleansed her by the washing of water with the word, so that he might present the church to himself in splendour, without spot or wrinkle or any such thing, that she might be holy and without blemish. In the same way husbands should love their wives as their own bodies. He who loves his wife loves himself. For no one ever hated his own flesh, but nourishes and cherishes it, just as Christ does the church, because we are members of his body. "Therefore a man shall leave his father and mother and hold fast to his wife, and the two shall become one flesh." This mystery is profound, and I am saying that it refers to Christ and the church. However, let each one of you love his wife as himself, and let the wife see that she respects her husband. (Eph 5:11–33)

The admonition that the church should abstain from the behaviour of an ungodly world is eventually linked to her calling as the bride of Christ. Such behaviour is, therefore, unworthy of her, and would bring shame to him who had given his life for her.

The use of the Isaiah 52:1 text is not casual but is intended to be a key to the ongoing typology that Paul has employed throughout the letter in which the church's experience is shown to be a typological fulfilment of the experience of Israel.[416] As Israel had been in exile and was urged to wake up from death and receive illumination, so Paul urges the Ephesian church not to be a victim of disobedience that leads to judgment. The members of the church had been dead in sin, but now they were alive in Christ (Eph 2:1–10), and so were to live in the light of the illumination they had been given, see also Isaiah 9:2.

The theme is drawing heavily on the example of Israel's unfaithfulness and the warning it provides for the new covenant bride. The reference to Christ making his church clean by his sacrificial death is linked by many scholars to the description of Yahweh washing Israel in the exodus (Ezek 16:9–11). Another exodus has taken place; the Passover victim has been slain, and the redeemed community has become the Lord's bride (Eph 5:25–27). Once again, justification is embedded in the narrative (see Rom 3:21–26) for all the themes in the passage—election, washing, innocence, and being presented as perfect—are part of the broader justification theme; and as we noted when we looked at Romans 5, the justification is corporate, it is something God has done for his people.

> Finally, be strong in the Lord and in the strength of his might. Put on the whole armour of God, that you may be able to stand against the schemes of the devil. For we do not wrestle against flesh and blood, but against the rulers, against the authorities, against the cosmic powers over this present darkness, against the spiritual forces of evil in the heavenly places. Therefore take up the whole armour of God, that you may be able to withstand in the evil day, and having done all, to stand firm. Stand therefore, having fastened on the belt of truth, and having put on the breastplate of righteousness, and, as shoes for your feet, having put on the readiness given by the gospel of peace. In all circumstances take up the shield of faith, with which you can extinguish all the flaming darts of the evil one; and take the helmet of salvation, and the sword of the Spirit, which is the word of God, praying at all

---

[416] O'Brien, *Ephesians*, 375.

times in the Spirit, with all prayer and supplication. (Eph 6:10–18)

The deliverance of the remnant of Israel from Babylon was their justification; it came about entirely as an act of God as he fulfilled his promise to his people. However, before the finalizing of this great salvation, when she will be presented before the father as his son's bride, she must engage the foes of darkness that will do their best to thwart the divine plan, as they had done with Israel. To protect her, Yahweh has provided his own armour for the church. This same armour had been offered to Israel in her exodus from Babylon, and it had brought the infant community safely through the desert until she came to her inheritance in Zion.

The mention of the armour of the Lord alludes back to Isaiah 49:2; 59:17 and again confirms that the text should be read against Israel's pilgrimage from captivity.[417] This links back to the exhortation of Ephesians 5:14 where Isaiah 52:1 was utilized in the appeal for the church to live soberly. This in turn brings all the great themes of Israel's exodus into the text Paul writes and amongst these themes is the promise that Israel was justified through her deliverance (see 1 Cor 6:10–11). It is because of this justification that the church will be presented without spot or blemish before the Father.

Philippians

Do all things without grumbling or disputing, that you may be blameless and innocent, children of God without blemish in the midst of a crooked and twisted generation, among whom you shine as lights in the world, holding fast to the word of life, so that in the day of Christ I may be proud that I did not run in vain or labour in vain. Even if I am to be poured out as a drink offering upon the sacrificial offering of your faith, I am glad and rejoice with you all. Likewise you also should be glad and rejoice with me. (Phil 2:14–18)

The appeal to the Philippians to be blameless is in a passage where Second Exodus imagery is used. It is generally agreed that the passage reflects Deuteronomy 32:5 where Moses urges the covenant community to live out its

---

[417] O'Brien, *Ephesians*, 457; Muddiman, *Ephesians*, 287; Cozart, *Present*, 233; Lincoln, *Ephesians*, 436. The Isaianic association with the armour is missed by Mitton, *Ephesians*, 220.

calling as the representative of Yahweh.[418] Paul applies this to the Philippian Christian community who, as children of God, are to live in the midst of a crooked and twisted generation. This echoes Israel's pilgrimage which took her amongst the nations who were in darkness and to whom Israel's light was to be a gracious guide. The church, like Israel, was to bring the word of God to those who were without understanding. Their call to be blameless recalls Israel's obligation to be true to Yahweh and echoes her status of having been justified by Yahweh's act of redemption.

> Look out for the dogs, look out for the evildoers, look out for those who mutilate the flesh. For we are the circumcision, who worship by the Spirit of God and glory in Christ Jesus and put no confidence in the flesh—though I myself have reason for confidence in the flesh also. If anyone else thinks he has reason for confidence in the flesh, I have more: circumcised on the eighth day, of the people of Israel, of the tribe of Benjamin, a Hebrew of Hebrews; as to the law, a Pharisee; as to zeal, a persecutor of the church; as to righteousness under the law, blameless. But whatever gain I had, I counted as loss for the sake of Christ. Indeed, I count everything as loss because of the surpassing worth of knowing Christ Jesus my Lord. For his sake I have suffered the loss of all things and count them as rubbish, in order that I may gain Christ and be found in him, not having a righteousness of my own that comes from the law, but that which comes through faith in Christ, the righteousness from God that depends on faith— that I may know him and the power of his resurrection, and may share his sufferings, becoming like him in his death, that by any means possible I may attain the resurrection from the dead. (Phil 3:2–11)

Paul lists the credentials he once trusted in for evidence of his moral character and religious affiliation. These things were once the basis of his hope that God would accept him. However, his encounter with the risen Christ made him see that he had put his confidence in the very law that judged

---

[418] Heathcote fails to see the link between the typological fulfilment of the church's exodus through the death of her Saviour and the exodus of Israel so cannot understand why the text has been chosen. J. Collange and A. Heathcote, *The Epistle of Saint Paul to the Philippians* (London: Epworth Press, 1979), 111. See also G. Hawthorne, *Philippians* (Waco: Word Books, 1983), 103 which concerns the influence to be from the Qumran community more than the experience of Israel on her pilgrimage. Eadie, *Philippians*, 139 notes that the people of Israel murmured on their journey through the desert as does G. Fee, *Paul's Letter to the Philippians* (Grand Rapids: Eerdmans, 1995), 245.

him, and which could never save him. The most ardent attempt to keep the law could not cancel out the true condition he was in as a member of a people who had rejected the mercy of their God. They also were in the same condition as the gentiles—under God's judgment—and religious works could do nothing about that sentence.

However, this reliance had changed. Paul had come to see that Christ (the Messiah) had died (Phil 2:6–11) to bring about the promised new covenant community. He turned from all that the law represented to embrace Christ by faith, thus entering the messianic community. Clearly the contrast Paul intends to convey by these words is how he once sought to be justified (accepted) under the law but now trusts Christ for justification.

Colossians

It is widely recognised that Ephesians and Colossians share a similar theological perspective even by those who deny Pauline authorship. One of the very positive things that Wright has brought many in the scholarly theological community to accept is that there is no reason to deny these letters to be Paul's because they continue his thoughts as found in the undisputed letters. They are therefore an important part of Paul's theological heritage for the church to cherish. The letter was one of Wright's first commentaries[419] and brought to the Christian community a young man with astute theological insight and gifting. He had written this before he had completed his doctoral studies.

In the first chapter, following the normal salutations that he made to the church Paul says:

> . . . giving thanks to the Father, who has qualified you to share in the inheritance of the saints in light. He has delivered us from the domain of darkness and transferred us to the kingdom of his beloved Son, in whom we have redemption, the forgiveness of sins.

He is the image of the invisible God, the firstborn of all creation. For by him all things were created, in heaven and on earth, visible and invisible, whether thrones or dominions or rulers or authorities—all things were created through him and for him. And he is before all things, and in him all things

---

[419] N. T. Wright, *The Epistles of Paul to the Colossians and to Philemon: An Introduction and Commentary* (Leicester: Inter-Varsity, 1986).

hold together. And he is the head of the body, the church. He is the beginning, the firstborn from the dead, that in everything he might be preeminent. For in him all the fullness of God was pleased to dwell, and through him to reconcile to himself all things, whether on earth or in heaven, making peace by the blood of his cross. (Col 1:13–20)

The passage is packed with Old Testament insights. The fact that the Colossians had been incorporated into the covenant community as gentiles, by being rescued from the kingdom of darkness and being brought into the kingdom of his beloved son picks up on the many Old Testament promises concerning the blessing of the gentiles through their acceptance by Israel's God.

This salvation was not an individual affair. They had not been brought out of darkness as individuals, but as a community. This deliverance and acceptance were only possible because of the death of 'his dear Son'. Joined to him in his death by the Spirit who has baptised all believers into Christ in his dying, they have all, believing Jews and gentiles, inherited everything that the Messiah's death had achieved, and all are rightly his because of who he is from before eternity. He died as their firstborn, a term that is rooted in the Passover event when Israel's firstborn was designated to bear the sins of their respective families and in so doing protected the nation from God's judgment.

But his death was not only for the redemption of his family. In Old Testament understanding only the Creator could redeem creation. His task was not only to bring his brethren out from the kingdom of darkness but to deliver the whole of creation from the curse that man's sin had brought upon the created universe.

Because, as the Messiah, the son of David, the one who is Israel's redeemer, has been raised from the dead so he has triumphed as the appointed Davidic king and conquered all of God's enemies, including death itself (1:18). Thus, all things have been made subject to him as the all victorious Redeemer king. This incredible work of redemption included the reconciliation of all things (1:20). Thus, Christ is presented as the firstborn redeemer king of the house of David, but he achieves what no earthly king could possibly achieve, he conquers death itself and reconciles all creation to himself.

The passage is introduced with a New Exodus motif in vv. 13–14[420] and this pointed to the way the hymn was to be read. It is a celebration of the work of salvation, as many of the Jewish Psalms had done. But this work of redemption was not nationalistic as in Israel's celebrations, it was not even about the celebration of the redemption of humankind. It went far beyond this. The Messiah has redeemed the whole of creation bringing it back to its pre-fallen state. The celebration is thus of an event which fulfilled the type of the exodus of Israel from Egypt and goes way beyond what any of the pilgrims could have anticipated being the liberation of the whole created order. All things, both in heaven and earth had peace made with God through the death of the firstborn son, the firstborn of all creation.

The reconciliation has been achieved, and resulted in the church being restored to the relationship man was created for:

> And you, who once were alienated and hostile in mind, doing evil deeds, he has now reconciled in his body of flesh by his death, in order to present you holy and blameless and above reproach before him, if indeed you continue in the faith, stable and steadfast, not shifting from the hope of the gospel that you heard, which has been proclaimed in all creation under heaven, and of which I, Paul, became a minister. (Col 1:21–23)

Like the Jews who had become alienated from their Creator and sent into exile, humanity in Adam had also abandoned its loving Lord and turned away in preference of a relationship with the prince of darkness. All that had caused the alienation has been removed and they were washed from the filth of sin to be made acceptable to God. The terms Paul has chosen to describe Christ's saving work are the key terms that the prophets used to describe Yahweh's saving activity to secure Israel's justification. Like Gomer she had been redeemed and presented holy and blameless and above reproach before the Father. The imagery is a clear echo of Ephesians 5:25–27 which is the grand finale of the justification of Israel when she is to be presented perfected to Yahweh as his bride. Again, without Paul using the term justification, he has drawn together all those glorious Old Testament themes that described this great saving activity of God in his work of justifying Israel as his people, but here it is not national Israel but the Israel of faith who have been saved and presented as faultless. All of this is exodus based.

---

[420] So also N. T. Wright, *The Climax of the Covenant: Christ and the Law in Pauline Theology* (Edinburgh: Clark, 1991), 109.

These themes of justification, reconciliation, deliverance from wrath, redemption (by his blood) are all found in a key text in Romans which goes on to show that the death of Christ achieved the deliverance of creation from bondage (Rom 8:18–22). Thus, Colossians 1:13–20 is a hymnal version of the theology of Rom 5–8. What these passages show is that justification is not essentially about being declared to be in the covenant, as Wright, but about the creation of and maintenance of the covenant, fulfilling all that the covenant promised Yahweh would bestow on his people and creation. The covenant brings together all of God's purposes and promises that the Creator has made to the true children of Abraham. He says in a passage saturated with New Exodus themes:

> For in him the whole fullness of deity dwells bodily, and you have been filled in him, who is the head of all rule and authority. In him also you were circumcised with a circumcision made without hands, by putting off the body of the flesh, by the circumcision of Christ, having been buried with him in baptism, in which you were also raised with him through faith in the powerful working of God, who raised him from the dead. And you, who were dead in your trespasses and the uncircumcision of your flesh, God made alive together with him, having forgiven us all our trespasses, by cancelling the record of debt that stood against us with its legal demands. This he set aside, nailing it to the cross. He disarmed the rulers and authorities and put them to open shame, by triumphing over them in him. (Col 2:9–14)

Like Israel was chosen to be the vehicle through which God's character was shown to the nations, so now the church has been chosen to make God known to the nations (Col 1:26). The message is for all peoples and Paul strives to fulfil his commission to make Christ known.

Paul's statement that the whole fullness dwells in Christ again stresses that the redeemer is no less than the Creator. He has not redeemed by decree but by putting himself forward as the paschal victim. His death has achieved more than forgiveness and redemption. His death has removed the believing community from the rule of Satan. Bound in a covenant relationship with sin (Satan) the elected bride has been released from the one who she had given herself to in the disobedience of Adam. It was that willing self-giving that created the relationship that had excluded God and embraced Satan. The elect must die to the relationship she was bound in. As his people's representative, he underwent a circumcision that rescued and changed the status of his chosen ones. In the moment of his death they ceased to belong to the kingdom of darkness and were embraced by the new covenant that Christ's death was about. As a circumcised people, they can share in the Lord's Passover and participate in the salvation that is in Christ their saviour. Inclusion in this baptism means that they have all together, as one body, received all the benefits of salvation. Raised, forgiven, freed from law observance as a means of salvation and united with Christ.

The theme of circumcision in the context of Passover is significant. Only circumcised people were allowed to keep the Passover, the event that was at the centre of Yahweh's saving activity. Thus, without circumcision Christ's death would have achieved nothing for no one could benefit from it. So, a representative circumcision was essential that meant that those who were outside of the covenant needed a redeemer who not only would die for them but would affect their acceptance by presenting them as circumcised in himself. This representative circumcision was carried out on Moses's son (Exod 4:24–26). The life of Moses was in danger as the angel sought to take his life and was only saved by his wife circumcising their son and throwing his foreskin at Moses feet. Moses was spared because of the representative circumcision performed.

Following this deliverance Moses was told to go to Pharaoh and call for Israel's release. This was only to happen after the Passover was celebrated. Israel was not circumcised, this had been neglected for decades. Her firstborn would have died as did the firstborn of the Egyptians, but for the fact they had been vicariously circumcised in Moses son's circumcision. The need of the new covenant community has been fulfilled in her greater circumcision in the death of Jesus which was 'the circumcision of Christ'.

> If then you have been raised with Christ, seek the things that are above, where Christ is, seated at the right hand of God. Set your minds on things that are above, not on things that are on earth. For you have died, and your life is hidden with Christ in God. When Christ who is your life appears, then you also will appear with him in glory. Put to death therefore what is earthly in you: sexual immorality, impurity, passion, evil desire, and covetousness, which is idolatry. On account of these the wrath of God is coming. In these you too once walked, when you were living in them. But now you must put them all away: anger, wrath, malice, slander, and obscene talk from your mouth. Do not lie to one another, seeing that you have put off the old self with its practices and have put on the new self, which is being renewed in knowledge after the image of its Creator. Here there is not Greek and Jew, circumcised and uncircumcised, barbarian, Scythian, slave, free; but Christ is all, and in all. (Col 3:1–11)

Paul's certainty that believers will appear with Christ in glory is contrary to the claims that Wright has made that there can be no assurance of salvation until the last judgment. This is not a law keeping certainty, it is a faith-based certainty that is God's covenant gift to His people.

1 Thessalonians

> Now concerning the times and the seasons, brothers, you have no need to have anything written to you. For you yourselves are fully aware that the day of the Lord will come like a thief in the night. While people are saying, "There is peace and security," then sudden destruction will come upon them as labour pains come upon a pregnant woman, and they will not escape. But you are not in darkness, brothers, for that day to surprise you like a thief. For you are all children of light, children of the day. We are not of the night or of the darkness. So then let us not sleep, as others do, but let us keep awake and be sober. For those who sleep, sleep at night, and those who get drunk, are drunk at night. But since we belong to the day, let us be sober, having put on the breastplate of faith and love, and for a helmet the hope of salvation. For God has not destined us for wrath, but to obtain salvation through our Lord Jesus Christ, who died for us so that whether we are awake or asleep we might live with him. Therefore encourage one another and build one another up, just as you are doing. (1 Thess 5:1–11)

Paul uses the language of Isaiah, where the people of Israel are described as children of the day who must not sleep but live soberly.[421] He refers to them putting on the breastplate and the helmet that Isaiah told Israel to wear during her exodus from Babylon. Paul clearly likens the Thessalonian community to Israel on her pilgrimage and transfers the features of her experience to the infant church to explain the significance of her suffering. The term 'Day of the Lord' is used without qualification; in the Old Testament, it was used by the prophets to alert the disobedient in Israel of coming judgment.[422]

Paul cites the Jews who lived in a false promise of peace before the exile saying 'peace, peace' when there was no peace, and this again reinforces his

---

[421] See E. Best, *First and Second Thessalonians* (London: Black, 1972), 206 who reviews Old Testament 'Day of the Lord' language.

[422] C. Wanamaker, *The Epistles to the Thessalonians: A Commentary on the Greek Text* (Grand Rapids: Eerdmans, 1990), 182; F.F. Bruce, *1 and 2 Thessalonians* (Waco: Word, 1982), 109.

dependency on the eighth-century prophets' tradition as they gave a warning which no one wanted to hear.[423] As Paul urges the Christians to keep alert, he echoes the imagery of Isaiah 52:1, again bringing Second Exodus themes into the passage.[424]

The Thessalonian believers would not come under this judgment for they were children of the light. They had made their exodus from the society which rejected the rule of God, and so they are recognized as a justified people— rescued from exile in the kingdom of darkness and making their pilgrimage in the strength and equipment that the Lord has provided.

2 Thessalonians

> The coming of the lawless one is by the activity of Satan with all power and false signs and wonders, and with all wicked deception for those who are perishing, because they refused to love the truth and so be saved. Therefore God sends them a strong delusion, so that they may believe what is false, in order that all may be condemned who did not believe the truth but had pleasure in unrighteousness. (2 Thess 2: 9 –12)

The theme of being deceived and put under a strong delusion echoes the signs that Pharaoh's magicians gave in answer to Moses's display of God's power, and the warning of Isaiah 29:4.[425] These are themes that are found in the Qumran documents (e.g. 1QpHab. 2:1, 2; 5:5, 11), but these references are likely to be from the earlier biblical sources. The passage again reflects the use of exodus and Second Exodus material which the story of the Christian community is seen as fulfilling. This sustains the claim that the church's experience of deliverance matches—on a far greater scale—that experienced by Israel when she was justified.[426]

---

[423] Echoing Ezekiel 6:14 and Ezekiel 13:10. See B. Witherington, *1 and 2 Thessalonians: A Socio-rhetorical Commentary* (Grand Rapids: Eerdmans,2006), 146.

[424] Wanamaker, *Thessalonians*, 184.

[425] Bruce, *Thessalonians*, 174.

[426] Not observed by D. Williams, *1 and 2 Thessalonians* (Peabody: Hendrickson, 1992), 130–131.

Chapter 13:
Reconciling Conflict and Review

Finally, I would like to offer a short explanation that might be a bridge between the two views of the law that Paul is thought to have. Wright, with other NPP theologians, would see Paul as having a positive view of the law as a source of blessing, while the Reformers would see it more as a source of condemnation; yet there is nothing to suggest that Paul may not have held both views in tension. Paul at times speaks positively about the law (Phil 3:3–6), yet at other times, he speaks of its role as judge (Gal 3:10–11). The resolution of this problem is possibly—and, in my understanding, likely to be—as follows.

From Philippians 3:6, we know that the devout young Rabbi Saul of Tarsus genuinely loved God. As a Jew, he had a very different understanding of sin from that which prevails in Western Christianity today.[427] Whilst he knew God to be holy, he had an unshakable confidence that all was well between himself and God because he belonged to the people whom God had chosen, and with whom he had established a covenant relationship. When Saul sinned, he knew that God had provided a way for this to be dealt with through the repeated temple sacrifices.

When Saul heard of the preaching of the followers of Jesus, he was outraged by their claim that the Messiah had been crucified by the Romans. This could not happen, for it damned Israel as those who had committed the world's most heinous sin. God, who loved Israel, would never do this! Naturally, his reaction was that this message of the crucified Messiah must not spread. It was blasphemous and shamed Israel. If the message of the followers of Jesus was true, it would have meant (in Saul's view) that there was no more hope for Israel, and all the promises of her prophets would be made void. There was no other possible response than to attack the message and its messengers to prevent it defiling Israel's faith, just as a surgeon would attack a tumour to save the life of his patient.

---

[427] For a critique and presentation of the understanding that Paul would have had from his Jewish inheritance, see Holland, *Divine Marriage*, 18–22.

And this is what Saul did with all of his might. However, we need to be clear that this response was very specific. It is totally wrong to interpret these actions as reflecting Saul's admiration of Phinehas, Elijah, or the Maccabeans;[428] the latter having clear military and nationalistic objectives. To overlay these examples from Israel's history on the rabbi from Tarsus is to turn him into something he never was![429]

However, when he met the risen Christ on his way to Damascus, Saul was forced to face the reality that the Messiah had not only been crucified, but that he had also been raised again as the conqueror of death. Saul realized that Israel had indeed rejected its Messiah and was continuing to do so. This forced Paul, now a disciple of Jesus, to face the problem of the law; for it had stated: 'Cursed is everyone who hangs on a tree' (Deut 21:23; Gal 3:13). Israel's Messiah had hung from a tree and, therefore, the law had condemned him. Israel's law—that is God's holy law—had sentenced Israel's Messiah to death!

This reality could do nothing other than drive Paul to search for a fresh understanding of what was going on, and this changed his outlook beyond recognition. Law itself had, from the very beginning, condemned Israel. This is what he says in 2 Corinthians 3:7–11. It is what Israel had conveniently forgotten, living as though nothing had happened. He saw that Israel had committed spiritual adultery on the very night of her marriage to her God at Sinai. She was a harlot, and the book of Hosea became particularly important to him along with the book of Isaiah which used the same imagery. In fact, the book of Hosea is used extensively throughout his thesis in Romans 9–11 to explain how Israel had not only forfeited her status as the bride but in doing so had allowed Yahweh to bring gentiles into what had until then been an exclusive relationship.

Paul, having discovered—or rather faced up to this interpretation, for he had known these Scriptures from childhood—realized that Israel was under God's wrath, and hence in the same position as the gentiles. He saw that the law, which had been given to bless Israel, actually condemned her because of

---

[428] As Wright does, *What Saint Paul Really Said*, 26–34.

[429] R. B. Hays, 'Adam, Israel, Christ,' in *Pauline Theology*, Vol. III, *Romans*, Edited by D. M. Hay and E. E. Johnson (Minneapolis: Fortress, 1995).

her sin of whoredom. The marriage night became a revelation of her adulterous heart.[430]

The marriage was never consummated! While the preparations were underway, and Moses was receiving the bridal gift from God (the Torah), Israel committed adultery by turning again to the Egyptian gods she had previously worshipped. She rejected the love of Yahweh and returned to the gods of Egypt.

What was Yahweh's response? He was going to blot her out of the book of life (Exod 32:32). He would fulfil the covenant curse by putting her away. The law was being applied in a way that was opposite to God's intention, which had been to bless rather than curse. Because of Israel's sin the law no longer protected the divine marriage but annulled it. At least, it should have done so, were it not for the vital intercession of Moses, who prayed that Yahweh would have mercy on Israel. Rather than remove Israel from the book of life, he pleaded that his own name should be crossed out instead (Exod 32:12–14). Moses reasoned that, if Israel were judged, the honour of Yahweh's name would be at stake, and the nations would accuse him of bringing Israel out of Egypt with the sole purpose of wiping her out (Exod 32:11–14).

When Paul wrote 2 Corinthians 3:5–18 (as discussed above) his sentiment appears very different to the positive statements he had made about the law elsewhere. How might we resolve such tension? I would suggest that we may only hope to do so by our reflecting on the divine marriage theme a little more deeply.[431]

The amazing thing is that God agreed to Moses's pleadings. However, he said that the matter had not been finalized. He would return again to this sin and bring judgment on his people, for they were a faithless and adulterous people. He made his intentions clear with these words:

> But the Lord said to Moses, "Whoever has sinned against me, I will blot out of my book. But now go, lead the people to the place about which I have spoken to you; behold, my angel shall go

---

[430] Wright misses the divine marriage dimension of Old and New Testament thinking relating to the law. For a fuller discussion see Holland, *The Divine Marriage* and forthcoming *Squaring the Circle*.

[431] Neither Wright, 'Romans', *NIB*, 446–448 nor Dunn, *Romans*, 1:280ff. have paid any attention to this important passage in their constructions of Paul's doctrine of justification.

before you. Nevertheless, in the day when I visit, I will visit their sin upon them." (Exod 32:33–34)

What Paul discovered following his conversion was that the confidence he and his people had in the law was entirely misplaced. Yes, Sanders had rightly identified that Palestinian Judaism mostly had a positive attitude to the law in the first century, but this optimism was only possible because parts of their history had been airbrushed out of existence. Paul was forced to reconsider the role of the law once he saw that it had sentenced the Messiah to death, for it said, 'Cursed is everyone who hangs on a tree' (Deut 21:23). He could not escape the fact that Jesus, the Messiah, had been hung on a tree (Gal 3:13). Paul had to reconcile the fact that the law, which is holy and true, had sentenced Israel's Messiah to death. The law was a decree of God and applicably to descendants of Adam, even to his incarnate Son. If Israel's guiltless Messiah did not bear her sin, then she would have had to bear the judgment herself.

Paul thus came to see that Jesus's death was crucial to save his people from the curse of the law that still had not been settled. By dying as the Passover sacrifice (1 Cor 5:7) Jesus fulfilled the role of the firstborn, who had been chosen to represent his family. Of course, in the original Passover, the firstborn was protected through the sacrifice of a lamb. Here, the firstborn could not be spared: he had to die, or his family (Israel), along with the whole family of Adam, would have had to bear the judgment.

Thus, I believe that Wright's overall doctrine of justification fails to deal adequately with all of the biblical material. As I have shown, his case has been built on selected texts which appear to support his case. To achieve his claims, he has ignored other equally valid texts which call his views into question. Actually, this is not Wright's own mistake—he has inherited the fault lines which are a characteristic of Sanders' covenantal nomism. Wright's method is also weak when he allows intertestamental literature to support his single reading for the term 'justify' and impose that one meaning on every use of the term, regardless of context.

I would suggest that the Reformers are better overall guides to the apostles' understanding, for they are much more careful in dealing with some of these possible levels of meaning I have highlighted within the term justification.

When we compare the understanding of the Reformers, we can see that they were not limited either to the forensic or the accounting understanding of justification. Since the time of the Reformers we have learned that Paul was dealing with terms that have a wider semantic domain than had been previously appreciated. These terms were available for Paul to use, being current terms in contemporary secular understanding, though Paul himself drew meanings for these terms from the Old Testament, which radically subverted the ideas of secular culture. Even so, because of the way in which Paul engaged with his audience, he could expect his readers to understand his message.

The exodus from Egypt was Yahweh securing a bride. The tragedy is, as Hosea went on to demonstrate through his own marital failure, Israel was an unfaithful bride, and this eventually brought her under judgment in exile.

Yahweh promised that he would create a new covenant with her and betroth her in righteousness (Isa 62:5; Jer 3:1–23; Hos 2:14–20; Matt 22:4, 25:10; 2 Cor 11:2; Eph 5:22–28; Rev 19:7). Into this new relationship the gentiles would be incorporated (Isa 2:2–4; 56:3–8; 66:18; Acts 15:14–19). A most important aspect of this incorporation was that the gentiles were to be accepted by Yahweh without them having to take on Israel's religious identity.

It is important to note how Paul avoided referring to the incredible passage of Isaiah 19:23–25 in his defence of exempting gentile believers from circumcision in Romans 2:28–29; 3:20. In these verses, he instead uses texts relating to Abraham's status when the covenant was made. Paul seems to deliberately neglect Isaiah 29 so as to stress what the Isaianic passage does not say, that Israel herself came into the covenant through Abraham without being circumcised. In other words, if Paul had used Isaiah 19:23–25, he may have given the impression that the gentiles were late to the party—an afterthought to make up the numbers, but not the preferred guests. By going back to the Genesis account, Paul stresses Abraham's gentile status when brought into the covenant; at the same time picking up on the promise to the nations to show that they had always been part of the plan of salvation. The gentiles were not invited as guests to the wedding but were to become part of the bride!

It is this incorporation of the gentiles that is one of the most important aspects of Pauline soteriology. The prophets had spoken of the divine marriage, but it was always only between Yahweh and Israel. The gentiles were mere observers of this wondrous event. However, Paul is clear; they were not observers but participators in the same way as believing Jews were. In this community that has died with Christ, there is neither Jew nor Greek

(Eph 2:15–22; 3:1–6; Col 3:1–11). The mystery that Paul speaks about in Ephesians is not the acceptance of the gentiles, but their equal inclusion in that community which is the bride of Christ. No other teaching in the New Testament can give us such assurance of the nature of the acceptance of the gentile believers by Christ. The gentile believers are loved as much as the Jewish believers.

Wright made clear what he intended to demonstrate regarding Paul's doctrine of justification. He wrote: 'What I am offering, in other words, is a hypothesis: try this framework on Paul, and see whether it does not make sense of the data we have, getting it all in with appropriate simplicity, and shedding light on other areas also—in other words, doing the things that all hypotheses have to do if they are to work'.[432] After this somewhat lengthy examination, I have to say that the hypothesis has proven to be wrong for the simple reason that it can only be verified if the texts that Wright has selected along with the readings he gives them are used. But to accept this means excluding crucial evidence which, when allowed to have its rightful place, challenges Wright's claim that he has constructed a hypothesis that leads us to the truth of what Paul taught and proclaimed.

Wright's Theological Method

At the heart of my concern—as I have explained throughout this book— are some of the methodologies which Wright employs to construct his theology. I have no problem with his orthodoxy, it is the position I would defend, but I have serious concerns about his methodology. He has based his entire case on what he has called historical realism. This method, he claims, keeps his interpretation of the New Testament firmly fixed in its historical context. He rightly argues that any proposal for understanding the text must fit into the historical framework that the text gives for itself. By this method the stated or implied date of the New Testament writers as they record the teaching of Jesus must be taken seriously and interpreted by careful reference to the historical and cultural context. In doing his exegesis in this way he sweeps away all those claims of interpretation which have lost the historical context and have finished imposing later understandings on the saying of Jesus which he could not have shared. This has left him with a clean canvas on which to paint his own version of Jesus.

---

[432] Wright, *Justification*, 67.

This method is very laudable and worthy of being followed. The only problem is that Wright has not followed his own methodological proposals. He certainly thinks he has, but he has most definitely failed to do so. Rather than keeping to the historical narrative of what Jesus knew from the culture and history he shared in, he has constructed his own narrative. What he has presented is one that is no longer recalling the history of Jesus from the days in which Jesus lived, but one that has been overlaid with the narrative of the books and traditions of Maccabees. Indeed, it is his version of the history of these events and the significance they came to have for later generations that have now, as a result of Wright's work, become the accepted version of critical realism for many. Wright's historical realism is nothing other than a rewritten history in which Jesus has been deeply influenced by the Maccabean exploits and claims. This is not critical realism, it is historical surrender!

Although Wright has stood against the confessional approach for interpreting Scripture, not allowing later confessional claims such as the creeds of the early church to be read back into the New Testament text, so he has unintentionally rewritten the text of the Gospels by interpolating another narrative, that of the Maccabees, into the New Testament text as a whole but especially that of the four Gospels. Rather than reading later confessional understanding back into the text, an error which he has rightly criticised, he has read into the New Testament texts that are faulty historical reconstructions of the influence of the Maccabean martyrs.

Furthermore. I find Wright's construction of Christian truth lacking the authority he has claimed for it. He has selected and merged materials of both secular and biblical origin with little to demonstrate that the outcome is apostolic in its understanding. He has claimed major foundational details to have been demonstrated as true when such is simply not the case. Saul being a zealot, the importance of the Maccabean story for interpreting Jesus and Paul, the claim to have stayed rooted in the Old Testament and the sweeping claims that his interpretation would have been obvious to a contemporary of Jesus or Paul (when they would only have been obvious if supplied with the faulty fabricated evidence that Wright has supplied his readers with). If the claims made by Wright are true then yes, there is a case for the narrative that Wright has constructed, but the hard evidence does not support Wright's construction. His version of critical realism is only possible by closing one's mind to the issues that have been ignored and that are raised here. It is this hidden eclectic narrative that he has created and seeks to exegete that has failed to provide a compelling case for the New Exodus tradition being in the text of the New

Testament. When this faulty reading is recognized and the original text provided by the apostles is read in the light of the Old Testament New Exodus tradition, then the pericopes they wrote glitter like diamonds in the sun and reveal truths that had been lost as a result of faulty methods, not only of Wright but of many others who have added to the biblical narrative and created a doctrinal system that was unknown to the apostles.

Wright's method of reading in which key teachings of Jesus and Paul are claimed to have their origin in the theology of the Maccabean movement has one important obstacle so far not considered as to its acceptance. The apostolic fathers were the leaders of the churches of the following generations after the apostles. I have argued that there is no evidence that either Jesus or Paul drew on these Jewish documents that are claimed to come from the period of the Maccabean wars. Indeed, I have challenged the widely assumed dating because the evidence is so weak. Supporting this concern, I turned to the writings of the apostolic fathers. Surely, having been taught by the apostles they would know the importance of this framework for understanding the message of Jesus and Paul.

The first church father was Clement of Rome.[433] In 1 Clement he urges Christians to stay faithful and to endure all suffering as followers of Christ. He gives a list of all the Old Testament saints who suffered greatly and then come to speak of the first-generation believers who paid for their testimony with their own lives. Not once does he refer to the example of the Maccabeans. The same is also found in all of the other early Patristic writings, the sufferings of the Maccabeans are not once referred to, not even in the writings of Justyn Martyr. This silence continues until we come to the writings of Cyprian, who became bishop of Carthage in 249. Clearly his pastoral letters would be after this date, thus almost two hundred years after Paul. It is not until these writings that a reference to the sufferings of the Maccabees appear.[434] Their introduction has no mention of how they supplied Jesus or Paul with their understanding of atonement or bodily resurrection as

---

[433] Clement, also known as Saint Clement of Rome, is listed by Irenaeus and Tertullian as Bishop of Rome, holding office from 88 to his death in 99. He is considered to be the first Apostolic Father of the Church.

[434] A.C. Coxe, *Ante-Nicene Fathers Volume 5*: Hippolytus, Cyprian, Caius, Novatian, Appendix. [Fathers of the Third Century] (Hendrickson Pub 1995) 49,504–509.

claimed by Wright, they are referred to solely as examples of righteous sufferers.

Now this is most suggestive, for I have earlier argued that that textual and historical evidence suggests that 4 Maccabees did not come into existence until much later than it is generally dated, and the silence of early Patristic writings supports this view. If this is correct, then 4 Maccabees did not exist in the time of the apostles, they were written, it would seem, as latter propaganda to support the Jewish war against Rome as an attempt to win favour from the wider population for the actions of the zealots of that time.[435] If this as a correct interpretation of the evidence, then it removes the possibility of Jesus, or Paul, being in anyway influenced by 4 Maccabees. And with this removal, Wright's whole argument concerning Christian origins comes crashing to the ground.

Reviewing Claim and Counter Claim

In chapter one I reviewed the relevant theological challenges that have been made against traditional Christian orthodoxy. In understanding these and their influence on a range of Christian thinkers I have sought to set Wright and his work against the battles the church has been battered by. I have sought to show that Wright has been a major contributor to restoring the trustworthiness of the Bible and for this important contribution we must be immensely grateful. Furthermore, he has also encouraged the church to recognise the importance of the Old Testament for understanding the New Testament. However, these important contributions are not to say that he is beyond challenge in the way that he interprets Scripture.

In chapter two, I discussed the case of Paul's pre-Christian identity and examined the way in which Wright reconstructs the traditional profile of the unconverted Saul of Tarsus, producing Saul as a young zealot who engaged in the zealot movement. I concluded that Wright's claim that Paul was a zealot could not be upheld with any certainty. The way in which Wright sees Paul's journey to Arabia as indicating that he identified himself with Elijah—a key model for the zealot community—is open to question. Indeed, it appears that much of the available evidence relating to this question has been

---

[435] The First Jewish–Roman War (66–73 C.E.), was the first of three major rebellions by the Jews of the Province of Judea against the Roman Empire. The second was the Kitos War in 115–117, which took place mainly in the diaspora, and the third was Bar Kokhba's revolt of 132–136 C.E.

insufficiently scrutinized; take for example the requirement to continually update his registration as a Roman citizen, and the improbability of a zealot agreeing to serve under a high priest who was in all but name a key servant of Rome in Jerusalem. The argument that Paul's post-conversion use of the term zealot as a description of his pre-converted self was also open to serious challenge, since it is apparent that Paul did not use the term in this sectarian way. Rather, he used the same expression to describe the devotion and love of the whole nation of Israel for the law.

If Wright is correct that Saul was a zealot, then in the days immediately following his encounter with the living Christ on the road to Damascus he must have experienced both an amazing transformation of his theological thinking and also the most excruciating identity crisis. His self-identity was being totally transformed. This seems unlikely, as there is little evidence that Paul needed to change his theology radically, and what is more, once he had realized that Jesus truly was the Jewish Messiah, he seems to have had little difficulty in accepting his call to evangelize the gentiles. If Saul had been a zealot, one might expect a reference to such a crisis of identity in his extant writings, but such references are noticeably absent. Wright needs to explain these details.

In chapter three I investigated Paul's theological identity by examining how he used the term of *doulos*, the slave or servant of Christ/the Lord. I found that while Wright shared my understanding that Paul saw himself as a servant of the Lord, he failed to apply this understanding consistently and sometimes reverted to the older understanding of Paul being a slave. Wright needs to justify why he sometimes opts for a slave status and at others for the servant status when the context has not suggested a change was needed; he should explain the basis on which he decides which reading to use.

In chapters four and five we considered how Wright uses supporting evidence from Greco-Roman sources to shape his exegesis of the New Testament. Like most other New Testament scholars, Wright has accepted the assumption that Palestine was Hellenized in the first century (as Hengel has shown), and Israel's religious understanding was influenced by Greco-Roman thinking (as Hengel has not shown but has assumed), so Paul must be interpreted in the light of this fact. In this chapter, I pointed out the danger of assuming that the dominant national cultural perspective was necessarily accepted by all of those living within the community it controlled. We looked at modern examples and saw that it is not unusual for people to live within cultures which they deeply resent. The true convictions of such people are often only known by their closest friends, so that only if we had access to correspondence between such individuals and those of like mind could we hope to understand how the individual's mindset agreed with or differed from the prevailing view.

Thankfully, of course, that is exactly what we have access to in the Pauline corpus; and having scrutinized Paul's letters for evidence of his imbibing the dominant culture we found nothing to suggest that he had. On the contrary, we found that the Jewish Scriptures acted as a counter-cultural formative influence on Paul's thinking.

Another question, of course, which arises as a result of the arguments of chapters one and two is, 'if Paul was a zealot, how did he become a "student" of Hellenistic culture and its literature?' Whatever his level of expertise in this area, Wright gives the impression of a man who deliberately looked for Hellenistic ideas that he could baptise into his teaching as a bridge to aid his readers and listeners. It was my argument that the only admissible evidence we have for understanding Paul's attitude to these intellectual and spiritual influences is to be found in his letters and the content of his speeches in Acts, and these—apart from the briefest of quotes from a poet when speaking to Greek philosophers on Mars Hill—suggest that Paul had no interest in framing his theological convictions in terms of Hellenistic arguments. Indeed, given the prevailing culture, the sheer absence of Hellenistic material in Paul proves his theology to be entirely counter-cultural and provides a substantial challenge to the prevailing assumptions that Wright articulates.

I also examined some of the texts which are widely seen to reflect this supposed Hellenistic intellectual absorption. I showed that by allowing the assumption of Hellenistic influence we are left with some irresolvable problems. On the other hand, when we considered these same texts in the light of their Old Testament contexts, these problems no longer arose. This discovery presented a powerful indication that we had correctly identified the true source of Paul's theological understanding, and in light of this, I suggest that the case for some of Wright's preferred exegesis is seriously weakened. While most of the examples examined were from Wright's own writings, there were some included that he did not specifically refer to but which I felt justified considering in view of the widespread assumption that the passages were rooted in Hellenistic practices and culture.

In chapter six I considered Wright's use of intertestamental literature as a key to understanding the teaching of the apostles. While I acknowledge the value of this literature for providing historical, cultural, and social information, I found a complete absence of citations and even allusions to these texts in the writings of Paul and concluded that there is no evidence to support Wright's claim that Paul had used these texts to undergird his teaching. The case has still to be made for understanding the theology of Paul in the light of these texts. Indeed, it was shown that the likelihood of the apostles being interested in the writings of heretical groups who denied and sometimes attacked apostolic teaching is simply untenable. Wright needs to make a much better case for using this material as a key source for his construction of Paul's theology.

In chapter seven I examined Wright's construction of Christology; especially regarding Jesus's own self-understanding. I found that Wright had completely ignored the evidence of the birth narratives and that his entry point into the discussion focused on Jesus seeing himself as a prophet who was called to preach to Israel about coming judgment. I found that Wright identified Jesus's sense of his unique relationship with Yahweh in terms of his realization that he was the promised Messiah, the King of the Jews, the son of David. This indicates that Wright has an evolving functionary Christology, wherein Jesus finally senses that he must die to save Jerusalem from the coming judgment at the hands of Rome. In this model of Jesus's self-understanding, which is discussed more fully in chapter eight, Wright says that Jesus had no idea that his death was for anyone other than for the Jewish nation. Wright needs to explain why he has excluded the evidence of the birth narratives, although he has said that he accepts their historical reliability. Secondly, he needs to tell us how the early church could be expected to trust someone who believed he was dying in God's will to achieve something which ultimately was not achieved—the protection of Jerusalem. Thirdly, he also needs to explain why Jesus, with his clear knowledge of the Second Exodus promises relating to the summoning of the gentile nations to worship YHWH, failed to consider that his death would have been to bring gentiles into the family of Abraham.

In chapter eight I considered how Wright's reconstruction of Jesus's self-understanding regarding what his death would achieve relied heavily on extra-biblical sources, in particular, the Maccabean literature, in which Eleazar prayed that his death would be an atonement for the sins of the people. Wright—although having mentioned the importance of the Passover for Jesus—failed to connect the merger of the sacrifices of atonement offered during the Feast of Passover in Ezekiel 45:21–24. It is because Wright has been unable—through Ezekiel—to see the Messianic Passover as providing

an atoning sacrifice, that he turns to Maccabees for his explanation; but
Wright needs to justify this position in the light of the Ezekiel prophecy.

We also saw that in appealing to the martyrdom theme of Maccabees
Wright has brought Hellenistic atonement concepts into the understanding of
both Jesus and Paul. This fact is not even reflected on. We also saw that his
claim that the Maccabean theme was widely known and powerfully formative
has been challenged by Jewish scholars.

Finally, in chapter nine I examined Wright's claims regarding Paul's
understanding of justification. I noted that Wright believes that the
Reformers—Luther particularly—misread the apostle's teaching because they
confused it with their own criticism of the Catholic Church's teaching on the
place of works in salvation. Wright claimed that the New Perspective had
demonstrated that Paul had a much more positive attitude to the law than the
Reformers had understood, by linking law intrinsically to the theme of
covenant.[436]

Moreover, Wright holds that the key to understanding justification is
found in the letter to the Galatians, where he believes that the issue being
thrashed out is not how someone gets right with God but how the true people
of God are to be identified. Thus, rather than the doctrine of justification
framing Paul's doctrine of salvation, Wright argues instead that it frames his
doctrine of ecclesiology. I see Wright's position here as entirely valid and
valuable; however, my concern centres on his claim that it is the only
meaning of the term justify in Paul and the way in which he uses this meaning
to reinterpret texts that the Reformers had called upon to support their own
understanding of justification.

Rather than there being only one meaning for this important term, my
survey has discovered that there are nine meanings within Paul; each of which
is rooted in the Old Testament. Furthermore, not only does Wright use Second
Temple literature to establish his idea of the meaning of justification in Paul
without following any recognized rules regarding admissible evidence, he
totally ignores a wide range of New Testament texts which run entirely

---

[436] Wright went on to change his emphasis saying that if Calvinism had been
the dominant scholarship instead of Lutheranism then the New Perspective
would not have been necessary, Wright, *Justification*, 53. Perhaps it is more
correct to say that if Dunn and Wright had known their church history better,
they would have realised that the New Perspective was a red herring for they
failed to grasp the breadth of what the Reformers held.

contrary to his argument without one word of explanation. It is clear that Wright needs to justify his method in dealing with these texts. It is equally clear that his conclusions on the subject of justification need to be reconsidered.

In his engagement with John Piper over the meaning of justification, Wright wrote the following:

> What I am offering, in other words, is a hypothesis: try this framework on Paul, and see if it does not make better sense of the data we have, getting it all in with appropriate simplicity, and shedding light on other areas also—in other words, doing the things that all hypotheses have to do if they are to work.[437]

I have examined Wright's claims concerning justification and I do not find that he has produced a convincing explanation for the meaning of the biblical doctrine of justification. He has failed to bring all of the evidence to the table leaving important texts on the side, not even mentioning their existence. I conclude that Wright has not achieved his claim of presenting *What Saint Paul Really Said*. Indeed, rather than the reformers confusing their debate with Rome regarding the law and reading it into Paul's debate with Judaism in how they are supposed to have wrongly understood it, it is Wright who has read his own construction of Judaism into Paul. This construction is heavily dependent on intertestamental texts that he has no right to manipulate to serve as evidence. In this it is Wright who is seriously guilty of what he accuses the reformers of. He has created his argument by manufacturing the evidence from secondary sources that do not belong to the Christian community to support his argument. And our study shows that apart from not seeing the full corporate dimension of justification, the reformers were absolutely right in their claims of what being made right with God entailed.

In chapter ten I offered an alternative reading of the biblical evidence in which I suggested that rather than Paul having one single lens concerning the meaning of justification he shared a much broader understanding of the doctrine which he had not invented but had developed from the Old Testament. At no point does Paul add anything to the Old Testament teaching which was fulfilled in the person and work of Jesus, whom he had come to worship and serve as God's Messiah, his eternal Son.

In chapter eleven I examined the doctrine of justification in the letters of Paul. The material was made more manageable by dividing it into two parts.

---

[437] Wright, *Justification*, 67.

Romans and Galatians, the two letters that specifically address the issues of justification were considered. We found that there were strong political factors over the demands that the gentiles have to submit to the Jewish believers, for it returned the keys of the kingdom back into the hands of the Jewish community. Only those that they approved of in respect to their keeping of the law and submission to its official teachers would be welcomed into the fledgling new covenant community. Paul rejected all such claims and insisted that believing gentiles had nothing to add to their faith in the same way as Abram was justified before he was circumcised.

In chapter twelve we worked through Romans and Galatians to follow how the theme of justification developed. We found that the issue that prompted Paul to expound this doctrine was that he wanted to deal with the pride of the Jews who thought of themselves as the only people that God loved and excluded the Gentiles from the covenant mercy that they had received. While Paul answered this claim carefully showing that Abraham had received his covenant membership as a Jew. The logic of this was that if Abraham was a Gentile when accepted by God, the gentiles continued to be welcomed and accepted. Paul used this fact not only to challenge the Jews concerning their pride but to encourage the gentile believers that God accepted them as children of the same promised that the Jews boasted in.

In chapter thirteen we discovered that the doctrine of justification permeates the letters of Paul. While the specific term might be missing, the outcomes and truths that accompany the doctrine are found in abundance. The new covenant community is not divided and there is absolute equality between believing gentiles and believing Jews. In this new creation, all distinctions have been brought to an end and all believers, both Jewish and gentile, are equally the children of Abraham through faith in the completion of God's promises that he had achieved through his Son's death and resurrection.

In chapter fourteen I offered an alternative reading of the evidence concerning Paul's struggle with the law and sought to show that there is neither inconsistency nor loss of assurance, as is claimed by many. Wright's failure to recognise the divine marriage theme at the heart of the New Testament narrative, as discussed in chapters ten and eleven, has left him with a version of salvation that has not brought assurance but a doctrine of works salvation, something that Paul was opposed to.

As I conclude I want to make it clear that Tom Wright has contributed greatly to the development of biblical theology which has been of immense blessing to the wider church. I respect his orthodoxy in that he values and holds to the great confessions of the church fathers. In many ways he has been a great example of a servant of Christ. My problem is that I don't believe that he can reach those positions via the arguments he has presented. He has been able to avoid the catastrophes that I fear that others will encounter, because many have never had the foundations put in place in their early years to keep them 'on the rails'. In following Tom Wright's methodology, without having his confessional underpinning, they will be in danger of even more fanciful exegesis than that which he has followed; one which will lead them away from their intended theological home. The edifice of Wright's confessional position looks majestic and commendable. The trouble is, as this study has shown, the foundations are not as sturdy as imagined. The surface is attractive, but the biblical core has no more substance than a building made not from concrete, brick or stone, but with polystyrene. Such a model for future generations to follow leaves me with real concern for the welfare for the church Tom loves so much. Sadly, in building terms, what has been achieved is a theology that is the equivalent of what was once known in the building industry as 'Jerry built'. A building that did not last because it violated the rules of building. Or, to use the words of Saint Paul:

> According to the grace of God given to me, like a skilled master-builder I laid a foundation, but someone else builds on it. And each one must be careful how he builds.

> For no one can lay any foundation other than what is being laid, which is Jesus Christ.

> If anyone builds on the foundation with gold, silver, precious stones, wood, hay, or straw, each builder's work will be plainly seen, for the Day will make it clear, because it will be revealed by fire. And the fire will test what kind of work each has done.

> If what someone has built survives, he will receive a reward.

> If someone's work is burned up, he will suffer loss. He himself will be saved, but only as through fire. (1 Cor 3:10–15).

Bibliography

Aernie, M. D., *Forensic Language and the Day of the Lord Motif in Second Thessalonians 1 and the Effects on the Meaning of the Text. West Theological Monograph.* (Oregon: Wipf & Stock, Reprint 2011).

Albright W. E. and C. S. Mann, *Matthew* (New York: Doubleday, 1984).

Anderson, G. P., *Paul's New Perspective: Charting a Soteriological Journey* (Downers Grove: Inter-Varsity Press, 2016), 92–152.

Anderson, H., '4 Maccabees', 531–564, in J. Charlesworth, ed. (1985) *The Old Testament Pseudepigrapha and the New Testament: Prolegomena for the Study of Christian Origins* (Harrisburg: Trinity, 1985; Second Edition 1998).

Barclay, J. M. G., *Pauline Churches and Diaspora Jews: Wissenschaftliche Untersuchungen zum Neuen Testament* WUNT I (Tübingen: Mohr Siebeck, 2011).

— *Paul and the Gift* (Grand Rapids: Eerdmans, 2015).

Barr, J., *The Semantics of Biblical Language* (Oxford: Oxford University Press, 1961).

Barrett, C. K., *A Commentary on the Epistle to the Romans* (London: A. & C. Black, [1957]).

Barth, M., 'Christ and All Things,' in Hooker, Morna, Stephen Wilson and C.K. Barrett, Paul and Paulinism: Essays in Honour of C.K. Barrett (London: SPCK, 1982)

Beattie, D. R. G., 'The Book of Ruth as Evidence for Israelite Legal Practice' *VT 24* (1974): 251–267.

Best, E., *A Commentary on the First and Second Epistles to the Thessalonians* (London: Black, 1972).

Borg, M. J. and N. T. Wright, *The Meaning of Jesus,* (New York: Harper One, 1999).

Bornkamm, G., 'The Revelation of Christ to Paul on the Damascus Road and Paul's Doctrine of Justification and Reconciliation: A Study in Galatians 1', in R. Banks, ed., *Reconciliation and Hope: Old Testament Essays on Atonement and Eschatology Presented to L. L. Morris on His 60th Birthday* (Exeter: Paternoster, 1974), 90–103

Braaten, C.E. and R. W. Jenson, Editors, *Union with Christ: The New Finnish Interpretation of Luther* (Grand Rapids: Eerdmans, 1998).

Bruce, F. F., *1 and 2 Thessalonians* (Waco: Word, 1982)

Bultmann, R. and K. Grobel, *Theology of the New Testament,* 2nd rev. edition (Waco: Baylor University Press, 2007)

Burke, T. J., *Adopted into God's Family: Exploring a Pauline Metaphor* (Downers Grove: InterVarsity, 2006).

Caird, G., *The Language and Imagery of the Bible* (London: Duckworth, 1980).

Campbell, D., *The Rhetoric of Righteousness in Romans 3:21–26. Journal for the Study of the New Testament 66* (Sheffield: Sheffield Academic Press. 1992).

Carson, D. A., *D. J. Moo and L. Morris, An Introduction to the New Testament* (Grand Rapids: Zondervan, 1992).

Carson, D. A., *Justification and Variegated Nomism Volumes 1 & 2* (Grand Rapids: Baker Academic, 2001, 2004).

Casey, M., (1991) *From Jewish Prophet to Gentile God: The Origins and Development of New Testament Christology* (Cambridge; Louisville, KT: J. Clarke & Co; Westminster/J. Knox Press.

Chadwick, O., 'All Things to All men' (1 Cor IX, 22) *NTS 1* (54–55) 261–275,

Chancey, M., *Greco-Roman Culture and the Galilee of Jesus SNTS* (Cambridge: Cambridge University Press, 2005), 134.

Charlesworth, J., *The Old Testament Pseudepigrapha and the New Testament: Prolegomena for the Study of Christian Origins* (Cambridge: University Press, 1985).

Chester, A., 'Jewish Messianic Expectations and Mediatoral Figures and Pauline Christology' in *Paulus und das antike Judeatum*, Editors. M. Hengel and U. Heckel (Tűbingen, 1991):17–89.

Ciampa, R. and B. S. Rosner, *The First Letter to the Corinthians* (Nottingham: Eerdmans, 2010).

Collange J. and A. Heathcote, *The Epistle of Saint Paul to the Philippians* (London: Epworth Press, 1979).

Conzelmann, H. and G. MacRae, *1 Corinthians* (Philadelphia: Fortress, 1975).

Coxe, A. C., *Ante-Nicene Fathers Volume 5: Hippolytus, Cyprian, Caius, Novatian, Appendix. [Fathers of the Third Century]* (Peabody, Massachusetts: Hendrickson Pub 1995)

Cozart, R. M., This Present Triumph: An Investigation into the Significance of the Promise of a New Exodus of Israel in the Letter to the Ephesians (Eugene: Wipf & Stock, 2013).

Davies, E. W., 'Ruth IV.5 and the Duties of the go'el' *VT 33* (1983): 231–234.

Davies, W. D., *Paul and Rabbinic Judaism: Some Rabbinic Elements in Pauline Theology.* 3rd edition. (Philadelphia: Fortress Press, 1980).

De Vaux, Roland, and John McHugh, *Ancient Israel: Its Life and Institutions* (London: Darton, Longman and Todd, 1961).

Dodd, C. H., *The Epistle of Paul to the Romans.* (London: Hodder and Stoughton, 1934)

— *According to the Scriptures: The Substructure of New Testament Theology* (London: Nisbet, 1952)

Dunn, J. D. G., *Romans 1–8* (Waco, TX: Word, 1988).

— *Christology in the Making: A New Testament Inquiry into the Origins of the Doctrine of the Incarnation.* 2nd edition. (London: SCM, 1989).

— 'Baptism in the Spirit: A Response to Pentecostal Scholarship on Luke-Acts', *JPT 3* (1993):3–27.

— *The Theology of Paul the Apostle* (Edinburgh: T&T Clark, 1993)

Eadie, J., *Philippians, A Commentary on the Greek text of the Epistle of Paul to the Philippians* (New York: R. Carter and Brothers, 1859)

Fee, G., *God's Empowering Presence: The Holy Spirit in the Letters of Paul* (Peabody: Hendrickson, 1994).

— *Paul's Letter to the Philippians* (Grand Rapids: Eerdmans, 1995).

— *Pauline Christology: An Exegetical-Theological Study* (Peabody, MA: Hendrickson, 2007).

— 'Wisdom and Christology in Paul' in *WWIS*, 251–79.

Fesko, J. V., *Justification: Understanding the Classic Reformed Doctrine* (Phillipsburg: P&R Publishing, 2008).

Finkelstein, L., *Akiba: Scholar, Saint and Martyr* (New York: Atheneum, 1975)

The Search for Truth

Fossum, J., 'The New Religionsgeschichtlíche Schule: The Quest for Jewish Christology' *SBL 1991 Seminar Papers*, editor. E. H. Lovering (Atlanta: Scholars Press, 1991),

Fuller, R., *The Foundations of New Testament Christology* (London: Lutterworth, 1965).

Goodrich, J. K., *Paul as an Administrator of God in 1 Corinthians. Society for New Testament Studies Monograph Series, volume 152* (Cambridge: Cambridge University Press, 2012).

— 'Sold Under Sin: Echoes of Exile in Romans 7. 14–25', *NTS 59.4* (2013), 476–95.

Green, G., *The Letters to the Thessalonians* (Grand Rapids: Eerdmans, 2002).

Hafemann, S. J., *Suffering and Ministry in the Spirit: Paul's Defence of his Ministry in II Corinthians 2:14–3:3* (Carlisle: Paternoster, 1990).

Hamer, C., *Marital Imagery in the Bible, An Exploration of Genesis 2:24 and its Significance for the Understanding of New Testament Divorce and Remarriage Teaching, Apostolos Old Testament Studies* (London, 2015)

Harmon, M. S., *She Must and Shall Go Free: Paul's Isaianic Gospel in Galatians. BZNW 168* (New York: de Gruyter, 2010).

Harris, M. J., *The Second Epistle to the Corinthians: A Commentary on the Greek Text* (Grand Rapids: Paternoster, 2005),

Hawthorne, G., *Philippians* (Waco: Word Books, 1983)

Hays, R. B., 'Adam, Israel, Christ', in *Pauline Theology, Vol. III, Romans,* Edited by D. M. Hay and E. E. Johnson (Minneapolis: Fortress, 1995).

— *Echoes of Scripture in the Letters of Paul* (New Haven: Yale University Press, 1989).

— *First Corinthians* (Louisville: John Knox Press, 1997),

— *The Conversion of the Imagination: Paul as Interpreter of Israel's Scripture* (Grand Rapids; Cambridge: Eerdmans, 2004).

Hengel M. and J. Bowden, *Judaism and Hellenism: Studies in their Encounter in Palestine during the Early Hellenistic Period.* 1st English edition. (London: SCM, 1974).

Henninger, L., 'Zum Erstgeborenrecht bei don Semiten' im E. Gaf (Editor.) *Fesschrift Werner Caskel zum Siebzigsten Geburstag* (Leiden: Brill, 1966).

Holland, T. S., 'The Paschal New Exodus Motif in Paul's Letter to the Romans with Special Attention to its Christological Significance' (PhD thesis, University of Wales, Lampeter, 1996)

— *Contours of Pauline Theology: A Radical New Survey of the Influences on Paul's Biblical Writings* (Fearn, Ross-shire: Christian Focus Publications, 2004).

— *Romans The Divine Marriage: A Biblical Theological Commentary* (Eugene, OR.: Pickwick Publications, 2011).

Hooker, M., *Jesus and the Servant: The Influence of the Servant Concept of Deutero-Isaiah in the New Testament* (London: SPCK, 1959).

Jewett, R., *Paul's Anthropological Terms: A Study of their Use in Conflict Settings* (Leiden: Brill, 1971).

Jobes, K. H., 'Jerusalem, Our Mother: Metalepsis and Intertextuality in Galatians 4:21–31' *WTJ 55* (1993):299–320.

Jonge, M. De, 'The Pseudepigrapha of the Old Testament and Early Christianity' in P. Borgen and S. Giversen, Editors., *The New Testament and Hellenistic Judaism* (Oxford: University Press, 1995)

Käsemann, E., *Romans* (Grand Rapids: Eerdmans, 1980).

Lander, S., 'Martyrdom in Jewish Traditions,' *A paper delivered to the Bishops Committee on Ecumenical and Interreligious Affairs and the National Council of Synagogues,* (December 11, 2003).

Lauer, S. E., 'Traces of a Gospel Writing in 1 Corinthians: Rediscovery and Development of Origen's Understanding of 1 Corinthians 4:6b' (PhD thesis, University of Wales Trinity Saint David, 2011).

Lincoln, T., *Ephesians* (Dallas: Word, 1990).

Malherbe, A., *The Letters to the Thessalonians in The Anchor Bible* (New York: Doubleday, 2000).

Mannermaa, T. and K. I. Stjerna, *Christ Present In Faith: Luther's View Of Justification* (Minneapolis: Fortress, 2005).

Marshall, I. H., review, 'Contours of Pauline Theology: A Radical New Survey of the Influences on Paul's Biblical Writings,' *EQ* 77.3 (2005): 270–272.

McGrath, A., *Iustitia Dei: A History of the Christian Doctrine of Justification* (Cambridge; New York: Cambridge University Press, 1986)

Menzies, R., *Empowered for Witness: the Spirit in Luke-Acts* (Sheffield: Sheffield Academic Press, 1994),

The Search for Truth

Mitton, C. L., *The Epistle to the Ephesians: Its Authorship, Origin, and Purpose* (Oxford: Clarendon, 1951).

Momigliano, A. and S. Berti, *Essays on Ancient and Modern Judaism* (Chicago: Chicago University Press, 1995).

Morris, L., *The Atonement: Its Meaning and Significance* (Leicester: InterVarsity, 1988).

— *The Epistle to the Romans* (Leicester: InterVarsity, 1988.

Muddiman, J., A, *Commentary on the Epistle to the Ephesians* (London: Continuum, 2001).

Neusner, J., W., Green and S. Frenchs, Eds., *Judaisms and Their Messiahs at the Turn of the Christian Era* (Cambridge: University Press, 1990).

Nicole, R., *Revelation and the Bible* (Grand Rapids: Baker, 1958), 137–151C.

Nicolet, C., *The World of the Citizen in Republican Rome* (Chicago: Chicago University Press, 1988),

O'Brien, P., *The Letter to the Ephesians* (Leicester: Apollos, 1999),

Oakes, P., 'Re-mapping the Universe: Paul and the Emperor in 1 Thessalonians and Philippians,' *JSNT* 27.3 (2005): 301–322

Oberman, H., 'Gemitus et Ratus: Luther and Mysticism' in idem, *The Dawn of the Reformation,* (Grand Rapids, Eerdmans 1992) 126–54.

Pamment, M., 'Kingdom of Heaven according to the First Gospel', *NTS 27* (1981), 211–232.

Piper, J., *The Justification of God: An Exegetical and Theological Study of Romans 9:1–23. 2nd Edition* (Grand Rapids: Baker, 1993).

— *The Future of Justification: A Response to N. T. Wright* (Wheaton: Crossway Books, 2007).

Porteous, N. W., 'Old Testament Theology', in M. Black, H. Rowley, and A. Peake, *Peake's Commentary on the Bible* (London; New York: Nelson, 1962)

Rad, G. von, *Old Testament Theology Vol. 2* (Edinburgh: Oliver and Boyd, 1965).

Reumann, J., 'The Gospel of the Righteousness of God: Pauline Reinterpretation in Rom. 3:21–31', *Int.* 20 (1966): 432–52.

— J. Fitzmyer, and J. Quinn, *Righteousness in the New Testament: Justification in the United States Lutheran-Roman Catholic Dialogue* (New York: Fortess Press; Philadelphia: Paulist Press, 1982).

Index of Authors

359, 360, 361, 362, 364, 365, 366,
367, 368, 369, 378, 380, 381, 383,
385, 386, 387, 388, 390, 391, 392,
393, 394, 395, 396, 397, 398, 399,
400, 401, 406, 408, 409

Ziesler, J.   101, 409

Index of Scripture and Ancient Sources

Ancient Sources

Other books by Tom Holland

If you have enjoyed reading this book by Dr Holland, you will enjoy:

- *Missing Lenses: Recovering Scripture's Radical Focus On Our Common Life In Christ*, ISBN 978-1912445066

- *Contours of Pauline Theology: A Radical New Survey of the Influences on Paul's Biblical Writings*, ISBN978-1857924695

- *Romans: The Divine Marriage: A Biblical and Theological Commentary*, ISBN 768-1608998098

- *Hope for the Nations: Paul's Letter to the Romans*, ISBN 978-1912445004

- *God and His Children: Learning about prayer through Christians in discussion (Volume 1)*, ISBN 978-1912445050

From www.Apiarypublishing.com